EDUCATING FOR DEMOCRACY

EDUCATING FOR DEMOCRACY

Preparing Undergraduates for Responsible Political Engagement

Anne Colby, Elizabeth Beaumont,
Thomas Ehrlich, Josh Corngold

o

Foreword by
Lee S. Shulman

THE CARNEGIE FOUNDATION FOR THE ADVANCEMENT OF TEACHING

JOSSEY-BASS
A Wiley Imprint
www.josseybass.com

Published by Jossey-Bass
A Wiley Imprint
989 Market Street, San Francisco, CA 94103-1741—www.josseybass.com

Jossey-Bass books and products are available through most bookstores. To contact
Jossey-Bass directly call our Customer Care Department within the U.S. at
800-956-7739, outside the U.S. at 317-572-3986, or fax 317-572-4002.

Jossey-Bass also publishes its books in a variety of electronic formats. Some content
that appears in print may not be available in electronic books.

Library of Congress Cataloging-in-Publication Data
Educating for democracy : preparing undergraduates for responsible political
engagement / Anne Colby... [et al.] ; foreword by Lee S. Shulman. — 1st ed.
      p. cm. — (Jossey-Bass higher and adult education series)
   Includes bibliographical references and index.
   ISBN-13: 978-0-7879-8554-7 (cloth)
   1. Citizenship—Study and teaching (Higher)—United States. 2. Democracy—
Study and teaching (Higher)—United States. 3. Political development—Study and
teaching (Higher)—United States. 4. Political ethics. I. Colby, Anne, 1946–
   LC1091.E38415 2007
   378'.01—dc22
                                                                        2007029350

Printed in the United States of America
FIRST EDITION
HB Printing   10 9 8 7 6 5 4 3 2 1

The Carnegie Foundation for the Advancement of Teaching

Founded by Andrew Carnegie in 1905 and chartered in 1906 by an Act of Congress, The Carnegie Foundation for the Advancement of Teaching is an independent policy and research center whose charge is "to do and perform all things necessary to encourage, uphold, and dignify the profession of the teacher and the cause of higher education."

The Foundation is a major national and international center for research and policy studies about teaching. Its mission is to address the hardest problems faced in teaching in public schools, colleges, and universities—that is, how to succeed in the classroom, how best to achieve lasting student learning, and how to assess the impact of teaching on students.

CONTENTS

To Lee S. Shulman
Inspiring Model of Open Inquiry

FOREWORD

THEY ARE CALLED the *lamed vav,* the thirty-six. The *Talmud* recounts that this deeply troubled world survives God's wrath because of the virtue of thirty-six anonymous men, "the hidden righteous," whose inherent goodness is sufficient to preserve all those around them. This legend became the basis for Andre Schwartz-Bart's novel of the Holocaust, *The Last of the Just.* The legend also fascinated the South American writer Jorge Luis Borges, who wrote in his *Book of Imaginary Beings:*

> On the earth there are, and always have been, thirty-six just men whose mission is to justify the world to God. These are the Lamed Wufniks. These men do not know each other, and they are very poor. If a man comes to realize that he is a Lamed Wufnik, he immediately dies and another man, perhaps in some other corner of the earth, takes his place. These men are, without suspecting it, the secret pillars of the universe. If not for them, God would annihilate the human race. They are our saviors, though they do not know it.

The roots of the legend may well lie with the narrative in Genesis of Abraham bargaining with God to prevent the destruction of Sodom and Gomorrah as punishment for its sinfulness. Abraham asks if the destruction can be forestalled if he can identify fifty righteous individuals. The response is affirmative. How about forty? The bar is lowered until, at ten, the negotiation ends. A decent society requires some critical mass of goodness, some threshold below which decency cannot be sustained. Out of this account may well have emerged the image of "the thirty-six" hidden righteous who constitute the lower bound needed for preserving the world.

Why do I refer to the legend of the *lamed vav* when reading *Educating for Democracy?* Perhaps it is the story of the late Otto Feinstein of Wayne State University with which the book opens. A Holocaust survivor, Otto devoted his academic career to creating university environments that would educate students who could use their knowledge and skill to nurture and lead democratic societies. Feinstein's family had been slaughtered at the hands of a nation whose higher education system had been the model for higher education reform in America. Some well-educated Germans had actively participated in the atrocities; others had stood aside and witnessed them without protest. We need to ask ourselves, how many engaged and participating souls does it take to sustain a democracy? And who is responsible for ensuring that the level of engagement and commitment the society requires is attained? This book makes the case that as many citizens as possible should be knowledgeable and responsible participants in the political processes of our democracy and that the college years represent a prime opportunity to prepare students for those important roles.

The challenge that those who educate for political engagement confront is to persuade as many of their students as possible to think of themselves as democracy's *lamed vavs*. They must begin to live their lives as if the fate of the democracy depended upon their willingness and ability to step forward and engage in political life in some significant manner. In the extreme case, what would happen if elections were held and no one bothered to vote? Or if good people were unwilling to step forward as candidates? These may be extreme situations, but are they unthinkable? Is there a threshold of engagement and participation below which democracies simply cannot function? Are there critical levels of political engagement below which democratic societies simply collapse?

We do not, of course, know the answers to these questions empirically. But we do know that some college and university programs are taking upon themselves a responsibility to educate their students for democratic participation. Thus, the research strategy for this work at Carnegie has been to seek out examples of faculty and programs that are already engaged in such efforts, to document carefully how they proceed and how students respond to such experiences, and therefore to offer existence proofs that such efforts can be successfully undertaken. The book is built around "visions of the possible" that are underway across the country, extracting the lessons that can be learned from their work.

For the past decade, much of the work of The Carnegie Foundation has pivoted around the role of education in fostering engagement, commitment, and responsibility among both college students and their teachers. We have come to understand the formation of character and values as an essential complement to the intellectual and technical achievements that properly capture the attention of educators. In our studies of education in the professions of law, engineering, the clergy, nursing, and medicine, we have emphasized the importance of the ethical and moral dimensions of professional development. We have dubbed that kind of learning "the third apprenticeship" in relation to the first two apprenticeships, the cognitive and the performative. In our work on doctoral education, we have similarly called special attention to "the formation of scholars" as we give special emphasis to the role of scholars as "stewards of the discipline." It should be no surprise then that in our work on the mission of under-graduate education, we should also give particularly close attention to the development of civically engaged, ethically committed, and personally responsible citizens.

As if teaching for serious political engagement and commitment were not a sufficient challenge, the authors stipulate an even more demanding standard. A liberal education must liberate, not indoctrinate. That is, faculty must teach students the tools they need for successful engagement, a deep appreciation for and understanding of the political process and its complexities, but must not shape the political beliefs of students to match their own. Indeed, one of the supreme tests of political formation is development of the capacities and dispositions to listen carefully and respectfully to the opinions of others, especially those with whom one disagrees. Such listening is a necessary condition for engaging in the dialogues and debates that are the intellectual backbone of the democratic process. This is where the political and the pedagogical intersect.

When John Dewey connected "education" and "democracy," he was not engaging in a juxtaposition of convenience. For Dewey, there was an inherent reciprocity between democracy and education, from the level of the society to the context of the classroom. And it was also no accident that for Dewey the classroom was a microcosm of democratic interaction and participation, a context of intense engagement for students with their subject matter, their fellow students, and with their teachers. These democratic interactions were not limited to the settings of student government or participatory decision making about school policies, as important as those settings were. They lay at the heart of understanding history and biology, mathematics and literature. "Truth" could only be ascertained through the open exchange of ideas, observations, interpretations, and values, with no claims disallowed. Inquiry proceeded through the democratic collision of opposing ideas, no holds barred. These were principles of pedagogy, not only of political engagement. For John Dewey, *Federalist 10* was a pedagogical manifesto as well as a civic one. In this sense, all teaching is potentially a pedagogy of political engagement, modeling the habits of mind and heart needed for effective democratic participation and leadership.

Professing Democracy

The authors of *Educating for Democracy* challenge educators to raise the bar substantially. They ask that we not only educate so that students understand the political process sufficiently to participate in it. They not only insist that students be taught the skills and strategies needed to act effectively within the political system. They ask that we teach all students in a manner that will lead to their engagement with and commitment to the political process. They thus ask educators to teach students to "profess democracy," to think like a citizen, to act like a citizen and to internalize an identity of democratic participation and engagement. They recognize that a major aspect of our ability to teach in that manner is that we, the educators, not only instruct in the traditional sense, but that we also model and emulate the very values and commitments that we teach.

According to versions of the legend of the *lamed vav,* were even a single one of the thirty-six to die without being replaced immediately, the world would end. Each and every one of the thirty-six is needed. Since neither they nor anyone around them knows the identity of a *"lamed vavnik,"* each of us must imagine the possibility that we are one of the thirty-six, and must therefore live our lives so as to be worthy of that status. Moreover, in a moral stance consistent with the philosophies of both Hillel's moral credo and Kant's categorical imperative, we must deal with every one of our fellow human beings as if she or he were one of the thirty-six. Thus, the tale is not only eschatological; it asserts the basis for norms of individual and group behavior. We are asked to treat others— their rights as well as their ideas—as if they were inspired, whether creatively or divinely. And our responsibilities as citizens are to help create a society and political system in which that kind of possibility becomes real. Ultimately, that is what "educating for democracy" entails.

The team of scholars who conducted this study and prepared this volume is itself a model of interdisciplinary collaboration. Senior scholar Anne Colby is a distinguished developmental psychologist who has devoted much of her career to the study of moral development across the life span. She joined the foundation ten years ago after nearly twenty years as director of the Henry Murray Research Center at Radcliffe College, Harvard University. Elizabeth Beaumont came to the foundation as a Stanford doctoral student in political philosophy and collaborated in our work on civic engagement. After completing her Ph.D., she remained as a research scholar to guide the effort on political engagement. She is now assistant professor of political science at the University of Minnesota. Senior scholar Tom Ehrlich was trained as a lawyer and has served as dean of the Stanford University Law School, provost of the University of Pennsylvania, and president of Indiana University, in addition to his appointment as the first president of the Legal Services Administration. Josh Corngold is a doctoral candidate in the philosophy of education at Stanford. He is working on problems of neutrality, objectivity, and tolerance as principles of democratic higher education. Psychologist, political scientist, lawyer/academic leader, and philosopher—this is the kind of team that is characteristic of the work we pursue at The Carnegie Foundation for the Advancement of Teaching.

I can only hope that the ideas and practices advanced in this volume can both energize and guide our colleagues in higher education, in community colleges and graduate schools, in professional schools and in liberal arts colleges, in state universities and in the growing legion of for-profit institutions, to raise their sights and broaden their missions. In these troubling times across the nation and the globe, the principles of democracy are in grave danger of being corrupted. The *lamed vavs* need all the help we can provide.

Lee S. Shulman
Stanford, CA

PREFACE

THIS BOOK IS WRITTEN for educators who want to help undergraduates become more knowledgeable and engaged participants in many arenas of democracy and public life. It is also written for those who are intrigued by the idea of educating for political development but are not quite sure what this would mean in practice or whether it can be trusted to be smart, effective, and unbiased. This is a practical book, built on the insights and experience of people who have been deeply involved in promoting the political understanding and engagement of undergraduates. A large portion of the book is devoted to sharing specific strategies for use in courses, in the cocurriculum, and in other campus activities.

This volume was first conceived as we were finishing an earlier study of undergraduate education for moral and civic development, a study that resulted in *Educating Citizens: Preparing America's Undergraduates for Lives of Moral and Civic Responsibility,* published in 2003. In the course of our research for that book, we were struck by the lack of attention to education for political engagement. On campuses across the country we saw many efforts relating to civic engagement more broadly, but much less concern with politics, even using a broad definition of the political domain. This seemed to us a serious gap, one that demands attention if American democracy is going to have the knowledgeable, skilled, and motivated citizens and leaders it needs—and if rising generations are to have the resources they will need to engage in public life in ways that reflect their values and goals and provide the many benefits of participation. In response to that gap, we designed what we came to term the Political Engagement Project (PEP). Our work with the students and faculty of PEP provided the material for this book.

Indeed, this book is strongly informed by our extended collaboration with a group of faculty and program leaders who teach not only to develop the capacities of their students for political engagement but also to provide an understanding of the political contexts and issues of the contemporary world that will inform the students' later work and personal lives as community members and citizens. These educators' own words, as well as our interpretations of their ideas and practices, are essential and highly visible threads in the texture of the book.

From the very outset, it was clear that the faculty and program leaders who participated in the project are deeply committed to educating for political understanding and engagement. For some this commitment emerged directly from their life experiences; for others it emerged from core beliefs that are foundational to their personal and professional lives.

In our first meeting, at the prompting of one member of the group, the participants shared the stories of how and why they became interested in promoting students' political engagement. This led to a fascinating set of tales. Although most of us did not realize it at the time, one person in the group was dying of cancer. Otto Feinstein, professor of political science at Wayne State University, died less than a year after that initial meeting. After hearing his story, we understood why he chose to spend a good part of the time and energy he had left to help us capture good teaching for responsible political engagement.

Otto was a young child growing up in a Jewish family in Austria just prior to World War II. His parents fled to the United States with Otto and his brother, escaping the Holocaust just before escape became impossible. Many in his extended family were killed. During the war, Otto tried to join the American military to fight against the horrors of fascism but was too young and was not accepted. After the war, he returned to Europe with his father, and together they located some cousins in Brussels. These cousins, who had spent their teenage years in concentration camps, were engaged in looking for and punishing notorious Nazi collaborators, and Otto wanted to join them in this. His cousins refused, telling him that he had not earned the right to take part and that, instead, he should spend his life doing whatever he could to prevent another such devastating breakdown of civilization and democracy. Otto understood his life's work as an educator as an effort to do just that.

It happened that Otto Feinstein was seated in our meeting next to Siegrun Freyss, a German immigrant to the United States, teaching government and public administration at the California State University, Los Angeles. Siggy spoke next, quietly explaining that her father had been a Nazi officer during the war—that her efforts to draw the university students, many of whom are from low-income families, into active democratic participation emerged from her desire to pay back in some small way the devastation that he and his cohorts had wrought in the name of the Nazi ideology.

Other faculty and program leaders had compelling, though often less dramatic, rationales for their work to help young people become more knowledgeable, thoughtful, capable, and dedicated participants in public life. We are grateful that we were able to draw on the work of these remarkable educators as we began to lay out what teaching for responsible democratic participation entails—the subject of this book.

We recognize that different colleges, universities, and other educational programs have different missions and serve different student populations. These differences influence their beliefs about what kind of political education is appropriate and the way that education should be carried out. We do not believe that every campus must have similar or similarly extensive efforts to promote students' political development, nor that every faculty member or program leader should be involved in education for political learning. We do, however, suggest that one goal of the formative college experience should be to help students become more politically knowledgeable and involved, and that all campuses should think about the best, most legitimate, and most effective way to support that development. We hope our book will contribute to that end.

Acknowledgments

In a very real sense, the leaders of the courses and programs in the Political Engagement Project were our partners in this book, and we are deeply in their debt for their collaboration. (Their names are listed, along with brief descriptions of their courses and programs, in Appendix A.) We have learned from all of them, though naturally none of them will agree with everything we have written. We are also grateful to the many students in these courses and programs who completed our questionnaires and talked with us about their experiences. We learned a great deal from them as well.

Over the three years of our research, John Bullock, Shubha Dathatri, Marivic Dizon, and Hahrie Han all served as research assistants, and we appreciate their many contributions. Our Carnegie Foundation colleagues helped us throughout the study that was the basis for the book and in its preparation: Lee Shulman, president of The Carnegie Foundation, Pat Hutchings, vice president, and Ann Fitzgerald, treasurer; along with Gay Clyburn, Mary Huber, Alex McCormick, Bill Sullivan, and Ruby Kerawalla. Jason Stephens, our colleague in our work on *Educating Citizens,* also assisted in the early stages of this work.

We are in debt to our colleague, Judith Torney-Purta of the University of Maryland, and her assistant, Jeff Greene, for their superb help in designing and implementing the student surveys and in making sense of the resulting data.

We received advice along the way from many people, and we underscore our particular thanks to Bill Damon, Bill Galston, Liz Hollander,

Scott Keeter, Les Lenkowsky, Peter Levine, George Mehaffy, Caryn McTighe Musil, Felice Nudelman, Craig Rimmerman, Carol Geary Schneider, and Laura Stoker. We are also immensely grateful to Ellen Wert for her excellent work editing the manuscript.

Finally, we express our gratitude to the foundations that supported our work: the Atlantic Philanthropies, the Carnegie Corporation of New York, the Center for Information and Research on Civic Learning and Engagement (CIRCLE), the Ford Foundation, and the William and Flora Hewlett Foundation.

THE AUTHORS

ANNE COLBY is a senior scholar at The Carnegie Foundation for the Advancement of Teaching, where she co-directs the Political Engagement Project, the Preparation for the Professions Program, and a new program on Business, Entrepreneurship, and the Liberal Arts. Prior to joining the Carnegie Foundation in 1997, she was director of the Henry Murray Research Center of Radcliffe College, an interdisciplinary social science research center and longitudinal studies data archive, now located at Harvard University. Her previous publications include six co-authored books, *A Longitudinal Study of Moral Judgment* (1983), *The Measurement of Moral Judgment* (1987), *Some Do Care: Contemporary Lives of Moral Commitment* (1992), *Educating Citizens: Preparing America's Undergraduates for Lives of Moral and Civic Responsibility* (2003), *Educating Lawyers: Preparation for the Profession of Law* (2007) and *Educating Engineers: Theory, Practice, and Imagination* (forthcoming). She is co-editor of *Ethnography and Human Development: Context and Meaning in Human Inquiry* (1995), *Competence and Character Through Life* (1998), and *Looking at Lives: American Longitudinal Studies of the Twentieth Century* (2002). A lifespan developmental psychologist, Colby holds a B.A. from McGill University and a Ph.D. in psychology from Columbia University.

ELIZABETH BEAUMONT is assistant professor of political science at the University of Minnesota and a senior fellow at the Institute for Law and Politics at the University of Minnesota Law School. Previously, she was a research scholar at the Carnegie Foundation, where she helped lead the Foundation's work on civic education. She co-directed the Political Engagement Project and was a partner on the Project on Higher Education and the Development of Moral and Civic Responsibility. Beaumont's research and teaching focus on the intersections of democratic and constitutional theory and practice, including political theory, civic engagement, and constitutional development. She co-authored *Educating Citizens* (2003) as well as several articles and chapters on civic education, and she is a member of the American Political Science Association's Civic Education and Engagement Committee. Her current projects include research on political efficacy and on civic engagement related to constitutional rights. She holds a Ph.D. in political science from Stanford University and a B.A. in English literature from Pomona College.

THOMAS EHRLICH is a senior scholar at The Carnegie Foundation for the Advancement of Teaching, where he co-directs the Political Engagement Project, the Project on Foundations and Education, and a new project on Business, Entrepreneurship, and Liberal Learning. He has previously served as president of Indiana University, provost of the University of Pennsylvania, and dean of Stanford Law School. He was also the first president of the Legal Services Corporation in Washington, DC, and the first director of the International Development Cooperation Agency, reporting to President Carter. Before coming to the Carnegie Foundation, he was a distinguished university scholar at California State University and taught regularly at San Francisco State University. He is author, co-author, or editor of eleven books, including *Higher Education and Civic Responsibility* (2000), *Educating Citizens: Preparing America's Undergraduates for Lives of Moral and Civic Responsibility* (2003), and *Reconnecting Education and Foundations: Turning Good Intentions into Educational Capital* (2007). He is a trustee of Mills College, and has been a trustee of the University of Pennsylvania and Bennett College. He is a graduate of Harvard College and Harvard Law School and holds five honorary degrees.

JOSH CORNGOLD is a doctoral candidate in the philosophy of education at Stanford University. His dissertation examines the moral and political grounds for regulating and funding religious schools in a liberal society. As a research assistant at The Carnegie Foundation for the Advancement of Teaching, he has worked on the Political Engagement Project as well as the Business, Entrepreneurship, and Liberal Learning project. He holds a B.A. degree in English literature and religious studies from Harvard College (1998) and an M.A. degree in political science from Stanford University (2005). He is a former high school English teacher and has worked extensively with diverse youth from California to New England.

INTRODUCTION

MANY COLLEGE-LEVEL introductory political theory courses begin with
the trial of Socrates in Plato's *Apology*. The fate of Plato's famous teacher
is well-known: Socrates, the gadfly of Athens, was condemned to death
by a jury of five hundred of his fellow citizens. He drank the hemlock,
preferring the death penalty to paying a fine or being exiled from a polity
to which he was deeply committed. As the class discussion proceeds, some
students interpret the *Apology* as a cautionary tale of democratic excesses
that result in the execution of a wise critic. Others see the example of a
philosopher who urges that the unexamined life is not worth living; still
others identify a lesson on the conflict between politics and love of truth.
But we can also understand and discuss the *Apology* as a dialogue on
what kind of education a democracy should want for its members and
how that education should—or should not—be pursued. We believe this is
an important conversation to have on college campuses, within and
beyond classrooms, and we have written this book as a contribution to
that conversation.

The considerations raised by Socrates' trial are as rich with possibility
and tension for classroom discussion as they are for scholarly reflection
on civic education: the challenge of maintaining legitimate political order
in the face of internal criticisms and external threats to democracy; potential conflicts between fidelity to a set of foundational values and virtues
and the commitment to rational deliberation about those values; the
mutual enlightenment and anger that can emerge from engaging in dialogue with others about cherished political ideals. It also raises questions
about what it means to consciously examine our own and others' values
and actions, including those of political leaders, in a democracy. This
Socratic practice can be seen not only as a significant method of illumi-
nation and learning but also as a way of influencing both values and
actions, and importantly, of holding both ourselves and those to whom
we delegate power accountable to the values we profess (Brickhouse and
Smith, 1994; Euben, 1997; Ober, 1998).

Of course, Plato's Socrates offers no definitive answers to the questions
he raises, placing the onus on us—educators and students—to creatively

imagine, discuss, compare, and evaluate our own best attempts to identify the kind of civic education democracies need and how that education might be conveyed. Although we are convinced that education for democratic participation can be a valuable, legitimate, and realistic goal for the undergraduate experience, we do not presume to answer all of the difficult questions this aspiration raises. Instead, in this book, we hope to call attention to a range of goals, conditions, and modes of education for political engagement, while providing practical suggestions drawn from educators.

The Public and Democratic Purposes of Higher Education

A college education serves many different purposes, some of which are very salient in the minds of students (and their parents), some much less so. Although broad educational goals pervade mission statements, fundraising strategies, and promotional materials, too few colleges invite students—or even most faculty or staff—to consider seriously the multiple purposes of higher education, including its public and democratic purposes. This is unfortunate: institutions of higher education have critical roles to play in helping to ensure the vitality and evolution of our culture and democratic system, and preparing students as thoughtful, responsible, creative citizens is an essential element in this. We know that a good college education can contribute significantly to this outcome, even without addressing it directly (see, for example, Kuh, 1993; Nie and Hillygus, 2001). But in this, as in other educational goals, if one really wants to give students the best chance to learn something, success is more likely if one is intentional about creating opportunities for that to happen.

In our previous book, *Educating Citizens: Preparing America's Undergraduates for Lives of Moral and Civic Responsibility* (Colby, Ehrlich, Beaumont, and Stephens, 2003), we made the case that moral and civic learning are important in undergraduate education and that they are achievable without sacrificing other goals. In this book, we elaborate on that position, focusing specifically on political learning that supports engaged citizenship in a pluralist democracy.

We begin from a developmental perspective on political engagement, understanding the undergraduate years and young adulthood as formative periods for political learning. At the core of this perspective is the recognition that responsible political engagement entails a multidimensional set of inclinations, competencies, and behaviors—we call these *political understanding, skill, motivation,* and *involvement*—that shape and are shaped by life experiences. We also begin from the conviction that there are compelling democratic and educational reasons why helping students develop the full range of these inclinations and capacities should be a serious goal of undergraduate education.

Meeting the Goals of College-Level Learning

Many educators acknowledge the importance of preparation for responsible citizenship but ask how we can possibly make this a high priority when there is already so much material to cover, so many intellectual skills and capacities to build. Fortunately, as the example of Socrates' trial illustrates, education for political understanding and engagement, if done well, intersects with education for many other important goals of academic learning in college, including creative analysis, application of knowledge to new contexts, and other hallmarks of deep learning that are not always achieved during the undergraduate years. In a recent statement about pressing challenges for American higher education, five of the most influential national education associations pointed to "some fundamental aspects of higher education" that "do not and should not change". "The most basic goals of an undergraduate education remain the ability to think, write, and speak clearly; to reason critically; to solve problems; to work collaboratively; to acquire field-specific knowledge; and to acquire the judgment, analytic capacity, and independence of thought to support continued, self-driven, lifelong learning and engaged citizenship"[1] (American Council on Education and others, 2006). As we describe it in this book, education for political development can address directly every one of these outcomes.

There is already compelling evidence from panel studies that the years from late adolescence through early adulthood are a particularly important period for gaining and integrating political values and habits (Jennings and Stoker, 2001). We also know that some aspects of the undergraduate experience, including curricular elements such as majoring in certain fields or taking courses that require keeping up with politics and extracurricular elements such as volunteer experiences, can influence civic and political development (Astin, Vogelgesang, Ikeda, and Yee, 2000; Eyler and Giles, 1999; Keeter, Zukin, Andolina, and Jenkins, 2002; Kuh, 1993; Kuh and others, 1991; Nie and Hillygus, 2001; Pascarella and Terenzini, 1991, 2005; Sax, 1999.)

Building on these foundations, we undertook the Political Engagement Project (PEP), a study of ongoing college-level courses and programs that focus on teaching for political understanding. Our research shows that high-quality education for political development can contribute to many aspects of general academic learning as well as increase students' political understanding, skill, motivation, and involvement. This political learning is valuable for many reasons. An understanding of the political contexts and issues of the contemporary world will inform students' later work and personal lives as well as their lives as community members and citizens. Indeed, we believe that having at least a basic understanding of the political and policy contexts in which people live and work is part of what it means to be an educated person.

This book is an effort to capture high-quality teaching for college-level political learning, which reflects some basic principles that are evident in good teaching more generally. In that sense, the book intends to articulate in some detail what it means to teach effectively for a complex and interconnected array of outcomes that include knowledge and understanding, skill or know-how, and several aspects of motivation—in this case in the domain of political development and democratic citizenship, broadly construed.

Current Inattention to Political Development

The stimulus for the Political Engagement Project was our perception that American higher education pays relatively little attention to undergraduate students' political learning. This is a lost opportunity: more than fifteen million Americans are enrolled in college, this group is increasingly diverse, and research suggests that colleges are well-positioned to promote democratic competencies and participation. The reasons for this inattention are complex, and serious discussion of their history and current power is beyond the scope of this book. (See Bennett and Bennett, 2003; Schachter, 1998; Snyder, 2001; Talcott, 2005.) We can only allude to a few of the many forces that may be operating.

One factor, no doubt, is that preparation for political engagement does not fall clearly into the boundaries of any particular department, field, or program on college campuses around which undergraduate education is organized. Political science or government departments may seem to be the obvious home for programs addressing students' political development. The focus that has dominated political science for the past half-century, however, is the objective, often mathematically driven study of political institutions and behavior rather than more normative goals or applied work of educating for citizenship. Nor is political engagement often a central goal of general education, for reasons we discuss in Chapter Two of *Educating Citizens*. It is noteworthy, though, that many colleges and universities today do choose to pay significant attention to various aspects of community engagement and civic participation, even as they devote minimal attention to specifically *political* engagement.

A review of college-level service learning programs—one of the fastest growing forms of civic education on American campuses—found that among six hundred programs, more than half involved direct service activities such as serving food at shelters, tutoring, blood drives, house renovations, or gardening (Robinson, 2000). Just under half (42 percent) involved educational and technical assistance programs, such as computer training. Only 1 percent of service learning programs included a focus on specifically political concerns and solutions, such as creating or working with groups to represent the interests of a community.

This disconnect between common forms of civic education and efforts for political engagement suggests that another factor, beyond some of the general organizational and historical features of academia, may be discouraging educators and institutions from addressing political learning—a concern that teaching for political engagement entails potential risks not posed by other forms of civic education. These risks include the sensitivity of many political issues and the concerns many educators have about being able to teach effectively topics that often engender strong reactions or disagreements. A somewhat different risk has been the topic of much discussion recently: political indoctrination. Some faculty worry about whether efforts to promote political development might, even if only inadvertently, bias students in favor of or against particular perspectives or ideologies. And some believe that steering clear of all political issues is the only way to avoid being suspected or accused of political bias. We believe these risks are very real and need to be taken seriously, as do the issues underlying them, such as the challenge of creating a climate of open-mindedness around political concerns. Chapters Three and Four of this book address these issues.

In those chapters, we do not resolve all of the tough questions this work raises about how to educate for political learning without imposing particular ideologies on students. We do, however, put forward our considered positions on some of those issues—issues that we believe must be confronted in order to do the kind of civic education we advocate responsibly and legitimately in a pluralist democracy. These include questions about what constitutes bias, the relationship between faculty professionalism and academic freedom, whether or not to impose constraints on speech that is perceived to be uncivil, and the like.

We are well aware that some readers will disagree with some positions we take. In fact, some of the faculty who took part in the Political Engagement Project view these issues quite differently than we do—it was the one aspect of the project about which there was considerable disagreement. There is room for legitimate differences of opinion on many of these questions, and we value an open climate that allows space to consider reasoned differences. The positions we have sketched in this book, although very much informed and influenced by participating faculty, represent only the views of the authors and are offered in the spirit of respectful and continued dialogue.

Our Understanding of Citizenship

In addition to raising highly charged issues concerning the ethics of teaching for political engagement, formulating a rationale and framework for this work also requires us to make some assumptions about the thorny questions of what citizens of a democracy need to understand and do. Does this book assume a particular normative conception of citizenship? The answer is a qualified "yes." Our work is clearly grounded in an assumption that, in order for democracy to flourish and for citizens to be capable of effectively identifying, expressing, and pursuing values and goals that are meaningful to them in the public arena, they ought to be at least moderately well-informed and engaged. That is, we do not believe that citizens are fundamentally incapable of making informed political judgments and therefore ought to consciously delegate or unconsciously abdicate as much political power as possible to political elites.

Likewise, we disagree with the arguments of some political radicals who hold that participating in any form of electoral or mainstream politics is inescapably counterproductive because it necessarily obscures or reinforces the powerlessness or inequality of many people in the current system and delays revolutionary changes that they consider essential. Finally, we also disagree with those, such as some libertarians, who believe that any form of civic education is illegitimate in a liberal pluralist society, because citizens should be left alone to develop their own political values and capacities—or not—based on their private lives and self-selected experiences.

To the extent that we have a particular conception of good citizenship it is this: it is important for pluralist democracy and for citizens themselves that as many people as possible possess a set of capacities that are intrinsically valuable and also support responsible citizenship by helping them thoughtfully evaluate political choices and effectively contribute to political outcomes. The notion of responsible citizenship means that our political choices and participation should be informed by knowledge, supported by skills, and guided by well-considered political values and commitments.

Thus, our focus on the multidimensional nature of political engagement is premised on the belief that responsible democratic citizenship should be understood and studied as involving more than regular or rote participation in basic electoral or partisan activities.

In this view of good or responsible citizenship, not every citizen needs to develop expertise in or passion for every political issue or participate in politics as frequently as possible. Nor must every citizen participate through all possible avenues of influence and action. Although political power, values, and choices importantly structure and shape many elements of our lives and communities and therefore warrant and need our attention and can generate value for us, the goal of responsible citizenship need not and should not crowd out other leisure and voluntary activities that make our lives meaningful, productive, and pleasurable.

Outside of these basic assumptions, however, this book does not adopt a highly specific ideal of good citizenship. As a result, our goals for civic education are largely consistent with ideals emphasized by representative democracy and broad-based interest group politics (Dahl, 1989; Verba, Schlozman, and Brady, 1995), but they are also consistent with many versions of deliberative democracy (Fishkin, 1995; Gutmann and Thompson, 1996; Mansbridge, 1983), as well as many versions of participatory democracy and strong democracy that emphasize a politics of widespread and direct participation, social movements, or mass mobilization (Barber, 1984; Lummis, 1996; Pateman, 1970). Likewise, we believe that a politics of collaborative public work toward common goals, which often occurs primarily outside formal political channels, is compatible with our goals of education for responsible citizenship (Boyte, 2001a). Thus, even though we do not accept all possible formulations of good citizenship, we operate under a broad umbrella with regard to democratic theory.

Within these broad boundaries, we leave open many specific questions and debates about ideals of citizenship. We do not presume to solve the age-old questions of how best to understand the roles of citizens in a democracy. Instead, we offer some broad-brush views on some of these questions, in the hope that our discussion will raise questions for educators and students to consider themselves. Those engaging in any form of civic education would do well to confront these issues—both the normative questions about conceptions of democracy and citizenship and the ethical questions about how best or most legitimately to pursue those goals. We believe it could be especially useful for educators, as well as their students, to do this in settings that allow them to discuss these issues with those from like institutions. It may be still more useful to discuss these issues with those from institutions that differ from their own along dimensions relevant to the issues at hand (bringing together, for example, faith-based and secular institutions, those that lean in more liberal and more conservative directions, those that draw students from particular types of backgrounds or with different types of career interests, and so on).

The Political Engagement Project

Because we wanted to better understand what kinds of learning experiences and educational practices may best promote key aspects of high-quality political engagement, a central purpose of the Political Engagement Project (PEP) was to document and investigate the impact of a range of promising educational efforts—interventions—on college students' political development. We were particularly interested in the development of key aspects of students' political knowledge, skill, motivation, and participation, the sum or integration of which we term *responsible political engagement*.

Like our assumptions about ideals of citizenship, our conception of the political domain is intentionally broad and inclusive, though not infinitely so. Our definition of the political includes deliberation about political values, collaborative public work, community and civic involvement that has a systemic dimension, various forms of engagement with public policy issues, as well as electoral politics at all levels.

Participating Courses and Programs

The Political Engagement Project documented the goals and teaching strategies of twenty-one courses and cocurricular programs, students' perspectives on their experiences in these courses or programs, and the impact of the experiences on key dimensions of political development. (See Appendix A for summaries of the twenty-one courses and programs that we studied.) Among the many strong courses and programs we considered, we selected a set that met the following six criteria:

- They had a central focus on political learning and a goal of promoting the important elements of students' political engagement (understanding, motivation, skills, and involvement).
- They included at least one active and interactive mode of teaching or "pedagogy of engagement" that showed promise for engendering political learning. These included extensive student discussion or reflection, interaction with political leaders or activists as guest speakers or in other venues, politically related internships, community placements or service learning, and research or action projects.[2]

○ The courses and programs had been ongoing for at least a year—
and in most cases for several years or more—at the outset of the
project. Moreover, their leaders expected them to continue in the
future, increasing the likelihood that they could benefit from our
mutual learning in the project.

○ The courses or programs were representative of the diversity of
institutional contexts for undergraduate education: large and
small, public and private, religiously affiliated and secular campuses, and one community college in addition to four-year institutions. Some of the interventions in the study took place at highly
selective institutions, others at institutions with moderate levels
of selectivity, and several at institutions that offer relatively open
access.

○ Courses or programs were representative of a wide range of student populations. In part as a result of the institutional diversity,
the students participating in these courses and programs were also
a very diverse group. The sample was representative of the larger
college student population in most respects, showing the full range
of parental educational levels—our proxy for socioeconomic status—and considerable racial diversity. Somewhat more than one-
third were racial-ethnic minorities, and 30 percent had at least one
parent who immigrated to the United States from another country.
In addition, 13 percent of the students were themselves immigrants.
As in higher education more generally, PEP included more women
than men (61 percent versus 39 percent). Thus, the interventions
drew many students from groups that tend to be less interested and
involved in political life, including many minorities, first-generation
college students, and women. (See Table 1 in Appendix B, "Survey
Scales and Results.") The largest share of PEP students majored in
political science, government, or public policy. These majors, however, accounted for only about a third of the sample. The rest of
the students majored in a wide array of other arts and sciences and
professional fields.

○ The courses and programs were representative of diverse course and
program types, varying in academic content, learning activities and
teaching methods, size, duration, and level of intensity. Although
the relatively small set of efforts we studied cannot capture all
important variations that exist, selecting programs that diverged
in many respects allowed us to increase the generalizability of our
findings. Some were intensive courses or programs that attracted

students already quite interested in politics. Others were more typical academic courses, including two introductory American government courses that met university requirements and other courses that involved little self-selection for political interest. The courses and programs ranged from summer institutes to a semester in Washington, D.C., from summer and academic year internships to credit-bearing courses in several departments, from extracurricular programs to multiyear living-learning programs.

Although the courses and programs were not selected for this reason, most were in fields with an obvious connection to politics: political science, government, public policy, American studies, urban affairs, and history, as well as some interdisciplinary programs that support leadership development and community service. Focusing on these disciplines made it easier to identify courses that give significant attention to political engagement.[3]

Methodology

We used several methods to document and learn from the PEP courses and programs. We interviewed and surveyed all the participating faculty and program leaders; reviewed syllabi, course assignments, and student work; conducted a survey of students before and after their participation (which we refer to as a "pre-post survey"); and interviewed a subset of both randomly chosen and faculty-nominated students about their experiences in the courses and programs subsequent to their participation.[4] We twice met for several days with all participating faculty and program leaders—at the outset of the project and again near its end.

This book is based mostly on these qualitative materials, especially the in-depth interviews with faculty, program leaders, and students. In the many quotations from these faculty and student interviews we use to illustrate our arguments, we do not provide reference citations, since these quotations are not drawn from published texts. In addition to this qualitative material, we offer a summary of key pre-post survey findings, because they provide evidence that the PEP courses and programs are successful in achieving their goals.

Findings About Student Learning

At the most general level, the survey results suggest that almost all of the participating students (just under 95 percent) felt involved with the activities of the course or program. The 5 percent who did not were disproportionately freshmen. Even more important, the survey indicates that carefully designed college courses and programs have significant effects on political engagement: knowledge, skill, motivation, and participation.

PEP COURSES AND PROGRAMS RESULTED IN POLITICAL LEARNING. Analyses of the pre-post student survey data provide strong evidence that the courses and programs do result in political learning along many different dimensions, including multiple indicators within each of the four clusters of outcomes we studied: political understanding, skills, motivation, and expected future political action.[5]

In analyses of the full sample, most of the outcome variables we studied showed statistically significant gains between the beginning and end of the courses and programs, with effect sizes indicating that the increases are practically as well as statistically significant. (See Appendix B, "Survey Scales and Results.") These outcomes included sense of politically engaged identity, internal political efficacy, and interest in reading about politics in the newspaper, several types of political knowledge, skills of political influence and action, and intentions to engage in activities expressing "political voice."

POLITICAL LEARNING DOES NOT CHANGE PARTY IDENTIFICATION OR POLITICAL IDEOLOGY. A notable exception to the general finding of developmental change in students who participated in the interventions is political party identification and political ideology (which, like many surveys, relied on self-ratings on a liberal-conservative continuum). Students entered these courses and programs with a broad spectrum of political beliefs, and the overall distribution of party identification and ideology did not significantly change as a result of participation, although some individuals shifted in one direction or another.[6] This finding is important for responding to the fears of some educators about the risks of political indoctrination and charges of bias that have been leveled at higher education, because it makes clear that these kinds of efforts to teach for political development do not guide students toward any particular party affiliation or ideological viewpoint.

SIGNIFICANT LEARNING GAINS WERE MADE BY STUDENTS WITHOUT INITIAL INTEREST IN POLITICAL ISSUES. The survey results also make clear that students have many different reasons for taking these courses and participating in these programs. Self-selection based on initial political interest played an important role for some students but was not a factor for others. For about half the students in this project, an existing interest in politics was an important motivation for joining the course or program. But the remaining half wound up in these courses and programs primarily for other reasons, including nearly a quarter who were strongly motivated by the fact that the course met a college requirement. Still other students enrolled in these interventions because the professor had a reputation for being lively; the students hoped that the experiences involved, such as internships or meeting political leaders, would boost their resumes; or the program offered the benefit of a semester away from regular college life.

To understand the experiences of both types of students, we took the group with less political interest to be relatively representative of the kind of political disengagement seen among many undergraduates and other young people, and we saw those with high initial political interest as representing a smaller but often disproportionately influential group of potential political entrepreneurs, networkers, and leaders who, if encouraged to continue along a path of political engagement, would be particularly well suited to motivating others and undertaking various kinds of leadership roles.

Both the low-interest group and the high-interest group made significant gains in a number of key dimensions of political engagement measured on the survey—including foundational knowledge related to political institutions and theories, knowledge related to current events, internal political efficacy, and skills related to political strategies and actions.[7] (See Appendix B, "Survey Scales and Results.") As predicted by much other research on democratic participation, students who began the course or program with little political interest had lower pretest scores on nearly all variables measuring important elements of political engagement. Although their scores did not rise to match the level of their more politically engaged peers on the posttest, the group with low initial political interest experienced significant increases along more dimensions of political engagement than their higher-interest counterparts, including gains in their sense of politically engaged identity and likelihood to engage in electoral and political voice activities in the future. The gains they experienced as a result of their participation were also more dramatic. (The effect sizes for the low initial interest group were consistently larger than those for the high interest group.)

Overall, it is clear that participating in these courses and programs helps shift low initial interest students toward the multidimensional set of competencies and capacities involved in responsible democratic citizenship. These results are particularly promising because low-interest students are more similar to the general undergraduate population, which tends to be quite disengaged from politics; thus, their growth suggests that many typical undergraduates could gain in important aspects of political development by participating in high-quality political engagement interventions. For those students with higher levels of interest, the effect of these courses and programs is to boost many aspects of their political knowledge and skills still higher Interviews with high initial interest students indicate that many of these students felt the course or program reinforced and encouraged their political interests and inclinations and helped them further develop strong intentions to be political leaders, innovators, and activists.

Educators' Goals for Political Development

Early on, we talked with participating faculty and program leaders at length about what they hoped students would learn in their courses and programs and how they tried to accomplish those goals. We continued exploring these questions throughout the project, through more in-depth interviews with the leaders, a survey, and an examination of their course and program materials. Despite many areas of divergence and diversity, we identified a number of common aims among the twenty-one interventions and found that most of the specific goals the faculty identified could be naturally grouped into three developmental dimensions we consider essential to political engagement: understanding or knowledge, skills, and motivation.

POLITICAL UNDERSTANDING. Political understanding is a central goal of all the PEP courses and programs, and often the most important goal from the faculty's perspective. In academic courses, this includes building students' political knowledge through much of the formal subject matter of the course.

Our ability to develop political goals and make informed decisions to advance them—our capacity to monitor the soundness of policies and to hold representatives accountable—depends on possessing a fair amount of political knowledge. Research suggests that when people are generally better informed, they tend to reach different political or policy decisions than when they are poorly informed (Althaus, 1998; Bartels, 1996). When national surveys study political knowledge, they frequently reveal surprising levels of ignorance about some important basic issues. This is true for all Americans, but it is often particularly true of younger generations. In a recent study of American young people, for example, 56 percent of youths did not know that only U.S. citizens can vote in federal elections (Lopez and others, 2006). Yet substantive knowledge about and understanding of political institutions, process, concepts, and issues is very important for responsible and effective political engagement.

Just what kind of knowledge should be considered essential—the core knowledge base—is more contested, and we do not try to resolve those debates, although it is clear that both foundational political knowledge

(knowledge of political theories, institutions, and organizations) and knowledge of current issues and events (current political and economic issues at local, state, national, and international levels) are important for democratic citizenship.

Both were explicit aims of the PEP interventions. In our pre- and post-participation surveys of students, we distinguished between these two types of knowledge and studied both. Students showed significant gains in both foundational and current issues knowledge from pre- to post-surveys, with low initial interest students increasing more.[8] (See Appendix B, "Survey Scales and Results.")

The great diversity in the content covered by the PEP courses and programs led us to focus in this book on crosscutting themes rather than on specific areas of political knowledge, as important as they are. These lessons the faculty hope students learn about political contexts and activities may be less explicit than the formal subject matter of the course, but they are nevertheless extremely valuable aspects of a more sophisticated political understanding.

These themes indicate that the faculty members whose courses and programs we studied are concerned about memorable and usable knowledge rather than short-term grasp of information. All use some form of active pedagogy of engagement in addition to lectures and assigned readings, because they recognize that although students may learn facts about American history or political events and institutions, this information will fade quickly from memory or not be enlightening in real political situations unless they see how it connects with real issues and appreciate its importance for their lives.

POLITICAL SKILLS. Like political knowledge, the universe of skills that can support responsible political engagement is far-reaching. Some of these skills are specific to the political domain, such as registering to vote or lobbying elected officials. Others are more widely applicable, such as analyzing political advertising, writing press releases, working with a group, or running meetings. Gaining political skills often involves having the opportunity to closely observe, and preferably, to practice some major subsets of the skills involved in participating in and influencing communities and political life, such as deliberation, advocacy, organizing, and campaigning. Because most people's everyday lives do not present them with sufficient opportunities to acquire political skills, incorporating this kind of learning into political engagement efforts can be critical.

Attention to these skills was evident in many of the PEP courses and programs, which addressed four categories of skills likely to support effective democratic participation across a range of activities, including elec-

toral politics (voting, volunteering for a campaign) and more direct forms
of democracy (working with a local school board, organizing people to
address a community problem, and so on):

○ *Skills of political influence and action:* such as knowing whom to
   contact to get something done about a social or political problem
   and persuading others to support one's political position
○ *Skills of political analysis and judgment:* including the ability to
   write well about political topics and the ability to weigh the pros
   and cons of different political positions
○ *Skills of communication and leadership:* for example, assuming
   leadership of a group and making a statement at a public meeting
○ *Skills of teamwork and collaboration:* such as helping a diverse
   group work together and dealing with conflict when it arises

We were not surprised that the category of skills for which students
reported lowest facility at the pretest were those of political influence and
action, followed by skills of political analysis and judgment; they felt most
confident about their communication and leadership skills. (See Appendix B, "Survey Scales and Results.") Students made statistically significant
gains in all four skills categories, showing the largest gains in the political influence and action skills, for which they had begun with the lowest
scores. This result is especially encouraging, because it is less likely that
students will gain these kinds of specific skills through other educational
areas or life experiences than the more analytical skills or communication
and group participation skills.

Moreover, our analyses of how specific learning experiences influence
students' gains in particular aspects of political engagement show that a
focus on teaching political action skills may be helpful for promoting
some other key outcomes. Holding all else constant, we found that interventions with a strong emphasis on teaching political action skills are
likely to have greater effects on students' internal political efficacy and
their interest in reading about politics in the newspaper than interventions
that lack this focus.

As in the case of variation in content knowledge across the PEP courses
and programs, the great variation in the types of skills students gained in
the different interventions led us to focus in this book on general principles involved in teaching for the development of skilled know-how rather
than to address the particularities of specific skills. The teaching of skills
is not a frequent focus of undergraduate education, especially in the liberal arts and sciences, and the teaching methods are necessarily somewhat
different from those used to impart knowledge.

POLITICAL MOTIVATION. Much research in political science shows that people who are more knowledgeable about politics are more likely to vote and to participate in the democratic process in other ways. Political knowledge not only helps citizens develop consistent opinions, rather than feeling uncertain about their views, but also helps them apply or convert their beliefs into meaningful voting and other political involvement (Delli Carpini and Keeter, 1996).

The pivotal role of political knowledge, however, is hard to separate from compelling motivations like political interest. People with higher political interest, for example, are more likely to seek out and retain political knowledge and also more likely to be politically active. We can also see the motivational role of knowledge by considering that more informed individuals are also more likely to understand the significance of political issues for their own lives and for people or values they care about; therefore, they are more inclined to want to influence decisions and policies connected with those issues. Likewise, politically motivated individuals will seek out or take advantage of opportunities to learn political skills and will have occasion to practice those skills, thus developing greater ease and expertise with many political activities than less motivated individuals. In the end, political understanding, skill, and motivation represent an interconnected complex of inclinations and capacities, all of which are constitutive elements of the kind of long-term, active, well-informed democratic participation we refer to as *responsible citizenship*.

The faculty and program leaders who took part in the PEP are well aware of the crucial role of political motivation in providing energy for and commitment to active political participation and to continued political learning. Their efforts to educate for political development were very much shaped by their desire to stimulate students' interest, concern, and excitement; to help them see the relevance of political issues for their lives; to support students' sense that what they think and do politically matters; and to develop a sense of themselves as politically engaged people.

Political motivation includes all of these qualities as well as emotions such as hope, compassion, and anger, and values we seek to embody through our choices or on which we feel compelled to act in certain ways. We saw in these interventions that political motivation can be strengthened by helping students develop constructive approaches to negative emotions such as cynicism, which can prevent the political participation of inexperienced students but can also grow out of engagement with the gritty world of political action once they begin to participate.

In both our qualitative and quantitative analyses, we pay particular attention to two aspects of political motivation that are key elements of long-term commitment to democratic participation: politically engaged identity and sense of political efficacy. In many discussions of citizenship and participation, *political identity* is used synonymously with identification with a particular group (such as women, or veterans, or Mexican Americans) or with partisanship or political ideology (such as an identification with the Green Party or with conservatism). We do not doubt the importance of these components, but believe that a central aspect of political identity has been largely overlooked—the idea of one's general identity as a politically concerned and involved person. To support responsible democratic citizenship, the importance of being politically informed and at least somewhat active should be central enough to citizens' sense of self that they do not consider political engagement entirely optional, to be pursued only when there is little or no cost attached or when there are potentially large or certain benefits to be gained. What we call *politically engaged identity* involves seeing or identifying oneself as a person who cares about politics and has an overarching commitment to political participation. This is likely also a person who has at least an emerging sense of his or her political values and views, which should evolve over time even as the overall sense of politically engaged identity remains relatively stable.

In our measure of this kind of motivation on the student survey, we found that sense of politically engaged identity represents a distinctive difference between low and high initial interest students. (See Appendix B, "Survey Scales and Results.") Although high initial interest students entered their courses and programs with a sense that being politically involved, concerned about government decisions and policies, and concerned about international issues was very central to their sense of self, this was not true of the other group. Although the low initial interest students' sense of politically engaged identity increased substantially from the pre- to the post-survey, the high-interest students did not show significant increases, probably because their scores were so high at the outset. In contrast, the two groups did not differ significantly on the pretest with respect to their sense of morally responsible identity—the extent to which they viewed being fair and unbiased, compassionate and concerned about all kinds of people, and honest or truthful as very central to their identities—nor did either change significantly in their sense of morally responsible identity as a result of their participation in the PEP courses and programs.

We also looked carefully at students' sense of internal political efficacy or political confidence. On this dimension, low and high initial interest students differed at the beginning and at the end of the interventions, and both groups' levels of internal efficacy increased significantly ($p < .001$), as measured through agreement with national survey items such as "I consider myself well-qualified to participate in the political process" and "When policy issues are being discussed, I usually have something to say."

Our analyses showed that some specific course and program features, such as an emphasis on teaching political action skills, predict greater magnitude of change in internal political efficacy.

We also examined several aspects of what we call *contextual political efficacy*, or beliefs people have about their ability to accomplish goals in particular political domains, including the campus, community, and political institutions. Efficacy in the campus domain was measured through questions about how hard it would be to work with others to achieve goals like "solving problems on your campus." The scale for efficacy in the community domain included items such as how hard it would be to achieve goals like organizing an annual cleanup program for a city park or how hard it would be to raise awareness of a political issue in the community. Finally, we measured efficacy in political institutions through questions about how hard it would be to do things like get the town government to build a senior center or how hard it would be to influence the outcome of a local election. The outcomes for these context-specific aspects of efficacy showed that participating in political engagement interventions, on average, significantly increased students' sense of efficacy for achieving collective goals on their campuses and in political institutions.[9]

Pedagogical Strategies Supporting Political Development

In surveying promising approaches to developing political engagement, we found five pedagogical strategies to be especially important: political discussion and deliberation, political research and action projects, invited speakers and program-affiliated mentors, external placements, and structured reflection. These approaches are, of course, familiar features of the higher education landscape—though by no means as widely adopted as lectures and seminars. We found that these learning activities can be specifically tailored to support goals of developing political engagement.

teaching elements

Two of these approaches—placements and structured reflection—call to mind the importance of service learning for civic as well as academic learning. Politically focused service learning is, indeed, a key pedagogy of this work. But not all service learning includes a political dimension and not all placements constitute service learning. Taken as a whole, the five pedagogies make the point that service learning is one valuable approach among several. This means that faculty have a wider array of options than some discussions of civic education might suggest.

Indeed, the full array of strategies used by PEP faculty goes beyond the five that emerged as especially important. In addition to these five and a number of other strategies that are relatively unfamiliar to most faculty, such as democratic decision making about the course itself, almost all of the PEP courses and programs use some version of lectures. PEP faculty stress the importance of lectures for their courses and programs, and our surveys and interviews with students confirm their valuable contributions to student learning.

Because lectures play a role in nearly all courses, we were interested to find in our survey data that they positively support several aspects of students' political development. One of the most important of these is students' intention to engage in political discussions in the future. All else being equal, courses and programs that rely on a higher percentage of lectures to convey political learning predict significantly greater gains in students' plans to discuss politics in the future than interventions that use lectures less. Student interview comments help explain this relationship: students often noted that they need to feel they have a working grasp of some elements *Lectures* of politics—or understand political concepts and issues in a more usable, relevant, or personally engaging way than they could gain from a textbook alone—before they feel comfortable or interested enough in political topics that they would want to talk about them with friends. Good lectures also present students with a kind of model for how they could frame questions and pose or weigh alternatives in a political conversation.

Key Sites of Political Learning

We found it striking that the academic courses and cocurricular programs participating in PEP shared the same goals and the same pedagogical strategies, although these took somewhat different forms depending on the structure of the program. These courses and cocurricular programs both strive to increase students' knowledge and understanding, help them develop politically relevant skills, and stimulate their interest, sense of efficacy, and other aspects of political motivation. Political deliberation, action projects, invited speakers, placements, and structured reflection are also common to both curricular and cocurricular efforts.

These commonalities may be surprising, given the sharp divide that usually separates academic and student affairs programs on most campuses. This unusual degree of common ground is probably due, at least in part, to the fact that we chose to include academic courses that engage students beyond the classroom and cocurricular programs that have the benefit of strong staff and faculty leadership. We believe that students learn a great deal from programs that have this kind of leadership and involvement by faculty and staff, although student-led extracurricular programs can also be valuable sources of political learning.

The similarities in the courses and programs should not, however, obscure the fact that PEP addresses two different domains or sites of college student experience. In *Educating Citizens* and other contexts we have written about the importance of taking full advantage of both the curriculum and the extra- or cocurriculum as essential sites of moral, civic, and political learning. The opportunities and challenges of the two are somewhat different even when they have some common aims, and both are essential to an optimal learning environment. Undergraduate learning for political engagement is significantly enhanced when the two domains are consciously connected.

A third site that can have a powerful impact is less well represented in PEP. That site, as we discuss at length in *Educating Citizens,* is the campus culture or climate—the many norms, rituals, socialization and other cultural practices; shared stories, values, and ideas; culturally significant physical symbols, settings, and features of the campus; and the many other implicit and explicit messages that help shape the educational experience for students—as well as for faculty and staff. Just as the right kind of campus culture can support moral and civic development more generally, we believe that it can also contribute to students' political engagement and growth.

In PEP we saw the importance of establishing a campus climate of political ferment combined with open-mindedness and civility. Many incidents of intolerance and contentiousness take place at the campus level rather than in particular courses or programs, so a broad focus on the institutional climate is essential in setting the context for constructive engagement. In addition, courses and programs are shaped by their institutional context to some extent, and that is one reason we made sure to include a diverse set of institutions.

Even so, our discussions of the goals and pedagogies of political development do not address explicitly the institutional context to any significant degree. This is largely because we studied individual courses and programs with an eye toward elements that could be extracted from the particular intervention or institution and used by faculty in very different settings. In addition, we did not encounter any colleges or universities in which the campus culture was thoroughly infused with opportunities for political development. It is just that kind of thorough infusion that we recommend, however, if educators want to have significant long-term impact on their students' responsible, effective democratic participation. We believe that the PEP courses and programs succeeded in promoting students' political development because they gave sustained attention to that goal, at least within the limits of a single summer or semester, which is the length of most PEP interventions. We believe that multiple experiences during undergraduate programs are even more effective—especially experiences that connect with and build on each other in the curriculum, the cocurriculum, and the campus more broadly.

We have written this book not only for individual faculty members who want to give more attention to political issues in their teaching but also for academic departments and curriculum committees thinking about both general education and the majors. If members of academic departments or curriculum committees work together to plan a cumulative, developmentally based sequence of experiences in political learning, it will almost certainly have a more powerful and lasting impact than any single experience can have. Similarly, leaders in student affairs may be able to help coordinate and create synergies among extracurricular programs, and working with their faculty colleagues, connect what students learn in their courses with their involvement in other activities. Likewise, institutional leaders are in a position to work with faculty and administrative leaders in both academic and student affairs to help shape a campus climate that supports growth toward effective citizenship.

Purpose and Organization of This Book

This book is organized into four sections: The first part (Chapters One through Four) examines the foundational theoretical and conceptual issues surrounding college-level education for political learning. The second part (Chapters Five through Seven) discusses central goals in political development that higher education should address. The third part (Chapters Eight through Twelve) focuses on key pedagogical strategies of teaching for political learning. The fourth part (Chapter Thirteen) offers concluding thoughts and recommendations.

The first chapter discusses what American democracy needs from its citizens, which includes some degree of informed participation and the adoption of some basic democratic values such as respect for majority rule and minority rights. In Chapter Two we define political participation broadly but distinguish it from nonpolitical civic participation, and present arguments for addressing students' political learning directly, rather than relying on civic engagement to support political development.

A key premise of this book is that education for political development is not legitimate in higher education unless it is conducted in a manner consistent with the core values of higher education institutions, which include intellectual pluralism, rational discourse, intellectual autonomy, open-mindedness, and civility. Chapter Three takes up questions of what this means and why it is important. Chapter Four suggests ways to create a college or university environment that supports respectful engagement across differences of opinion.

The second section addresses goals for political development in college. Each chapter describes in some detail how faculty actually approach the goals, offering "lessons learned" about what political learning means in practice and how it is best supported.

The third part focuses on each of the five key pedagogies for political teaching and learning. We describe, in concrete terms, what the approach entails, why faculty use that pedagogy—what they see as its goals and potential benefits—and how to use it to best advantage.

Our perspective on college students' political learning is an optimistic one, but we know that success in this endeavor depends on the availability of quality programs. With this in mind, in the final chapter, Chapter Thirteen, we review principles of effective teaching for political development and common challenges for that teaching, both of which emerged from our interviews with PEP faculty and students. These principles reflect some well-established findings of research on teaching and learning. We also offer recommendations for framing the educational goals in a multidimensional way to increase the likelihood that the political learning achieved in college will last past graduation.

The PEP Document Supplement

This book is meant to be a practical resource. With that in mind, we have compiled a set of documents from the twenty-one PEP courses and programs that make implementation easier as well as convey a concrete sense of how the recommended teaching strategies work in practice.[10] These documents, which we call the PEP Document Supplement, are available on the Internet at http://www.carnegiefoundation.org/educating_for_democracy/docs. We have also included footnotes throughout the book pointing readers to supplementary materials that connect with that section. These supplementary documents do not offer a full picture of the courses and programs from which they are drawn. They were chosen not for that purpose but rather because they are readily adaptable for use beyond the originating course or program.

We have organized the supplementary documents into eight sections, beginning with a preliminary section describing the Political Engagement Project, followed by a section on "getting started," which includes activities that some PEP instructors use at the beginning of their courses to introduce students to the political realm. In one of these introductory exercises, for example, students share their first memory of a political event. The next four sections correspond with four of the key pedagogies outlined in the handbook: discussion and deliberation, political research and action projects, placements, and reflection. These sections include such diverse materials as instructions for running simulation exercises and sample contracts with organizations hosting placements.

The next section focuses on the evaluation of courses and programs or their components. The main documents in this section are the questionnaires we administered at the beginning and end of the interventions and our interview protocols. These are available for use by other researchers and are accompanied by information about variables, scales, and psychometric properties of the survey instrument.

Finally, the document supplement includes selected student reports, essays, and other written work that illustrate high-quality responses to some of the class assignments. This student writing also shows the degree to which political learning in higher education is intellectually serious and demanding work for faculty and students alike.

NOTES

1. The organizations were the American Council on Education, American Association of State Colleges and Universities, American Association of Community Colleges, Association of American Universities, National Association of Independent Colleges and Universities, and National Association of State Universities and Land-Grant Colleges.

2. Based on their analysis of factors that were important for high school seniors' civic knowledge, Niemi and Junn (1998) recommend that rather than relying on traditional lecture formats, more interactive teaching strategies should be used, including more discussion of politics as revealed in current political events. The term *pedagogies of engagement* is sometimes used to describe general educational practices associated with gains in dispositions of citizenship as well as gains in critical thinking and problem-solving. Some distinguishing features of pedagogies linked to civic gains include an open classroom climate for discussions and sharing opinions, cooperation among students, active learning projects and activities, prompt and extensive feedback, and high expectations on the part of faculty (Amadeo and others, 2002; Chickering and Gamson, 1987; Ehman, 1980; Pascarella and Terenzini, 1991).

3. We are also aware of many courses in other fields that address political and policy issues. In *Educating Citizens* we described some efforts to incorporate civic and political issues into sociology, education, art, science, nursing, and other health care courses. Many specific policy issues can be relevant subjects for students who are majoring in business, engineering, and other professional fields as well as students in arts and sciences disciplines.

4. More detailed accounts of the research questions, survey instrument, analyses, and findings are being reported separately, including an initial set of findings discussed in a special issue of the *Journal of Political Science Education* (Beaumont, Colby, Ehrlich, and Torney-Purta, 2006).

5. At 70 percent, the matched-pair response rate for the survey was strong, and much higher than that seen in standard survey research: 863 students completed the presurvey, representing a response rate of 86 percent of total course and program enrollment; 732 students completed the postsurvey, representing a response rate of 76 percent; 680 students completed both pre- and post-surveys for a 70 percent matched-pair response rate. Our regression analyses (HLM) rely on a somewhat smaller sample of 626 students because we removed students from two long-term programs whose pre- and postresponses did not reflect the actual beginning and/or end of the intervention. Our repeated measures analyses of variance (ANOVA) are based on a sample of 481 students: we drew a random sample of 60 students from an introductory American government course of more than 200 students in order to prevent the possibility of skewing the data too much in favor of the effect of one intervention.

6. For political ideology, repeated measures analysis of variance showed that students did not shift significantly along the liberal-conservative spectrum from pre- to post-survey.

7. The smaller gains made by the high initial interest group, in terms of number of indicators on which they changed and the effect sizes of their changes, can be partly explained by the fact that those students were often near the top of the scales at the pretest and thus showed some ceiling effects. But, as the interviews with some high-interest students demonstrated, many of them were changing in ways that were not detectable by the kinds of general items included on the survey, particularly in the area of intentions for future political involvement.

8. Because of vast differences in academic content across the programs, we had to measure political knowledge indirectly, through self-report, rather than ask substantive questions that would assess knowledge directly. Other research has shown that for various learning outcomes, including knowledge, there is a high correlation between actual and self-reported attainment as long as self-report questions are crafted carefully, use clear reference points for levels of self-rated expertise, and refer to specific topic areas. (See, for example, Anaya, 1999; Dumont and Troelstrup, 1980; Kuh, 2005; Torney-Purta, 1998.)

9. The analysis of variance showed a main effect for pre-post change with significance level of $p = .002$ for efficacy in campus contexts and $p<.001$ for efficacy in political institution contexts. Efficacy in community contexts just missed a statistically significant main effect at $p = .061$. (See Appendix B, "Survey Scales and Results.")

10. For another source of useful ideas and strategies for integrating civic education into undergraduate education, see *Quick Hits for Educating Citizens: Successful Strategies by Award-Winning Teachers* (Perry and Jones, 2006).

CITIZENSHIP, POLITICS, AND CIVIC ENGAGEMENT

BY DEFINITION, DEMOCRACY IS a creative work in progress. Three-quarters of a century after Abraham Lincoln's Gettysburg Address identified government of, by, and for the people as "unfinished work," John Dewey argued that creating democracy remains "the task before us" during the "critical and complex conditions of today" (Dewey, [1939] 1988, p. 225). While acknowledging the danger of external enemies of democracy such as Nazism, Dewey stressed that the gravest threats are internal: the failure to cultivate an understanding of democracy as a way of life involving personal commitments and actions reflecting those commitments. Democracy's persistence, Dewey urged, will ultimately hinge not on military protections or the formal mechanics of elections but rather on our devotion to ideals such as those that Lincoln identified and "the attitudes which human beings display to one another in all the incidents and relations of daily life" (p. 225).

The struggles of both fledgling and established democracies confirm Dewey's insight: democratic institutions are only as sound as the citizens, actions, and goals that animate them. Democracies need a culture of ideals and practices that can support citizens' involvement in and control over social choices and directions. They also need a culture of responsible participation that can engender and sustain fair, trustworthy, and appropriately accountable political institutions—whether legislative assemblies, courts, or police forces. Although democracy means many things to many people, as we see it democracy is fundamentally a practice of shared responsibility for a common future. It is the always unfinished task of making social choices and working toward public goals that shapes our lives and the lives of others.

What Do Democracies Need from Their Citizens?

We start with the assumption that reasonably well-informed, capable, engaged, and public-spirited citizens are essential if a democracy is to flourish. To some, this may seem like a given, but in fact, in the realm of political study it is contested. Even the question of what it means for a democracy to flourish is open to debate. Nevertheless, a number of outcomes are fairly widely acknowledged as implicit in the notion of democratic vitality. They include reducing the potential for tyranny and corruption among those with leadership responsibilities; increasing the responsiveness of the system to the public and to a notion of the common good; improving the quality or fairness of political decision making and outcomes; expanding citizens' horizons, opportunities, and general well-being; and striving to maintain a sense of the overall legitimacy of the system and to avoid political injustice or crisis.

Citizen Participation

Even if they come to a rough agreement on the characteristics of a well-functioning democracy, students of politics differ in their views of citizens' proper roles in contributing to democratic health. Some assume that control by political elites is not only inevitable but also beneficial: an egalitarian and active democratic culture is not a core component of a healthy democracy. Others argue that, whether or not informed participation would be a good thing in principle, the average citizen does not possess the basic intelligence or civic-mindedness to participate in an informed way (Campbell, Converse, Miller, and Stokes, 1960; Converse, 1964; Neuman, 1986; Truman, 1971). And in the aftermath of World War II, amid fears of totalitarianism and mass populism, a handful of scholars argued that widespread citizen participation could be dangerous and perhaps should be discouraged (Berelson, Lazarsfeld, and McPhee, 1954; Huntington, 1975, 1981; Lipset, 1962; Truman, 1959). Dye and Ziegler, for example, suggested, "Political apathy and nonparticipation among the masses contribute to the survival of democracy" (1970, p. 38). These and other scholars express considerable skepticism about the "democratic public" and the potential for ordinary people to participate competently in politics. The influential Austrian economist Joseph Schumpeter warned, "The electoral mass is incapable of action other than a stampede" (quoted in Pateman, 1970, p. 5).

Although skepticism toward the "democratic public" has not completely disappeared, for many influential modern scholars of democracy, relatively broad-based participation is the defining characteristic of democracy qua democracy (Hanson and Marcus, 1993; Pateman, 1970). It provides basic legitimacy to a democratic polity by demonstrating popular sovereignty—as opposed to oligarchy or rule by a technocratic or tyrannical elite—as rule by the people based on relatively inclusive and egalitarian participatory norms and practices. Political theorists also point to the positive impact of broad-based participation on the health of communities and the quality of decisions. Both theoretical and empirical work suggests that political and many forms of civic participation promote the kind of cooperative orientations that support democracy, such as social trust, reciprocity, and the ability to see beyond one's own narrow interests or perspectives and recognize broader public goals.

Recent research on deliberative democracy, for example, suggests that participating in deliberations about political outcomes leads people to discard inaccurate perceptions of the facts and rigidly held political views, and may yield a greater sense of the overall legitimacy or acceptability of the ultimate outcomes, even if one personally disagrees with them (Barabas, 2004; Ferejohn, 2006; Fishkin, 1995, Rosenberg, 2007). Various forms of participation in public life can also foster more immediately tangible benefits, such as lower crime rates, lower taxes, and stronger schools. (See Gutmann and Thompson [2004] and Mansbridge [1983] for theoretical perspectives on democratic deliberation; see Putnam [1993, 2000], Schlozman [2002], and Schlozman, Verba, and Brady [1999] for descriptions of empirical research.)

Morris Fiorina (1999) and others offer further justifications for encouraging broader-based and responsible participation, pointing to the negative impact of increasing polarization and very narrow bands of political engagement on democratic norms and political culture. While many Americans are disengaged from politics today, those who are participating are more strongly partisan and ideological than at any point in the past fifty years (Bartels, 2000). The increasing polarization of the electorate and political leaders is producing a political landscape many find troubling for democracy: greater political mistrust and alienation, less likelihood of talking across differences, greater likelihood of rhetoric associated with "culture wars," an inability to compromise, and distorted public judgment or a decreased ability to learn from new information that should influence public opinion (King, 1997; Mutz, 2002; Mutz and Mondak, 2006; Shapiro and Bloch-Elkon, 2006; Uslaner, 1993; Wolfe, 2006).

Fiorina argues that in spite of the increased opportunities for average Americans to get involved in politics, individuals who "come disproportionately from the ranks of those with intensely held extreme views" are more motivated to do so. The result is "a politics that seems distant from the views of ordinary people" (1999, p. 418). Yet if we encourage broader political engagement—Fiorina suggests finding innovative ways to reduce the time and energy costs of participation—those who attempt to influence public affairs are more likely to include the full range of political perspectives, including more moderate views. Thus, increased breadth of political engagement can have a tempering effect on a political system that seems to be growing more polarized. If a basic premise of democratic politics is that it is valuable for people to consider and evaluate different viewpoints, then we should be concerned about political trends toward more selective participation, which work against this premise and undermine the open and civil consideration of a range of opposing views.

Informed, Responsible Citizens

Despite political scholars' differences about the value of citizen participation and the goals of this participation, even relatively minimalist or procedural conceptions of democracy focused on voting assume, either implicitly or explicitly, that people should be politically informed. This basic need to remain politically informed presupposes that citizens have also gained the basic competencies they need to understand the issues, contextualize current events, and make reasoned decisions about political alternatives presented by officials or the media, as well as the motivation to maintain a minimal level of awareness.

Being politically informed, it turns out, is closely related to being politically engaged: implicit in the goal of having a politically informed populace is the assumption that citizens possess political knowledge and reflective judgments that are useful in guiding their voting or other political activities. This means people need to care enough about or have enough interest in politics that they are willing to invest energy in gathering, interpreting, and applying relevant information.

Most political theorists also point to the importance of public adoption of, or at least compliance with, some basic democratic values. These essentially moral values include an endorsement of individual worth, equality, and rights; a willingness to support majority rule in accordance with constitutional principles; and a commitment to pluralism and political tolerance that permits nonviolent means for resolving differences. The idea of *responsible* citizenship also conveys the sense that we consider questions of a greater or common good, consider the importance of values or long-term goals beyond our own narrow self-interest, and take personal responsibility for our commitments and actions.

Obviously, the way one defines *democracy* shapes the way one thinks about what kind of citizens democracy needs and what roles educational institutions should play in forming citizens. We operate from a relatively pluralist definition of what a good citizen is or does in American democracy, but we do not believe, as some do, that democracy can be healthy without widespread participation or on the basis of well-designed institutions or expert elites alone. Political egalitarianism requires that as many people as possible possess basic democratic competence and that institutions whose missions include supporting democracy should find ways to contribute actively to this essential goal. This notion reflects not only our own perspectives on democracy but also those adopted by important educational policy initiatives. For example, the national education goals of the Goals 2000: Educate America Act of 1994 included the goal of adult literacy and lifelong learning, which mandated that every American adult possess the knowledge and skills necessary to exercise the rights and responsibilities of citizenship (Center for Civic Education, 1994).

What Counts as Political?

Clearly, we align ourselves with the political theorists who see broad-based political engagement as a good thing for democracy and for individuals themselves, at least when that participation is thoughtful, well-informed, and grounded in core democratic values. But this conclusion begs the question of what exactly we mean when we talk about specifically *political* engagement—understanding, skill, motivation, and participation.

Of course, electoral politics—voting, participating in campaigns or political parties, contacting elected officials, running for office, and the like—is an important part of the political domain. Indeed, many political scientists' conceptions of political activity focus particularly on actions related to the electoral and representative component of democracy—actions intended to influence the selection of public officials and their political decisions (Brady, 1999).[1] Early studies of political participation defined democracy in terms of electoral components, often measuring participation primarily as voting in national elections (Campbell, Converse, Miller, and Stokes, 1960).

Expanded notions of political participation include direct, local, or nonconventional political activities, such as citizens' personal involvement in community decision making, and informal political discussions through which citizens refine their own views or influence the views of others (Barber, 1984; Boyte, 1980; Mansbridge, 1983; Pateman, 1970). Notions of participatory and deliberative democracy highlight the value of the processes as well as the outcomes of political interactions, including collective decision making in venues where many influential choices and goals are pursued, such as workplaces or community groups. Deliberative democracy particularly emphasizes the value of discussing public problems under conditions that are inclusive and respectful, conducive to reasoned reflection, and premised on mutual willingness to understand others' perspectives and involve the possibility of refining values around common interests and developing mutually acceptable solutions (Bohman and Rehg, 1997; Dryzek, 2000; Elster, 1998; Gutmann and Thompson, 1996).

We endorse these broader definitions of political engagement, including what Harry Boyte (1980) and others have called "the citizen politics of public work," building on the belief of John Dewey ([1927] 1988, p. 212) that "sharing in common work" is a crucial element of human life. The notion is that citizens work together to mediate differences so they can establish and achieve shared goals that contribute to the public good. This form of political engagement may intend to influence government action, but often it does not. Thus it goes beyond the definition of political participation focused primarily on electoral politics and representative democracy put forward by Verba, Schlozman, and Brady (1995). In this view, political actions are not limited to selecting representatives, influencing their choices, and holding them accountable, but can occur at different structural levels and through a range of informational or communicative channels or social networks, using many different strategies for political expression and influence.

A Broad Definition of Political Participation

This wider view of democracy embraces efforts to participate through informal or nongovernmental institutions as well as those seeking to influence public officials or formal government entities. Thus, sketched broadly, political participation can include working informally with others to solve a community problem; serving in many types of neighborhood organizations and groups that have a stake in political policies or outcomes; supporting political causes or candidates financially; participating in public forums on social issues; discussing political issues with family and friends or trying to influence coworkers' political opinions; working on a campaign for a candidate or issue; writing letters or politically oriented electronic journals (blogs); signing petitions and participating in various forms of policy advocacy and lobbying; raising public awareness about social issues or mobilizing others to get involved or take action through rallies, protests, sit-ins, street theater, or public awareness campaigns; participating in collective consumer efforts intended to achieve political goals, such as purchasing or boycotting particular products or making investment decisions in support of social-political causes; and of course, voting in local or national elections or perhaps even running for public office.

A broader understanding of the variety of ways that people can exercise their political voice and will recognizes that the form as well as the substance of politics shifts over time. Television broadcasts of early civil rights protests in the 1960s, for example, not only provoked realization of the shameful inequality experienced by black Americans but also created awareness of the political effectiveness of methods of protest politics and the power of gaining public attention for political messages and goals. As a result, sit-ins and other forms of civil disobedience introduced by civil rights activists in the late 1950s have become common tactics among many U.S. social movements, ranging from right-to-life activists to supporters of same-sex marriage (see, for example, Gorney, 1998; Moats, 2004).

A broader definition of political activity that includes things like wearing a political message on one's T-shirt or participating in sit-ins or street theater implies that political action cannot be defined solely in terms of the instrumental goal of pursuing political interests in the electoral arena. In this broader conception, political actions frequently involve expressive goals or efforts to identify shared principles or common concerns, to challenge or shape others' political ideas, or to express or develop one's own political understandings and views (Chong, 1991).

Political Participation as Conceived in the Political Engagement Project

The conception of political participation that informs the Political Engagement Project takes elections to be central to representative democracy. However, it also values these broader understandings of the modes and contexts of democratic activity and the more expansive understandings of the goals of political activity they suggest. Although the political realm can be described by characteristic features, including particular contexts (the voting booth, the candidate's fundraising breakfast), activities (petitioning, lobbying, protesting), or targets of action (the governing board of the university, the town council), the core meaning of the term *political* is not ultimately derived from its association with any finite set of domains, undertakings, or focal points. Rather, the defining feature—what makes a given activity *political*—rests on the political nature of the goals or intentions animating the activity: goals connected to individual and group values, power, and choice or agency, and the desire to sustain or change the shared values, practices, and policies that shape collective life.

Generational Shifts in Concepts of Politics

Taking a broad view of the political domain is especially important in research and interventions involving college students, because, insofar as they are politically involved at all, many young people seem to be drawn more to direct participation in the public sphere than to electoral politics. A group of students who participated in a Kettering Foundation study in the early 1990s, for example, expressed the belief that traditional politics is all but irrelevant to their lives and said they would be interested in participating only in a "different kind of politics," such as one that brings people together at the community level (Creighton and Harwood, 1993). More recent college students have voiced similar skepticism toward conventional politics (Longo and Meyer, 2006).

Technological changes have contributed to the ways in which today's young people experience, understand, and participate in politics (Rimmerman, 1997; Zukin and others, 2006). As recent elections have shown, the Internet is not only an important source of political information but also a nexus for political action (Zukin and others, 2006). Among those young people who are politically active in some way, Web sites, blogs, MySpace pages, electronic petitions, and online discussion groups can provide outlets for political expression. The work of young "netroots" activists (grassroots activists who participate in politics via the Internet) is believed to have assisted a number of candidates in recent years, particularly Democrats (Schneider, 2005). Technologies such as e-mail and text messaging are also used to mobilize support for real and virtual protests, such as demonstrations against U.S. military involvement in Afghanistan and Iraq (see, for example, Associated Press, 2003). Thus, although these and other modern-day demonstrations have roots in the protest politics of the 1960s, their form and focus are being reshaped by modern technologies and political concerns.

Other modes of political participation have special appeal for the younger cohorts that some have termed the Dot-Net or Millennial Generation (or Generation M)—for example, consumer politics, boycotting or buying *(buycotting)* particular goods because of the producer's internal or external policies (Zukin and others, 2006). In addition, compared with the general population, high school and college students are more likely to select—or create—clothing or accessories to call attention to their social and political values, such as wearing "identity bracelets" and T-shirts advocating social causes.

More Forms of Participation, Lower Rates of Participation

This rich array of new strategies for political action is an important reminder that some young people *are* highly politically engaged and that college can be a particularly fruitful time for developing such interests and habits. A number of the students who participated in the courses and programs we studied in the PEP fall into this category. Still, these important initiatives and opportunities tend to reach only small numbers of students, and active participation in politics, particularly electoral politics, remains more the exception than the norm among young Americans, including undergraduates and recent college graduates. Although not all evidence points consistently in the same direction, there is persuasive research suggesting that current generations of young people are less knowledgeable about and interested and involved in politics than were prior generations at the same age (Putnam, 2000).

Overall participation rates are lower now than they were for earlier cohorts of college students. Interest in and discussion of politics has dropped since the 1960s. Although rates of political interest and involvement have increased since 2000, they have not reached the levels shown in the 1960s and 1970s, even taking into account the full range of activities defined as political under a broad conception of that domain (Sax, 2004). Although some studies suggest that this political disengagement is often accompanied by deep skepticism or hostility toward conventional politics (see Walker, 2000), more recent research indicates that most politically inactive young people cannot articulate a clear reason for their lack of participation (Zukin and others, 2006).

Civic Engagement as an Apolitical Alternative

Studies of young people in the most recent cohorts suggest interest, instead, in what could be called an *apolitical* alternative to politics. Perhaps as a result of their distrust of conventional politics, many undergraduates believe volunteering is a more effective outlet for their energies. For example, in a national survey, a majority of students said that doing volunteer work for organizations that help the needy can bring a lot of change, whereas much fewer believed that conventional political activity could do so (Peter D. Hart Research Associates, 2001). This is consistent with surveys carried out by the Higher Education Research Institute at the University of California, Los Angeles, showing that community service volunteer work has increased to more than 80 percent among incoming college students in recent years, even as political engagement has declined (see Sax, 2004).

Similarly, in some qualitative studies, such as those conducted by the Harwood Group, students say that they can make a bigger difference on social issues through direct service volunteer work than through conventional political activities, implying that community service might be seen as a particular strategy through which to pursue political or quasi-political goals (Creighton and Harwood, 1993). Student leaders from twenty-seven campuses issued the statement titled "The New Student Politics" after participating in a conference on civic engagement. In this passionate statement, they argue that "community service is a form of alternative politics, not an alternative to politics. Participation in community service can be undertaken as a form of unconventional political activity that can lead to social change" (Long, 2002, n.p.). The prevalence of this view on college campuses is supported by survey data; more than a quarter of students in the Harvard University Institute of Politics Poll (2005) said they believe volunteering for community organizations *is* a political activity.

Clearly, civic and political engagement shade into each other; the boundaries between them are not sharp. Civic engagement is valuable in its own right and some forms of community involvement can have important political dimensions. Even so, we do not believe that *all* community service counts as or can be automatically equated with political activity. We believe that it is important to distinguish between political participation and nonpolitical civic participation, while acknowledging that the two represent different points on a single continuum and contribute to each other in a number of ways. It is important to make the distinction as best we can, because nonpolitical civic engagement does not guarantee political participation (Galston, 2001). The sources of motivation for the two are often different, the skills they require overlap, but not completely, and the two frequently take place in different kinds of institutional settings.

Relationship Between Civic and Political Participation

Despite its relatively broad scope, our definition of politics does not include all civic participation. Although we think it is critical to take young people's understanding of politics into account, on this point we must disagree with a fair number of them. The boundaries of the political realm are often permeable, but emphasizing the role of political goals and motivations focused on networks of power and accountability, public choices and public work, and policy issues and the systemic dimensions of social issues and problems helps us understand the dividing line between political and nonpolitical undertakings that may otherwise share similar contexts or actions.

Applying these criteria, we do not count as political many common forms of community service, such as tutoring children, cleaning up a public beach, volunteering at a senior center, or stocking shelves in a food pantry. Our definition also excludes organized social and civic activities that may be important for building social capital and individual satisfaction, such as book clubs, athletic leagues, or religious organizations, except when those groups take on political goals.

Our definition of politics also excludes individual lifestyle choices and personal commitments such as energy conservation, recycling, or organic food consumption or gardening unless these are intended and structured to contribute to broad social or institutional change, such as through identifying one's actions with broader movements working on these issues, participating in related groups, supporting related causes, or selecting leaders who hold favorable views on these issues.

For example, at a recent showing of Al Gore's film on global warming *An Inconvenient Truth,* young people greeted patrons outside the theater with brochures about modest changes they can make in their homes or driving patterns to help reduce global warming. Although they were not attempting to influence policymakers, we would include these young people's activities in our conception of politics because they were intended both to raise awareness of these issues and directly change other individuals' behavior. In contrast, if film patrons followed a suggestion in the brochure—switching to energy-saving lightbulbs, for example—we would not count that action as political unless they joined a larger movement to help shift public behavior more generally. It is noteworthy in this regard that in their 2006 study of political participation, Zukin and his colleagues found that 90 percent of those who reported having engaged in consumer activism said that they saw it as an individual activity rather than as part of an organized campaign.

Does Voluntarism Lead to Political Participation?

It is important to understand the complex nature of the relationship between civic and political participation if we are to develop strategies for preparing students for high-quality political participation. If civic voluntarism prepares students well for and is causally related to later political participation, then we ought to have relatively little concern for the current generation of young people, because so many of them participate in direct service volunteer work. The question, then, is whether the high rates of volunteering that characterize today's students and young adults will translate into high levels of political engagement as they move further into adulthood.

There are both empirical and theoretical reasons to believe that something like this may be going on. A number of political scientists have pointed to what Verba, Schlozman, and Brady refer to as "the embeddedness of political activity in nonpolitical institutions of civil society" (1995, p. 40). Both political scientists and developmental psychologists point out that experience with civic voluntarism contributes to political participation to a significant degree (Putnam, 2000; Verba, Schlozman, and Brady, 1995; Youniss and Yates, 1997).

There are several reasons for this connection. First, organizations can operate as sites of recruitment into political activity, with participants being more likely to receive requests to take part in campaigns, rallies, or other activities; to contribute money; or to join a letter-writing effort. Participating in civic activities incorporates people into social networks that may encourage or invite their political activity, or encourage them to develop a particular political stance or act on a political issue.

Civic engagement also often exposes participants to political knowledge and stimuli, potentially increasing their interest in and concern about political issues "as when a minister gives a sermon on a political topic or when organization members chat informally about politics at a meeting" (Verba, Schlozman, and Brady, 1995, p. 40). Or, as Richard Brody has suggested, although a typical bowling league is likely to begin as an apolitical social group and to remain that way indefinitely, it could become politically active if, say, the town government sought to use eminent domain to purchase its space and construct a public parking lot, just as one's elk-hunting or trail-running club might engage in a letter-writing campaign if the state decided to change the use conditions in state forests (Brody, personal e-mail to one of the authors, September 17, 2001).

Another important point of connection is that various forms of civic engagement pursued by adolescents and adults can provide opportunities for participants to develop civic capacities, such as communication, organizational, or advocacy skills, which serve as resources for political participation, effectively reducing the barriers posed by a lack of political competence (Battistoni, 1997; Mann and Patrick, 2000). Possession of the types of skills that can be acquired from involvement in clubs and community organizations is among the most important predictors of political participation (Verba, Schlozman, and Brady, 1995). In line with these theoretical formulations of the relationship between civic and political participation, scholars have found empirically that politically active individuals are more likely than their inactive peers to have participated in community service, clubs, and other organized activities in high school (Smith, 1999; Verba, Schlozman, and Brady, 1995; Youniss, McLellan, Su, and Yates, 1999).

Necessary Conditions for Developing Political Capacity

The relationship between nonpolitical civic participation and political participation is more complicated than this analysis suggests, however. It is clear that organizational involvement *can* build civic skills, expose participants to political issues, and successfully recruit members into political activity, but it is also clear that this happens only under some circumstances. The degree to which organizational involvement leads to the development of important political capacities and civic skills depends on the nature of the organization or other setting for participation, and even more, on the role of the participant in that organization or setting.

If participation is to lead to the development of politically important skills, the role should be one in which the individual needs and therefore practices those skills. Key activities that support the development of politically important skills (those identified by Verba, Schlozman, and Brady, 1995), for example, include writing letters, taking part in decision making about institutional matters, planning or chairing meetings, and making presentations. Some kinds of volunteer work or organizational participation, as well as many roles in the workplace, require the participant to develop or exercise these sorts of skills, but many kinds of volunteer work and organizational participation do not.

Similarly, some organizations raise political issues in more compelling ways than others, and thus increase the political knowledge, interest, and concern of their members. Organizations with explicit political agendas, such as the Sierra Club and the National Rifle Association, are more likely than garden clubs or self-help groups to invite some degree of political engagement.

It follows, then, that there is a much greater chance that civic participation will lead to political participation if the volunteer activity offers opportunities to develop political knowledge and high-level organizational and communications skills, which in turn support a stronger sense of political efficacy. When the activities also draw participants' attention to political or policy issues, they can be valuable in increasing their political interest and concern, which are key components of political motivation.

Unfortunately, this does not happen in many of the volunteer service activities in which high school and college students usually participate. This is especially true for the so-called drive-by voluntarism in which many students engage—a day spent cleaning a public beach or serving meals in a soup kitchen. In line with this analysis, research suggests that in younger generations these forms of civic involvement often remain separate from political engagement and do not alleviate their alienation from political institutions and processes (Gray and others, 1999; Mason and Nelson, 2000; National Association of Secretaries of State, 1999).

PEP Faculty Reflections on Political and Civic Participation

When we interviewed faculty and students who participated in the Political Engagement Project, we asked about their personal experience and perceptions of the relationship between relatively apolitical volunteering or community involvement and political engagement. Their comments reinforce the picture we have outlined: civic participation can potentially contribute to political development but often it does not realize that potential.

The PEP faculty feel strongly that it is important to distinguish between political engagement and nonpolitical civic engagement even if it is sometimes difficult to identify precisely the line separating the two. In their ongoing observations of and work with students, they are clear that these two sets of activities are different in important ways and that performing community service will not necessarily ensure that students develop interest or expertise in the political domain.

As Adam Weinberg, former director of the extracurricular program Democracy Matters, put it: "When I wanted my daughter to learn how to swim, I didn't give her bike-riding lessons, I gave her swimming lessons." Weinberg is pointing to a theme we heard in many of the faculty interviews: some political skills can be learned from taking part in community service but most cannot—or at least they are not typically developed in the kind of community service that the great majority of students perform. If you want students to develop political skills, it is much more effective to engage them in overtly political activities than to hope that they will gain these skills through a set of activities that is likely to be quite removed from political action.

Many faculty made the point that connecting direct community service with political learning can be extremely productive but that this connection seldom happens spontaneously. For fruitful connections to happen, faculty need to be intentional about fostering a better understanding of the relationship between their direct service activities and related political and policy issues.[2]

Faculty noted several ways that community service and political engagement can enhance each other if these connections are made. If students are guided to learn about and engage with policy issues that are directly related to the community service they are doing, the service activities provide graphic illustrations of the social issues the policies are meant to address, giving students an immediate and often emotionally compelling sense of how these issues are manifested in people's everyday lives, what they look like "on the ground." Connecting these concrete manifestations of social issues with systemic, political analyses of related concerns "raises macro-level questions about micro-level issues" and vice versa, according to PEP faculty participant, Ross Cheit, who teaches the course Children and Public Policy at Brown University. (See Appendix A, "Course and Program Summaries.") These concrete experiences with real people coping with the broader social issues under consideration often increase students' interest in and motivation to engage with the political or policy-level analyses, which can otherwise seem rather remote and abstract.

PEP Student Understanding of Political and Civic Participation

Interviews with PEP students make it clear that they see the relationship between community service and political engagement in much the same way that faculty do. Many, though not all, of these students had previously taken part in community service, as most of today's high school and college students do at some point (Sax, 1999). There was a consensus among undergraduates in our study that students usually do not make the connection between civic and political engagement on their own and are seldom helped to make those connections by the faculty or program directors who are involved in overseeing experiences like service learning, volunteering, or participating in student clubs or organizations. These students found their experiences in the Political Engagement Project courses and programs to contrast sharply with their previous volunteering and community service experiences. In the PEP courses and programs, faculty went out of their way to make those connections, and students universally found this extremely enlightening and productive.

In addition, direct service activities are most often performed in connection with local or national nonprofit organizations—organizations that are sometimes directly tied to political initiatives or goals and other times are indirectly tied to politics and public policy through the problems they seek to address. Thoughtful faculty find ways to help students become more aware of this fact and its implications, paying particular attention to the role of nonprofits in the wider political economy, both in the United

States and abroad. As one student in the Model United Nations course taught by Dick Reitano explained, "I don't think I would have recognized, prior to Model UN, that small organizations really can have a big impact."

In thinking about the needs addressed by nonprofits, students often mentioned that political work is needed if systemic problems or short-comings that gave rise to those needs are going to be addressed in a comprehensive way. This kind of response reveals both the advances and the limitations represented by students' emerging understanding of the relationship between the immediate needs addressed by community service and the policy environment, which can profoundly affect the social problems that generate those needs. Recognizing the importance of this relationship is clearly an advance in understanding over that of students who provide direct service without any awareness of the wider phenomena those individuals' challenges represent, the impact of political affairs on those phenomena, and the potential for political agency and action around those phenomena. Yet students still have a limited understanding if they believe there can be an effective and broadly acceptable governmental solution to every social issue. At the very least, this perspective represents one particular position with regard to the appropriate role of government (National Association of Secretaries of State, 1999), one that is not acknowledged or examined by these students—or, in some cases, their teachers.

It is worth noting that this formulation of the role of legislation and government action is consistent with research findings on young Americans' conception of citizenship as carrying a wide array of rights and benefits but entailing very limited obligations. A number of studies have found that young people expect that public institutions will meet the needs of the populace but have not thought much about what this would mean or about the range of alternative conceptions of the role of government. In our view, this points to the need to explore with students a wider range of perspectives on the complex relationships among a variety of private, nonprofit, and public institutions that share functions in a complex political economy. These conversations can also profit from attention to the full array of forces that can contribute to systemic change, including but not limited to government action. For example, the environmental protection movement involves everything from lobbying for government-based public policy, attempts to change consumer behaviors such as demand for high mileage cars, and raising awareness about other behaviors of communities and individuals, such as recycling.

But from what students in the PEP reported, as well as what national surveys suggest, it appears that students are seldom encouraged to consider the full range of options available for addressing the issues and problems they care about. Instead of imagining an often complementary spectrum of civic and political actions that can be brought to bear on any given problem, they tend to think instead in bifurcated terms of the direct service volunteer work they are most familiar and comfortable with on the one hand and government action on the other.

The Role of Structures and Incentives

Because civic engagement does not automatically prepare students for effective political participation, it seems clear that more explicit attention to political learning is necessary if we are to take full advantage of higher education's opportunities to prepare thoughtful, skilled, and active citizens. Indeed, that is the central premise of the Political Engagement Project and this book.

Believing that a better understanding of the reasons for the gap between rates of community service and political engagement can help inform our efforts to engage students in politics, we asked the PEP students why, in their opinion, they and many of their peers are so much more likely to participate in service than in politics. Many offered explanations that are familiar from the research literature on the topic: It is easier to see that you are having an effect when you help individuals; the rewards are often more reliable and immediate. We don't see the relevance of politics for our lives. We don't trust politicians or the political process (See, for example, Creighton and Harwood, 1993; Sax, 2004.)

A Route to Political Engagement

Yet these familiar responses were not the most dominant theme in our conversations with PEP students about the disparity between civic and political engagement. A different point came up over and over, in both the student and the faculty interviews: students are offered a great wealth of opportunities to do community service but they perceive very few opportunities and little encouragement to become politically involved. Students are strongly encouraged to do community service—even required to do so in many high schools and some colleges. Community service is incorporated into many college courses, and there are well-elaborated infrastructures on every college campus. The route to becoming politically engaged, however, remains unclear to many students. It is unfamiliar territory, whereas community service has become almost as familiar as going to school. As one student at the Sorensen Institute for Leadership put it: "There was always more pressure toward community service, and more opportunities available. High schools promoted community service activities, but never, ever, promoted a political engagement activity. I don't remember that happening even once. Community service is just so much more emphasized to our generation."

The PEP faculty also pointed to the many opportunities for community service that students are exposed to throughout high school and college compared with the few available for political involvement. Like many of the faculty, Marshall Ganz, who teaches courses on community organizing at Harvard, commented that the community service model is so powerfully inculcated in students throughout many years of their schooling that it has become familiar and comfortable, whereas more politically focused engagements with communities are entirely novel to most college students.

It is often assumed that people feel varying degrees of motivation to participate in either community service or politics and become involved to the degree that they are motivated to do so. This implies that our task as educators is to motivate them in order to ensure that they become engaged. Youniss, McLellan, and Yates (1997) have suggested that this model has the causality reversed—that motivation is largely the *result* of engagement rather than the cause. Young people are recruited to participate in civic or political institutions and processes for many different reasons, including incentives that may have little to do with intrinsic motivation. Then, in the course of participating, they develop relationships that inspire them and make demands on them, gain satisfaction that they could not foresee, and begin to expand and reshape the values and goals that led them to participate, often shifting their sense of identity in the process.

If there is any truth to this alternative formulation of motivation and engagement, the relative absence of opportunities and encouragement for political engagement, in contrast with the plethora of opportunities to engage in nonpolitical service, may provide a more powerful explanation for the disparity than the usual accounts—that students are turned off to mainstream politics, and so on. It may be that young people's high levels of involvement in community service but not politics is less a story of their natural inclinations and choices and more a story of structures of opportunity and incentives provided by adults. The imbalance can be read as a striking success story about efforts to encourage young people to give back to their communities and about the lack of any comparable effort to get them politically involved. This interpretation is consistent with Sax's interpretations of the rise in volunteerism, based on her research using the Higher Education Research Institute surveys. Sax offers three explanations for the rise in volunteer experience among incoming college students: "(1) the increasing numbers of service programs supported by federal and state governments; (2) the increasing numbers of service learning opportunities at the elementary and secondary levels; and (3) the growing numbers of high schools requiring community service for graduation" (2004, pp. 67–68).

Creating Pathways to Political Engagement

We know that well-organized efforts to strengthen political participation among undergraduates and other young Americans can succeed, suggesting that young people will respond favorably to being treated seriously as potentially powerful political agents. In recent years, nonpartisan efforts to turn out the youth vote, such as the World Wrestling Entertainment's partnership in Smackdown Your Vote and Hip-Hop Summit Action Network, seem to have contributed to an increase in young people's political participation in the 2004 and 2006 elections, boosting political awareness, voter registrations, and voting, particularly among groups who tend to participate less, including young blacks. (See, for example, Student PIRGs' New Voters Project, 2006.)

We believe that the domain of political engagement—and thus, the citizenry necessary for a healthy democracy—is ripe for just such a success story if educators and others in control of opportunity structures and incentives begin paying serious attention to this important domain. This would involve creating structured opportunities, offering encouragement, and providing other incentives for reducing known barriers to and increasing familiarity with political participation.

NOTES

1. For example, Verba, Schlozman, and Brady define political engagement as "activity that has the intent or effect of influencing government action—either directly by affecting the making or implementation of public policy or indirectly by influencing the selection of those people who make those policies" (1995, p. 38).

2. For concrete examples of how PEP faculty and program leaders are encouraging their students to draw connections between service experiences and larger political issues, see the "Research/Action Projects and Simulations," "Placements," "Reflection and Journals," and "Examples of Student Work" sections of the PEP document supplement at http://www.carnegiefoundation. org/educating_for_democracy/docs/.

2

THE ROLE OF
HIGHER EDUCATION
IN PREPARING CITIZENS

THERE ARE COMPELLING REASONS to make education for responsible democratic participation a stronger thread in American undergraduate education. The United States is going through what seems like a rocky time, and it has gone through many such times before. The United States is not alone in this. The unfortunate truth is that collective existence is not easy, either inside or across national boundaries. It often feels that it takes more goodwill, wisdom, and competence than human beings possess for them to live and work together productively and peacefully toward the good of all. In democracies, the goal is for individual citizens to be, as much as possible, part of the solution to the complexities of collective existence rather than part of the problem. Considering how hard it is to make that goal a reality, we believe that citizens need all the help they can get.

Higher education is far from the only avenue for preparing citizens to be as politically thoughtful, skillful, and active as can reasonably be expected, but it does present valuable opportunities to do that. In quite a dramatic shift from the past, a very large share of the population now attains at least some college education. The reach of these institutions is much broader than it used to be—and also much broader than it is in most other countries today. With more than seventeen million students in 2005, enrollment in college is at an all-time high. Although issues of equal access remain a concern, two-thirds of all 2004 high school graduates enrolled in colleges, and enrollments for minority, low-income, and first-generation college students are also at an all-time high and are projected to grow (Longo and Meyer, 2006; U.S. Department of Education, 2006).

Yet we fear that, to a large extent, these opportunities to help an increasingly diverse group of young people become more politically thoughtful and engaged are being wasted. Although higher education does prepare students for some aspects of responsible citizenship, it could do much more. As we noted in the previous chapter, although both college and high school students have many opportunities for nonpolitical civic participation, they often have little encouragement or opportunity to engage politically. This situation could be different if educators would pay specific attention to political knowledge, skill, motivation, and participation—the four dimensions of learning for responsible political engagement.

We know that this is a controversial claim. Skeptics suggest that promoting democratic learning is not the business of higher education. Some believe that if political learning is to be represented in schooling at all, it belongs only in primary or secondary school social studies or civics courses. Others argue that, given the strong correlation between advanced education and political participation, colleges already seem to serve this function effectively, even if it is not an explicit focus of the curriculum. Still others express concern that if political learning were addressed more fully in undergraduate education, it would be a diversion from more important academic goals. The most vocal and passionate opposition comes from those who argue that if students' political development becomes an explicit goal of undergraduate education, political bias and indoctrination are inevitable, violating basic liberal democratic norms. Because this final concern is such a complicated and important issue, we will set it aside for now and address it at length in Chapters Three and Four. For now, let us explain why we believe the other concerns to be ill-founded.

Secondary School Civics: The Educational Foundation

Ideally, preparation for active, capable citizenship begins much earlier than during the college years. Parents often play important roles in civic formation, yet we know that not all families are equally positioned to encourage political learning or active participation (Center for Information and Research on Civic Learning and Engagement, 2002). In part because political learning in the context of the family is not sufficient for preparing citizens, middle and high schools have historically taken responsibility for civic education, primarily by teaching students about American history and government.

How effective are these courses? A number of reviews in the last several decades concluded that civics courses do *not* contribute significantly to political knowledge or other aspects of political socialization (Anderson and others, 1990; Jennings and Niemi, 1974; Langton and Jennings, 1968; Torney-Purta, Oppenheim, and Farnen, 1975). More recently, however, research on the impact of civics education shows that, under some circumstances, these courses do have a statistically significant positive impact on political knowledge.

For example, Niemi and Junn (1998) found that the recency and extensiveness of civics courses, the breadth of topics addressed, and the extent to which the courses include open discussions of current events made significant contributions to knowledge. Zukin and colleagues (2006) found that open discussions of political issues and direct teaching of and practice in performing civic skills led to increased political engagement among a large proportion of the students who had these experiences. Despite this evidence that such courses at the high school level can make a difference in political learning if they incorporate good practices, these educational practices are far from universal, and the majority of students in this study said that their interest in politics did not increase as a result of the civics courses they had taken.

Other research also shows that, for most students, high school civics does not impart sufficient political understanding for responsible participation. Studies of high school graduates make it clear that even their political knowledge—usually the strongest outcome of secondary civics education—is shockingly weak in many areas. For example, a 2005 survey of California high school seniors who had taken a state-mandated twelfth-grade U.S. government course found that although a high percentage of these students said that they planned to vote, most did not feel well-enough informed to vote responsibly (see California Campaign for the Civic Mission of Schools, 2005). They had little knowledge of major political issues or current events, half could not correctly identify the function of the Supreme Court, a third could not name even one of California's two U.S. senators, and 41 percent did not know whether the Republican or Democratic Party is more conservative. This study is consistent with national data. For example, in the 1998 Civics Assessment of the National Assessment of Educational Progress, three-quarters of high school seniors performed at basic or below basic levels. More than a third were below basic, and only 4 percent performed at the highest level, proficient (Lutkus and others, 1999).

Informal Political Education: Scaffolding Lifelong Political Learning

Fortunately, education for political knowledge, commitment, and expertise need not stop after graduation from high school, even for those who do not go on to college. Important sources for political learning lie outside formal educational settings altogether. There is no question that people can learn a lot about politics throughout life, especially if they pay some attention to the media and other forums where political discussion takes place or if they are inclined to talk about politics with others. Civic skills are often gained through community involvement in clubs or religious organizations, and workplaces (Verba, Schlozman, and Brady, 1995). Those who participate actively in electoral politics and those who work to address local issues in their neighborhoods and communities gain both political knowledge and political skills.

Even those who avoid more demanding types of political engagement are exposed to political events, politically relevant information, political opinions and interpretations, and political debate from many sources— from television coverage of news, issues, and candidates; public radio and commercial "talk radio"; print and electronic newspapers and magazines; participation in many community groups or activities; informal discussions with acquaintances, friends, and family members; mailings of political flyers and other literature; and even telephone solicitations from political fundraisers. Of course, individuals vary in the attention they pay to these sources of information and opinion. Some ignore all but the most inescapable of the messages, whereas others, the relatively rare "political junkies," pursue political information with all the fervor of addicts. But most people have at least some modest awareness of the political environment, locally, nationally, and even internationally, and most form at least some tentative opinions on the main issues of the day.

This kind of ongoing informal education is critical for an informed and thoughtful electorate. Media sources, books, public lectures and debates, and other educational opportunities can be of the highest quality and are essential mechanisms of lifelong education for democracy. But overall, informal political education is hit or miss, and ultimately, inadequate in most cases. What we might think of as consumer-driven political education tends to reach most fully only the subset of people who are already concerned about and engaged with politics, providing much less to those who are not already interested and inclined to pay attention. In the general population, political knowledge is not high, even during or right after presidential elections. Delli Carpini and Keeter (1996), for example, reported that in the 1992 presidential election between the senior George Bush and Bill Clinton, only 15 percent of those surveyed knew that both candidates supported the death penalty. Very sizable minorities could not place the two candidates relative to one another on their positions on abortion (39 percent), defense (44 percent) and other key issues, or on overall ideology (36 percent). Similarly, a large minority of those surveyed could not place the two main political parties relative to each other on key issues or overall ideology. Surveys conducted around the time of the 2004 presidential election similarly showed that nearly 60 percent of Americans had heard little or nothing of the controversial Patriot Act and 70 percent were unaware of George W. Bush's prescription drug bill, the most expensive new government program in forty years and a critical piece of his domestic policy agenda (Somin, 2006).

Moreover, we know that relatively easy access to political information is insufficient for supporting responsible citizenship. Without a strong foundation of institutional knowledge, or an ability and willingness to evaluate information critically and with an open mind, it is far less likely that individuals can learn as much from media or political debates, assimilate new information about political issues, put international events in political context, or allow their opinions to be shaped by pertinent information (Popkin and Dimock, 1999; Rahn, Aldrich, and Borgida, 1994; Shapiro and Bloch-Elkon, 2006). Most people do not seek out in-depth information; consider multiple points of view; engage in sustained deliberation about political institutions, processes, and issues; or develop a wide array of political skills.

It is time-consuming to pursue political understanding and engagement in a serious way, and many people feel their lives are busy enough without this kind of additional time commitment, even if only a few hours a week to keep up with the newspaper or television news. Furthermore, we know that younger generations are much less likely to pay attention to traditional news sources, and although they are more likely to rely on the Internet and entertainment programs drawing on current events (such as the satirical news program *The Daily Show* with Jon Stewart), their overall attention to politics remains relatively low (Harvard University Institute of Politics, 2005; Sax and others, 2003; Zukin and others, 2006).

In addition, the quality of much informal political information is questionable. Political advertising, many blogs, and most commercial talk radio shows make no claim or pretense of being unbiased. In fact, some of these sources knowingly or unknowingly disseminate misleading or incorrect information. Much television news coverage is notoriously superficial, and may not sustain the attention of viewers in any case. Communications research indicates that even the intense public information efforts of political campaigns succeed mostly in reinforcing the entrenched prior beliefs of their target audiences (Jamieson, 2000). In addition, some research suggests that people may be too willing to defer to the views of "opinion leaders" who are neither expert on complex public policies nor committed to providing a fair or unbiased consideration of competing perspectives. One experiment, for example, found that on the issue of crime control, most liberal voters were willing to follow the views of liberal talk show host Phil Donahue while most conservatives were willing to follow those of conservative talk show host Rush Limbaugh, even though neither is an expert on crime (Lupia and McCubbins, 1998).

Contemporary Higher Education and Political Knowledge and Participation

How well, then, does a typical American college education prepare students for the complex demands of informed and active citizenship? There is no question that formal education is a powerful predictor of political knowledge, civic values, and active engagement in the political realm. This has been shown in study after study and in numerous reviews of the literature (Delli Carpini and Keeter, 1996; Nie, Junn, and Stehlik-Barry, 1996; Pascarella and Terenzini, 2005). Educational attainment, especially the attainment of a college degree, clearly has a substantial positive association with many key attributes of effective citizenship, including knowledge of the principles of democracy, political leaders, and other political concepts and information; political interest and attentiveness; frequency of voting; participation in high-demand political activities; and essential democratic virtues such as tolerance.

Indeed, studies of the relationship between educational attainment and political knowledge and behavior make it clear that the wealth of informal opportunities for lifelong learning in the political realm tend to magnify rather than diminish disparities between those with and without a college education. Although this is troubling from the perspective of democratic equality, it also suggests the role that higher education can play in promoting the cognitive skills required to acquire, process, and analyze relevant political information, as well as the motivation and the opportunity to do so (Delli Carpini and Keeter, 1996; Nie, Junn, and Stehlik-Barry, 1996). As Delli Carpini and Keeter underscore, "All education, but especially college, has a powerful effect on political knowledge through the development of skills and orientations that make it easier for the well schooled to comprehend and retain political information" (1996, p. 192). Similarly, Nie and colleagues emphasize that "formal education has a dramatic impact on the ability of individuals to gather information on a variety of subjects, organize facts meaningfully, and efficiently process additional and related knowledge" (1996, p. 41).

These findings not only point to the importance of strengthening political learning at the secondary school level but also suggest that investments in college students' political sophistication and concern will pay compounded benefits as those individuals proceed through life. It stands to reason that the more we prepare young people to appreciate high-quality sources of informal political information, to evaluate political messages carefully, and to actively seek further learning throughout their lives, the better able they will be to benefit from high-quality sources of political information and protect themselves from biased and unreliable sources.

Strong correlations between college attendance and civic or political participation are probably not entirely due to the direct effect of higher education, however. For one thing, there is evidence that a significant part of the relationship can be accounted for by a selection effect—that is, the students who are most likely to be civically or politically engaged are also more likely to attend college. Research on high school students indicates that those who later go on to college are already higher in political interest, efficacy, sophistication, and knowledge before they matriculate. Thus, colleges attract or select applicants who are more civically and politically engaged than their peers (Jennings, 1993; Jennings and Niemi, 1981; Torney-Purta, Barber, and Wilkenfeld, 2006). This may be due in part to the fact that college-bound students are more likely to come from families who are educated themselves and who value political engagement more than families of students who do not go on to higher education.

Despite this selection effect, most political scientists believe that the statistical relationships between educational attainment and various civic and political indicators also represent some real effects of education. But only a portion of this influence is a *direct* result of education. Direct effects include the development of cognitive skills such as communication, critical thinking, and formal reasoning, as well as substantive learning about historical, economic, and social processes, which make it easier to understand and remember complex political ideas and information. It appears that the indirect effects of higher education are at least as important. It is well-known, for example, that individuals with greater economic and other resources are more likely to participate politically than those with fewer resources. Because higher education attainment is positively related to income and social status, and these resource variables predict political participation, some of the statistical relationship between educational attainment and political engagement can be attributed to the mediating effect of these resource variables.

According to Verba, Schlozman, and Brady (1995), another important mediator of indirect effects of education is workplace experience. These authors show that, among all the nonpolitical settings they considered, the workplace offers by far the most opportunities to learn and practice civic skills. But access to these opportunities is more stratified in the workplace than in any other setting. The extent to which one's paid work involves learning and exercising civic skills, such as organizing and leading meetings, writing persuasively, or mobilizing others, is strongly related to the job's status in the organization and the amount of responsibility (and therefore compensation) it entails. Clearly, workers with the lowest levels of education will have the fewest opportunities to develop civic skills on the job. In sum, more highly educated workers will be more likely to develop skills that facilitate their political engagement.

A Paradox

The indirect effects of education on political knowledge and engagement help explain a striking paradox: political knowledge and engagement have not increased in the past fifty years (indeed, according to some indicators, they have decreased) while the proportion of the U.S. population attending college has increased dramatically. Delli Carpini and Keeter (1996), for example, found that over the half century addressed in their study— the 1940s to the 1990s—overall levels of political knowledge did not increase, even though the proportion of individuals attending college more than doubled. In fact, they report, "Today's college graduates are roughly equivalent [in political knowledge] to the high school graduates of that earlier epoch [the 1940s]" (pp. 197–198). This does not mean that education has no impact: the political knowledge of non-college-educated individuals in recent cohorts has also declined. Delli Carpini and Keeter report that those with a high school degree now are roughly as knowledgeable as high school dropouts of the mid-twentieth century.

Several interpretations of this paradoxical phenomenon have been proposed. Nie and colleagues (Nie, Junn, and Stehlik-Barry, 1996) stress that it may not be the learning that results from higher education that increases participation but, instead, higher education's sorting function—one's location in the social structure, which is connected with access to scarce resources such as income and other aspects of high-level jobs. In this view, it is one's relative rather than absolute educational attainment that matters, meaning that even as the average educational level in the United States increases, rates of political engagement remain static. Other explanations for the paradox focus on factors other than education to help explain political participation, factors that have changed so as to decrease participation, thus offsetting the population increase in educational attainment. These include things like greater political alienation, declining participation in communities (social capital), and demographic shifts such as generational effects.

These generational effects are especially relevant to our own analysis, because they show that college-age students of the current generation are less politically engaged than those who preceded them. So, for example, only a third of college freshmen in 2003 and 36.4 percent in 2005 said that "keeping up to date with political affairs" is essential or very important; this compares with 60 percent of freshmen in 1966 (Pryor and others, 2005; Sax and others, 2003).

Bennett and Bennett (2003) report that the statistical strength of the long-standing relationship between higher education and some aspects of political participation seems to have weakened in recent years. They attribute this shift in part to the fact that college-educated young Americans are not as politically active as previous cohorts were at their age, so the political engagement advantage experienced by college-educated versus non-college-educated individuals is diminished: "The data . . . show some differences among young Americans, depending on whether they have or have not had some college experience, but by and large one is not impressed by college-educated young people's psychological involvement in public affairs and political activism" (p. 9).

Bennett and Bennett (2003) stress that attending college still had a statistically significant impact on civic and political participation in 2000, as it did in 1972. But the effect is smaller, with exposure to higher education having less impact, showing, for example, that exposure to higher education had a stronger differential effect on news consumption in 1972 than in 2000. The failure of rising levels of college attendance to boost political knowledge or participation suggests that we cannot count on mere involvement in higher education alone to adequately support young people's political development.

In addition, much research finds that political knowledge and participation are unevenly distributed across the population, even when education is held constant. Delli Carpini and Keeter (1996), for example, found large group differences in political knowledge, with women, African Americans, low-income people, and younger Americans showing the lowest levels of political knowledge. Most of these knowledge gaps have remained stable over time, but there was no gap between younger and older cohorts in midcentury, whereas by 1989, the cohort difference (post–baby boom versus others) had become substantial. Understandably, individuals who expressed less interest in politics were also lower in their political knowledge.

In light of these group differences, it is important to note that larger percentages of groups that tend to have lower levels of political knowledge and involvement are now enrolled in college. Reflecting this general trend, the students who participated in the Political Engagement Project included somewhat more women than men, sizable percentages of first-generation college students, racial minorities, students whose parents were immigrants, and students who had low levels of political interest at the outset of the PEP course or program. As we presented in our summary of findings in the Introduction, the positive impact of the courses and programs tended to be greater for these groups than for groups that have historically shown higher levels of political knowledge and participation.

Benefits of Education for Political Engagement: Cognitive Development

One of the most widespread objections to increasing the attention on political learning in undergraduate education is the belief that this emphasis will detract from other, more important academic goals (see, for example, Murphy, 2004). But the evidence is reassuring on this score. Research on service learning makes it clear that incorporating civic participation in the curriculum can increase rather than decrease academic achievement (Astin, Vogelgesang, Ikeda, and Yee, 2000; Eyler and Giles, 1999), and we believe that the same is true for more specifically political participation.

When students are educated for political understanding, skill, and engagement, they benefit from learning a wide array of communications, interpersonal, research, and other intellectual skills, as well as developing important personal qualities such as persistence, responsibility, and tolerance. All of these outcomes are widely considered central to a good undergraduate education. The general educational benefits of attention to political learning are especially evident in the area of cognitive development, which is undeniably one of the two or three most central goals of undergraduate education. Virtually all colleges aspire to teach their students how to think in a more sophisticated way about complex issues, which is a key aspect of their cognitive development, and education for political development is well-suited to contribute to this cognitive goal.

A close look at well-documented cognitive-developmental goals, including reflective judgment and critical thinking, helps illustrate the ways in which political learning and other kinds of academic learning are mutually reinforcing. Reflective judgment and critical thinking are essential for responsible political and civic engagement. They are equally important for understanding substantive material in academic disciplines, for professional work, and for a wide array of roles in which individuals engage as private persons over the course of their lives. It is no wonder they are centrally represented in the mission statements and educational goals of virtually every American college and university. Because cognitive learning in this sense represents such a clear intersection of political and other academic learning, we will consider it here in some depth.

Reflective Judgment

The dimension of college students' cognitive capacities that is most relevant to that intersection is captured in the extensive work of Patricia King and Karen Kitchener (1994, 2002), which connects with related work by Perry (1970), Knefelkamp (1974), Baxter Magolda (1992), and others. King and Kitchener have described the development of what they call *reflective judgment,* which refers to the judgments individuals make about ill-structured problems for which there are multiple possible solutions. As individuals develop more mature reflective judgment, they exhibit changes in their epistemological assumptions, in their ability to evaluate knowledge claims and evidence, and in the ways they justify their claims and beliefs, all of which are central to learning to think and communicate clearly about this kind of ill-structured problem.

King and Kitchener (1994, 2002) describe stages of increasing maturity in reflective judgment. At the lowest level, individuals imagine knowledge to be certain and absolute, though they are aware that not everyone has knowledge in any given area and sometimes the truth about an issue is not yet known even to authorities. At the next level, individuals recognize that some problems are ill-structured and inevitably include elements of uncertainty. At the highest level, individuals "recognize that knowledge is never a given but rather the outcome of inquiry, synthesis of evidence and opinion, evaluation of evidence and arguments"; they recognize that "some judgments are more solidly grounded and defensible than others"; they judge beliefs "with respect to their reasonableness, consistency with the evidence, plausibility of the argument, and probability in light of the assembled information"; and they recognize that "judgments may be reviewed and altered on the basis of new information, perspectives, or tools for inquiry" (Pascarella and Terenzini, 2005, p. 38).

Courses addressing political understanding and engagement entail discussion of exactly the kinds of issues that King and Kitchener call ill-structured problems. Students at the *prereflective level* (King and Kitchener, 1994, 2002) will not be able to make sense of some aspects of political discussion that are crucial to that discourse—awareness of these problems' inherent uncertainty and lack of a single authoritative answer, along with the need for careful evaluation of evidence and plausibility of argument. By contrast, students do have the requisite cognitive abilities to engage in these activities once they reach the *quasi-reflective level,* although they need to reach the *reflective level* if they are to be fully proficient.

College students almost universally need to develop in this area, because most come into college with very simplistic conceptions of knowledge, rational discourse, and related issues. Students entering college show significant variation in the maturity of their reflective judgment, but most enter at the prereflective level, believing that knowledge is gained through personal experience or by finding out the right answers from authorities. Although students at this level lack the prerequisites for a reasoned approach to dealing with ill-structured problems, their growing "recognition that knowledge is sometimes uncertain and [their] increasing need to justify beliefs reflect a growing ability to differentiate categories of thought and signal movement toward more complex stages of thinking" (Pascarella and Terenzini, 2005, p. 37). Fortunately, students' reflective judgment does advance during college, with most reaching the quasi-reflective level. This is a critical transition, because at this level they are able to use reason and evidence in forming, evaluating, and justifying judgments.

Critical Thinking

A related construct of particular relevance to deliberation and judgment about political issues is *critical thinking.* Although researchers use many different definitions and measures of critical thinking, most address students' capacity to "identify central issues and assumptions in an argument, recognize important relationships, make correct [in]ferences from data, . . . interpret whether conclusions are warranted based on data, evaluate evidence or authority" (Pascarella and Terenzini, 2005, p. 156). Like reflective judgment, critical thinking develops significantly during college but does not reach full proficiency by the end of the senior year.

Some investigators have looked not only at the *ability* to think critically but also the *disposition* to do so—that is, the inclination to be open-minded, ask challenging questions, follow reasons and evidence wherever they lead, and appreciate complexity and ambiguity. This disposition to think critically is also an important dimension of high-quality political discourse. Fortunately, students' disposition to think critically also increases during college, making a notable jump between the freshman and sophomore years.

A student in one of the PEP programs, the University of Maryland's CIVICUS Living-Learning Program, which begins in freshman year and extends over several years of college, described the change in her experience of political learning from the first to the later years of the program in terms that reflect exactly the kinds of developmental distinctions King and Kitchener and others have described. Although this student attributed much of the change to differences in the program itself over the years, it seems at least as likely that she was noticing a change in her own capacity for reflective and critical thinking. It is telling that in freshman year she considered terms like *social capital* and *civil society* to be "information" that needed to be memorized, whereas later these same terms represented "topics and issues" that needed to be understood in terms of their contexts and implications:

> The details of the first year are a little sketchy to me. I remember the first class we had to take, when we were freshmen. It was a lot of information. . . . But as we took more classes, we actually took in the information more and could relate it to our lives better. [By information] I would say all the concepts we were learning about—civil society, social capital, things like that. All those things were thrown at us, and we kind of felt like we had to memorize a lot of information. But it wasn't really relatable to what we were actually doing. But as we went through the program, we had a little more sense of like the contexts of those topics and issues. [In the first year] it was so much information that I wasn't really grasping it at first. As we actually talked about these issues and read about more current issues and articles about it, I understood it better.

Synergy Between Cognitive Development and Political Learning

Even though, on average, reflective judgment and capacity for and disposition toward critical judgment develop during college, the research also indicates that students vary in the rates at which they advance. (A detailed review of the factors that support more significant advances in these aspects of cognitive growth is available in Pascarella and Terenzini, 2005.) The basic outlines of that research are worth considering because they illustrate so well the potential synergy between political learning and general cognitive development. It is noteworthy that the educational experiences associated with more significant growth in reflective judgment and critical thinking include all of the key pedagogies and general approaches to teaching and learning that we found to be especially salient in the work of the PEP faculty and program leaders.[1]

The key factors identified as contributing to greater advances in reflective judgment and critical thinking by Pascarella and Terenzini's comprehensive 2005 review include the following:

○ Students' perceptions of their institution as emphasizing critical, evaluative, and analytic judgment

○ Purposeful instruction and practice in deliberation about ill-structured problems, along with reflection about epistemological assumptions such as credibility and warrant

○ Experience arguing about significant topics of controversy

○ Constructivist and cooperative pedagogies, in which students are actively involved in their own learning experiences

○ High-quality service learning—that is, service learning in which challenging service experiences are well integrated with academic course content and accompanied by ongoing structured reflection

○ Both in-class and out-of-class discussions with peers whose personal values, political beliefs, religious beliefs, or national origins are different from their own

○ Faculty who are accessible to students and concerned about student growth and development

○ Extracurricular involvement in organizations and clubs, especially those that encourage the application of classroom learning to the organization's activities

We found all of these factors well represented in the PEP courses and programs, which we believe are ideally suited to teaching for reflective judgment and critical thinking.

Public and Private Benefits of Political Learning

In addition to contributing to other educational goals, political development is itself a goal of great value to communities and to students themselves. As important as it is to cultivate competent, responsible citizens for the sake of a strong democracy, this is not the only reason to educate college students in political affairs. Preparation for active and informed citizenship is also a private good—that is, it directly benefits the students themselves. Providing the kind of education that inspires and supports informed, effective participation can be endorsed simply because it helps individuals promote or achieve their own political preferences or makes them more effective political actors (Aldrich, 1993). Political knowledge and skills are understood by many political scientists as valuable resources that are differentially available to people (Delli Carpini and Keeter, 1996; Niemi and Junn, 1998).

Possession of these resources makes it more likely that individuals will be able to understand how political choices affect their real interests—that is, the choices they would make if fully informed, and more capable of pursuing those interests effectively. In addition, more highly skilled and knowledgeable political action is likely to be more productive in achieving results that are in the actor's interest, thus increasing the value of time invested in political activities. For example, participation helps people pursue their own particular political interests and issues, whether they be neighborhood improvement or Social Security, by getting them on the political agenda and increasing the chances that government will respond to their concerns (Berry, Portney, and Thompson, 1993; Campbell, 2003).

Moreover, a number of political scientists and psychologists have pointed to broader personal rewards of political engagement. Overall, the cultivation of political capacities related to political understanding and skill represents an important aspect of the development of the individual's full human potential, an idea that has held currency since the days of Plato and Aristotle. Both classical and more contemporary advocates of democracy highlight the valuable educative, enlightening, creative, self-actuating, or self-realization effects that political involvement can have for individuals, particularly involvement that goes beyond the voting booth (Barber, 1984; Mansbridge, 1999; Pateman, 1970; Thompson, 1970).

Participating in politics can expand our intellectual capacities or engender a meaningful sense of personal fulfillment or identity. Writers as varied as Rousseau, de Tocqueville, and Arendt identified psychological processes by which political participation engenders individual development such as improving our capacity for reasoning, compassion, courage, and enterprise. John Stuart Mill argued that the interactive exchanges involved in political participation produce "the capacities moral, intellectual, and active," by expanding one's sense of one's own interests (Mill, 1862, n.p.).

A number of empirical studies have also pointed to the personal rewards of political engagement. Verba, Schlozman, and Brady (1995), for example, found that their respondents often stressed the civic and social gratification they gained from political participation. Political activity can be fun or exciting, and it can offer the chance to spend time with other people and gain their esteem. In addition, some political actions are intrinsically satisfying and perhaps better understood as expressive rather than instrumental in nature, with the benefit deriving from performance of the action itself rather than (or in addition to) deriving from its expected consequences. Pursuing something they believe in, acting with a sense of higher purpose, is for many people at least as gratifying as accomplishing an extrinsic goal.

Verba, Schlozman, and Brady (1995) investigated the types of gratification that politically active individuals cited as resulting from their involvement in politics. They found, not too surprisingly, that respondents mentioned different kinds of gratification depending on the nature of the political activity. Overall, they found that potential career advantages and other material benefits were seldom part of the equation. Those who engaged in political activities performed in a social context frequently cited the gratification of working with others. For all forms of political activity, civic gratification played a significant role, with many respondents referring to the satisfaction of doing their part or furthering a cause they believe in.

Ethical Legitimacy of Educating for Political Engagement

Believing that both American democracy and the students themselves will benefit, we advocate including many aspects of political learning as serious goals in undergraduate education and contend that learning for political engagement should be included in the curriculum as well as in extracurricular student life. Education for political development not only contributes to other key undergraduate learning goals but is a feasible way to increase political involvement: students do show gains in many dimensions of political understanding, motivation, skill, and expected participation if they take part in courses and programs that make these goals a priority and use effective teaching methods to achieve them.

Several critically important questions remain: Is educating for political development ethically defensible? Or does this set of goals run too great a risk of being political indoctrination? Is it compatible with not only the *educational goals* of undergraduate education but also the *values* of academic institutions? These questions are being hotly debated at the moment. Critics are raising questions about whether higher education faculty are trying to indoctrinate or proselytize, imposing their own political views on students. If proselytizing is unavoidable in education for political development, then we would agree with these critics' conclusion that it does not belong in the academy. We turn to these questions in the next chapter.

NOTE

1. For examples of how PEP faculty and program leaders put some of these key pedagogies to work, see the "Deliberation, Discussion, and Debate," "Research/Action Projects and Simulations," "Placements," and "Reflection and Journals" sections of the PEP document supplement at http://www. carnegiefoundation.org/educating_for_democracy/docs/.

3

THE OPEN INQUIRY IMPERATIVE

IF WE ARE TO TREAT education for responsible political engagement as a serious goal, then it must be integrated into the curriculum, as well as into extracurricular programs and the campus more broadly. Yet many people both inside and outside the academy disagree. They say that political issues do not belong in the classroom, that serious abuses are inevitable if they are allowed in, and that it is preferable for individuals to find other ways to educate themselves for political engagement. We believe, however, that it is possible to create a harmonious relationship between the political development goals we advocate and the special character of higher education.

As we discussed in Chapter Two, many forms of informal political education—such as political advertising, partisan blogs, and some radio and television shows—are often deeply biased and of poor quality. In contrast, the kind of political education we advocate for the college curriculum and campus should resemble the best kind of journalism: nonpartisan and unbiased, open to multiple points of view, grounded in a deep knowledge base and serious deliberation, and civil in tone. We believe that efforts to educate for political development must aim to help students understand a wide range of perspectives and positions, learn skills that are useful in the service of their own self-defined political goals, and develop their motivation to pursue those goals.

There have long been questions about whether and how colleges and universities can prepare students for their roles as responsible, politically engaged citizens without imposing particular ideologies, but they take on special urgency now that some conservative commentators and activists have charged that the academy carries a pervasive liberal political bias. Among the various recommendations these critics have made is to exclude discussion of political and policy issues from the classroom altogether.

Similarly, some educators prefer to steer clear of education for political—as opposed to more broadly civic—engagement because they fear that education for political development cannot avoid charges of bias and indoctrination. We believe these attitudes reveal a misunderstanding of the nature of high-quality education for political development and its compatibility with key academic values.

Core Academic Values

Including education for political development explicitly in undergraduate education, especially in the curriculum, is legitimate only if it is consistent with the core values of higher education institutions. What are these core values? Although there is room for differences of emphasis and interpretation, few would dispute that scholarship, teaching, and learning in higher education should be guided by intellectual integrity, mutual respect and tolerance, a willingness to listen to and take seriously the ideas of others, public consideration of contested issues, and a commitment to rational discourse, procedural impartiality, and civility. These values are essential to the central tasks of higher education, but their importance is not entirely instrumental. They are also critical to the moral legitimacy of the educational enterprise, and represent a core ethical commitment of that enterprise.

Intellectual Pluralism and Diversity of Perspective

The values of intellectual pluralism, open-mindedness, and respect for diversity of perspective lie at the heart of higher education's dual mission: the advancement of knowledge through research and the education of students. Freedom to pursue unorthodox ideas is essential if creativity and innovation, which underlie the advancement of knowledge, are to thrive. Diversity of perspective also contributes to a vibrant educational context, enhancing students' depth of understanding, intellectual vitality, and critical capacities.

In his classic essay "On Liberty," John Stuart Mill underscored the importance of open-minded consideration of diverse points of view through arguments that connect directly to the university's educational and knowledge-building roles. He pointed out that "it is only by the collision of adverse opinions" that the "whole truth" has any chance of emerging, that even a correct position unless it is defended in the face of vigorous challenges, will "be held in the manner of a prejudice with little comprehension or feeling of its rational grounds," and that the meaning of a particular teaching will be "lost or enfeebled" without such challenges (Mill, [1859] 2002, p. 54). Because of its importance for truth-seeking and deep understanding, Mill recommended a rich intellectual context that has come to be known as the *marketplace of ideas*.

Respect for diversity of opinion and open-minded consideration of opposing views are essential for the legitimacy of courses that educate for political engagement. In general, faculty choices about whether and how to include diverse perspectives on an issue depend on the topic and its place in the field being taught. For some issues, there are alternative perspectives that are credible and important enough to warrant inclusion; for others, controversies surrounding the issue have been resolved, at least for the moment. When it comes to teaching for political understanding and engagement, however, it is important to provide multiple credible points of view whenever possible. We realize that judgment in this realm is key, and we are not suggesting that faculty give "equal time" to views they consider to be without merit. Although there are surely exceptions, however, we generally think that faculty who have passionate political convictions and personally find all opposing views to be without merit have a responsibility as teachers to include what they (or other experts in the field) see as the best alternative perspectives. In this sense, the press to teach about and consider multiple points of view constrains academic freedom in the name of good teaching. This is just one of many tensions among positive values that have to be negotiated when teaching for political understanding and engagement.

We are suggesting that faculty, in their roles as teachers, ought to help their students develop a quality of openness to new ideas as well as the capacity to make and evaluate arguments and justifications for their own and others' positions. These two goals are linked, because students need some basis on which to make judgments about the new ideas they are considering. One way to teach for these goals is to model this kind of discourse. If faculty want to be effective models of open-mindedness in the political domain, it can be worthwhile for them to think about their own potential vulnerability to ideological prejudice and to be self-conscious in cultivating a genuine openness to and respect for different, even opposing, perspectives.

Academic Freedom

For Mill, pursuit of truth through the open-minded consideration of diverse perspectives provided the central rationale for freedom of opinion and expression. This value—academic freedom—is one of the central commitments of the modern university. Academic freedom means that faculty are granted wide latitude to formulate and express opinions, including controversial opinions, toward the goal of high-quality scholarship, which is recognized to depend on intellectual exploration, integrity, and creativity.

These core academic values of freedom of expression, along with a corresponding respect for others' intellectual autonomy, have important implications for curricular efforts to foster students' political development. Conservative critics have said that many faculty bring into the classroom political issues that are not relevant to the subject matter and that this practice is neither legitimate nor protected by academic freedom (American Council of Trustees and Alumni, 2004; Horowitz, 2004a, 2004b). This raises the question of whose prerogative it is to determine whether a topic is relevant to a given course.

Of course, faculty members' academic freedom as teachers is not unlimited—the undergraduate curriculum cannot be simply a loose collection of courses representing their personal interests. Within the boundaries of departmental and institutional needs, however, it is up to faculty to determine the specific goals and content of the courses they teach and to decide what material and assignments will best accomplish those goals. This includes making judgments about whether and how to address controversial issues in whatever domains are relevant to the course. This is not only a faculty prerogative but an essential feature of learning in higher education. We have seen that political or policy issues can be relevant to a wide range of courses and that students can benefit from encountering these issues across many sectors of the curriculum.

Many controversial issues concern theoretical and other debates within academic disciplines or fields and have little to do with the kinds of political or social issues that have been receiving public attention in recent years. Controversy is unavoidable in academic life, and diversity of opinion is essential in all areas of scholarship, including areas that have nothing at all to do with politics. It is also important to recognize that many questions of social and public policy do not raise intensely emotional, controversial, "hot-button" issues for most students. In fact, faculty who incorporate a political focus in their courses often make a point of staying away from divisive issues such as abortion. The reason for this is not so much fear of controversy and conflict as recognition that very contentious discussions are rarely terribly productive.

Standards of Academic Discourse

As important as they are, open-minded consideration of alternative perspectives and the academic freedom to pursue ideas wherever they lead do not fully capture the special quality of academic life with which formal education for political development must be aligned. Both of these central values are inextricably bound up with the essential cluster of academic values that establishes standards for the kinds of expression that should be taken seriously or considered academically legitimate, both in scholarship and in teaching. Open-minded consideration of diverse ideas is meaningless without some way to evaluate competing perspectives. Academic freedom is empty if it is not guided by a commitment to intellectual quality. Although the particular features of scholarly and scientific standards are discipline-specific and often contested, at a more general level they represent a shared understanding of academic discourse as requiring *reasoned justification of claims, presentation of evidence, and consideration of plausible alternative explanations of the evidence and of objections to proposed interpretations.*

When education for political development is introduced into academic coursework, it is obliged to conform to these standards of academic discourse, just as any other subject matter is. In this way, academically based education for political development contrasts with political advertising and proselytizing and with much informal political discourse in everyday life. Often, those nonacademic forms of political persuasion use all available means to achieve their goals, whereas education for political understanding in the academy has to be shaped by reasoned argument, warrant or evidence for one's views, consideration of alternative points of view, and a knowledge base that is as free of ideological bias as possible.

A central dimension of educating for political understanding and engagement is to teach students to bring these standards of deliberation and argumentation to their political thinking and discourse, to subject their own and others' claims and opinions to critical analysis and evaluation. This means being curious, intellectually honest, and open to new ideas discrepant from one's own, and not simply closing off consideration of these ideas based on prejudice. These essential personal qualities and intellectual skills are among the most important goals of education for political development.

If students master these skills, it will help protect them from illegitimate persuasion both during college and later in life. As noted in the statement "Academic Freedom and Educational Responsibility" issued by the Association of American Colleges and Universities (2006, n.p.): "Building such intellectual and personal capacities is the right way to warn students of the inappropriateness and dangers of indoctrination, help them see through the distortions of propaganda, and enable them to assess judiciously the persuasiveness of powerful emotional appeals. Emphasizing the quality of analysis helps students see why unwelcome views need to be heard rather than silenced. By thoughtfully engaging diverse perspectives, liberal education leads to greater personal freedom through greater competence."

These shared standards for academic discourse have a number of important implications for what students can legitimately expect from faculty and what faculty can expect from students. These implications are important for teaching and learning in almost any subject area and are especially critical when highly charged political, social, and religious issues are involved.

SETTING LIMITS FOR ACADEMIC FREEDOM. First, standards for intellectual discourse serve to anchor and ground academic freedom, even sometimes placing boundaries on the academic freedom of faculty in their roles as scholars and teachers. These standards are critical for assessing or demonstrating the value of ideas, and they are institutionalized in processes, conventions, and structures that regulate academic opportunity, performance, and advancement. These institutional structures mean that faculty do not have absolute license, because there are standards of discourse and scholarship against which their work—both research and teaching—is judged. In good teaching, faculty back up their claims and assertions and take seriously alternative points of view for which a credible case can be made. The responsibility to teach in conformity with standards of academic discourse also means that students are free to put forward ideas that conflict with positions taken by the faculty member, and those ideas will be judged on their merits.

SETTING LIMITS FOR STUDENTS. Standards of academic discourse establish limits for students as well. Sometimes students want faculty to devote serious attention in their courses to positions their teachers believe to be without merit. Of course, making this kind of judgment is not always straightforward, and faculty should not hastily rule a topic out of bounds without taking students' concerns seriously. Ultimately, though, it is not possible for faculty to follow every suggested tangent. Some positions are not supported well enough to warrant coverage, and some are simply irrelevant to the subject at hand. When student suggestions are credible but not central enough to the subject matter to take the time of the whole class, some faculty suggest readings or special projects interested students might pursue on their own. Ultimately, though, faculty must be the judge of whether and how to address topics suggested by students.

Sometimes it is necessary not only to leave out topics that some students want to cover in a course but also to include issues and assignments that make some students uncomfortable. Because it is up to the instructor's judgment to determine the subject matter's intellectual credibility and relevance to course goals, students do not have the right to insist that credible positions that are unsettling to them be excluded from the classroom.

A May 2005 article in the *Chronicle of Higher Education* describes a situation in which students made this kind of demand. Ann Bahr, a philosophy and religion professor at South Dakota State University, described a number of incidents in which some Christian fundamentalist students in her courses demanded that particular readings and perspectives be included in the syllabus and others excluded (Bahr, 2005). In one case, a group of religiously conservative students claimed that two books on Evangelical Christianity that Bahr had assigned were biased against that religious movement and should be removed from the reading list. One of the books was written by a respected Evangelical scholar, the other by a highly regarded scholar whose religious identity is less clear. Because the books were not particularly critical of Evangelical Christianity, Bahr surmised that it may have been "the objective, scholarly tone of the books that upset [her] students." In her view, these students seemed to be hoping for a more devotional stance toward religion in this Religion in American Culture course. Bahr kept the readings in the syllabus, over her students' protests. Similar kinds of incidents have been reported in the political domain and at the intersection of religious and political concerns—an area of particular salience on campuses today.

Teaching students to understand and value the kind of "objective, scholarly" perspective that Bahr's students found objectionable—a discourse governed by standards of reason and evidence—is a central educational function of colleges and universities. Both developmentally and culturally, many students arrive with little understanding of this defining feature of academic life. The challenge is to help them gain both appreciation of and facility with this kind of discourse, however resistant to it they may be. Participation in reasoned discourse is not discretionary in higher education. Opting out of this essential quality of the academic enterprise is, in essence, opting out of the enterprise itself.

In fact, students are very likely to encounter discussions, readings, and ideas that make them uneasy when they come to college. Disequilibrium and discomfort are almost inevitable when students are confronted with new ideas and new ways of thinking and communicating. This can be especially disconcerting when they are expected to use these unfamiliar modes of thinking to grapple seriously with new perspectives on important intellectual, social, political, and religious issues. But this discomfort cannot be avoided.

In response to a controversy about diversity of political perspective at Duke University in 2004, then-president Nan Keohane (2004, n.p.) urged both faculty and students to recognize the educational value of experiences that take students beyond their comfort zones: "Our classrooms are impoverished if the expression of diverse views is discouraged, either by the faculty member or by fellow students. . . . Clear statements of well-articulated, provocative views stimulate deeper thought, and more discussion, than the cautious expression of ideas designed not to make anyone uncomfortable."

Civility

When courses do involve serious engagement with provocative ideas and multiple perspectives on controversial topics, students' views are likely to differ sharply from one another and from the teacher's point of view. Maintaining a respectful and civil tone in this kind of discussion is another hallmark of the best academically based political communication, which unfortunately contrasts boldly with much political communication outside (and even sometimes inside) the academy. This key value of academic discourse, admittedly sometimes honored in the breach, is important both in the classroom and on the campus more generally. We believe the goal is achievable, having seen many cases of faculty and students working together to create a classroom climate of mutual respect, providing a supportive context for conversations in which participants strongly disagree. Maintaining a climate of civility and respect for difference requires faculty to monitor and manage the classroom climate and also to model civility themselves, toward each other and toward their students. This includes exhibiting and insisting on sensitivity to the diversity of views represented in the student body, especially sensitivity toward minority opinions.

We said earlier that some commentators have criticized faculty for bringing irrelevant political issues into the classroom, and we argued that academic freedom gives faculty the right to decide what kinds of issues and topics are appropriate for inclusion in their courses. But the explosive campus incidents that have been reported in recent news accounts suggest that problematic references to political issues by some faculty are less a matter of thoughtfully incorporating education for political understanding and engagement into their teaching and more a matter of casual asides, jokes, and comments that are meant to lighten up or personalize the class. Teachers at all levels often refer briefly to events or topics that are not relevant to the subject matter, such as commenting on recent sports news, for example. Usually students appreciate the levity and no one objects. But when this kind of comment or joke is about politics, religion, or other highly charged subjects, it runs the risk of offending someone without serving any educational purpose. In essence, faculty are failing to treat their students with respect and civility when their comments establish camaraderie with an in-group who have similar beliefs, excluding others. This is very different from putting forward and carefully arguing a position that is not shared by all as a considered part of the course content.

We do not mean to suggest that every conversation about politics, every experience of political engagement, has to be deadly serious and earnest. Satire is a time-honored political tactic and should be represented among the array of skills students learn to appreciate and exercise. One way to motivate students' politically is to show them how much fun political involvement can be, and surely humor plays an important part in the fun of politics. The popularity of television shows like Comedy Central's *The Daily Show,* which lampoons both Democrats and Republicans, is just one indication of how powerful satire can be in stimulating young people's interest in politics. Among the many challenges for faculty in teaching for political engagement is to help students take each other seriously and avoid demonizing those with whom they disagree without taking the whole process so seriously that it loses its spark, its sense of the absurd, and its fun-loving spirit.

Classroom and campus climates become tangible in part through small behaviors that are experienced as carrying larger significance. For that reason, it is helpful for students to become more aware of the things they do that others read as expressions of respect or disrespect. Conversations that allow students to talk across lines of political affiliation and other important differences about what behaviors connote disrespect or intolerance can be very valuable learning experiences for all involved. But there are also risks attached to an overemphasis on interpersonal sensitivities. One risk is that students may become hypervigilant or oversensitive about perceived slights. Although students need to be respectful toward one another, if they are going to become and remain politically engaged, they can also benefit from developing a fairly thick skin. A sense of general goodwill and solidarity in a class can contribute to both civility and a bit of toughness.

SPEECH CODES. Unfortunately, some acts of incivility go well beyond poor manners and interpersonal tension. Ugly incidents of racism, religious prejudice, and other forms of bigotry come up all too regularly on college campuses. In an effort to insist on human respect and civility, many institutions have established formal speech codes, which restrict certain kinds of speech, with significant penalties attached to violations. For example, in 1988 the University of Michigan established a policy that prohibited speech that "stigmatizes or victimizes an individual on the basis of race, ethnicity, religion, sex, sexual orientation" and a number of other categories (Gould, 2005, p. 13). By the end of the 1990s, hundreds of higher education institutions had adopted speech codes—as many as half of American colleges and universities, by some accounts.

This solution has not proved workable, at least not as originally conceived. Formal speech codes raise a number of problems. College speech codes have been challenged legally on First Amendment grounds and have been struck down in many states as vague and overly broad. Although not directly on point, in *R.A.V. v. St. Paul*, a 1992 decision, the U.S. Supreme Court held that public bodies (in this case a city) could not impose "special prohibitions on those speakers who express views on the disfavored subjects of 'race, color, creed, religion, or gender'" (Gould, 2005). Enforcement of speech codes is troublesome in a number of other ways as well. Because it is almost impossible to draw clear boundaries between hate speech and expressions of objectionable or repugnant ideas, problematic interactions often result in multiple, conflicting interpretations. When speech codes are enforced, conflicts often turn legalistic and procedure-driven, obscuring the moral obligations we all have to treat each other with respect. Legalistic approaches to forcing civility do not generate goodwill or address the real problems these incidents reveal.

Following the Supreme Court decision in 1992, the American Association of University Professors issued its statement "On Freedom of Expression and Campus Speech Codes." This statement acknowledges how profoundly objectionable hate speech is and its destructive impact on institutions as well as individuals. But it goes on to argue that speech codes cannot avoid constraining freedom of expression, which is "the very precondition of the academic enterprise," and therefore cannot be justified in higher education institutions (1994, n.p.). The statement suggests other means of dealing with "incivility, intolerance, offensive speech, and harassing behavior," recommending, among other things, that institutions of higher education adopt "a range of measures that penalize conduct and behavior rather than speech, such as rules against defacing property, physical intimidation or harassment, or disruption of campus activities." The AAUP statement also urges colleges and universities to educate their students about the issues and to strongly condemn "serious breaches of civility."

A number of institutions have indeed revised their policies on nondiscrimination and intolerance along the lines that the AAUP recommends, some in response to lawsuits, others without that kind of external pressure. In a recent shift, for example, the Pennsylvania State University changed its policies to clarify what constitutes harassment and protected speech on its campuses. As described in the *Chronicle of Higher Education,* "Under the new definition of harassment, physical or verbal conduct directed at an individual on the basis of race, religion, sexual orientation, or similar personal characteristics must be 'sufficiently severe or pervasive so as to substantially interfere with the individual's employment, education, or access to university programs, activities, and opportunities' to qualify as such. The conduct must also 'be such that it detrimentally affects the individual in question and would also detrimentally affect a reasonable person under the same circumstances'" (Jacobson, 2006).

Notwithstanding the court decisions, the recommendations of the AAUP, and decisions by leading private and public universities to drop their speech codes, many higher education institutions have continued to adopt speech codes or kept existing codes in place. In practice, however, it seems that these codes generally serve more as statements of expectation and representations of campus norms than as real regulatory mechanisms. Research on speech codes indicates that they are seldom enforced in contemporary higher education (Gould, 2005). Thus, there may be more convergence around the kinds of recommendations put forward by the AAUP than it might seem if one looks only at the number of institutions that retain formal speech codes.

From our perspective, the move from formal speech codes to clear statements of expectation about civility and mutual respect is a positive development, reflecting an awareness that civility cannot be precisely defined or legislated. We believe the approach that is most effective and most compatible with basic academic values is to adopt clear statements of expectations, which are regularly reinforced by senior administrators and faculty, and to reserve penalties for criminal conduct (such as defacing property or threats of violence) or substantial interference with access to university programs and resources, as in Penn State's new code. The more the expectations for mutual respect and civility can be bolstered by establishing a sense of general will on campus, the more powerful those norms will be.

RESTRICTING SPEECH IN THE CLASSROOM. Not all faculty and administrative leaders agree that suppressing objectionable speech by students raises too many problems. For example, in a 2003 journal article, "Social Justice, Democratic Education, and the Silencing of Words That Wound," Barbara Applebaum begins with an anecdote about a Christian student in her graduate-level course on democratic education and diversity who remarked in a class discussion that she would have no problem with homosexual students in her prospective work as a school administrator because she had learned to "love the sinner but hate the sin" (p. 151).

After relating this anecdote, Applebaum goes on to argue that the Christian student's speech is "an instrument of subordination as much as it is an expression of her viewpoint" (p. 157). In her view, such speech not only harms gay students but also leaves a deep impression on heterosexual students, reinforcing norms of heterosexist domination.

Applebaum argues that "the liberal belief in freedom of expression and a marketplace of ideas is compelling only if all viewpoints have an equal opportunity to have their voices matter" (p. 159). Teachers should employ an "affirmative action pedagogy" with the aim of disabling "the system of privileges and deprivations created and sustained by the norm of heterosexuality" (p. 160). Returning to her earlier example, Applebaum writes, "I will . . . silence these dominant voices when necessary" (p. 161).

Although Applebaum's desire to protect the feelings of homosexual students is understandable, her means of accomplishing that goal involves suppressing the views of the Christian student. It would not be surprising if the Christian student felt that, in the academic context, her views on homosexuality do not represent "the dominant voice" and that she was the one being "denied equal opportunity for her voice to matter." In fact, Applebaum acknowledges that the student did try to claim the right to express her religious beliefs, a claim that "astonished" Applebaum by its "brazenness" but failed to convince her of the claim's validity (2003, p. 152).

A commentary on the Applebaum article by John Petrovic (2003) takes the argument for censorship a step further, calling for "censorship of silence." Petrovic claims that "Applebaum's focus on explicit 'utterances' and 'expressions of beliefs' is too narrow, leaving out silence, especially the silence around sexual orientation in school curricula. Silence is a speech act that serves the reproduction of power and promotes harm just as powerfully as the other speech acts Applebaum is willing to censor; and so she begs the question: Can we forget to censor silence in the fight against heterosexism?" (p. 163). One wonders what other silences we would need to censor if we were to follow Petrovic's advice. We could no doubt fill the curriculum with material that is there for the purpose of censoring those silences. In our view, both Applebaum and Petrovic are mistaken in promoting censorship of student views. They are modeling behavior that has no place in the academy.

Clearly, these questions of speech codes, censorship, and whether or not some voices should be silenced are themselves contentious issues. Dilemmas of this kind present real challenges, because in these as in many other ethical dilemmas, positive values conflict, and what counts as an adequate solution is a matter of judgment. Answers to these dilemmas do not follow neatly from a commitment to procedural justice or to the values of tolerance and respect for persons. In our judgment, though, the contending values in these dilemmas are potentially reconcilable, and strong efforts should be made to achieve that reconciliation.

Concern for the welfare of all students is clearly important, but Applebaum's and Petrovic's arguments for censorship are, in our view, useful illustrations of the risks attached to a strong emphasis on protecting students' feelings. In most cases, we do not believe that faculty need to sacrifice freedom of expression and diversity of opinion in the classroom for the sake of civility or protection of vulnerable students. Those goals can be accomplished more effectively and in a deeper and more lasting way through efforts to help students truly understand each other's points of view, which is not possible when differences of opinion are suppressed. In the end, students on both sides of contentious issues may experience some discomfort, but if handled well, the experience will be a positive one from a developmental point of view.

In the case Applebaum described, for example, there are a number of options for a productive discussion following the Christian student's comment. We are not suggesting that the class could profit from talking about whether homosexuality is, in fact, a sin. But a discussion of the meaning of professionalism as a school administrator when confronted with students, parents, teachers, or other colleagues whose values or commitments are fundamentally discrepant with their own could be valuable for all of the students. The kind of situation Applebaum's student described, albeit with a wide range of content, is very likely to arise in the future work lives of many in the class.

A perceived need to suppress free expression is not the only risk of an overemphasis on civility. A much more pervasive problem is that students become so fearful of offending each other that they refuse to engage in strenuous argumentation and debate. Students often confuse an attitude of respect for and openness to others' views with a belief that all points of view are equally valid. When this happens, the stakes drop out of ethical and political deliberation and students are less likely to take it seriously (Ricks, 1999; Trosset, 1998). This is a particular problem in the political domain, because the sometimes rough-and-tumble world of politics requires a tolerance for some conflict, the push and pull of opposing agendas, values, and beliefs. As PEP faculty member Marshall Ganz said: "Conflict is important. Students are more into relativism than pluralism. I want to get them off relativism and into pluralism. There is a real reluctance to challenge people you disagree with. There is no tendency to demonize within my course; everyone is too afraid to confront each other. But they need to do that, because vigorous pluralism is about challenging each other."

It is important for faculty teaching for political development to find ways to create a civil and respectful atmosphere without making students conflict-averse. In Chapter Four we suggest some strategies to help accomplish this.

Faculty Roles and Professionalism

What do the values of academic freedom, diversity of opinion, and standards of reasoned discourse and civility mean for faculty roles and professionalism with regard to educating for political development? Respect for diversity of opinion and the academic freedom of students does not mean that faculty have to be politically neutral.

In thinking about advocacy by faculty, it is important first of all to distinguish between advocacy in which faculty engage as private citizens, as scholars, as members of a professional community, and as teachers. As private citizens, faculty vote, participate in or donate money to political parties and campaigns, and write political opinion pieces, among other things. In their roles as scholars, faculty sometimes speak about important social or policy issues that connect with their research. An economist might write a feminist critique of prevailing economic theories, an educational researcher might prepare a policy briefing in support of school choice and vouchers, a political scientist might advocate for increased public deliberation about important policy questions. As a member of a professional community, a faculty member might advocate for or against high-stakes testing in higher education or for or against the use of embryos for medical schools' stem cell research, and so on. All of these roles are quite different from the role of teacher, and different norms apply to advocacy in the different roles.

The Multiple Roles of Faculty Members

Some of the recent public discourse on the politics of university faculty has failed to distinguish between faculty members' roles as teachers and their various other roles. Recent conservative critiques of liberal or left-leaning faculty have tended to focus on their personal political activities (especially political party affiliation and campaign donations), on strong and provocative statements they have made in their scholarship, or on advocacy they undertake in their disciplinary communities. (See, for example, Horowitz, 2006b; Jones, 2006a, 2006b; Zinsmeister, 2005. For examples of responses to these critiques, see Free Exchange on Campus, 2006; Jaschik, 2006; Makdisi, 2006.)

These critiques make an assumption that we believe is unwarranted—that faculty members' political activities in their other roles necessarily affect their teaching. The important question for us is not what faculty do as private citizens or scholars but what they do as teachers. This is an empirical question, and one that has barely been addressed at all. We turn to it in Chapter Four.

FORMS OF ADVOCACY IN TEACHING. There is, however, reasonable agreement about what faculty *should* do as teachers with regard to their own political convictions and opinions. Philosopher Robert Newton Jr. offers one statement of these norms. Newton distinguishes among several forms of advocacy, which, in his view, vary in legitimacy. As we have done, he distinguishes between forms of advocacy that are legitimate in the context of teaching and those that are appropriate as a scholar or private citizen. In teaching, Newton particularly highlights the legitimacy and usefulness of *critical advocacy,* in which both faculty and students are free to present arguments for their positions on the issues in question, and *dialogical advocacy,* which intends to broaden or deepen the conversation—for example, challenging students to rethink unsubstantiated claims or arguing for positions they personally do not hold, playing devil's advocate to make sure the full range of positions are well represented or to challenge a too-simple formulation that has not grappled with possible objections (Newton, 2003). The purpose of dialogical advocacy in the classroom is to teach advocacy skills.

Newton (2003) contrasts these forms of advocacy in teaching with abuses such as proselytizing and indoctrination, both of which intend to bring students to one's own point of view, sometimes using means that are not open to challenge or critique, rather than strengthen their ability to make independent judgments. This can certainly happen in courses that address political issues, but it can also easily happen in areas that have nothing to do with politics—for example, with regard to a rival theoretical formulation or other heated debates in a discipline or field of research. The straw man problem extends well beyond the political domain and is objectionable wherever it appears, both in teaching and in scholarship. The keys to legitimacy when it comes to advocacy in the classroom, for both political and nonpolitical issues, are that students be exposed to multiple perspectives and encouraged to express dissenting views and make their own judgments about the issues at hand, and that positions put forward by both the teacher and the students be judged on their merits.

PEP FACULTY EXPERIENCE WITH ADVOCACY. PEP faculty think carefully about whether concealing or revealing to students their own political beliefs would best uphold those ideals. They have differing responses to this question, and either choice is consistent with an open classroom climate as long as faculty are careful to provide and encourage multiple perspectives, including those with which they personally disagree. Some choose not to tell students about their own political affiliations and their students confirm that by the end of the course they still do not know what their teachers believe politically. Students say that they appreciate and respect the reasons for this choice.

Other faculty feel that it is preferable for a number of reasons for them to tell students where they stand on the issues and why. This decision is based on a desire to model the process of taking and justifying a position, to be honest about their beliefs and possible biases, and to avoid seeming to endorse a position of extreme moral relativism. These faculty believe that explicating their own views is perfectly compatible with respect for diversity of opinion as long as they are careful not to impose their views on students and make serious efforts to ensure that opposing views are well articulated. As Ganz said, "[My commitment to open inquiry] begins with truth in advertising. I need to say to them, 'This is where I am coming from.' I can't avoid that because [political organizing, the topic of the course] is values-based work, values matter. But the course is about translating values into action and that crosses the political spectrum."

Practicalities of Professionalism: Grading and Other Assessments

It is obvious that faculty should not discriminate against students on the basis of political opinions when they are grading essays, presentations, and other work that expresses political views. We would add that, when it comes to assessment, not only fairness but also *the appearance of fairness* is crucial. When students complain about faculty bias, they are often referring to what they imagine to be unfair grading. Because students often do not understand their teachers' grading criteria very well, they may think their work is being evaluated based on the political views it expresses rather than its quality, even when this is not true. For this and other reasons, which concern good teaching more generally, it is essential to make assessment criteria explicit, illustrate them with examples of good work whenever possible, and provide as much feedback as possible on student work in relation to the criteria.

A challenge for ensuring that assessments are unbiased judgments of quality is the relatively subjective nature of many assessments, such as evaluations of student papers, presentations, and other open-ended work. This means that faculty need to be alert to the possibility of subtle biases in their judgments of work that expresses political beliefs. Psychological research shows that people tend to resist challenges to their own political beliefs in part by subjecting these challenges to greater scrutiny than arguments and information that are consonant with their own beliefs. For example, a study that asked participants to critique articles for and against the death penalty found that the subjects were far more successful in identifying the flaws in the article expressing a viewpoint different from their own than the one with which they agreed (Lord, Ross, and Leeper, 1979). Studies of this phenomenon have not to our knowledge included samples of intellectuals or academics who are trained to separate critical analysis of presentation and argumentation or credibility of evidence from personal assessment of conclusions, so it is not clear whether faculty are as vulnerable as the general public. Nevertheless, the research sounds a cautionary note and suggests that faculty are well advised to be self-conscious and alert in their efforts to discount any possible biases against dissenting views.

Complicating Factors

Using the core values of academic life as guidelines for teaching about politics makes sense in principle and represents a broad consensus around which people from a wide array of political perspectives—both critics and defenders of the academy—can come together. In general, there is wide agreement on the importance of diversity of opinion, academic freedom, reasoned discourse, and civility and on the power of these principles to protect the educational process from possible bias. In June 2005 the American Council on Education (ACE) issued a statement responding to the ongoing controversy surrounding the question of political bias on college and university campuses, and the Association of American Colleges and Universities issued its 2006 statement shortly thereafter. Our own thinking on these issues was informed and influenced by these thoughtful statements. The leaders of many colleges, universities, and education-related organizations have signed on to the ACE "Statement on Academic Rights and Responsibilities," and some of the most vocal conservative organizations have urged higher education institutions to implement the principles it sets out. This is a significant achievement, considering the vitriolic character of current debates about politics in higher education. Unfortunately, this consensus on guiding principles does not resolve the matter. When dealing with issues as contested and consequential as politics, it is necessary to negotiate some complications. It is to these complications that we turn next, in Chapter Four.

4

CREATING ENVIRONMENTS
OF OPEN INQUIRY

ALTHOUGH THE CORE VALUES of the academy demand an environment of open inquiry, it is challenging to create such an environment, particularly around political ideas. Several features of higher education, politics, and political development complicate the effort. First, both academic disciplines and political perspectives of faculty and students carry explicit and implicit ideological assumptions. This inescapable fact raises questions about the extent to which these assumptions are acknowledged, open to challenge, representative of a wide range of views, and compatible with the educational goal of engaging students with diverse perspectives on contested issues. Second, to a large degree, a climate of vigorous debate and open-minded pursuit of truth requires all participants to have a sophisticated epistemological understanding and well-developed intellectual skills. But many students have not yet developed the cognitive skills necessary to argue their positions effectively or to understand the grounds for evaluating others' claims. Third, if students are to be prepared for active political engagement, the strong focus on reasoned, considered analysis that lies at the heart of open inquiry can be a barrier to decisive judgment and passionate, committed action. Finally, a general climate of political polarization off campus can also invade the campus culture and the attitudes of both students and faculty.

In this chapter, we look closely at these four challenges that complicate efforts to create and sustain an environment of open inquiry. We then turn to suggestions for addressing them at the level of the campus as a whole and in individual courses and programs.

Allegations of Political Homogeneity in the Academy

There is broad agreement across a range of constituencies on the importance of intellectual and ideological pluralism, but there are sharp disagreements about how much *actual* diversity of political opinion there is in the academy, at least with regard to the representation of conservative views. Conservative critics charge that this marketplace of ideas sells only one brand. They argue that students are not exposed to a diverse enough range of political perspectives, and that the imbalance in the direction of more liberal views is, in effect, proselytizing of a sort, whether intentional or not.

The research evidence is quite clear in showing that more higher education faculty members describe themselves as politically liberal than conservative. However, most of the studies reporting these numbers (or the proportions of Democrats and. Republicans) look at faculty in only a few institutions, and the figures vary considerably across these studies (see, for example, Klein and Stern, 2004; Klein and Western, 2004; Rothman, Lichter, and Nevitte, 2005). To our knowledge, the most recent studies of faculty political identification that have large, national samples are those conducted by the Higher Education Research Institute (HERI) at the University of California, Los Angeles.

Every three years since 1989, HERI has conducted large-scale surveys of the attitudes and beliefs of higher education faculty. The most recent of these surveys, conducted in 2004–05, included 40,670 full-time faculty from 421 institutions (Lindholm, Szelenyi, Hurtado, and Korn, 2005). Although the study indicates that there are indeed more liberal than conservative faculty, especially in some disciplines, the imbalance is much less extreme than some of the smaller studies would lead one to believe.

In the full sample of faculty from all institutions in the HERI study, 51 percent of respondents identified themselves as liberal or far left, 29 percent as "middle of the road," and 20 percent as conservative or far right. The figures vary to some extent across institutional types, with private universities just slightly more liberal than public universities, and four-year institutions more liberal than two-year colleges. So, for example, for faculty in two-year colleges, the figures are 38.6 percent liberal or far left and 26.3 percent conservative or far right. In considering these figures, it is important to bear in mind that most students attend two-year colleges and public four-year institutions. Many fewer attend the kinds of institutions that typically have the highest proportions of liberal faculty.

Although these numbers indicate something about the political makeup of the faculty, they do not tell us much, if anything, about intellectual pluralism in the academy as it affects the experience of students. As a number of university presidents have pointed out, the key question for universities as educational institutions is not how faculty vote, but how they teach. While she was president of Duke, Keohane wrote, "The real issue is not the personal political views of members of the faculty, but the quality of their scholarship and their teaching, which includes welcoming diverse and contrary viewpoints in the classroom" (2004). If faculty are not proselytizing or indoctrinating, and if they are, instead, working to ensure representation of and respect for diversity of opinion, it matters a lot less what their political party affiliations are.

Effect of Faculty's Political Attitudes in the Classroom

Unfortunately, there is little or no systematic research on the degree to which faculty who address political issues in their courses provide or encourage students to express a diverse range of views. The one relevant study that we have seen, "Politics in the Classroom," conducted by the Center for Survey Research & Analysis for the conservative American Council of Trustees and Alumni (ACTA), is flawed in a number of ways, but it does give a general sense of the extent of open inquiry in classrooms in which faculty refer to political issues.

Before considering the study's findings, however, it is important to understand its flaws: the first concerns the sample. This study surveyed students in the universities and colleges ranked as the top fifty by *U.S. News & World Report* (Center for Survey Research & Analysis, 2006). Because the proportion of liberal faculty in a college or university is correlated with its selectivity (Astin and Denson, n.d.), the sample for this study represents institutions whose faculties are more likely to be self-described liberals than the national average. The response rate for students has not been made available, so it is impossible for us to know whether the sample is at all representative of students at these institutions. The survey was administered shortly before the 2004 presidential elections, so it is quite possible that the timing could have affected students' responses as well.

In addition to sample selection and timing, the item format is also problematic. Items in the survey follow a standard format: "On my campus, some professors [are intolerant, etc.];" "On my campus, some courses [present issues in an unfair manner, etc.]"; or "On my campus, some panel discussions and presentations [seem one-sided, etc.]." For each item, students are asked to rate how strongly they agree or disagree with the statement. Because of the way the items are phrased, when a student says that she agrees with the statement, "Some faculty make negative comments in class about conservatives," for example, we do not know whether the student has ever heard a faculty member do this or whether she assumes that it sometimes happens based on conversations with her friends or even based on news stories about alleged bias. Likewise, we have no indication of what students mean when they endorse an item that says "Some faculty" or "Some courses." They might be referring to a very small minority or to many faculty (or courses). But presumably, when students say they *disagree* that "Some faculty do *x*," they believe that the phenomenon in question is absent or close to absent on their campus.

For the most part, the results of this survey indicate that although nontrivial minorities of students believe there are some politically biased faculty or courses on their campus, most students *do not believe* the campus has some biased faculty or courses. For example, more than three-quarters of the respondents do not believe "There are some professors who are intolerant of certain [political or social] viewpoints." Similarly, more than two-thirds disagree that some "present social and political issues in an unfair and one-sided manner." A larger percentage of students, though still a minority at 48 percent, feel that among all of the panel discussions and presentations addressing political issues that take place on their campus, "Some seem totally one-sided," though this does not imply that the perceived one-sidedness is always skewed in the same direction.

In evaluating student survey data, it is important to bear in mind that students are not objective observers of political behaviors in their teachers. April Kelly-Woessner and Matthew Woessner (2006) have studied students' perceptions of their professors' political perspectives (liberal-conservative and Republican-Democrat) and evaluations of those faculty in relation to the match or mismatch between students' perspectives and faculty's perspectives as attributed by the students. Kelly-Woessner and Woessner found that when students perceive their professors' politics as different from their own, they rate the course and the instructor less positively than when they perceive their professors as political allies. This is so whether the students or the faculty are liberal or conservative.

We need to interpret the results of the ACTA survey cautiously in light of this evidence that students' own political perspectives affect their evaluations of their teachers. In fact, the authors of the ACTA report acknowledge that "self-described conservative students reported bias in significantly higher numbers" (Center for Survey Research & Analysis, 2006, p. 3). Even so, the data seem to indicate that some, though generally not most, students at these institutions believe that at least a few of the faculty on their campus make partisan comments in class or fail to exemplify tolerance of multiple perspectives and to ensure that those perspectives are well represented in their courses.

In light of our earlier discussion of principles of good teaching and their relationship to teaching political issues, if these students' beliefs are an accurate representation of their campuses, then it appears that some faculty need to be more careful to honor diversity of perspective and more sensitive to the feelings of students who have different political perspectives. Even if the students' perceptions of bias are not accurate, higher education institutions would do well to address those perceptions.

Impact of Faculty Political Orientation on Students

Another important issue is what impact faculty political orientation has on students' political orientation.

The PEP survey data provide a preliminary answer to this question. The PEP survey assessed students' political orientation and political party identification before and after their participation in the PEP courses and programs. These data show no net change in the students' self descriptions on the liberal-conservative dimension or in the proportions of students that identified themselves as Republicans and Democrats. Because students in the PEP study enter the courses and programs with a wide range of political orientations and the majority of PEP faculty, like faculty nationally, are politically liberal, we should have seen an overall shift toward more liberal self-descriptions in the students if faculty political orientation was influencing student orientation.

But most of the PEP courses and programs are not all-encompassing, and (with a few exceptions) they last for only a semester or a year at most. What about the impact of four years of college spent on a campus with high proportions of liberal faculty? Do students at these campuses tend to become more liberal?

Fortunately, Astin and Denson recently completed a careful longitudinal study of this issue. The study (n.d.), "Long-Term Effects of College on Students' Political Orientation," looked at the effect of both faculty and peers' political orientations on students' political orientations at the end of college and six years later, as well as the effect of the college experience as a whole at these two points.

For these analyses, Astin and Denson used a large national longitudinal database to track undergraduate students from their entry to college in 1994 to graduation four years later, and then reassess them six years after college, in 2004. At all time points, students rated themselves as far right, conservative, middle-of-the-road, liberal, or far left. Overall, the study showed a slight shift to the left in college students by the time of graduation. But this effect disappeared completely during the immediate postcollege years. Respondents became more polarized in their self-described political orientation over time, but there was no change in overall political balance over the ten-year period of the study.

Astin and Denson's analyses also show that by far the strongest predictor of postcollege political orientation is students' political orientation when they enter college, leaving a relatively small amount of variance attributable to college characteristics and experiences, including both faculty and peer political orientations. In addition, mean entering student political orientation is very highly correlated with the college's mean faculty and student political orientations. In fact, most of the association between the political orientations of college graduates and the orientations of their former peers and faculty is the result of self-selection—the correspondence is already there when students enter as freshmen.

But not all of the variance in college graduates' political orientation is accounted for by self-selection, and multivariate analyses are able to disentangle the independent contributions of peer and faculty effects during college. These analyses show that mean faculty orientation does not contribute to graduates' political orientation, whereas mean college peer political orientation does contribute independently to that outcome. That is, the political orientation of students' undergraduate college faculty has no effect on college graduates' political orientation once the influence of the student peer group is taken into account.

Interviews of PEP students conducted after their participation in the courses and programs provide some impressionistic data that may help us understand the absence of a faculty effect on students' political orientation. Although many PEP faculty did choose to reveal their own political leanings to their students, they were by and large quite careful to represent a wide range of positions in the course or program. Even in the few cases where students felt the coverage was tilted in one direction or another, these students were not passive recipients of that material, parroting what they read or heard from faculty. College students think about and evaluate the political views they encounter. Some may shift slightly to the right, even in a course with a politically liberal professor, because of readings they find compelling, experiences with speakers or placements, or interactions with a wide range of peers. Conversely, some students in a conservatively focused program might shift in a more liberal direction for the same reasons. In the end, though, any tendencies to shift toward more liberal or more conservative directions cancel each other out.

In addition, students tend to push back when they feel that coverage is not balanced. Most students did not experience the PEP course or program in which they participated as one-sided, but among the few who did, we saw push-back in both political directions, with students criticizing what they saw as the more conservative stance of some programs and the more liberal stance of others.

These studies suggest that there is little cause for concern that imbalances in college faculty's political orientations constitute "indoctrination" or lead to systematic shifts in students' political orientations. In our view, however, these findings should not make institutions of higher education complacent about ensuring that students encounter a diverse array of political perspectives. Consideration of multiple points of view and an atmosphere of open-mindedness and searching inquiry are important in their own right, even aside from the question of whether faculty perspectives influence students' political ideologies.

Values Assumptions Implicit in Academic Disciplines

In part because of the power of like-minded enclaves, both faculty and students sometimes seem unaware of the values and beliefs that are implicit in their approach to a subject. Perhaps because of the familiarity of these beliefs or their prevalence in the discipline, some faculty assume that their assumptions are politically neutral or even simply factual, even if they are experienced by others as ideologically laden. For this reason, they may not raise their assumptions to an explicit level for acknowledgment and examination.

This can occur at any point on the political spectrum. For all the recent talk of liberal bias on college campuses, one of the most prevalent values permeating a number of disciplines is extreme individualism. The preponderance of research in economics and political science, for example, builds on a model of rational choice. This model assumes that individuals try to maximize their perceived interests and that social phenomena represent the aggregate of individuals pursuing this self-interested strategy. Sociobiology and some branches of psychology are characterized by a similarly self-interested view of human nature. Courses in economics, public policy, and business (currently one of the most popular undergraduate majors) often begin from the related assumption that free market capitalism is the best solution to social problems and may not consider alternatives to this ideology. At the other end of the political spectrum, some courses in other fields, including the social sciences and humanities, take for granted an assumption that economic inequities are in every case the result of oppression and marginalization of some groups by others.

We are not suggesting that every course needs to take up the field's epistemological and values assumptions as an object of study or that faculty have to include in every course alternative bodies of research and theory based on fundamentally different assumptions. We do believe, though, that it is useful for faculty to be aware of and to acknowledge the ideological assumptions they are making, even if serious consideration of those assumptions and alternatives to them is not appropriate to the nature of the course. It can also be useful for departments to offer some courses that do take on the epistemological and values questions directly.

When a course specifically addresses public policy and political issues, it is almost always worthwhile to take some time to consider values assumptions that might otherwise be invisible. When important implicit assumptions are not acknowledged and examined, faculty are less likely to notice the absence of alternative points of view. This is a particular problem for courses that attempt to foster political understanding and engagement, because they need to be especially careful not to proselytize for a particular political ideology. A useful antidote to inadvertent narrowness is for faculty to communicate with colleagues who may not share their assumptions as they examine their course goals and assignments through the lens of open inquiry as a goal.

When ideologically laden language and unexamined assumptions come up repeatedly in a number of courses in an institution, this can leave some students feeling quite frustrated. One such belief, for example, is that contemporary society is bifurcated into oppressed and oppressing groups, and that it is important for students to be aware of their relationship to these categories. Especially for students who feel they are often classified as oppressors, even despite a lack of evidence for this in their own behavior, this can be a demoralizing experience. As one PEP participant at a notably liberal institution said about his undergraduate experience there:

> Whenever we went to talk politics, it would degenerate into how evil white people had been. And for me and my friends, who are white, it sort of, the people in the class didn't distinguish between white settlers in 1870 and 1890 and us. It was "white people." And so we'd be in class having a discussion about politics and all of a sudden one person raises her hand and says something like, "You know, after hearing about this I really have disdain for white people and what they've done." It doesn't make for nice, calm, rational discussion when you're being insulted. This was very much a campus phenomenon. An exam-

ple is the first year seminar—a freshman writing course we were all required to take. One of the things they focus on in those classes seems to me to encourage racism and sexism. Just so many instances of professors wanting papers on how whites oppressed Hispanics or how men oppressed women. It really makes you feel that by the end of your time [here], you're either going to end up hating white men, or, if you're a white male, hating yourself for all the things that you—that is you because they don't make any time distinction—did to all these people.

The kind of statement this young man attributes to his classmate could serve to open a very enlightening conversation about stereotyping, the notion of collective responsibility and its limits, the question of how best to use historical understanding to illuminate contemporary issues, and so on. But especially when the topic concerns the sensitive issues of race and class, it is very hard for students like the one we just quoted to find the courage and the precision of language and ideas to speak up, and especially to do so in a way that would be persuasive and thought-provoking rather than defensive. The challenge, then, is to create a campus climate that is self-aware about language and concepts that carry ideological baggage, at all points on the political spectrum, and that presses back against all versions of narrowness and polarization.

Students' Developmental Limits

In laying out the guiding principles for academically based political education, we have stressed the importance of intellectual autonomy; open-minded consideration of multiple perspectives on complex issues; quality of argumentation, evidence, and other aspects of warrant in evaluating or establishing the merit or credibility of a position; the value of students' challenging each other's claims and positions and those put forward by their instructors and others in positions of authority; the inclusion or exclusion of material and issues from a course, based on their relevance and intellectual credibility; the separation of judgments of ideological agreement and disagreement from quality of evidence and argument in the assessment of student work; and the desirability of teaching for deliberative capacity and personal qualities of open-mindedness and civility in the face of difference. We also outlined what we—and others—understand to be legitimate and illegitimate faculty advocacy and reported on a study of students' perceptions of teachers' advocacy, evenhandedness, and bias.

Every single item in this array of principles, goals, and considerations presumes a high level of intellectual sophistication and maturity. Insofar as the principles we have laid out are intended primarily as guidelines for faculty and higher education administrators, that assumption of intellectual sophistication should not present a problem. But the situation is more complicated than that. Students also need to have a reasonable grasp of these principles and goals if they are to understand their teachers' rationales for making judgments about course content, grades, and whether and how to put forward their own opinions on political issues.

If students are going to challenge faculty and each other through reasoned discourse, they also need to see how credibility can reside in evidence and rationale rather than role or position (teacher, expert, or other authority figure) and appreciate what does and does not count as a credible justification. Students also need a reasonable degree of what psychologists call a "disposition toward critical thinking" if they are to exhibit the important qualities of civility, open-mindedness, and reasonableness that are essential to political education in the academy.

All of this is a tall order, and the research on college students' cognitive development, including reflective judgment and both capacity for and disposition toward critical thinking, raises serious questions about whether their intellectual development, at least in the early undergraduate years, is advanced enough to grasp these complex and subtle matters. As we noted in Chapter Two, most students, even many of those who are returning adults, enter college with simplistic epistemological assumptions that cannot support a reasoned approach to dealing with ill-structured problems. This is both a complication for the ideals of academically based education for political understanding that we have sketched out in this book so far and also an indication of what a rich and powerful opportunity for intellectual growth political education can be. It is a real challenge for educators to determine how best to mitigate the complication and take advantage of the opportunity.

As we noted in our discussion of reflective judgment, few students come to college with an understanding of or appreciation for the nature of academic discourse, including the intellectual processes and standards that regulate academic freedom, determine which positions need to be taken seriously, and form the basis for reasoned deliberation, including deliberation about political issues. It is important to find out how students understand these issues, in part by being alert to their confusions, misconceptions, and lack of understanding.

The well-known limitations of students' cognitive sophistication have implications for their intellectual autonomy as well. As long as students are encouraged to disagree and put forward objections or opposing views, in principle, it is entirely within the bounds of faculty professionalism for instructors to present and argue for their own views on issues discussed in class, including political issues that are addressed by the course. But the research on students' cognitive development underscores the fact that students and faculty are not on an equal footing when it comes to articulating and making the case for their positions. Thus, even when students are encouraged to put forward perspectives that differ from those presented by the faculty member, they are not usually able to defend their views as well as faculty members can.

Supporting Students in Articulating Their Positions

Many faculty recognize that this means they will often need to teach students how to make the best possible case for their position, providing coaching and scaffolding to help them argue effectively—even if their position is in opposition to the faculty member's cherished beliefs. Recognizing that students are often not in a strong position to argue for alternative perspectives, many faculty take the initiative in making as compelling a case as they can for views they do not actually hold. It is especially important to do this if no students in the class represent those alternative views.

But making a strong case for a position that is opposite to one's own strongly held views is not easy to do. Even when faculty want to encourage open debate by drawing out students with minority opinions, they are sometimes so convinced of the superiority of their own political positions that they cannot imagine how one might make a really persuasive opposing case. This makes them poor guides for students who are struggling to articulate such a view. Because this role of guide is so important, it is worth some extra effort on the part of faculty to investigate a range of opinions on issues they plan to cover and seek out the best articulations of those opinions.

Sometimes when a faculty member or an especially articulate student has made a powerful case for a particular position, another student may have a strong intuition that the conclusion reached is not right but be unable to say why—unable to identify exactly what is wrong with the evidence or argumentation. Although it is incumbent on the dissenter to identify the flaws in the case, faculty would do well to recognize that this can be very, very hard to do, especially for undergraduate students, and they often need guidance in this effort. If students who sense that a position has weaknesses that they cannot yet identify are encouraged to seek additional evidence and consult with experts who represent the view they intuitively favor, this kind of situation can be a powerful opportunity for learning.

Sometimes, though, a student's developmental level is not yet mature enough to rise to this kind of challenge. This raises the question of whether a lack of maturity in students' grasp of epistemological issues might sometimes lie behind their unwillingness to accept judgments that seem quite reasonable to the professor.

Consider the experience of Ann Bahr, who wrote about her conservative Christian students' demand that books on Evangelical Christianity be removed from the syllabus (2005). Students in another of her courses protested even more strenuously when she responded to their request to cover the Bible's position on homosexuality by outlining multiple scholarly interpretations of the relevant passages. Students were particularly incensed when Bahr responded to their request to give her own evaluation of a book that draws unqualified conclusions about the Bible's condemnation of homosexuality. Bahr said that though she appreciated the author's analysis and linguistic work, she did not believe his basic argument could withstand close scrutiny, and she explained why. Tempers flared, and though Bahr invited her students to discuss the matter further after class or during office hours, no one took her up on the offer.

If we consider that these students may see knowledge as absolute and transmitted by authorities, we can better understand their strong reaction when what they believe to be received wisdom of the most important sort is opened to question in a way that they have no framework for understanding—multiple legitimate interpretations of essentially indeterminate material, assessment of the plausibility of argument, and the like. When this lack of epistemological expertise is combined with an immature grasp of widespread conservative accusations of liberal bias in the academy, students may leap to condemn their teachers for bias rather than struggle to understand the complex process of scholarly debate.

But the good news is that, as long as they remain engaged in the struggle to understand, students can develop more mature reflective judgment and critical thinking abilities in college. Academic institutions, programs, departments, and faculty benefit from being intentional and explicit in their efforts to provide guidance, practice, and feedback as students learn to look for and evaluate evidence, make and critique arguments, and generally engage in the process of deliberation. High-quality education for political understanding and engagement involves just exactly those experiences that have been shown to support these dimensions of cognitive growth: service learning and other pedagogies of engagement, deliberation about controversial issues, engagement across differences, and so on. In this way, political education contributes not only to more well-prepared citizens but also to the central intellectual goals of a liberal education.

Analysis Paralysis

Educating for political engagement is rather like professional education. In politics as in professional work, it is often necessary to act without full knowledge of the relevant background and parameters. Efforts to attain a fully developed, complete analysis before making a judgment or taking action can be paralyzing. In public life, both in professional work and in political engagement, it is often necessary to make judgments and take action in the face of considerable uncertainty.

The high-quality political thinking and deliberation that is the goal of education for political engagement requires the capacity for and inclination toward careful thought and deliberation, deep knowledge, and open-minded consideration of multiple views. But emphasis on intellectual development carries the risk of disconnecting thinking from commitment and action.

An important question, then, for educators who want to support political engagement is how to help students achieve passion and commitment to act that is accompanied by open-mindedness and critical deliberation. This means helping students reconcile commitment and open-mindedness, which can sometimes seem incompatible.

Not long after a crisis at Columbia University about alleged faculty bias against pro-Israeli students, President Lee Bollinger delivered the "Cardozo Lecture on Academic Freedom," in which he stressed the importance of academic freedom and the need for faculty, "not external actors, [to] determine professional standards for the academy" (Bollinger, 2005, n.p.). In articulating the rationale for academic freedom, Bollinger spoke of the academic inclination toward deep skepticism of certitude. He went on to stress that, however important skepticism and recognition of uncertainty are for intellectual life, other hallmarks of the scholarly profession, including intellectual openness, imagination, and mental courage, suggest that the academy is more than "a place of deep skepticism."

These comments point to an inherent tension between skepticism and commitment, passion, and action. It may be, in part, too great a reliance on the academic value of skepticism that leads many thoughtful people to take no action. We need to think carefully about what kinds of certitude we should be skeptical of and the proper limits of skepticism in the domain of action.

Although it may seem paradoxical, open-mindedness can be combined with firm, passionate, sustained commitment to action. In fact, in a study of people who had shown exceptional moral and social commitment over the course of many decades, Anne Colby and William Damon (1992) found that these people exhibited exactly this combination of qualities. These individuals, who had all worked for many years to support civil rights, fight poverty, advance peace and religious freedom, and the like, showed a distinctive quality of certainty about their commitments but were not dogmatic or rigid. These "moral exemplars" tended to listen to their critics, thinking seriously about what they said and trying to understand the perspectives of people who fundamentally disagreed with them. In the end, though, they often had to say, "I just don't buy your core assumptions."

We offer these examples to underscore the importance of teaching for both careful deliberation accompanied by open-minded consideration of alternative perspectives and also passionate commitment. If we are to accomplish both of these outcomes, it is valuable for students to become skilled in analytic discourse about political issues, but it is also important for them to recognize that other forms of discourse are both appropriate and useful. Political participation often involves personal testimony and witness, compelling narratives, prophetic preaching, civil disobedience, mass protest, or silent resistance. One goal of political education is to help students gain an appreciation of the diversity of expression these modes of participation represent.

Climates of Political Polarization

College and university leaders agree that educating students in the practice of open-minded inquiry is a key component of undergraduate education, and most recognize that political issues cannot and should not be excluded from the mix. But creating a classroom and wider campus climate that is truly open to multiple perspectives on contested political issues is not easy. This is true whether the majority opinion on campus is conservative or liberal. Unfortunately, in most settings, people with strong political opinions talk almost exclusively to those who agree with them. College campuses should be an exception, but generally they are not, so neither students nor faculty are accustomed to communicating across ideological divides. And demonization of the opposition is so thoroughly woven into contemporary American politics that it is no wonder students fear being harshly judged if they speak up for an unpopular view.

As hard as a faculty member might work to create a classroom open to inquiry and supportive of committed action, both faculty and students are operating in and influenced by the broader campus context and culture—in fact, by the political culture outside the campus as well. A general climate of polarization and intolerance makes it difficult, inside the boundaries of a single course or extracurricular program, to help students absorb the values of open-mindedness and respect for perspectives different from their own, not only seeing intellectually the importance of these values but also changing engrained prejudices and habits. Furthermore, it is less likely that questions of ideological diversity and open inquiry will be self-conscious concerns for faculty if they are not salient values in the campus culture. If the campus pays little attention to these questions, some faculty may offer their students a slanted view without even realizing it, not having thought much about the ideological assumptions their teaching conveys.

An Academic Bill of Rights?

One strategy for addressing these issues that has received a great deal of media attention in the past year or two is a call for legislation that would require colleges and universities to adopt an "Academic Bill of Rights," along with mechanisms to enforce its provisions. The bill, which has been introduced in many state legislatures but has yet to be approved in any, would challenge colleges and universities to adopt voluntarily procedures that the sponsors claim would encourage a diversity of political perspectives among faculty, campus speakers, and student organizations.

For the most part, the specific provisions of the Academic Bill of Rights (Horowitz, 2006a) are in line with the statements of principle issued by the American Council on Education (2005) and Association of American Colleges and Universities (2006). They include, for example, "Students will be graded strictly on the basis of their reasoned answers and appropriate knowledge of the subjects they study" and "Faculty will not use their courses for the purposes of political, ideological, religious, or antireligious indoctrination" (Horowitz, 2006a, n.p.). As we have said, these are among the norms of faculty professionalism that are strongly endorsed by institutions and by faculty themselves.

Despite the uncontroversial character of many of the Academic Bill of Rights' specific provisions, however, we believe that this legislative strategy for ensuring academic freedom and respect for diversity of opinion is seriously misguided. Perhaps most importantly, this kind of legislation threatens the time-honored (and legally protected) freedom of academic institutions from outside political interference. As Bollinger said in his lecture (2005, n.p.), the idea that "faculty members, not external actors, should determine professional standards for the academy . . . is the foundational principle of academic freedom." Along with Bollinger, William Bowen (1987) and others have written persuasively about the importance of freedom of higher education from outside intervention, so we will not dwell on that issue here.

Even aside from this very basic concern for the independent status of higher education, we believe that the proposed legislative solution will not work. The problem with a legislative approach to ensuring open inquiry is that it casts the issue in negative terms, as a matter of policing the faculty—and the campus more broadly—to stamp out "indoctrination." Given the complexity and ambiguity of both political and academic discourse, this kind of policing would be impossible to implement objectively. And cast in negative terms, the effort itself would be destructive to the goal of civil discourse across ideological boundaries. By contrast, a positive approach, in which administration, faculty, and students from different political perspectives join together to develop strategies for the positive pursuit of open inquiry, can itself contribute to a climate of open-mindedness, respect, and cooperation.

Strategies for Creating an Environment of Open-Minded Inquiry

At the level of general principles, there is wide agreement that, if it is to be legitimate and effective, education for political understanding and engagement has to be compatible with the central values of the academic enterprise—academic freedom, reasoned discourse, open-minded consideration of alternative perspectives, and civility. But the consensus tends to break down when principles are applied to actual cases. In truth, these are difficult, complicated, and contested issues. They cannot be resolved by simple, crisp guidelines. Instead, educators need to adapt general considerations to particular dynamic and shifting contexts through ongoing monitoring and adjustment, always keeping in mind the underlying ideals.

Balancing the Tensions

Along many dimensions, faculty and administrators need to keep balancing and rebalancing competing goods, which remain in inherent tension with each other. This requires thoughtful awareness, wise judgment, and pedagogical skill. What are these tensions that must be so skillfully negotiated to achieve an environment of open inquiry?

CIVILITY AND ITS RISKS. Teaching about political issues often means engaging controversy. The norms of academic life require civility in these engagements, both in the classroom and beyond. Bringing civility to controversy entails balancing along a number of dimensions at once. How can we require mutual respect without suppressing freedom of expression? How can we insist on civility without becoming legalistic? How can we support sensitivity to others' feelings while encouraging students to be tougher and less ready to take offense themselves? How can we under score the value of multiple perspectives without pushing students toward relativism and disengagement? How can we recognize issues that are just too divisive to be productive without avoiding hard questions that need to be explored? These are the multiple balancing acts that skillful teachers perform all the time when they teach for political development.

REFLECTION AND ACTION. Bringing education for political understanding and engagement to undergraduate education is important in large part because it can lead to a thoughtful, knowledgeable, reasoned approach to politics. But careful investigation and deliberation can go on forever. Ambiguity and uncertainty are seldom completely resolved. Even so, political engagement requires action—often action in the face of uncertainty. How then can we instill habits of careful deliberation and considered judgment, along with decisive action at the right moment? A related question is how to foster passion and firm commitment without dogmatism. And how are we to combine open-minded regard for new or different ideas with steadfast resolve and stamina?

SERIOUS COMMITMENT AND A LOVE OF THE GAME. Finally, how can we make sure that politics is fun—at least some of the time—while also taking it seriously? A light touch, some humor, and a sense of fun change the tone in a class, making it easier to negotiate the many other tensions inherent in this work. Passion and a competitive spirit make politics fun for some players. And laughter often comes from reducing the opposition—and sometimes even ourselves—to absurdity. The question here is how to combine this fun-loving spirit with goodwill and good-natured generosity, how to be sure that we do not take ourselves too seriously though the issues involved are matters of vital concern.

Implementing Campus-Level Strategies

Most of the recent conflagrations around political issues in higher education have taken place at the campuswide level, so it is important to put strategies in place for fostering open inquiry not only in individual courses but also in the campus as a whole. This requires attention to the campus culture. Campus cultures, which are multiple and dynamic in any one institution, are embodied in an array of cultural symbols and practices with which participants in the culture engage actively.[1] Among the most important of these are public spaces and other physical features of the campus, iconic stories that are told over and over, shared ideas and philosophies, rituals of various kinds, and socialization practices directed toward people newly entering the culture, like first-year students and new faculty. Strategies to create a campus climate that truly values open inquiry and respect for ideological diversity can draw on all of these cultural practices. We offer here several of the campuswide strategies we saw at work in the Political Engagement Project, as well as in our previous studies.

RAISE THE ISSUE IN PUBLIC. This means, first of all, that faculty and administrative leaders on a campus should be self-conscious in raising the issue of open inquiry, fostering conversation about what it is, why it is important, and what the principle of open inquiry should mean in practice. The goal is to have a searching discussion of these issues, recognizing that there will be differences of opinion, but looking for common ground that will allow real respect for open inquiry to become a more palpable element in the institution's identity. Although this should not be a top-down endeavor, messages from the highest levels of the institution's leadership are essential to its success, and campus leaders should use multiple opportunities to explicate and support these goals.

As we have noted, presidents of a number of colleges and universities have made powerful and inspiring statements in response to recent crises around political issues on campus (see Bollinger, 2005; Keohane, 2004; Stewart, 2005). The texts of these statements are generally published in campus newspapers or other media and circulate widely on and beyond the campuses. Especially if institutions can find ways to encourage engagement with the key ideas in these statements, their messages can greatly increase the visibility and salience of the issues they address. Of course, a crisis atmosphere heightens student and faculty interest in this kind of statement, providing the opportunity for a powerful "teachable moment." But cogent articulation of values like academic freedom and open inquiry need not wait for a crisis. As long as they can find ways to bring the issues alive in a vivid way, administrative leaders can begin fruitful conversations about these issues at regular occasions throughout the academic year and embed them in the various events and rituals that take place on campus.

SOCIALIZE NEW STUDENTS. It is especially useful to pay attention to the socialization of new students. Materials sent to newly admitted students should set an expectation that the campus will be a community of discourse and that students will be exposed to diverse opinions about many issues, including political issues. Opening convocations can also help set the tone for both entering and returning students and faculty by embodying intellectual flexibility and openness to new ideas.

A common practice on many campuses today is to ask all entering freshmen to read the same book during the summer before they start college and then talk about the book in discussion groups during orientation week. Often these books convey fairly obvious ideological messages, and it sometimes seems that those who choose the books have not thought very much about the one-sidedness of those messages. If, instead, the chosen books embody a passionate commitment to inquiry and truth-seeking rather than a particular (hidden or not-so-hidden) political slant or a bland "on the one hand, on the other hand" approach, students will get a glimpse of this key aspect of academic life even before arriving on campus. Alternatively, some institutions ask students to read an array of compelling essays rather than a single book, and this too allows wider latitude to include multiple points of view.

INVITE DIVERSE VIEWS AND MODEL CIVILITY. Another place for establishing a campuswide respect for diversity of opinion is in the choice of campus speakers and in guidelines for their treatment. University officials do not control all of these invitations, but they do control some, and those invitations can be planned in order to emphasize the openness of the institution to a spectrum of differing views. For example, sponsoring debates between outstanding advocates of different sides on controversial issues can be a lively and informative approach and is often a very good choice. But it is not always the best choice—debates often reinforce a sense that issues are dichotomous, and the discourse they generate does not always exemplify tolerance and civility.

Depending on the issues being addressed, it can be even more useful to sponsor sessions in which participants hear not "both sides" of an issue but multiple sides. These events can also draw attention to the fact that many issues—such as immigration policy, for example—generate many different perspectives *within* as well as across political parties. Invited guests should also include individuals who exemplify political engagement as cooperative public work in a community, regardless of ideology, and others who represent positions and accomplishments that are hard to classify on a simple left-right dimension. Many local issues are less likely to be reducible to simple right-left categories than are national issues, so they are especially effective in helping students think about politics in a less ideologically driven way.

If campuses want to foster respect for diversity of perspective, speakers should also include respected exemplars of open-mindedness and civility who (despite their own convictions at one or another point on the political scale) truly believe that effective, engaged citizens need to be skilled at communicating and forming alliances with people whose perspectives differ from their own.

This kind of thinking was evident during Terry Gross's interview with the Democratic senator Ted Kennedy, which was heard on National Public Radio's *Fresh Air* in April 2006. Kennedy's remarks highlight the importance of bipartisan cooperation, collegiality, and good humor despite political conflict:

KENNEDY: We're continuing to work now with Senator McCain on the issues of immigration and immigration reform. Right after that, we're going to work with Senator Specter on the voting rights extension, which is so important. . . . I've worked with Orrin Hatch on the Ryan White legislation that dealt with AIDS, about the CHIP program, the Children's Health Insurance Program. . . . So we tried to do that and we had some success.

INTERVIEWER: I wonder if it's hard to develop relationships of trust in modern Washington.

KENNEDY: Well, we joke both with [Republican] Senator [Alan] Simpson and Orrin Hatch. We used to say if we sponsored each other's legislation, usually one of us hasn't read it. But, you know, I'd find, for example, I'd be fighting with Orrin Hatch on the floor of the Senate on fetal transplantation, . . . with regard to basic research and NIH funding . . . in the morning, and then I'd be going down in the afternoon working with him on the Religious Restoration Act, which we eventually got passed, about state and federal impediments on terms of religious practices. . . . So, even though you differ one time, you try and find ways of working at another. And I think unless you have that kind of temperament, if you're just going to get upset with somebody that's going to oppose you, you're in the wrong business.

A rich education for political engagement should include opportunities to hear from people who believe that polarization and vitriol are destructive and unattractive and make it clear that they believe this not because they lack the toughness or conviction to be hard-hitting political actors but because they understand that solutions to complex social and economic problems require the wisdom that comes from listening to and drawing on a variety of viewpoints, rather than a simplistic or moralistic approach (Boyte, 2004).

Students select many of the speakers who come to campus, so helping students think about how to choose speakers, and how to treat them once they arrive, is also extremely important. In fact, a common trigger for political disputes on higher education campuses is an invited speaker who is controversial. This happened in the 2004–05 academic year, when Hamilton College invited an extremely outspoken and divisive figure, Ward Churchill, then professor and chair of ethnic studies at the University of Colorado, to speak about prison issues as part of a campus series titled Class in Context. A couple of months before he was scheduled to speak, a Hamilton faculty member drew attention to a little-known paper that Churchill had written shortly after the 9/11 attack, where Churchill tried to justify the actions of the hijackers, even calling the World Trade Center victims "Little Eichmanns," who were implicated in the oppression wrought by U.S. foreign policy. The president of Hamilton, Joan Hinde Stewart, and the dean of the faculty worked with the group that had invited Churchill to turn the event into a panel discussion in which his views on 9/11 would be challenged. But when the national media took up the issue a firestorm ensued, including many threats of violence. Although President Stewart strongly believed, and continues to believe, that principles of free speech require an invitation to be honored once it is issued, in the end she cancelled the talk regretfully because of serious safety concerns.

Stewart's thoughtful response to the incident highlights the core values of the academy, which provide useful guidance on how to think about this kind of incident, including the question of how opponents of the invited speaker should behave. As Stewart pointed out (2005), the academic value of freedom of expression affirms the right of a speaker to make controversial statements as well as the right of opponents to boycott or protest the speaker. But freedom of expression conflicts with denying the speaker the opportunity to be heard. If a campus is to create an environment that upholds respect for diversity of opinion, protesters should not be allowed to silence speakers with whom they disagree.

The values represented by *academic standards* can also play a role in the highly charged issue of controversial speakers on campus. In her response to the controversy at Hamilton, President Stewart forcefully affirmed that the principle of academic freedom requires that faculty members and invited speakers be free to express differing, and even unpleasant, views. However, she also pointed out that "academic excellence and intellectual diversity must go hand in hand" and suggested that invitations should be extended to those "who are thought-provoking and not merely provocative, who challenge us intellectually as opposed to being merely outrageous" (Stewart, 2005, n.p.). Helping students understand and appreciate this distinction, while also respecting their autonomy, is a valuable educational opportunity.

SUPPORT CAMPUS ORGANIZATIONS, ENCOURAGE COOPERATION. Unlike teaching about politics in the curriculum, it is acceptable for extracurricular programs that concern politics to be partisan in their focus and membership. Some of these organizations are explicitly so—the Young Republicans and Democrats being the most obvious examples. Other groups may represent the Palestinian or Israeli perspectives on the ongoing conflict in the Middle East. Still other organizations serve students of particular religious denominations or national origins. As long as a wide range of perspectives is represented, this partisanship is perfectly legitimate in the extracurricular domain and is useful in supporting students' passion for deeper engagement. Campus leaders can encourage a wide range of organizations and encourage them to cooperate across ideological differences.

In spite of strong feelings students may have about the issues their group is addressing, it can be a powerful learning experience when groups whose members feel they have opposing interests find ways to work together by cosponsoring panels, debates, or other events, collaborating in other ways, or communicating about areas of conflict. This does happen with some regularity—for example, when Young Republicans and Young Democrats cosponsor candidate debates during political campaigns. If student groups are going to move toward cooperation rather than conflict, they need to identify a common agenda that means more to them than the issues that separate them.

We saw this happen in the PEP program Democracy Matters, for example, in considering the role of money in American politics. This is a multicampus program that is explicitly nonpartisan, but some campus chapters have included mostly Democrats, while others are predominantly Republican. Students in one of the more liberal chapters talked with great appreciation of the valuable learning that resulted from their collaboration with a conservative student group that shared their interest in campaign finance reform.[2]

Democracy Matters is one of many extracurricular programs that are nonpartisan, at least in intent. Although some of these programs are, in reality, quite politically homogeneous, others draw students from a range of perspectives who share a concern for a particular set of issues, such as environmental sustainability. The more these groups are able to be truly politically diverse, the better they can support the development of open mindedness and respect for multiple perspectives.

Implementing Course- and Program-Level Strategies

As important as it is to strengthen the cultural norms of open-mindedness and respect for diversity of opinion at the campus level, if faculty who address political issues in their courses do not ground their teaching in those ideals, the wider invocations will ring hollow. Given the complicated dynamics of contemporary political discourse, this is not easy to do. It takes real effort and will seldom happen without conscious attention. In our study, we saw that most PEP faculty realize this and use a wealth of strategies to help students' think more broadly, collaborate across difference, and manage conflict without animosity and intense conversations with at least a modicum of equanimity. We offer some of their strategies and experiences.

REPRESENT DIVERSE POINTS OF VIEW. Most faculty work hard to make sure that students encounter a wide array of perspectives on the political and policy issues addressed by their courses. They often begin by talking very explicitly with their students about the value of engaging with perspectives different from their own. When he was director of Democracy Matters, Adam Weinberg advised students from the outset that "politics is not about preaching to the choir." Alma Blount, director of Duke's Service Opportunities in Leadership program, tells her students that too many people who care about politics allow themselves to become isolated in their own small circles and that it is important to "put themselves more into the mix of diverse interests, values, and perspectives." She urges them to make it a habit to talk often with people who don't agree with them.

Some faculty rely mostly on discussions drawing on diversity of opinion among the students or on spontaneous opportunities to speak up for minority opinions themselves in order to accomplish the breadth they are seeking. Others take a more active and deliberate approach to introducing material that represents a range of perspectives, beginning with a carefully crafted syllabus. A well-planned course syllabus can ensure the consideration of diverse points of view through its choice of lecture and discussion topics, reading and writing assignments, projects, and other activities.

One of the most straightforward ways to ensure diversity of perspective is to include readings that represent those perspectives. Students find it gratifying to learn about unfamiliar points of view and appreciate faculty efforts to include readings that introduce political ideas that are new to them. A politically liberal African American student in the Mills College Civic Leadership Program, for example, commented on how much she learned from reading the works of well-known black conservatives.

Depending on the particular focus of the course, ensuring that multiple perspectives are represented in the reading assignments can take real effort. In any field, both within and well beyond the political, it is easier to identify high-quality work that is consistent with one's own point of view than to find what seem like really good statements of alternatives. As we have already mentioned, people are generally less knowledgeable about that body of work, and whether they intend to or not, are likely to read it with a more critical eye than they bring to more congenial writings. Mechanisms to help faculty share reading lists in their own institution and across institutions can be a big help in this process.

Inviting a wide range of guest speakers is another engaging and vivid way to represent and stimulate discussion of diverse political perspectives, and students often comment on how much they learn from these speakers. Locating speakers who can do a good job presenting the various points of view can be challenging, however. Faculty sometimes find that they need to reach beyond people with whom they have personal connections in order to find some who represent perspectives different from their own. The institution can help by supporting faculty efforts to do this.

Diversity of perspective can also come from students. Political diversity among students varies across institutions and across courses and programs in any one institution. Students in some PEP courses and programs are very politically diverse, in others they are less so. A key to taking the best possible advantage of whatever degree of diversity is present is to make sure to support and draw out students who, on any given topic, seem to hold a view different from the majority. In courses and programs that are fairly homogeneous this can be a special challenge, because student opinions may not cover a wide range and those few students who do see the issues differently are small minorities, and naturally feel more reluctant to speak up than they would if their numbers were larger.

Our interviews with PEP students made it clear that most of them sincerely value the chance to engage a range of perspectives. Among the most frequent comments were expressions of enthusiasm about lively discussions that engage significant differences of opinion. Diversity of opinion and animated debate in these courses may center on questions relating to partisan politics, but often they do not. A Providence College student reflected on one that did not entail a liberal-versus-conservative debate:

> We were having a discussion about participatory democracy and Dr. Battistoni brought up the question, "How important do you think voting is?" And some person said voting is just like a tool for show that doesn't really mean anything. I came out as like, "That's obviously not right." I brought up discussion about participatory democracy and how we needed it, and how voting is one of the main forms of participation in politics, and how it's very necessary. And we went back and forth for a little while, and finally we came to a happy medium and we settled with that.

Just as students in the more diverse programs comment on how much they gain from the group's breadth of opinion, students in more homogeneous groups often say they had wished for more diversity. As one Portland State student said, "I think the course would have been really interesting if there were half Republicans and half Democrats. If there had been more diversity, I think there would have been more energy."

In fact, it was much more common for students to express frustration with the limited diversity in point of view among their peers or a fellow student's ideological rigidity than with perceived bias on the part of the instructor. Students said that they sometimes stopped listening to classmates who never seemed to consider others' points, responding to every issue with the same, apparently knee-jerk, ideological reaction. It is also worth noting, though, that in the rare cases where students felt that the course was slanted and the instructor intolerant of opposing points of view, they complained bitterly. Students are quick to notice closed-mindedness in either peers or teachers, and they almost always find it extremely objectionable. This is no doubt one reason they are seldom persuaded to adopt the opinions of the offending party.

ESTABLISH A CIVIL ATMOSPHERE AND MANAGE CONFLICT EFFECTIVELY.
In order to foster an atmosphere of open inquiry and diversity of perspective, it is important to be clear from the outset about the high value placed on open-mindedness, civility, and mutual respect.

Of course, not all students are open-minded and respectful of others' opinions. We heard from some faculty that a few students enter their courses or programs with entrenched intolerance for perspectives other than their own and a habit of expressing their animosity toward those views. This is especially common in courses or programs that tend to attract or explicitly select for politically committed students. These students, who can come from any point on the political spectrum, may not even be aware of their lack of civility or may see it as evidence of their passion and commitment. Unfortunately, even a significant minority of such students can wreak havoc with the tone of a classroom. One faculty member described struggling with a group like this with only mixed success: "We get kids who self-select, and last year that really happened. We wound up with a group of 'political correctness police.' It was just five students out of twenty-two, but they were a real pain. It was horrible for me and the other students. . . . They treated others rudely, would roll their eyes when the more moderate students spoke. . . . I would call them on their behavior both in class and privately. . . .We chose the group differently this year. We looked for students who we believed were really open to learning from others different from themselves."

In the effort to maintain a respectful atmosphere, many PEP faculty enlist students' help by creating formal roles for them to play in class discussions. In several of the courses and programs we studied, students take on the role of moderator or overseer of the discussion's tone and productivity. At Providence College, Rick Battistoni, for example, assigns one student to be moderator for each discussion and another to be what he calls a "vibeswatcher," letting participants know when they need to calm down a bit or watch their tone of voice.[3] Students take turns playing these roles, and many commented on the special value of having a vibeswatcher. The very act of creating a role like this calls attention to the process and character of productive deliberation. Teaching students to be effective moderators can have the same effect.

Both students and faculty find ways to use humor to break the tension when discussions get too intense. Students often told us how much they appreciated it when their professors used humor to "lighten things up." PEP faculty often make a point of helping students understand that some degree of conflict is all right, that political life often involves engaging and managing conflict. One of Sue Briggs's students in the CIVICUS program at the University of Maryland describes how Briggs got this point across in a particularly heated discussion: "A lot of us were frustrated that she didn't say much. We were frustrated by the amount of tension that was allowed to continue. But by the second or third class she explained to us that issues like this arise every day in politics. If you go to the city council meetings, town council meetings, a lot of them erupt in this amount of tension. She wanted to give us a hands-off approach at first, but then she helped reconcile the two sides and explained what she thought was going on."

Describing the course he teaches at Harvard, Marshall Ganz says, "Fear of conflict doesn't have a place in a democratic polity. Pluralism involves challenging each other's positions." Several PEP faculty noted that they are able to create a civil atmosphere without making students conflict-averse by building a sense of community in the class. When students get to know each other and have a sense of group solidarity, it is easier for them to disagree without generating feelings of animosity, to confront each other's claims vigorously without being afraid that the listener will take offense.

According to both students and faculty, the issues most likely to generate high levels of tension concern race, religion, sexual orientation, and other aspects of individuals' core identity. When discussions call up sensitivities around these identity issues, it can become very difficult to maintain civility and deliberate productively. Students sometimes choose to stay away from extreme hot-button issues, realizing that some topics are more likely to bog down than to move forward. In describing the process, Tony Perry (formerly with the Urban Agenda program at Wayne State, now a faculty member at Henry Ford Community College), says, "Students often feel that they need to set aside issues like abortion or gay marriage because they squeeze out other issues they care about—education, the war in Iraq, health care, the economy, and so on. They don't want the hot button issues on which people seldom change their positions to prevent them from focusing on other problems."

When tensions arise around race, religion, or other sensitive issues, the conversation can become productive if there is a basic level of trust and goodwill in the group as well as skillful faculty intervention at opportune moments. Addressing very divisive topics is a high-risk undertaking and can lead civility to break down or leave some students feeling hurt or angry. Gerald Shenk described a memorable, though difficult, incident that took place during a course he taught at California State University, Monterey Bay. The conversation was about the strong emotions raised by our most visible and contested political symbol, the American flag:

> As part of a political action project in that course, I had a student who wanted to burn the flag. We went outside and no one knew what he was going to do. Then when he pulled out his lighter, with the flag in his other hand, I noticed that the other students looked horrified and turned ashen. I stopped him and suggested that we go back inside and talk about it. It was probably the greatest discussion I've ever been part of with students. Nearly everyone cried as they talked about or heard about what the flag meant to them. Some associated it with the death of relatives in what they believed were meaningless wars, others with freedom for ancestors who had immigrated here. It was the most tolerant, respectful, powerful discussion I've seen students have together. Ultimately, a distinction was made between what was legal versus

what was the ethical or moral thing to do. They felt that though the student had the legal right to burn the flag, it would have been insensitive to the feelings of the class and others in the community.

UNDERMINE STEREOTYPES AND REDUCE DEMONIZATION. Even though conflict is an unavoidable part of the political process, this does not mean that engaged citizens need to succumb to the polarization and demonization of the opposition that often seem to characterize contemporary electoral politics. An important goal for many PEP faculty and program leaders is to work with their students to undermine unfounded stereotypes that political groups have of each other and reduce the tendency to demonize the opposition. Many of them raise this issue with students directly. Often students come to realize the humanity of those on opposing sides of tough issues simply by getting to know for the first time people who very much disagree with them.

The Sorensen Institute takes an interesting and unusual approach to dispelling stereotypes, and it could probably be adapted for use in other programs. This intensive thirty-day summer program involves a wide array of educational sessions teaching students the substance, skills, and social, ethical, and historical contexts of Virginia politics. It culminates in a mock state assembly session, in which students work in teams to try to pass legislation. In the opening meeting of the program, the director, Greg Werkheiser, asks students not to reveal their own political party affiliations (if they have them) until that mock assembly session. It is somewhat surprising that students are able to comply with this request, and in most cases, not deduce each other's party loyalties in the course of their many discussions, but in fact that seems to be the case. This withholding of information and then revealing it in the end is a very salient aspect of the experience for many students and their comments about it are universally positive. An important related goal for many of the courses and programs is showing students the inadequacy of using simplistic left-right categories to think about politics. The PEP courses and programs use a variety of approaches to get this message across, including making the point in many contexts that for most political and policy issues, there are more than two viable points of view. One student from the Sorensen Institute highlighted this as one of the things that, in her view, kept the debates from becoming overly contentious. As she put it: "There were never hard feelings. . . . I think it was because the issues were never just black and white. There were always lots of different groups and lots of variation in what people thought."

In the Wayne State American government course that involves students in the Urban Agenda Project, faculty members Otto Feinstein and Tony

Perry made it a point to talk to students about the ways that electoral politics in Michigan defy simple preconceptions about liberals and conservatives. As Perry pointed out, showing the students in detail that "Michigan has a really divided electorate and elected officials often don't line up with the national party on every issue . . . is a visible mechanism for making the point."

Another good way to make the point about the limits of a simple left-right analysis of political issues is to focus on local issues, which are often harder to stereotype than the national issues that take on such a partisan tone. Courses that focus exclusively on local politics are in an especially strong position to do this. In Dick Simpson's Chicago politics course at the University of Illinois, Chicago, for example, students often engage in spirited debates about local issues that directly affect their own communities. Although one could link the issues to broader ideological categories, it seems that the more personal experience students have with the issues, the less likely they are to frame the debate in partisan terms.[4]

SUPPORT NONDIVISIVE ENGAGEMENT. Several of the PEP courses and programs use pedagogical approaches that are especially well-suited to engaging students politically while carrying only minimal risk of ideological divisiveness. For example, the Urban Agenda asks students to study local issues in order to become knowledgeable about them, and then to work in small groups to identify issues they feel are most important for citizen groups and elected officials to address. The groups come together in a large convention and arrive at a single agenda, which is then used as the basis for engaging with high school students and other grassroots groups and with candidates and the press.[5] This approach is exciting and empowering for students, yet does not require them to argue through their differences about preferred solutions to the issues.

Simulations can also be helpful in building political knowledge and skills while avoiding contentious ideological divisions. The Model United Nations program, for example, involves students from around the world. Each class is assigned to a particular country, and students develop agendas, position papers, resolutions, and the like from the perspective of that country. At the end of the semester, groups of students from all over the United States and a number of foreign countries gather in New York to join in a simulation of a United Nations General Assembly.

This approach ensures that students understand international issues and the domestic issues of another country from that country's point of view. Because they are not reacting to the issues from the perspective of American foreign or domestic policy, they are less likely to line up along the usual ideological divisions. Through the simulation, participants also engage with students representing many other countries and thus come to understand multiple perspectives and gain a more complicated and full-bodied sense of the issues. Students are also exposed to multiple perspectives on the United Nations itself. Although the course does begin with the assumption that international cooperation is a good thing, it does not ignore the fact that the United Nations itself is often a target and source of controversy.

A third approach, which offers the sharpest contrast with the usual rancor of partisan politics, is the public work model developed by Harry Boyte and his colleagues at the University of Minnesota. Boyte describes "the citizen politics of public work" as fundamentally different from the dominant conception of politics and citizen action (2001a, n.p.). The dominant view centers on electoral politics, which pits the forces of good against the forces of evil and entails mobilization around predefined agendas, with clear winners and losers. This view leads naturally to demonization of the opposition, which is often seen as a necessary element in efforts to mobilize large numbers of people on one side or another. The politics of public work shares with the dominant view of politics a recognition that individuals and groups in a democracy have different, often conflicting interests, but instead of a win-lose approach to conflict, the politics of public work involves negotiating these diverse interests and points of view so that citizens can work together to accomplish shared goals that contribute importantly to the common good. In public work politics, "[F]orming alliances and learning to understand the experiences, interests, and worldviews of others, including those we disagree with profoundly, are foundational skills. Political energy is generated by the ability to improvise, try new things, and develop new relationships. A rigid division of the world into saints and sinners makes that impossible" (Boyte, 2001b, p. 6).

These teaching approaches that deemphasize partisan divisions often have a distinctly pragmatic tone. As Jim Farr of the University of Minnesota said: "I am a democratic pragmatist." Perry uses the same word to describe the Urban Agenda approach: "The approach is pragmatic. Let's figure out how these issues can best be dealt with."

Building on the Foundation

We have devoted considerable discussion to questions of how to conduct college-level political education in ways that are morally legitimate and consistent with core academic values. We have done so because we believe that no endeavor to educate for political engagement should be seriously biased or out of step with fundamental academic values. We know that education for political engagement *is* sometimes biased, but we strongly believe that it need not and should not be.

Our basic assumption that education for political development is legitimate only under specific circumstances—is the foundation for the rest of this book. We turn now to more extended discussions of the specific learning goals of these educational efforts—that is, how faculty who are teaching for political development understand its goals and their insights about how to achieve them, and five key pedagogies that effectively support political development in college students.

NOTES

1. For an in-depth discussion, see *Educating Citizens* (Colby, Ehrlich, Beaumont, and Stephens, 2003), pp. 83–95.

2. For more information on Democracy Matters, see documents 27, 28, and 29 in the PEP document supplement available at http://www.carnegie foundation.org/educating_for_democracy/docs/.

3. For Battistoni's brief description of the "discussion leader" and "vibes-watcher" roles in classroom discussions, see document 8 in the PEP document supplement online at the address shown in note 2.

4. For examples of local issues that students confront in Simpson's course, see documents 19 and 20 in the PEP document supplement online.

5. For a detailed description of the agenda-setting process, see document 11 in the PEP document supplement online.

5

TEACHING FOR POLITICAL KNOWLEDGE AND UNDERSTANDING

POLITICAL KNOWLEDGE AND UNDERSTANDING form the linchpin of responsible political engagement. Our abilities to identify and articulate our political interests and goals, to make thoughtful decisions and take informed action, to make sense of political communication, to judge and monitor the soundness of policies, and to hold representatives accountable, all depend on the adequacy of our political understanding (Nie, Junn, and Stehlik-Barry, 1996). Political knowledge and understanding do more than affect the quality of political judgments; they help people convert their opinions into many forms of meaningful political involvement and are powerful predictors of political participation (Althaus, 1998; Delli Carpini and Keeter, 1996; Popkin and Dimock, 1999).

The more people know about politics, the better able they are to sort, interpret, and remember new information they encounter (Bennett, 1994; Fiske, Kinder, and Larter, 1983). Conversely, the less people know, the more difficult it is for them to make sense of the news or participate meaningfully in political conversations, and the less likely they are to be interested in politics. Thus, positive and negative feedback loops result in a cumulative effect over time. Longitudinal studies confirm this, showing that the political knowledge gained during formative periods, such as high school and college, is particularly important because it establishes a strong base on which individuals continue to build over the course of their lives (Jennings, 1996).

Because political knowledge and understanding play such a critical role, they are widely acknowledged as among the most important goals of civic education. The PEP courses and programs are no exception to this: when

asked to describe their goals, both faculty and cocurricular program leaders talked first about imparting substantive knowledge. Students also identified gains in political knowledge and understanding as highly salient
benefits of these courses and programs.

Foundational and Current Events Knowledge

Gaining and maintaining political knowledge and understanding, like any
kind of learning, requires attention and effort (Lupia and McCubbins,
1998; Luskin, 1990). When people do pay attention to politics, it is usually because they have come to find it personally enjoyable or rewarding
or because they feel a responsibility to keep up with politics (Delli Carpini
and Keeter, 1996). Recognizing this, PEP faculty are centrally concerned
with fostering students' desire for political knowledge. They hope that by
making politics feel more important, interpretable, and relevant, or by
encouraging students to pay attention to current events that are related
to the course, students will gain greater political interest and be inspired to
continue learning about political issues after the course or program ends.
The course is intended as a building block to deeper and broader political understanding in the future.

In conjunction with stimulating students' interest in politics, most PEP
faculty work to build two types of political knowledge in their students—
general or foundational knowledge and knowledge of current issues and
events (Delli Carpini and Keeter, 1996; Gilens, 2001; Zaller, 1992). Foundational political knowledge includes the kinds of theoretical, conceptual,
and institutional understanding that help people organize and interpret
new political information and ground their judgment in a grasp of institutional forms, purposes, and processes. Foundational knowledge includes
the base of knowledge about U.S. government often associated with civic
education in middle or high school, such as what the main branches of
government are and what they do, what the concept of checks and bal-
ances means and why it is important, or how the roles of state and federal government differ. But, particularly at the college level, foundational
political knowledge involves linking this relatively static understanding of
American government to a range of contextual, historical, and comparative knowledge that can help put these basic concepts in perspective and
foster greater insight into their meaning.

Attention to this contextual dimension of foundational political knowledge allows students greater insight into civic institutions like the Bill of
Rights by teaching how civil liberties protected by the U.S. Constitution
were interpreted during the McCarthy era, for example, or in what ways

and for what reasons they may differ from the protections for civil liberties in other countries. This kind of political knowledge can also involve learning how political groups or movements have operated, such as religious and other antislavery groups prior to the Civil War.

Promoting current events knowledge is also extremely valuable, and research shows that civic education works particularly well when it includes discussions of current events. Frequent discussions of current issues can increase overall levels of political knowledge as well as democratic values and propensity to participate (Niemi and Junn, 1998; Torney-Purta, Lehmann, Oswald, and Schulz, 2001). Without keeping somewhat abreast of current issues and events, citizens are unable to develop their own opinions about and responses to the issues that concern them. If foundational knowledge is analogous to learning the rules of the game, then current issues and events knowledge is more analogous to following the flow of the game—the pressing issues and debates facing us—sufficiently that we feel connected to or invested in it and capable of participating.

The PEP courses make it a priority to connect substantive classroom learning with learning about related current issues and events. In his Children and Public Policy course at Brown University, for example, Ross Cheit uses an electronic bulletin board to post newspaper articles, his own commentary about the significance of the articles, and links to other resources about the same policy issues students are studying and experiencing in the internships they do in connection with the course. Cheit uses both local newspapers, which help connect students to local issues, and national newspapers like the *New York Times*. He told us that this use of current periodicals was one of the most engaging and productive aspects of the course: "There was an important New York court decision about the custody rights of battered women, for example. I posted the *New York Times* article about the case and a link to the decision. Because a number of students were working on issues related to custody and domestic violence, they were really interested in this case. My commentaries helped make connections to course concepts and pose questions. We had a great discussion about that case."

All of the PEP courses and programs also seek to impart foundational knowledge about politics, such as how institutions like state assemblies, the United Nations, local governments and school boards, juvenile courts, or markets actually work, or the history of the nation's founding, the progressive or civil rights movements, or the implications of different moral and political ideas and theories for political choices. Thus, they help students build specific aspects of foundational knowledge on American or international politics or policy, focusing on structures and institutions, the political process, political theory, and policy formulation and implementation.

Both the specific content covered and the balance struck between foundational and more policy-oriented or current events knowledge are intentionally extremely varied in PEP. The courses and programs cover a wide array of topics, including child and family policy; campaign finance reform; the local politics of Chicago and San Francisco, and the state-level politics of the Commonwealth of Virginia; classical and contemporary political theory; free market economic systems; the United Nations; and the environmental history of California. (See Appendix A for summaries of each of the twenty-one courses and programs we studied in PEP.)

Despite its diversity, even this range is limited compared to the full scope of undergraduate education. Courses in most disciplines and in pre-professional programs such as teaching, engineering, business, or nursing can contribute to students' development as citizens if they connect major topics in the field with relevant public policies and other civic concerns. On most campuses, faculty in many disciplines and programs that one would not normally associate with civic education try to promote students' political understanding. They do this by placing the topics they centrally address, whether in biology or art or nursing, into a broader institutional or historical frame, asking how they interact with or are affected by social and political institutions or issues.

Our survey results show that increases in political knowledge were among the most important contributions of the interventions: on average, students made significant gains in both foundational political knowledge and knowledge of current events. (See Appendix B, "Survey Scales and Results.") And students who began their interventions with the lowest levels of political interest—which is typical of many college students and other young Americans and is usually related to low levels of political knowledge—made the greatest gains in both types of political knowledge. Moreover, it appears that interventions targeting students of lower socioeconomic status (as indicated by average level of parents' educational attainment) may be particularly effective in boosting foundational political knowledge.

Goals for Teaching Political Understanding

As we talked with PEP faculty and students about the process of teaching and learning political understanding, we saw five common goals emerge. Some of these highlight the importance of both foundational and current issues knowledge, along with an understanding of the complexity and contingency of democratic politics. Others address the intersection of political understanding with motivation, describing, for example, how to help students find political knowledge intriguing and relevant or see the concerns of the political realm as involving issues and values they care about. We can think of these crosscutting goals as relating both to *what* students know and understand about politics, and also to *how* students think about, conceptualize, frame, and reflect on their political knowledge and understanding.

Increased Depth and Breadth of Political Knowledge

Depth of substantive knowledge is important to effective democratic engagement, and many PEP courses and programs embody this understanding, providing extensive coverage of selected issues. Cheit's course devotes a semester to public policy regarding children. Adam Reich, who took the course himself and has also served as teaching assistant in the course, explained that, through Children and Public Policy, he realized that policy questions need "more than a week's worth of discussion. . . . The course highlights the importance of taking the time to deal with issues in their complexity."

Other programs and courses provide similar depth on other issues. The Democracy Matters program engages students for a year or more on campaign finance reform and related issues. In Dick Simpson's course at the University of Illinois, students delve deeply into policy issues affecting the city of Chicago. In Duke's Service Opportunities in Leadership program, students select their own focus issues and develop extensive "social issue research portfolios" on them.[1] Experiences like these underscore the substantive specificity of social and public policy and the value for effective participation of deep knowledge of particular issues.

Helping students develop a broad base of political knowledge is also important. Courses and programs that cover a wide range of issues lead many students to feel more knowledgeable about and more interested in politics. As a student noted following his participation in the Sorensen Institute for Political Leadership: "When I go back to school this year I'm going to really know what I'm talking about when issues come up. I've established positions on some issues now that I didn't even know enough about to attempt to have a position before. We covered topics in one month that we never discussed in my three years at Virginia Tech. . . . And before, I wasn't one to watch the news, but I watch it now, because I want to know what's going on. . . . It's important to me."

Although faculty use many different approaches to help students develop in-depth exposure to one or more specific areas or issues, the teaching strategies almost always include carefully chosen readings, accompanied by discussion. In a number of cases readings were not only discussed but connected to written reflections. Students frequently remarked that they were deeply moved by a memorable book or article, as well as learning both substance and fundamental concepts. A comment by this Berea College student in Meta Mendel-Reyes's course is typical: "One thing I remember most is a book we read, a pamphlet really, by Jamie Hilbert. It was called 'Singing the World into Existence.' It said 'Be the change you want to see,' which is a quotation from Gandhi. That will stay with me."

In addition to readings, all PEP faculty use lectures and intermittent "mini-lectures" to teach for substantive knowledge and understanding. In this sense, teaching material that prepares students for informed democratic participation is not different from teaching academic material more generally. But faculty and program staff educating for democratic participation are also aware that imparting *usable* knowledge requires both incentives to use the knowledge and practice doing so. This involves connecting academic knowledge and understanding with students' personal interests and concerns.

There are many ways to do this. Otto Feinstein and Tony Perry created a forum for their Wayne State University students to develop an agenda of issues that the students themselves saw as critical for the local Detroit community. The students could think through which policy issues were important to them and then learn a lot about alternative perspectives on how best to address those issues. When students are establishing the priorities themselves, they feel a personal investment in pursuing solutions.

Imparting *usable* knowledge also requires that students actually apply the substantive material they are learning in action or research projects, placements, simulations, or other pedagogies of engagement. This increases their desire to learn and teaches them how to use their academic knowledge in real situations. Students speak of a sense of urgency about learning material they need to use in carrying out actions they really care about. Work that entails collaboration among students can heighten this urgency, making many students feel they need to keep up with their partners and not let them down. As one student in the Model United Nations course said, "My partner was on top of his game more than I was, I think. So when he would bring up an interesting point, that would make me want to look that up so we could talk about it intelligently."

In addition to the common array of readings, lectures, discussions, and writing opportunities, some faculty found it particularly valuable to use political research projects to help students gain democratic knowledge and understanding.[2] Although some of the research projects were typical of many academic courses, such as a research paper on a specific political topic, some were more ambitious. In Alma Blount's Service Opportunities in Leadership program, for example, many students conduct what Blount calls community-based research projects in conjunction with their summer internships.[3] The projects address real needs of the organizations for which the students are working and result in reports and other products that are genuinely useful to the agency. The products include survey data, documentary articles, and feasibility studies.

Students in Simpson's course on the city of Chicago conduct research on a city or state governmental department or organization, creating a detailed report on what the organization does.[4] As one student put it, "Everything from its mission statement and genesis to its current and past year budget cycle, its operating versus capital costs . . . its key issues and focus . . . and how decisions are made." Students often describe these projects as one of the most valuable experiences in the course.

A Broader Conception of Democratic Participation

A goal shared by many PEP faculty is to help students understand democratic participation in broader terms than partisan battles and voting in national elections.[5] More than half the students in PEP reported that "expanding or redefining" their view of politics had been very important to their learning. Many described as a major revelation their new awareness of the many avenues for active citizenship, including involvement in local politics, grassroots participation, a diverse array of nonelective roles in government, and various kinds of policy-related work. Expanding students' conceptions of politics is closely linked with the development of political motivation, because these forms of participation often seem less remote and imposing than electoral politics on the national level.

Roudy Hildreth, who worked with Jim Farr on the University of Minnesota course Practicing Democratic Education, identified expanding students' conception of democratic participation as a key goal of the course, in which college students serve as coaches in the Public Achievement program originally established by Harry Boyte and his colleagues. Hildreth emphasized that combining classroom teaching with the practicum helped reframe the students' view of the political realm around Boyte's notion of citizen politics. In this view, ordinary people work together to pursue collective goals and accomplish outcomes of public value, or public work. "In class, we expand the domain of the political to the everyday. We speak not just of formal institutional politics but of everyday activity. The practicum helps to drive this home," said Hildreth.

Deliberative and Reflective Capacities

Many aspects of political knowledge and understanding shade over into intellectual skills that are central to democratic participation, such as reflective judgment and critical thinking. A whole range of political judgments, evaluations, and decisions are closely connected to what we know, or think we know, about politics, and to what are sometimes termed *metacognitive skills* related to how we reason about the relation of our knowledge to the world and our goals. For example, to be prepared for responsible democratic participation, students need to learn how to evaluate the evidence others present and recognize and evaluate implicit assumptions in their own and others' arguments. They need to learn how to find information and use it to evaluate alternative positions on political or policy issues, to formulate and defend their own positions, and to evaluate and respond to others' positions.

Students also need to be able to see and evaluate issues from alternative perspectives. Providing opportunities for students to engage with peers who see things differently than they do is a very effective way to support this learning. A student in the Model United Nations course said, "When I read the (opposing side's) position paper, I could understand why they had made a decision to support something. It opened me up to understanding that there are perspectives other than my own."

Evaluating competing arguments in this way causes students to think harder about things they have previously taken for granted. This often leads them to change their minds about issues or to take a more nuanced and qualified position than they had before. In fact, in our survey, 88 percent said that they had changed their thinking about a political issue during the PEP course or program. Students often attribute the shift in their thinking to discussions with classmates who hold views very different from their own. When students make a strong and convincing case for the positions they hold, they are able to influence the views of others in the class, even on issues that evoke strong opinions and emotions.

Sometimes exposure to new views comes from readings rather than from talking with classmates. A student in Mills College's Institute for Civic Leadership talked about undertaking a research paper on black conservatism that led her to a different understanding of some important issues connected with political ideology and political party affiliations. In the process of reading and writing about black conservatives, she was struck by their emphasis on self-reliance and empowerment and found herself grappling with the implications of these ideas for her own political identity as a young African American.

Courses that provide practice grounding judgments and arguments in substantive knowledge can lead to new habits as well as new understanding. As one Model United Nations student said, "This course has changed how I interact with people. I can cite numbers, specific agreements; I can give reasons. Because of the class, I'm more likely to want to get specific information about why I believe what I believe." Likewise, a student in Otto Feinstein's American government course referred to habits of mind he picked up: "The method of thinking and examining situations that my professor taught me—I carry it into all of my other classes and all corners of my life, just a certain way of examining things, not just accepting what's being said by experts, but trying to find out what the underlying principles are."

A More Realistic Understanding of Politics

In their study of civic knowledge at the high school level, Niemi and Junn (1998) emphasized that, too often, gaining traditional textbook knowledge of civics means that students have a naïve view of political institutions that "glosses over the fact that democratic politics is all about disagreement and attempts to settle quarrels peacefully, satisfactorily, and in an orderly manner" (1998, p. 150). In contrast, PEP courses and programs are specifically concerned with helping students learn about how politics "really works." Niemi and Junn note that this approach leads students to see politics as more relevant and interesting as well as understand it more clearly. We saw three important approaches to this goal at work in the PEP courses and programs: helping students appreciate the complexity of political issues and social concerns, helping them recognize that political and policy choices require trade-offs, and helping them experience the way the democratic process "really works."

HELPING STUDENTS APPRECIATE THE COMPLEXITY OF POLITICAL ISSUES AND SOCIAL CONCERNS. A goal that often coincides with gaining in-depth knowledge or more multifaceted perspectives on politics is helping students understand that political and social policy issues are complex, but that this is part of what makes them important and intriguing. As Dick Reitano said about his Model United Nations course, "The issues are complex, difficult to resolve, and don't lend themselves to easy answers. The course stimulates far more awareness of cognitive complexities in understanding how countries work and why they act the way they do in global politics."

This appreciation of complexity is one element of the kind of mature understanding that is foundational for responsible democratic participation. Mendel-Reyes also stresses appreciation of complexity as a goal of her course, Introduction to Service, Citizenship, and Community: "Part of what I hope to do is help students unlearn their expectations or stereotypes [about communities, service, and politics] so they can learn a more complex, more realistic, more motivating approach."

HELPING STUDENTS RECOGNIZE THAT POLITICAL AND POLICY CHOICES REQUIRE TRADE-OFFS. A number of PEP faculty address the complexity of politics by stressing that policy formulation and implementation require the reconciliation of competing sets of values and interests, all of which may seem desirable but which, in practice, must be traded off against each other. Others emphasize that in a pluralist democracy, treating political goals and values in zero-sum or all-or-nothing ways can lead to deadlock and despair. And even well-formulated policies designed to gain as much consensus as possible have unintended consequences. Further adding to the complexity is that both the formulation and implementation of policy are carried out by real human beings, who bring to the work complicated profiles of motivations, constraints, talents, and limitations. For example, describing the goals of his course Children and Public Policy, Cheit said:

> Sometimes I think I have the same goal in all of my courses—appreciation of complexity. I want the students to understand that there are always trade-offs, which is a key concept in public policy. They need to understand what's being traded off. In juvenile justice, for example, there are conflicting goals—punishment, rehabilitation, protection of society, and so on. You can't do them all equally. In child protection, there are type I and type II errors—taking kids out of the home when they should be left there and leaving them there when they should be taken out. If you minimize one, leave more kids in the home to avoid taking them out unnecessarily, you also leave more in their homes incorrectly.

HELPING STUDENTS EXPERIENCE HOW THE DEMOCRATIC PROCESS "REALLY WORKS." In contrast with the streamlined version of civics taught in many secondary schools, these courses introduce students to the ambiguities, irregularities, and contingency (often referred to as the "messiness") of the political process. Adam Weinberg considered this an important goal for Democracy Matters: "We're interested in helping students figure out what it really means to change laws."

Similarly, Rick Semiatin, of American University's Washington Semester Program, said his course is about how politics really works: "I want students to experience the reality of politics from the inside . . . to understand that politics is messy. It doesn't fit into boxes and is often more process than form." A student in Simpson's City of Chicago course echoes this thought, saying he considers it "the best political science I've taken in terms of being real" as opposed to his other courses' tendency to "talk on abstract and academic levels."

Unfortunately, showing students the messy reality of the democratic process entails risks as well as benefits. Some say that you should never watch laws or sausages being made, and a vivid introduction to *realpolitik* does sometimes reinforce students' cynicism, discouraging a sense of efficacy and a desire for engagement. As one Engalitcheff Institute student said of her Washington, D.C., internship: "I was proud to be an American before I came, but going to D.C. might have diminished that pride . . . because you see people that you're not exactly proud to be affiliated with." Another said, "I guess working on Capitol Hill was disillusioning in that I think a lot of politics works because of the machinery in politics and is actually quite divorced from the wants of the constituents." Although none of the faculty and program leaders believe it is useful for students to become so cynical that they opt out of politics, a number do feel that some degree of frustration or disillusionment may be an inevitable part of gaining greater political knowledge and sophistication.

Most faculty, however, make a conscious effort to mitigate or compensate for the more extreme elements of political cynicism that some students develop when they experience politics at work. In particular, many view opportunities for reflection about disconcerting experiences as critical for ensuring that "learning how it really works" will make the democratic process come alive without leaving students disillusioned and disheartened. Somewhat paradoxically, if handled well, exposure to the realities of the democratic process can actually help temper some students' cynicism. Professor Doug Morgan of Portland State, for example, says that everyone leaving his class should have a greater appreciation for the competing and conflicting values that elected officials must reconcile. He believes that if students understand better the necessity of compromise in the political process, they will appreciate the hard choices elected officials face and see the process as legitimate even when it does not conform to their idealized notions of it.

Action Despite Limitations of Knowledge

Even as students become more knowledgeable and more aware of the complexity of social issues and the democratic process, they also become more aware of the limits of their understanding. Sometimes their growing appreciation of the wealth of knowledge that could potentially inform their thinking about an issue can lead them to feel overwhelmed and immobilized rather than empowered. As students come to see that experts devote decades, even whole careers, to a particular set of issues, some may begin to wonder how they could ever hope to know enough to make choices or take action.

A student participating in the Metro Urban Studies Term, sponsored by the Higher Education Consortium for Urban Affairs, talked about feeling frustrated with discussions of economic issues, feeling that neither he nor his peers could ever know enough to make truly informed judgments about some of the issues of urban poverty covered in his program: "I've had some economic training, . . . but when you're looking at an entire economic system, I might as well have no training because they're just such complicated issues. That can be a frustrating thing—to feel like you want to understand so much more in order to really have a substantial view of what we should do."

For courses and programs to support students' active democratic engagement, faculty need to be sensitive to this pitfall and help students learn that knowledge and understanding are always partial, and yet we have to act anyway, not only in the political arena but also in many other domains. When the course or program involves taking some action on the issues under consideration or becoming a competent public spokesperson, it can help students learn that, as important as it is to be reasonably well-informed, ultimately one has to act even without full knowledge.

NOTES

1. For a description of the various parts of the social issue research portfolio, as well as an example, see documents 26 and 56 in the PEP document supplement at http://www.carnegiefoundation.org/educating_for_democracy/docs/.

2. For examples, see the "Research/Action Projects and Simulations" section of the PEP document supplement at the online address cited in note 1.

3. For a description of the steps involved in completing a community-based research project, as well as an example, see documents 23 and 55 in the PEP document supplement online.

4. For a description of this project, as well as a model, see documents 19 and 20 in the PEP document supplement online.

5. For a few examples of how PEP faculty encourage students to think about democratic participation in broader terms, see the "Getting Started (What Is Politics?)" section of the PEP document supplement online.

6

TEACHING DEMOCRATIC PARTICIPATION SKILLS

IN A DEMOCRACY there are a host of political activities in which people can engage to express their views and work toward political goals. These activities require various levels of personal initiative and expertise, ranging from basic electoral involvement (such as seeking information and voting) to higher-initiative electoral involvement (such as campaigning, lobbying), as well as issue advocacy, community organizing, and other kinds of direct democracy. Each of these requires a particular set of skills if it is to be done well. Even responsible participation in basic electoral politics requires at least a minimum of expertise, such as knowing how to register to vote and find one's polling place, finding and making sense of information about candidates or resolutions, and so on. The more complex political activities entail the capacity for collaboration, various aspects of leadership, and many specific skills like writing press releases, organizing others to support a candidate, and so on.

Most college students have few opportunities to learn skills that are important in politics, which include some that are general, such as running meetings or speaking in public, and some that are more specifically political, such as contacting elected officials or lobbying the legislature. Yet political skills are essential to democratic participation, and studies show they are strong predictors of political involvement. Like the benefits conferred by political knowledge, a toolbox of skills for political engagement is a valuable resource individuals can draw on to make their participation easier and more effective. When students do have opportunities to learn concrete political skills, they find it satisfying as well as novel. As a student at Berea College said, "I have been involved in a lot of activities and groups. But I have never had this kind of thing before—'Here's the tools you need. Here's what makes citizen action powerful.'"

Acquiring Essential Tools

Political skills cannot be easily separated from political understanding and motivation. These three categories of goals interact dynamically, often in mutually reinforcing ways. Students' mastery of political skills supports their motivation to participate, and reciprocally, political participation often results in greater political skill.

Conventional wisdom points to alienation and apathy as the reasons why young people do not participate in the political process. Yet the feeling that they do not know how to get involved may be a bigger barrier to political engagement for young people (and others) than either of these. We know, for example, that although some young adults are quite cynical about or uninterested in politics, many *do* care about political affairs and see political action as having positive results. Recent surveys of undergraduates found that although about 30 percent believed "Political involvement rarely has any tangible results," the majority disagreed, believing instead that political involvement can be an effective method of solving problems (Harvard University Institute of Politics, 2003). Large numbers of American teens say they intend to participate in civic and political activities like voting, collecting signatures for a petition, or participating in a nonviolent protest march, even though current participation rates suggest that their desire to participate does not always translate into future involvement (Torney-Purta, Lehmann, Oswald, and Schulz, 2001; see Chapter Six, Table 6.3, showing that 85 percent of fourteen-year-olds in the United States plan to vote, 50 percent plan to collect signatures for a petition, and 39 percent plan to participate in a nonviolent protest).

This disconnect between young people's desire to be politically involved and their actual involvement is partly attributable to their lack of political skills. If students gain not only skills but also a sense of themselves as skilled and capable of learning new skills they may need in the future, they will also feel more politically efficacious. In fact, our survey shows that courses emphasizing skills of political action lead to substantial increases in internal political efficacy and also to higher levels of political interest (specifically, interest in reading about politics in the newspaper).

Political skills are also inseparable from political understanding. In fact, skills must be grounded in understanding if they are to be more than mindless, mechanical, or reflexive actions. This intellectual grounding is especially evident in skills of deliberation, negotiation, written communication, public speaking, and other forms of persuasion. All of these require a rich knowledge base about the issues under consideration together with a range of intellectual and interpersonal skills.

Most of the skills addressed in PEP courses and programs are politically infused variants of skills that, in slightly different forms, are central to academic discourse in the disciplines, many forms of professional practice, and many other life pursuits. If skills related to democratic participation can be learned in robust and flexible forms, they can be adapted and transferred to enhance students' development and functioning in other domains as well.

Researchers have traditionally paid less attention to understanding the role of civic and political skills than other factors in political participation. In the past decade, however, the path-breaking work of Verba, Schlozman, and Brady (1995) on the Citizen Participation Survey spurred greater appreciation for the ways in which acquiring civic skills, particularly at a formative age, may put people on a trajectory toward greater political engagement throughout their lives. This research and other studies suggest that many people first begin to acquire skills that are important for civic participation in adolescence—at home and at school, especially extracurricular experiences—and continue developing them into adulthood through work and participation in civic and political groups (Glanville, 1999; Verba, Schlozman, and Brady, 1995). Participating in organized groups as a young adult is found to be particularly important for predicting later civic engagement, perhaps because these early experiences allow young people to learn and practice hands-on skills, such as various communication and organization skills, that facilitate their future involvement in community and political affairs (Yates and Youniss, 1998).

Along with Verba, Schlozman, and Brady (1995), others have pointed out that some types of organizational involvement can better boost political skills and participation than others. In one national longitudinal study, for example, Glanville (1999) found that high school extracurricular experiences that were "instrumental" or connected to working together toward group goals, such as student governments, political clubs, school newspapers, or youth organizations in the community, were associated with greater increases in early adult political participation (voting, attending political rallies, working for a campaign, or contributing money to a campaign) than "expressive" activities like choirs, athletics, or honor societies.

Although membership in civic groups is an important means of learning and practicing relevant skills, it is not sufficient. Participation in voluntary activities is unequal across different demographic groups and is highly self-selected, so it is neither wise nor fair to concede that only young people who are inclined to join civic skill-building organizations should gain the political skills they need for future democratic participation. The idea of using educational interventions to build civic skills in a larger and more representative group of young people is not new. Indeed, this is a key justification for some kinds of civics courses, required volunteering and service learning programs, and national programs such as the Corporation for National Service's AmeriCorps and VISTA.

There is already evidence that educational programs can provide some of the same kinds of skill-building opportunities afforded by civic group participation. National surveys of young people's civic and political engagement find that those who report having been taught skills like letter-writing or debate in high school or college participate more in politics than those who did not learn those skills. In fact, learning these kinds of skills is more important for later participation than more general academic activities related to politics, such as being required to follow current politics and national affairs (Keeter, Zukin, Andolina, and Jenkins, 2002; Zukin and others, 2006).

A number of studies have shown that the single greatest predictor of high-level expertise in a complex skill is the number of hours devoted to practicing the skill (Ericsson, 1996; Ericsson and Charness, 1994; Ericsson, Krampe, and Tesch-Romer, 1993). This research also suggests that people are surprisingly good at developing new skills, including skills that seem to require innate abilities they believe they do not have, like having an exceptional memory (Ericsson, 2003). Together with research on the role played by involvement in civic groups, research on expert performance and skill acquisition suggests that the skills of political engagement are widely accessible, given the right opportunities to learn.

Impact of PEP Courses on Skills Acquisition

We wanted to know whether and how students' experience in the PEP courses and programs contributed to various kinds of political skills, so our student survey addressed four important and distinct categories of civic and political skills:

- Skills of political influence and action
- Skills of political analysis and judgment
- Skills of communication and leadership
- Skills of teamwork and collaboration

Because studies show that, under appropriate conditions, self-reports on outcomes like skills and knowledge correlate highly with direct assessments (Anaya, 1999; Dumont and Troelstrup, 1980; Kuh, 2003), and because it was not feasible to assess directly this wide range of skills, we examined political skills through students' self-ratings. Students were asked to indicate on a 6-point scale to what extent they believed they could enact several specific skills within each category, ranging from "can do this very well" (6) to "cannot do this" (1).

For all four categories, we analyzed the survey data for the full sample and also compared the effects of the interventions for students who entered with higher levels of political interest with the effects for those who entered with lower levels of political interest. We found that in the full group analyses, students showed statistically significant gains in all four categories of skills. (See Appendix B, "Survey Scales and Results.") When we separated the students into two groups based on their lower or higher initial interest in political issues, we found some consistent patterns across the four skill types as well as some differences. For all four sets of skills, students with higher political interest at the outset showed higher levels of skills on the presurvey, and their self-ratings remained higher at the end than those of their peers who entered the courses and programs with less political interest. But the students who entered the courses and programs with less interest in politics showed larger gains in all four categories of skills.

Skills of Political Influence and Action

Notably, the skills category that showed the largest gains from pre to post is arguably the most explicitly political in focus: skills of political influence and action. At the beginning of the interventions, students' skills of political influence and action were lower than their skills in any of the other categories, but they increased significantly for both groups, those with low and high initial political interest. For students who began with less interest in politics, the change was quite large, whereas increases for the high initial interest group were more modest. Gains in these skills are particularly important, because students are less likely to learn these kinds of high level, domain-specific skills in other courses or from general life experience.

Skills of Political Analysis and Judgment

We also saw substantial gains in skills of political analysis and judgment, or the ability to develop reasoned opinions and informed judgments about political concerns. Among students who began the courses and programs with little interest in politics, these gains were quite robust, whereas students who entered the courses and programs already very interested in politics showed smaller (but still significant) increases.

Skills of Communication and Leadership

Interpersonal, group process, and collective decision-making skills are important in many civic and political contexts and are also valuable in school, the workplace, and other settings. Communication and leadership skills are important for many aspects of democratic participation, particularly in connection with direct and local democracy. It is very difficult to advance political goals, for example, without some degree of comfort and facility in publicly expressing political views and opinions to others. For this category of skills, both the low and high political interest groups showed statistically significant increases, but the sizes of these increases were somewhat lower than for political analysis and judgment or skills of political influence and action.

Skills of Teamwork, Collaboration, and Compromise

Skills related to group process and decision making are particularly important for political life in a pluralist society, especially when collective action is needed to accomplish one's political goals. Differing priorities and conflicting interests can exist inside and across organizations, and the capacity to collaborate or compromise with others in the face of differences and disagreements is central to successful political action.

The pattern of learning for this skill set differed from that of the other three we examined, because only students in the group that had lower initial political interest made significant gains, and those gains were quite small. It is possible that these political skills are somewhat harder to learn or improve on than the others. Research on college students suggests that they prefer to avoid conflict and are not prepared to navigate the kinds of environments of conflict that often surround politics in a diverse democracy (Hurtado, Engberg, Ponjuan, and Landreman, 2002). Thus, students may be somewhat less open to practicing these skills than political skills that feel less personally risky.

Overall, the survey data show that the courses and programs are remarkably effective in increasing students' sense that they have mastered a wide array of politically relevant skills. It is especially encouraging to see robust changes in students who enter the courses and programs with relatively little prior interest in politics. Of course, it is harder for the high initial interest students to show substantial gains, because their scores for these variables are so much higher at the outset than those of their peers. But even these students saw significant gains in three of the four categories.

Goals for Teaching Democratic Skills

A familiar model for the teaching of complex skills is the apprenticeship. Apprenticeships involve a master—a highly skilled practitioner of the domain—paired with a novice, who watches the master's expert performance, attempts to replicate it, and is offered corrective feedback by the master, often along with explanations grounded in guiding principles. The teaching of skills in academic settings draws on a loosely similar pattern. Research on the teaching of complex skills and our discussions with students and faculty suggest that effective teaching of skilled know-how, in politics as well as other domains, involves three key elements: representations of expertise, practice, and informative feedback. Together with these essential elements, the process of learning skills should be concrete, context-specific, conceptually grounded, and to the greatest extent possible, connected to students' real goals, with consequences for the attainment of those goals. These common learning principles apply across the four categories of skills we examined through our survey and the diverse array of specific skills addressed by the PEP courses and programs. The students and faculty described a number of ways to combine representations of expertise, practice, and informative feedback to build political skills and put them in context.

Representations of Expertise

To call something a *skill* is to say that it can be done with greater or less expertise. Helping students develop skills of political engagement means helping them move toward more competent, sophisticated, comfortable, or expert performance. This seems obvious but requires mention because some faculty use the term *skills* loosely, referring, for example, to the *skill of listening* when they are talking about listening *more of the time* rather than developing greater *expertise* in listening.

Exactly what constitutes greater expertise in a particular skill is not always obvious or uncontroversial, so an important first step in teaching democratic skills, one that is often neglected, is to convey to students what mastery looks like for that ability. This means not only identifying the skills students should develop, but articulating, modeling, or showing in some other way the key dimensions of performance at lower and higher levels of competence.

So, to continue with the example of the skill of listening, teaching this important democratic skill requires having, and conveying to students, a picture of what more effective listening entails. The skill of listening was a goal for many PEP courses and programs, because faculty recognize the critical role that listening well plays in political activities such as negotiation, community engagement, and political discourse. Faculty mean many different things by *learning to listen well*. It is not essential that they all agree. What is crucial is that they convey to their students the major dimensions of their conception of expert listening. Some, though not all, of the PEP faculty did this quite explicitly.

A student in an environmental history of California course at California State University, Monterey Bay, noted two important dimensions of listening effectively that he had learned in the course. One was the ability to set aside one's strong initial judgments or emotional reactions while listening to others. This ability is important for fully understanding others' perspectives and for formulating thoughtful, civil responses. The student said that, like many of us, he generally had trouble listening to "comments or information that I don't agree with and actually make me upset, not angry, but really affects me emotionally . . . and responding in a way that is still collected and professional." The class helped him learn to "just take in what someone is telling you, listening to the comments they're making, and not developing your own opinions about it until they're done and you've heard everything they had to say." This stance helped the student "step back and process the information we were getting, develop the way I feel about it, and turn that into a response."

The second dimension of listening well that was stressed in the course, the students noted, was accurately grasping and representing what another person is saying. As he explained, the class did several exercises that "made us realize that most of us don't listen very carefully and that we absolutely need to do that." He said the class offered good practice for this skill, including an exercise in which students pair up to share their opinions on a political issue. Each restates his or her partner's positions, and the partner responds with feedback regarding the accuracy of the paraphrase. Watching others in the class do this made it clear that people vary in their ability to represent others' views accurately.

Opportunities and Encouragement to Practice

Along with a grasp of what constitutes greater expertise, a key to learning skills in any domain is practice, and many PEP faculty emphasize the critical value of practice when teaching political skills. For example, in his University of Minnesota course connected with the Public Achievement program, Jim Farr stresses the value of a "coaching" approach that allows college students to practice democratic skills at the same time that they are guiding school children in community action projects. As Farr said, "Our pedagogy is learning by doing." Students recognize the value of practice too, and they appreciate that these courses and programs provide novel opportunities to practice political skills offered by few other college experiences.

Feedback from Multiple Sources

As important as it is, however, practice alone is not the most effective method for gaining expertise. Just as one cannot usually become an accomplished pianist merely through unguided practice, but rather through a combination of practice and expert feedback, students need guidance on practicing skills of democratic citizenship. As Adam Weinberg, former director of Democracy Matters, said, "The only way students learn is by doing it and then having someone to call and really talk through the problems. In a way, this is coaching, more like a model of athletics than classroom teaching."

This kind of informative feedback or coaching can come from many sources: faculty and program staff, other experienced people, peers, and experiences of success and failure, through which the outcomes of one's own performance serve as important feedback. Ideally, programs combine some elements of all of these types of feedback to help students build skills. Students in Democracy Matters talked about how much expertise with political skills they gained from feedback loops that included several sources: "Talking to people and getting ideas and having them work with you really helps. There's always something to learn from somebody. That's how I see it. Nobody really knows everything. You might be an expert in one thing. They can be an expert in another. You guys can swap ideas. It comes from meetings. Asking newcomers questions all the time, like what they thought about the meeting. What they think I should do better. What they would like to see happen."

Probably the most obvious sources of expert feedback on students' performance are faculty, program staff, and teaching assistants; all were important in the PEP courses and programs. This is clearly the case in Democracy Matters, as Weinberg describes:

> As an ongoing process, Democracy Matters leaders sit down on a weekly basis to talk about each campus chapter, where they are, what's working or not working, and we try to get onto each campus at least once a year. . . . I was on a campus recently where an antiwar teach-in

had been scheduled at the last minute for the same night that I was there to talk on campaign finance, so not many people showed up. And I used it as a moment to talk to students about that—it's OK to cancel an event at the last moment—talk through with them why they didn't make that decision, and then we try to take that experience to other chapters.

Weinberg and other program leaders try to convey this kind of feedback in monthly newsletters and e-mails sharing obstacles and ideas for addressing them, such as an article identifying ideas for responding to critics, which arose from students in one campus chapter saying, "We don't know what to say to critics," or "We don't know how to respond to this."

It was clear from faculty and students that offering meaningful guidance is much more like coaching than "cheerleading." It is sometimes most useful when it is quite critical. A student in the Model United Nations course described the intensive learning he and others gained from this feedback: "We were kind of molded throughout the course to achieve diplomacy. It was very intense. Every time someone was not using a diplomatic tone, we were told right then. . . . We got a lot of feedback from the professor and the TAs. And it was not sugar-coated."

Unfortunately, offering intensive feedback sometimes creates logistical and resource challenges and can place boundaries on the optimal size of a political engagement program. Weinberg talks about how Democracy Matters' "mentoring model" of extensive guidance to campus coordinators has caused growing pains, leading the group to consider halting the expansion of chapters: "If someone said to describe what you do in two sentences, I'd say we're running tutorials on democracy and organizing, and you can't do that without the real, rich, deep contact." In recent years, the program has limited the number of students attending an annual summit in order to maintain a high level of instructive feedback from program staff: "We do an exercise to talk about struggles and successes they're having on their campuses, but that doesn't work unless Democracy Matters leaders are there at the table with them. It requires that kind of really deep, rich, reflective feedback."[1]

Instructive guidance on skill-building can take the form of direct feedback from program leaders and faculty on students' practices or activities, as some of these examples show, or it can involve outside experts offering tips on how to handle situations students are facing or steps students can take to accomplish political goals. Sometimes faculty and even students themselves recruit outside experts to provide this kind of feedback. A Democracy Matters student described actively seeking guidance from experienced people outside the program: "We've sought it out. In our group, we invited the Cornell lobbyist to teach us how to lobby. And we invited a former state legislator to teach us how to talk to state legislators. That has been very valuable. . . . There are ways of getting expertise. And usually the people who have it are very eager to share it."

Mutual feedback among peers is equally important across most PEP programs and courses and is particularly effective when it operates in conjunction with feedback from faculty or experts. Farr's course relies on peer feedback as a primary method for promoting development of democratic skills. Students gather in weekly debriefing meetings in which they present the successes and challenges they face and ask each other for help. Farr describes the sessions this way: "We are tacking between talking about it and putting it into practice. Sometimes there are little things you can do to model things. Some people are very good about knowing how to get through a bureaucracy. We ask them, 'How did you do that?' 'How did you research?' 'Let's take time to talk about it.' Some skills we promote by sharing best practices or best recent good luck stories. Some students are quite good about articulating these things."

Marshall Ganz's Harvard University course in community organizing relies on a similar type of peer feedback. Students do regular presentations on their political projects and then their peers evaluate things that are working well and areas that need attention. Such exercises contribute to the skill development of both the peer evaluators and the presenters, including learning to analyze political goals and strategies objectively and to give usable feedback effectively. As Ganz said, "The students learn to make their evaluations less judgment and more information. And the presenter learns to take feedback as information and not as judgment."

As students engage in political action, simulations, classroom deliberations, and the like, they can also gain feedback by paying attention to the outcomes of their actions. When students are learning skills of persuasion, for example, they can often tell from their classmates' reactions how well they have succeeded in convincing them. In this sense, feedback is embedded in the task itself if students learn to assess the outcomes of their actions.

Sometimes the political efforts succeed; sometimes they do not work out as planned. Both students and faculty emphasized that one can learn at least as much from mistakes and unforeseen or undesired consequences as from successes, even when failures are quite public or painful. One Democracy Matters student told us about learning from "messing up" the prior week. The campus group had planned a major information and recruitment event with a band playing, but "the band bailed on us."

"That's very demoralizing. . . . The rest of my crew were mad. They started cussing. Because they put a lot of work into it. So what we did was just tabled, talked to people. We still got our petitions signed. . . . It's more of accepting you've messed up, but moving on, and doing better the next time. So next time, we said, OK, we're going to start off with something small. . . . Maybe show the movie *Bulworth*. . . . I guess it's like [a] hurting and healing, type of thing."

Monitoring their own incremental gains in political skills helps students see that they are making progress, thus building their confidence and sense of efficacy. Another Democracy Matters student said, "Seeing that a lot of people come to the meetings is very motivating. Having more efficient meetings is very motivating. To see that I do something that I've done before but I do it better."

The Value of Metacognition

The preceding example dovetails with research findings showing that learning from experience is enhanced—including the depth of learning, its persistence over time, and its usefulness in new contexts—by activities in which students consciously step back to take stock of their learning and levels of mastery. As one student said, "Making mistakes and doing things better the second time. I think when you first start doing something. . . . When you do it, and you evaluate yourself and you see where you didn't do something right, the next time you want to do it better."

Cognitive scientists use the term *metacognition* to refer to this kind of self-assessment and reflection on "what worked and what needs improving" (Bransford, Brown, and Cocking, 2000, p. 12). Without this kind of reflection, it is almost impossible for people to learn from their own experience.

We saw the goal of developing students' ability and inclination to evaluate their own experiences threaded through many of the PEP courses and programs. In Ganz's course, critical reflection papers require students to evaluate what they are doing by using a conceptual lens drawn from class readings. Ganz explains how requiring students to critically analyze their experiences can help them figure out "how to learn from practice."

Showing students how to be more reflective or self-conscious about their learning can also help them apply political skills to new contexts and mitigate the inherent limitation that any one political engagement intervention can address only a subset of the many skills supporting democratic participation. If students develop skills in such a way that they also understand that they are learning the *process* of gaining political skills and expertise, they will see that they are acquiring core learning principles that apply beyond the particular skills acquired in their programs. They can learn to look at complex political problems and goals and see that to be effective in those situations, they need some specific capacities, many of which can be identified through careful observation of or discussions with relevant experts. Students also need to learn that most kinds of expertise *are* learnable—not a matter of special talent beyond the reach of the average person, as we often tend to assume, thinking, "I'm just not good at public speaking" or "I'm just not good at leading groups."

Putting Political Skills in Context

Learning political skills entails gaining concrete, specific, and contextualized facility and expertise rather than generic capacities understood at a high level of abstraction and inclusiveness such as "critical thinking" or "communication skills." In the broader academic context, this insight underlies recent efforts to teach particular kinds of skillful writing (writing scientific reports, essays, or journalistic accounts, for example) rather than assuming that all good writing is the same. PEP faculty and program directors are quite aware of this specificity of skills in the political domain. Greg Werkheiser, who was directing the Sorensen Institute for Political Leadership at the time of our study, was one of many program leaders who emphasized that, as real political engagement operates in specific contexts, conceiving of and teaching democratic skills in a particularistic way is the best way to support effective political action:

> So we teach how to lobby the Virginia General Assembly, not generic "how to lobby." We teach people how to work with media in Virginia, and so on, all the way down the line. Now, the lessons that are learned there can be transferred to a certain extent to different contexts. For example, to learn about welfare policy, it doesn't make sense to study it only at the national level because it's very different in each of the states. To understand it meaningfully, you should first understand it on the state level, and then take those lessons and try to think how it could manifest itself differently in different states, or on a national level.

Emphasizing to students at Vassar College and Dutchess Community College the particularity of skills involved in different political activities, Dick Reitano guides students to learn that not all skills gained from other political experiences, such as activism or debate clubs, are equally useful for simulating the activities of the United Nations. One student described how he and his classmates learned that success in the context of Model United Nations requires skills of diplomacy, especially achieving a compromise to which all parties can agree, rather than engaging in activism or "winning a debate": "For diplomacy, listening is key. Making it work for both parties. . . . If you're serious about finding a solution, there's usually some way to make it work. This was a big change. Watching the debate team make that transition was so interesting. Going from winning the argument to wanting to find a solution."

This student's awareness of the need to adapt a skill learned elsewhere to the specific needs of the current context reveals a finely tuned perceptiveness about the important features of effective action in a given context. It is the kind of specific feedback and reflection on action described earlier that helps students develop this kind of awareness.

Imparting a Sense of Urgency

As these and other examples from our interviews indicate, students in PEP embrace opportunities to learn political skills, and some even seek them out. One thing many of these courses and programs have in common is that they involve either real political action or intensely engaging simulations that *feel* very real to the students, such as the Model United Nations or an exercise in the Sorensen College Leaders Program in which students simulate the Virginia Assembly.[2] This kind of learning context leads students to feel a motivating sense of immediacy about learning relevant political skills. The students see that they *need* these skills in order to succeed in something they care about and want to do. Thus, they are more inclined to pay close attention, practice, and look for help in gaining expertise.

Some programs also include relatively highly structured workshops on specific skills such as speechwriting or various components of a political campaign, often taught by experts. Skills workshops can be particularly useful if students feel they are learning things that will allow them to accomplish things they want to do and if they have opportunities to use the skills relatively soon.

Using Conceptual Frameworks to Scaffold Practical Political Skills

To gain meaningful expertise, students have to learn specific skills connected to particular civic or political contexts. But context-specific learning is in tension with the goal of wanting students to be able to adapt what they learn to new contexts. Fortunately, there are strategies faculty can use to help students adapt political skills to new settings, including grounding the learning of specific skills in a conceptual framework that allows for deeper learning and greater transfer (G. L. Blasi, 1995; Bransford, Brown, and Cocking, 2000).

If direct experience is accompanied by identification of key principles and multiple examples of those principles, students learn from experiences more efficiently than they can without this theorizing. Identifying the operative principles or key elements of important political skills—such as the two components of the skill of political listening we noted earlier— can be usefully achieved through reflections by more experienced practitioners, thoughtful guidelines, or well-elaborated conceptual frameworks. A popular example of this is the book *Getting to Yes* (Fisher, Ury, and Patton, 1991), which conveys the basic principles of negotiation as formulated by the Harvard Negotiation Project. The role that conceptualization plays in enhancing skill development underscores the inseparability of the two categories of goals we call *understanding* and *skills*.

The value of making explicit what would otherwise be so embedded in experience that it is invisible is illustrated by a memorable study of people whose job is to determine the sex of baby chicks. In the egg industry, it is important to know early on which chicks will become roosters and which will become hens. This is a difficult discrimination to make because male and female chicks look almost exactly alike. Traditionally, "chicken sexers" have learned their craft through long apprenticeships during which they compared their judgments to those of experts, slowly becoming more and more accurate. It was assumed that there was no way for them to learn more quickly. But when a researcher asked experienced chicken sexers to articulate the basis of their judgments, what they paid attention to and what they ignored, this generated principles and guidelines that greatly decreased the time it took for new apprentices to become highly skilled (G. L. Blasi, 1995).

Likewise, many PEP courses and programs teach democratic skills by combining political engagement experiences with a focus on key principles or concepts embedded in that experience. Often they draw on well-established literatures identifying important themes in political involvement or on faculty members' or other experts' experiences in the political domain. For example, students in Duke's Service Opportunities in Leadership program read widely on concepts of leadership and discuss them in connection with their summer internship experiences.[3] Program director Alma Blount highlighted a central idea in that literature:

> I want them to get a new understanding of what leadership is. I present a framework on leadership and tell them to test it out. They will be dealing with a world of complicated, messy problems where nothing is

clear-cut. In the dominant paradigm on leadership, the leader is a person with a vision who influences others to follow. This conception is inadequate for the real work that goes on in organizations. Instead, I talk about leadership as an activity, not just a person. Different people at different times with different roles can exercise leadership. There needs to be a match with the task.

Like many other faculty teaching for political engagement, Blount also focuses on the concept of political power and how important understanding power is for being an effective political actor. As she put it: "I try to help them understand how power works. . . . In the Industrial Areas Foundation [with which she worked], they stress that power is never abstract. It is always connected with real human beings. The question is, 'Who has power regarding a particular issue? Who has the power to help us?'" This way of thinking about power is new to most of her students, and they find it very useful as they formulate strategies for achieving their political goals.

Breaking Complex Skills into Components

Integrating experience with conceptual frames can be enhanced by breaking macro-level and complex skill sets such as leadership into smaller, more manageable or familiar components—a kind of building-blocks approach. Grossman and Compton call this process *decomposition of practice,* and their observations of professional education demonstrate how important this practice is in training professional practice skills in seminaries, clinical psychology programs, and schools of teacher education (Grossman and Compton, 2005). Similarly, faculty and other mentors teaching political skills often help students break down complex and potentially overwhelming tasks into steps that are more manageable and potentially learnable—and in some cases more similar to things the students already know how to do.

Quite often, a high-level or complex political skill or undertaking can be seen, on closer scrutiny, to be a cluster of more specific skills, each of which can be learned with the appropriate guidance, practice, and feedback. So, for example, community organizing entails many component tasks such as making connections with others around shared goals, setting up and running effective meetings, developing materials for publicizing the effort, identifying individuals with the power to assist the agenda, and so forth. Because the component tasks have greater specificity, it is easier to teach them than the larger, more amorphous macro-level skill of community organizing.

A Democracy Matters student's description of solving a problem illustrates how effective a building-blocks approach can be. He was trying to figure out how to get media coverage for his chapter's work on campaign finance reform. He was at first baffled and rather overwhelmed at the prospect of this goal: "I was like, 'How are we supposed to do that?' Because I've never dealt with that before." Several graduate students with more experience and his adviser helped him break down this task into more manageable components. He needed to learn what kinds of media people to contact for coverage in the press, television, and radio. He needed some specific contact names. And he had to learn how to write a press release—what to cover and how to say it. His mentors also suggested that sending e-mails to journalists is usually less effective than conversations, either in person or on the telephone, so he needed to learn how to pitch his ideas to the press orally. In the end, he said: "Now I know how to get media coverage. That is one of the things I've learned that will benefit me in the future."

When basic elements of political skills or tasks are identified, carefully identifying and naming them can also help students see how those elements relate to broader conceptual frameworks. Naming a key element of a complex macro skill shows the element's centrality to the broader task at hand and its potential applicability in other contexts. The students we interviewed from Ganz's course on community organizing all mentioned how much they appreciated having learned to conduct "one-on-ones," or individual relationship-building, as a critical step in community organizing. As one said, "[One thing I learned] is the idea of one-on-ones, where you meet with people individually and get to know them and what their interests are and how you can build upon those interests toward shared goals. . . . How that can build a movement. . . . I thought that was a really useful skill."

An Institutionally Integrated Approach

A great challenge in supporting the development of political skills is that it takes a long time to achieve even competent, let alone expert, performance of these complex skills. Students in Otto Feinstein's Introduction to Government course had opportunities to learn several key skills of democratic citizenship in the Urban Agenda component of the course.[4] But the course met only four hours a week for one semester, and the experience was not reinforced elsewhere in the university. Students finished the course more interested in politics and often more efficacious, but such a brief exposure could give them only a beginning in practicing democratic skills. This is one area in which extracurricular programs like Democracy

Matters can have a comparative advantage, because students can be involved as intensively as they like for as long as they want.

A realistic view of the time investment required to learn complex skills points to the importance of an institutionally holistic and intentional approach to fostering political understanding and engagement. To have a lasting impact on students' democratic capacities, campuses should find ways to offer multiple, intersecting opportunities for students to learn key political skills and apply or practice them in different settings. One way to accomplish this is through planning efforts that identify a set of democratic skills relevant for several courses, programs, or activities that are already underway. Some candidates for crosscutting democratic skills might be persuasive writing and public speaking about political goals and policies—such as presentation of political positions based on finding, choosing, and presenting evidence or analysis of political arguments or critiquing political positions in terms of logic, factual substantiation, and rhetoric—or interpersonal skills such as collaboration and negotiation connected to political issues or ends.

This planning and integration can take place in the context of general education and academic majors, in student affairs, and in the potential connections among them. For example, departmental faculty might agree on several key democratic skills central to the goals of the major or profession, identify courses in which some of those skills are already taught or are "likely suspects" for teaching them, and decide how the department could build on or connect to extracurricular experiences that foster related skills.

NOTES

1. For more information on Democracy Matters and the role of campus coordinators, see documents 27, 28, and 29 in the PEP document supplement at http://www.carnegiefoundation.org/educating_for_democracy/docs/.

2. For examples, see the "Research/Action Projects and Simulations" section of the PEP document supplement at the online address shown in note 1.

3. For a description of how inquiry about leadership fits into the various components of the Service Opportunities in Leadership program, see document 21 in the PEP document supplement online.

4. For more information on the Urban Agenda, see document 11 in the PEP document supplement online.

7

FOSTERING POLITICAL MOTIVATION

WE ALL KNOW WELL-EDUCATED PEOPLE who fail to pay attention to politics or even vote. However knowledgeable or skilled people are, they will not be politically engaged unless they are motivated to be. There are many competing demands on everyone's time and energy, and political involvement seldom yields evident instrumental rewards, such as knowing that our actions made a crucial difference in a political outcome we care about. This means that even if people have the ability and opportunity to participate they will not do so consistently over time without more intrinsic motivations, including political interest, passion, commitment, or sense of civic duty (Barry, 1970; Gamson, 1968; Riker and Ordeshook, 1968).

Motivation for democratic participation includes qualities as varied as being interested in public affairs, feeling personally responsible for collective outcomes, or having a commitment to active participation—to doing one's part. One's inclination to act politically can include many particular, issue-specific interests—such as wanting a specific candidate to win an election—as well as broader or longer-term values and commitments related to democratic institutions and processes, such as a commitment to individual rights or equality, a belief that informed voting is essential for democracy, or a desire to act in ways that can help improve community welfare. Some of the most important forms of long-term motivation include fidelity to democratic ideals, seeing democratic participation of some sort as among the central features of one's sense of self, a belief in the overall legitimacy or general responsiveness of the political system, and a sense of political empowerment or confidence in one's ability to act effectively.

Motivation for democratic participation includes emotions, such as hopefulness about the future and indignation about injustice. People can be motivated by positive feelings toward a group with which they identify or by compassion or concern for people who are unlike themselves (Hoffman, 1981). Emotions like anger about or passion for a particular issue or problem can also sometimes inspire people who have never before been politically active to become intensely involved (Dahl, 1961). Conversely, attitudes like anti-institutional beliefs and emotions like cynicism, distrust, or alienation are likely to reduce participation (Levi and Stoker, 2002).

Factors Influencing Political Motivation

Many factors that affect political motivation at any given time are situational or contextual; they are part of the shifting cultural, social, and political environment rather than stable characteristics of individuals. Some of these factors relate to the contingencies in the political domain—predictions that a particular electoral race will be extremely close, for example, or intensive media coverage of a political scandal. Among the most powerful situational influences on political behavior is being explicitly asked to participate in some way by political parties and other groups or by friends or family (Huckfeldt and Sprague, 1992; Leighley, 1996; McAdam and Paulsen, 1993). Research shows that peers exercise particular motivational influence over college students and young adults (see Green, Gerber, and Nickerson, 2004).

Unfortunately, these situational factors are not necessarily sources of long-term political motivation. In one longitudinal study of college students, for example, Sax found that many who became more politically engaged during college, apparently as part of a peer culture that supported activism, did not remain engaged after college (Sax, 1999). In order to have an enduring impact on political engagement, participation in response to contextual influences has to become habitual or lead to changes in individuals' dispositional characteristics through influences on their commitments, sense of identity, deeply held values, or sense of political efficacy.

The good news is that sustained political engagement can lead to changes in these more stable habits, attitudes, and dispositions. For example, when, for whatever reason, students participate in political activities over a period of time, they develop habits that support continued political involvement. A number of studies have indicated the powerful influence of habit formation for political engagement, particularly when habits are established at a young age (Gerber, Green, and Shachar, 2003; Miller and Shanks, 1996; Plutzer, 2002).

Involvement in politics and political education programs can also lead to greater political interest, values, and commitment. Participation in political activities through peer groups, social networks, civic volunteerism, and mobilization efforts can introduce or reinforce political goals as well as more general democratic values. Participants are influenced in part by the way they learn to appraise the importance of a political issue or orient themselves to social problems and by the psychological rewards they reap through their interactions with these groups, which broadens their political interests and concerns and leads them to care more about others' welfare.

Clearly, political socialization begins early in life (Easton and Dennis, 1967; Hess and Torney, 1967), but the range of motivations that support political participation is not fully formed by our families or other early experiences and can change considerably over time, especially during early adulthood (Jennings and Stoker, 2001). Recent research suggests that some of the most important democratic dispositions, such as political efficacy and trust, are open to influence in adolescence and young adulthood and can be increased through relatively short-term experiences such as civic education programs (Brehm and Rahn, 1997; Finkel, 2003).

Key Aspects of Political Motivation

Two key aspects of political motivation are *political identity* and *sense of political efficacy*. In the research literature, these two are of central importance theoretically and empirically, and we found they were prevalent goals of the PEP courses and programs we studied.

Political Identity

A sense of oneself as a politically engaged person is a key mediator between individuals' civic or political values and their behavior and also contributes to stability of civic and political commitment over time (Colby, Ehrlich, Beaumont, and Stephens, 2003; Conover and Searing, 2000; Flanagan and Sherrod, 1998; Verba, Schlozman, and Brady, 1995). For example, Youniss and Yates (1997) show that the long-term impact of youth service experience on later political and community involvement can best be explained by the contribution these service experiences make to the creation of an enduring sense of oneself as a politically engaged and socially concerned person. Later forms of political and community involvement derive, in part, from these important definitions of self.

When values, ideals, and commitments that relate to democratic participation are central to one's sense of self, we speak of that person as having a *politically engaged identity*.[1] Having a politically engaged identity involves seeing oneself as "the kind of person" who cares about politics and is committed to some kind of political participation. Individuals with politically engaged identities also have at least an emerging sense of their own political beliefs and values, although these particular beliefs can and probably should evolve over time. For these people, being politically informed and at least somewhat active are central enough to their sense of self that they are likely to act even when it entails significant cost and when their actions may not make any tangible difference.

Sense of Political Efficacy

Another pivotal motivation for political engagement is having a strong sense of political efficacy. This does not mean one believes political action will always have an immediate impact or will necessarily have the desired impact even in the long term. People who participate in civic actions are often driven by the *possibility* of change, not the certainty of success (Harwood Group, 1991). But if people are going to participate politically, they have to believe that their political judgments and activities matter, that some kind of change is possible, and that there is a relationship between their actions and positive outcomes (Bandura, 1997). A long line of research demonstrates the important role a sense of political efficacy plays in supporting democratic participation and its relationship to other predictors of participation, including education, political knowledge, interest, civic trust, and attention to politics in the media (Abramson, 1977; Almond and Verba, 1963; Easton, 1975; Iyengar, 1980; Langton and Karns, 1969; Madsen, 1987).

More recently, it has become clear that sense of political efficacy should not be considered a single construct—it is important to distinguish between *internal political efficacy* and *external political efficacy*, or faith in government responsiveness. Sense of internal political efficacy refers to "beliefs about one's own competence to understand and to participate effectively in politics" (Niemi, Craig, and Mattei, 1991, p. 1407). In contrast, external political efficacy or sense of government responsiveness represents one's assessment of the degree to which current government institutions or authorities are responsive to citizens' demands. The two concepts are related, but it is possible to have a strong sense of internal political efficacy while also believing that the current political system is relatively impervious to change. An individual could also feel that political institutions and authorities are open to citizen influence but that she is not herself sufficiently informed, skilled, or powerful to make a difference.

Research on political efficacy has shown that internal political efficacy is a more stable characteristic of individuals than their sense of government responsiveness or external efficacy (Niemi, Craig, and Mattei, 1991; Pollock, 1983). Internal political efficacy is also more strongly predictive of some kinds of political participation. In light of this research, it is understandable that the PEP courses and programs did not by and large take increasing external political efficacy as a goal but were consistent in identifying students' internal political efficacy as one of the key dimensions of political development they hoped to strengthen. Helping students see themselves as capable of grasping complex political and policy issues, contributing to the public sphere, and making some kind of difference was an objective of all the participating courses and programs.

Impact of the PEP Courses on Political Motivation

The PEP student survey assessed several dimensions of motivation for democratic participation, including political interest and attention; norms of citizenship; general concern for various public issues like education, national defense, and race relations; internal political efficacy; and a sense of politically engaged identity.

Political Interest and Attentiveness

Interest in public affairs (Verba, Schlozman, and Brady, 1995) is clearly a part of motivation for political participation. Many college students are just not interested in politics, so they have little desire to become better informed or more active democratic participants. But students' interest in policy and other public issues, politics, and the democratic process can increase when they learn about how the issues affect their lives, when they connect participation with concerns or values that are important to them, and when they become more knowledgeable and actively engaged.

In fact, many students reported increased enthusiasm for public affairs as a result of their participation in PEP courses and programs. Interest in reading the newspaper (either online or in print) and general levels of political interest increased significantly among students who entered the

PEP courses and programs with lower levels of political interest. (See Appendix B, "Survey Scales and Results.") Students who began the course with higher levels of interest maintained this interest. These students reported reading the newspaper at least six days a week—on their own, not as an assignment.

Politically Engaged Identity

Fostering students' sense of politically engaged identity, the extent to which being politically engaged is central to an individual's sense of self (Hitlin, 2003), was an objective of most of the PEP courses and programs. As we expected, students who entered the PEP interventions expressing higher levels of political interest already had a very strong politically engaged identity at the outset and so did not experience significant changes in this regard. (See Appendix B, "Survey Scales and Results.") Clearly, political interest and a strong sense of self as an engaged citizen are mutually supportive motivations and each is likely to enhance the other.

Those who entered with lower levels of political interest also showed notably lower levels of political identity at the outset and experienced a significant shift toward a stronger sense of politically engaged identity by the end of the PEP experience. For these students, being politically concerned and involved became much more central to their sense of self than it had been before. Even so, this increase was not large enough to bring them up to the very strong sense of self as political agents that characterized those who entered PEP with high levels of interest.

Sense of Internal Political Efficacy

Our measure for sense of internal political efficacy, or political confidence, is similar to measures of this construct typically used in political science research (Craig, Niemi, and Silver, 1990). Students respond to questions tapping various elements of political confidence, including the sense that they can understand important political issues, are well informed, and are well qualified to participate. Following the general pattern we saw for most outcomes, the students who expressed little political interest at the outset of the interventions also had considerably lower initial levels of internal political efficacy than their more politically interested peers. (See Appendix B, "Survey Scales and Results.") These students who came in with lower political interest showed significant increases in internal political efficacy as a result of their participation. Those who entered with higher levels of interest maintained their high levels of efficacy but did not show a significant increase. Consistent with prior research, we also found that internal efficacy predicts intentions to participate in a number of important democratic activities, including voting and other aspects of conventional electoral politics, as well as political discussions and working with community groups.

Students' sense of internal political efficacy increased more in courses and programs that included politically related service learning or community placement experiences, and those that placed greater emphasis on learning skills of political action (Beaumont, Greene, and Torney-Purta, 2007). These results suggest that several different types of civic education models can be very effective in increasing students' political efficacy, particularly when students come into the experience with little prior interest.

Among the effects of course activities, emphasis on skills of political action had the most notable impact. This is important, because teaching political skills is often neglected in civic and political education efforts. This is a serious oversight not only for political expertise but also for political motivation, for, as we discussed in the previous chapter, there is an important reciprocal relationship between developing knowledge and skills and feeling efficacious in the political domain. A *sense* of political efficacy (confidence in one's capacity to grapple with political issues and so on) is distinct from *actual expertise* (skill and knowledge, as they might be measured from a more objective standpoint), but naturally the two are closely related. When students gain political skills and knowledge, this will not only strengthen their capacities in these important areas but will also contribute to their motivational development, giving them a stronger sense that they are capable of participating in the political process and that they have something important to contribute.

Goals for Teaching for Political Motivation

In the courses and programs we studied, we saw in the design and teaching explicit goals for developing students' political motivation, including a politically engaged identity and a sense of internal political efficacy. We explore each of these two goals, in turn.

Fostering Political Identity

Faculty in the PEP courses and programs addressed two aspects of students' *political identity*. First, they hoped that one or more modes of democratic participation would become an important part of their students' sense of who they are. Second, they hoped that students would gain increased self-knowledge around political values, goals, propensities, and assets. As PEP faculty tried to meet these teaching goals, their use of models and mentors figured prominently.

MAKING POLITICAL PARTICIPATION CENTRAL TO SELF-IDENTITY. The PEP faculty share a concern for building responsible citizenship into the core of students' identity. Alma Blount, for example, wants students in Duke's Service Opportunities in Leadership program to "develop a public self. I talk about this and it sounds strange to them. We say that having an exemplary personal life is not enough." Pointing to another aspect of a public self, Kristi Schutjer-Mance expects that participation in Mills College's Institute for Civic Leadership will "help students develop a stronger leadership identity."

Students we interviewed also described a shift in the centrality of basic democratic values and engagement in their sense of self as an important outcome of their participation in the PEP courses and programs. As a Democracy Matters student told us: "I've always known what would count as politics or what being politically involved would mean. Democracy Matters helped me *become* what I've thought being politically involved means." A student in the Citizen Scholars Program at the University of Massachusetts put it a bit differently: "I'd say I've developed a very strong political identity. Probably more political than a lot of people wish I would be."

POLITICAL SELF-EXPLORATION AND SELF-KNOWLEDGE. Through exploration that challenges assumptions and encourages open-minded, thoughtful consideration of possibilities, students in many of the PEP courses and programs come to a clearer sense of *what kind of* democratically engaged people they are or want to be and what values are central commitments for them. In Otto Feinstein's American government course at Wayne State University, for example, as students worked to establish priorities for a policy agenda affecting the Detroit area and debated and discussed these issues, they were "coming to grips with their own values."[2] Feinstein would tell them, "This is not a course about debate skills; it is a course about you."

Students often talk about self-knowledge as a valued outcome of their participation in a range of course and program activities. As a Mills College student said, "I think I've grown a lot, and . . . it's been a lot about refining who I am and having the confidence to be who I am." Sometimes the self-exploration involves resisting simplistic categories and labels.

Another Mills student talked about developing a strong sense of political identity but also said that some labels she had previously adopted without giving them much thought no longer seemed appropriate: "I don't have to push myself to fit into a box that doesn't feel genuine." In other cases, students come to a clear sense of what they are and are not, as this Duke University student explained, "The 'hippie activist' or the 'grassroots organizer,' that's not where my strengths are. I'm someone who really enjoys the macro level and writing policy and writing the speeches . . . maybe even holding office. . . . I think it solidified my self-identity as a realistic idealist."

MODELS AND MENTORS. In their efforts to strengthen a sense of political identity, PEP faculty often connect students with models, mentors, and others they can identify with or be inspired by. If students identify with these models through what psychologist Hazel Markus calls their *actual selves* ("She's like me") or their *ideal (desired) selves* ("I want to be like him"), the experience can change the way they experience themselves, making them feel empowered, committed, or inspired (Markus and Nurius, 1986). Often the PEP courses and programs connect students with political actors directly, through invited speakers, mentorship programs, and collaborative political action. Some courses and programs also use biographies and autobiographies to engage students with inspiring lives of political commitment.

When students are able to learn about and connect with engaged individuals with whom they can identify, they come to see democratic participation as less forbidding and more accessible than they had imagined. They find new ways to think about themselves as engaged citizens by identifying with the people they meet, and they become more confident of their own potential for contributing, thus also increasing their sense of political efficacy.

Interactions with guest speakers often give students a more concrete sense of what political participation entails, broaden their understanding of modes of political action, and provide models of people from backgrounds like their own who have found ways to make a difference on issues they care about and with whom students can identify. As a student in Dick Simpson's Chicago politics course commented: "The speakers were really . . . inspiring—seeing them as real people and being able to envision myself as someone like them in the future. Mike Quigley, a Cook County commissioner, helped me see that a career in politics is made up of small steps and not necessarily some grand plan. I guess it's putting a face on political leaders."

As noted, some students connect with guest speakers or mentors because these models seem more ordinary than they had expected—people much like themselves. As one California State University, Monterey Bay, student said, "I sat in class with the mayor of Marina and I realized she's just a regular person like we are. And Lupe Garcia was just a mom with kids in the educational system . . . and now she's this big political voice in Salinas." Other students identify with speakers or other models by connecting them with what they hope to be like someday, their ideal selves. These students typically find the mentors and models inspiring, as this Mills College student does: "My mentor got me into a political fundraiser event with Barbara Lee, and at other events I saw Dolores Huerta, Dee McKinney, and a couple of other really strong, powerful women in public service. It's always really reassuring and empowering to see them and think, 'Yeah, I want to be like her!' I came away from the Barbara Lee event just floating, thinking, 'I want to be like this lady.' She's in politics, but she stayed true to her ideals, and she's just so inspiring."

Fostering a Sense of Internal Political Efficacy

Increasing students' sense of internal political efficacy is an important goal for all the PEP courses and programs. It involves working to build students' confidence in their ability to understand complex political issues and processes and participate in the political realm. It includes efforts to promote their sense of inclusion or belonging with regard to the political domain (this may be especially important for students who come from low-income backgrounds or who are recent immigrants); to give them the sense that by acting individually or (more often) collectively, they can accomplish political goals or contribute to political change on some level; to counteract their cynicism; and to help them develop resilience in the face of setbacks so they will not be deterred by disappointing short-term outcomes of their efforts.

The PEP courses and programs use many different strategies to accomplish these objectives. Readings, classroom discussions, and lectures can help students better understand the political process, important social and political issues, and the role of individuals and groups taking part in political action at both local and national levels, thus contributing to political self-confidence. Likewise, more active or community-based pedagogies build skills and understanding, thus contributing to students' sense that they are efficacious in the political domain. In the main, faculty used four strategies to achieve this goal: shifting students' understanding of political participation and effectiveness; engaging students in political action; helping them gain political expertise; and tempering cynicism about the political system.

SHIFTING UNDERSTANDING OF POLITICAL PARTICIPATION AND EFFECTIVENESS. One approach that faculty use to strengthen students' sense of political efficacy is to change the way they think about political participation—to reframe it conceptually. We observed three ways, in particular, that faculty in PEP programs tried to shift, or reframe, students' understanding of political participation:

- Broaden their understanding of politics, leadership, and what it means to "make a difference." Faculty often talk about the value of helping students move toward a broader conception of democratic engagement.[3] If students can see that meaningful participation includes some relatively accessible activities, they will be more likely to see themselves as having the capacity to participate. Blount sees this as a central goal of her program: "If you can broaden students' concept of leadership and make it more accessible, they have a greater chance of feeling efficacious." Student comments reinforce this insight. A Metro Urban Studies Term student remarked: "I used to think that politics was this high-flown thing. And now I realize that anyone can be politically involved. . . . And being politically involved doesn't mean just campaigning or being involved with the government or things like that."

- Demystify politics, making political participation more transparent. In addition to providing a more capacious definition of democratic participation, faculty also stress the need to give students a more concrete sense of how politics works, to demystify the skills of political participation. Blount, for example, stressed the importance of making sure students understand how political change takes place, what it means to have power, and "how power works." A San Francisco State University student described the shift she experienced as she came to understand what it is like to engage politically: "I definitely came away with a sense that I can make a difference. It is easy to get connected in politics. For example, one of the students in this program is working in city hall as an intern. I thought you had to be pretty active to do this. But in fact the opportunity is right there. I really am looking at this."

- Talk with students directly about efficacy—giving them new ways to think about why political participation is important. Faculty also take on the issue of political efficacy directly, talking with students about why democratic participation is important. The ways these faculty frame the issue are often new to students and appear to make a memorable impression on them. Gerald Shenk of California State University, Monterey Bay, said: "I try to get them to see that, whether they do it intentionally or not, they are always political actors shaping history."[4]

Students say that this kind of message changes the way they think about their responsibility to be active participants in a democracy. A Democracy Matters student pointed to an important shift in his thinking about what it means to make a difference and why political participation can potentially make an even bigger long-term impact than community service:

> [The problem with] community service hours is that they're Sisyphian efforts. You're pushing a rock up a hill, and it's just going to come right back down unless you change the pitch of the hill. That is why working on something foundational like campaign finance reform is much more appealing to me than feeding people at a soup kitchen. I mean, that can be very gratifying and I think for some people it's a lot more gratifying and certainly a lot less scary than lobbying the state legislature, but for me, there's something very important . . . [about] concentrated political action.

ENGAGING STUDENTS IN ACTION PROJECTS. Another powerful approach to fostering political efficacy is to engage students in political action projects of various sorts.[5] Action projects provide experience with democratic participation and often lead students to feel that their efforts are being taken seriously and might have some impact. But taking action in a way that feels worthwhile and effective is not easy, so faculty need to direct and support students in ways that maximize the positive benefit they get from their participation. PEP faculty had several suggestions for increasing the contribution of action projects to political motivation.

   o *Help students set achievable goals.* One thing that can be useful
     in preventing discouragement and burnout is to help students be-
     come more sophisticated about where they are and are not likely
     to succeed. When they set realistic goals, they are less likely to get
     discouraged. A student at Duke talks about the importance of this
     for her learning:

I think that I'm just more aware of places for hope and also places where it seems like there's not much hope on things. Like for my welfare reform project, my instructor made the good point that there are certain things that I wanted to change about welfare reform that were unlikely to change. [The teacher] was like, "Well, these things are politically impossible. That is not going to happen." To realize that there are some things that can't be changed was really sad. But then to think about some of the issues that can be worked on, I think that's really inspiring.

○ *Help students take satisfaction in small successes.* During a single course, it is not reasonable to expect that students' political engagement will have a notable impact. Even the longer-term involvement afforded by participation in multiyear or extracurricular programs seldom achieves more than modest goals in the context of real-world politics. One way to make sure these experiences are beneficial nevertheless is to help students recognize and enjoy even small accomplishments. Adam Weinberg illustrates this point:

If we can get students to see some of the more subtle things as progress then we've made a huge impact on them. And that's probably one of the best indicators that they'll stay involved in politics forever, because they've redefined success. [If you ask them to describe successes,] I think they'd say, "We made money in politics a major issue on our campus, that Democracy Matters became a known entity on campus." They'll point to concrete things they've done like we went into a local high school, we went to the legislature to lobby, had a successful evening event, had a great article in the newspaper.

Students appreciate this approach and seem to experience a great deal of satisfaction when the process is framed this way. As a Mills College student said, "It was a lot of little things, little accomplishments that I would get excited about. Even my job—the quilt project [for her internship at a youth arts program], putting together the proposal, executing a proposal to finishing it."

○ *Take students' work seriously.* We saw that the faculty members in the PEP courses and programs maximized the educational value of active democratic participation by making every possible effort to ensure that the work students do is taken seriously and that students are aware of that attention and consideration. This effort is doubly valuable, because student projects are more authentic and better learning experiences when they serve a real need, and the various audiences for the work will be more likely to take the contribution seriously if it has been designed from the outset to serve a real purpose. Brian Murphy made this a high priority for student projects in his course, The Politics of San Francisco: "The first thing is that we want to create practical projects that actually serve communities. We want people to produce things that have public value."

○ *Help students experience the power of collective action.* More often than not, effective democratic participation requires people to work together. Many students do not understand this, and making them aware of it often helps them feel more efficacious. Even if students cannot imagine making a difference by working alone, they can see that by working with others, they could have an impact. For this reason, many faculty help students gain experience with collective action.[6] Some students told us that even seeing others work together toward successful outcomes can be empowering. As one young woman at Berea College said: "I learned that you can be part of something as a whole that can change things dramatically. I met community people who got together and got a law changed." When asked, "What effect did it have on you?" she replied: "The world isn't as big. People can make a difference if they get together with others."

HELPING STUDENTS GAIN POLITICAL EXPERTISE. We observed that PEP faculty also focused on helping students become more skilled or knowledgeable as a strategy for developing their sense of political efficacy. Of course, feeling politically efficacious is related to actually *being* more efficacious. It comes as no surprise that when students master skills of democratic participation and become more knowledgeable, they are more confident about their capacity to contribute and therefore more likely to become engaged. This is important because even if students are interested in politics and would like to get more involved, if they lack political skills and knowledge, it is unlikely to happen. Greater expertise, which then feeds into motivation, is a central goal for the Sorensen Institute. As Greg Werkheiser explains: "Knowing how the system works helps reduce fear and build confidence, being confident in the defensibility of what you believe, and having the skills necessary to compete. We try to offer all of those things in our program."

TEMPERING CYNICISM AND MAINTAINING HOPE. We saw that PEP faculty's efforts to foster a greater sense of political efficacy in their students face a number of challenges, one of which is the students' widespread skepticism about politics. This skepticism can be especially intense among some student groups. Siegrun Freyss, at California State University, Los Angeles, often teaches recent immigrants from Mexico and Central America. As she says, "For students who have connections with illegal immigrants, the government is seen as the enemy."

Education for political engagement should not encourage naïve, superficial, or uncritical acceptance of the status quo. At the same time, this education needs to take on the challenge of tempering extreme cynicism about politics and aspire to create citizens who are willing to act as guardians for their own and others' interests, and for democratic values, institutions, and processes. One way to navigate this tension is to combine an appreciation of the ideals of our democratic system—that democracy is unrealized but not unrealizable—with a realistic sense of where we have fallen short of those ideals and a belief that these ideals are worth striving for (Gutmann, 1996; Rahn, 1992). People actually tend to be particularly engaged when they feel quite politically efficacious themselves but also have a healthy measure of skepticism toward political institutions, leading them to believe that political "influence is both possible and necessary" (Gamson, 1968, p. 48). But healthy skepticism is not the same as disengaged cynicism, and the latter needs to be addressed if students are going to be motivated to participate.

Sometimes students' cynicism is initially increased when they begin participating more actively in politics. They arrive in a PEP course or program with unrealistic idealism and can become disillusioned when they engage with the gritty reality of political life. As Brown faculty member Ross Cheit put it, "Some students come in with unrealistic expectations. They get frustrated if they haven't changed the world in a semester." Students can also become overwhelmed when they are dealing with very complex issues and discouraged if the actions they take on are unsuccessful. And Feinstein was not alone in pointing out, "Some of the students work on [political] campaigns and can get burned out if their candidate loses."

Faculty use a wide array of strategies for tempering students' cynicism about politics, some of which we described in Chapter Five. For example, they help students get to know people in public life at both community and national levels, learn about and come to identify with community or political organizations, and develop a more nuanced understanding of the dilemmas and constraints that public service entails. We observed two additional approaches that help support students' stamina and persistence when the going gets tough:

- ○ *Establish a hopeful tone.* Although PEP faculty and program leaders take a sophisticated view of the political realm, recognizing how difficult it is to achieve change, they also work to convey a sense of hope and realistic optimism. When faculty and program leaders are self-conscious about sending balanced messages—such as recognizing both the inevitable difficulties and the opportunities for small and incremental successes—they are more likely to have a positive effect than if they are overly optimistic. As Adam Weinberg says of Democracy Matters: "While we are critical (of the current campaign finance system), we are not doomsayers. Students struggle with that as well—hope versus despair."

- ○ *Connect students with models of long-term political engagement.* One challenge in the effort to increase students' sense of political efficacy is that effective participation is a long-term proposition and inevitably involves defeat as well as success along the way. Stamina and persistence are critical to long-term commitment, yet they are hard to maintain. Exposing students to people who are involved in political action for the long haul and have weathered defeats can help protect them from becoming discouraged, as can experience with people whose long-term commitments show persistence in the face of challenge. For this reason, it can be extremely useful for students to interact with some old-timers who have themselves found ways to keep up their energy and determination in the face of challenges. As Weinberg says of some of the mentors who work with Democracy Matters students, "The older people teach the younger ones that it's a marathon, not a sprint."

NOTES

1. This definition of politically engaged identity is distinct from definitions typically used by political scientists, who tend to associate political identity with either group- or category-based identities (that is, one's identity as an American, a woman, a Hindu, a disabled person, a liberal, a conservative, and the like). These kinds of particular group identities will, of course, inform one's overall political identity by informing the specific kinds of political action one takes or the specific issues one cares about.

2. For more information about the development of this policy agenda, see document 11 in the PEP document supplement at http://www.carnegie foundation.org/educating_for_democracy/docs/.

3. For a few examples of how PEP faculty encourage students to think about democratic participation in broader terms, see the "Getting Started (What Is Politics?)" section of the PEP document supplement at the online address shown in note 2.

4. For an example of how Shenk and his colleague David Takacs encourage students to view themselves as political actors, see document 3 in the PEP document supplement online.

5. For examples, see the "Research/Action Projects and Simulations" section of the PEP document supplement online.

6. For examples of how PEP faculty and program leaders are helping students gain experience in collective action, see documents 11, 14, 15, 27, 28, 29, and 54 in the PEP document supplement online.

8

LEARNING THROUGH DISCUSSION AND DELIBERATION

DISCUSSION AND DELIBERATION ARE UBIQUITOUS in education at all levels, and are especially important in higher education. The terms represent not only a valuable set of educational activities but also an important set of learning outcomes. Similarly, intellectual skills, including the various skills of deliberation, are just as important as substantive knowledge for thoughtful political engagement.[1]

Those with well-developed skills of political deliberation engage differences of opinion, see issues from multiple points of view, explore and evaluate competing claims, and recognize and evaluate the implicit assumptions in their own and others' arguments. They know how to offer and evaluate evidence, and to form judgments that are well reasoned and supported by arguments that conform to standards of rational discourse. They can find reliable information and use it to evaluate alternative positions on political or policy issues, to formulate and defend their own positions, and to evaluate and respond to others' positions. They also know how to listen actively, ensure that others understand their viewpoints, compromise without abandoning their convictions, and work toward consensus under conditions of mutual respect.

Individuals who lack deliberative capacities are at a serious disadvantage not only in the political realm but also in their education, their work, and other areas of their lives. For example, reasoned argument is central to the entire enterprise of higher education, so it is hard to progress without this important ability. In fact, deliberation quintessentially represents the application of exactly those academic standards that we pointed to in Chapter Three as thoroughly integral to the whole fabric of the academic endeavor.

Teaching strategies that include thoughtful political discussion and deliberation the focus of this chapter—help students learn the whole range of capacities involved in political deliberation, because *practicing* deliberation is the best way to develop the *skills* of deliberation. Practice is especially effective when it is carefully and strategically structured and guided by the teacher and accompanied by informative feedback.

Political Deliberation Skills

On the most general level, engaging in reasoned and inclusive discussions means that when we face complex political questions, we pause to listen to, reflect on, and discuss alternative outcomes, considering the perspectives held by those around us and trying to come to a well-supported position that takes this variety of perspectives into account. Students need to begin by learning to operate within these fundamental parameters.

Understanding Argument

To develop deliberative skills, students need to learn the basics of what counts as a well-reasoned argument, the ground rules of public discourse. The norms of argument will be a new concept to most of them. In our study of the PEP courses and programs, both faculty and students point to an initial lack of understanding about forms and uses of argument and gains in understanding what counts as a reasoned argument as an important learning outcome. Doug Morgan, of Portland State University, focuses directly on this goal in his course The Ethics of Leadership:

> Students are not good at deliberation when they start the class. . . . Just expressing your first opinion instead of your second and sober opinion is not what the public space is about. It is not a forum for each individual to just stand up and air his opinions. [Students] don't understand the unique character of public discourse. . . . Public discourse is governed by "rules of the game," and it is important to understand what the rules are and why they are in place. I do this to reinforce the idea that political engagement and discourse are special activities that require a peculiar set of competencies and skills.

At a more advanced level, students need to learn about paying careful attention to the logic of the argument as well as the presentation of several varieties of evidence, including empirical data, historical analysis, and personal experience. They need to understand that deliberation frequently involves challenging the bases of others' reasoning, raising questions of what should count as acceptable starting assumptions, valid supporting evidence, or legitimate authorities on any given political problem or issue. Narrative arguments based in stories and personal perspectives can be used in thoughtful political discussion, including political deliberation, as long as they are contributed in the spirit of mutual respect and treated as illustrations or considerations to be discussed rather than as a way to circumvent reasoned discussion. Students need to learn that in following the norms of deliberation, their arguments based on moral appeals and personal stories will not be taken as definitive, and like other arguments, will be open to critical questioning and competing claims.

It may be even more important for students to understand that some forms of argument are *not* valid. Many of the kinds of discussions they are used to hearing on television or "talk radio" do not constitute reasoned deliberation. Reasoned deliberation precludes the use of ad hominem attacks, stereotypes, and gross generalizations, as well as the kind of bombastic and aggressive grandstanding sometimes referred to as cross fire–style argument, in which the participants talk past each other and there is no real exchange of views. As students learn that assertions that are intentionally one-sided or misleading are clearly out of bounds, they also need to learn to use rhetorical forms that are honest and respectful as well as persuasive. That is, they must learn that deliberation and other discussions in the context of educational programs must embody the core values of academic discourse that we stressed in Chapters Three and Four.

Careful Listening

Active listening is one of the most important skills of political deliberation. Morgan insists that his students learn to listen to each other carefully so that they can accurately represent each other's statements before responding to them. As he said, "One key element of deliberation is the seemingly simple—but really not simple at all—importance of listening to other people and getting it right. 'Getting it right' means accurately understanding and characterizing the arguments of others." When this step in the deliberative process is pulled out and addressed directly, through a number of simple exercises, students can become much more self-conscious about learning to really listen to other people's ideas. In the surveys and interviews, the PEP students frequently pointed to the ability to *listen actively* as among the most valuable things they have learned.

Considering Competing Claims

One aspect of thoughtful political deliberation is the consideration of competing interpretations or conflicting perspectives on the issues. In reflecting on their experiences in these courses, students were well aware of learning to "consider different points of view before making decisions," as a student in Dick Simpson's Chicago politics course put it. A student in Duke's Service Opportunities in Leadership program also articulated the importance of this ability: "[We learned] to use the skills of holding people to their ideas, forcing them to develop them, putting two competing ideas up against each other, putting them back and forth . . . in order to develop something useful, and following through with that."

Grounding Opinions in Knowledge and Evidence

High-quality deliberation, argumentation, and judgment not only require careful reasoning but also depend on substantive knowledge. Coming into the PEP courses and programs, students generally lack this knowledge but learn a great deal as they formulate positions on the issues and develop supporting arguments. Students in Dick Reitano's Model United Nations course, for example, become very knowledgeable about the country they are representing and the issues of their mock United Nations committees. As a student said: "This course has changed how I interact with people. I can cite numbers, specific agreements, I can give reasons. Because of the class, I'm more likely to want to get specific information about why I believe what I believe."

Of course, there is a limit to the depth of understanding students can achieve in a single course or program, and they sometimes mention being aware of those limits. Nevertheless, they appreciate it when they feel prepared for the deliberations in which they engage. As a Sorensen Institute student said: "Even though none of us were necessarily experts, I think when we discussed things we had really thought about it."

Evaluating Underlying Assumptions, Premises, and Biases

Another important aspect of political deliberation is the ability to uncover and evaluate the assumptions—both one's own and others'—on which an argument is based or the interests it serves. This ability is crucial in evaluating information, especially information available on the Internet, and in understanding and responding effectively to arguments put forward in course readings or classroom discussions.

Ideally, students should apply this critical assessment to their own opinions as well as to those of their political opponents. When positions that students take for granted are challenged, they need to think more deeply about the basis for their beliefs. A student in the Sorensen Institute program began to look more closely at her own assumptions after engaging with a speaker with whom she disagreed: "Someone came and gave a talk from the Family Foundation, a pro-family lobbying organization. She had a lot to say that sparked discussion and led to debate amongst us about things she had said or claims she had made, like about homosexuality and abortion. I think that it really made a lot of us think about what our own reasons were for the views we had."

If students develop not only the ability but also the habit of critically evaluating the positions and arguments they encounter, it can increase the rigor of their thinking in many domains. As a student in Otto Feinstein's American government course remarked: "The method of thinking and examining situations that my professor taught me, I think personally I carry it into all of my other classes and all corners of my life. It's a certain way of examining things—not just accepting what's being said to me by experts but actually trying to find out what the underlying principles are . . . and to find what the different views on it are."

ENGAGING DIFFERENT PERSPECTIVES WITH CIVILITY AND RESPECT. Other features of high-quality political deliberation go beyond analytic rigor and substantive knowledge to include personal qualities, such as a willingness to be courteous and respectful, even in heated exchanges. Virtually all the PEP faculty stressed the importance of engaging with civility and respect for others' views—"not simply shooting down other people's thoughts before giving them a fair hearing," as Sue Briggs of the CIVICUS program put it.

For students in the Sorensen Institute, this was an aspect of the experience that they particularly appreciated. For example: "Talking to some classmates, there were some sharp differences, but people were very diplomatic about how they voiced it; they'd say, 'You know, I really pretty much agree with so-and-so about this, but where I disagree is. . . .' So I think that was a really constructive approach to disagreement."

LOOKING FOR COMMON GROUND. In the process of deliberating about challenging issues in a group context, students learn not only to listen to each other and maintain civility but also to look for areas of agreement in the midst of considerable disagreement. Requiring students with differing perspectives to work together collaboratively can be especially useful for teaching this skill. As Reitano said about students in his course: "Collaborative work is the primary means for teaching deliberation, such as students collaborating on a UN committee. Some students start off disagreeing on everything and can be disruptive, but often after spending enough time talking, they discover that they do have things in common and can respect their differences."

BEING GENUINELY OPEN TO RECONSIDERING ONE'S OWN POSITIONS. Sometimes, this kind of careful, respectful listening leads students to change their minds about issues or to take a more nuanced and qualified position than they had before. This Sorensen Institute student talks about how her perspective on one hot button issue shifted:

> Some of my opinions changed because I respected the people who made the opposite argument, respected them enough to actually listen to what they had to say and try to understand their points of view. I sometimes wound up agreeing with them on some points in the end. . . . [For example,] I used to think that affirmative action was a great fix, but now, I still see it as a fix, but not as such a great one. And that's a pretty huge issue for someone to change positions on. . . . This happened . . . through debate in the classroom. And at first I would get so angry at people; I remember getting so angry, thinking "What are they talking about? How can they say this?" But then at the end I started to understand their arguments because they really established their positions well, and I had to agree with some of their criticisms.

BALANCING OPEN-MINDEDNESS WITH PASSION AND COMMITMENT. As important as it is to maintain an open mind and a degree of humility in political deliberation, it is also important for students to develop passion and commitment. Passion adds spirit and energy to the discussion, which inspires other students, like this one from the Sorensen Institute: "The level of passion and involvement of the other students really brought a lot to the table." In addition, many of the PEP courses and programs help students begin to differentiate the beliefs or values they feel they cannot compromise from those on which they are ready to shift if someone presents a convincing case for doing so.

Rewards of Building Political Deliberation Skills

Research on political discussion shows that without encouragement to be open-minded and really listen to multiple perspectives, merely talking with others about a complex political issue, such as Social Security reform, is not likely to help participants improve the thoughtfulness of their views in light of a broader range of information (Barabas, 2004). This research suggests that educational programs need to pay particular attention to helping young people appreciate and take seriously views that are different from their own, whether in obvious or more subtle ways. In our study, we saw that all of the PEP courses and programs recognize this goal as central to their purposes.

Of course, it would be unrealistic and unwise to suggest that every time students talk about politics they adhere to rigorous deliberative standards. They should be encouraged to engage in other kinds of political discussions that are also worthwhile, including casual conversations with family, friends, and coworkers (Huckfeldt and Sprague, 1987; Mutz, 2002; Young, 1996, 2000). The norms for talking among friends or family, for example, do not include expectations about full inclusion of different perspectives, as in deliberation. Informal conversation, however, encourages students to express their ideas and contributes to both their political interest and their sense that politics matters in their lives and things they care about.

The PEP student and faculty surveys show that faculty and program leaders spend a considerable amount of time on political discussion, including discussions of course topics and materials and discussions of current events. On average, faculty report spending nearly one-third of all course time on discussion, making it the most consistently and intensively used teaching technique in these courses and programs. This focus on discussion has important benefits, as we learned from both the survey results and our interviews with students and program leaders.

Students who participated in these politically focused courses and programs made important gains on a number of outcomes related to political discussion and deliberation.

Stronger Skills

Our analysis showed that whether they entered the programs with low or high interest in politics, students made significant gains in skills of political analysis and judgment. (See Appendix B, "Survey Scales and Results.") For example, they were able to "weigh the pros and cons of different political positions" and "recognize conflicting political interests," skills that are highly relevant for political deliberation. Both groups of students also showed significantly increased confidence in a set of skills related to communication and leadership that support deliberation, such as the ability to "articulate my ideas and beliefs to others" and "talk about social barriers such as race."

Greater Interest, Changed Attitudes

Our data also show that students with low initial political interest entered the courses and programs saying they discussed politics with others much less in a typical week, had less confidence in their ability to "explain my political views to others," to "persuade others to support my political opinion," and to be able to "reach a compromise" and were less likely to say they would "discuss political problems with friends" in the future than students who began the courses and programs with high levels of political interest. The low-interest group experienced significant gains on all of these items, whereas the high-interest group maintained the same high levels they reported for these items in the presurvey. Both groups came to view political discussion as a more important form of political activity during the course of the interventions. Both low and high initial interest students made significant gains in their belief that good citizens are those who "engage in political discussion" and that raising awareness of political issues through discussions can be an effective way to promote political change.

Strategies for Teaching Discussion and Deliberation

As we studied both the academic courses and cocurricular programs of the PEP, we saw faculty use a number of different strategies to provide experiences with thoughtful political discussion or deliberation.[2] We also saw the practical steps they took to make these activities and assignments effective. In this section, we describe the main teaching strategies we observed, share the PEP faculty's practical approaches, and discuss the challenges faculty confront in using political deliberation as a teaching tool.

Chief among the strategies we saw were face-to-face discussion and deliberation, discussion and deliberation in simulations, technology-enhanced deliberations, and reasoned consideration or "internal deliberation" through writing assignments.

Face-to-Face Discussion and Deliberation

The most common approach we saw in both classrooms and extracurricular programs was some version of face-to-face discussion. The discussion can be structured as a response to readings, speakers, issues or case studies presented by the teacher or other students, or by films and other media. Ross Cheit talked about the importance of using rich accounts of cases as the basis for discussions in his Children and Public Policy course at Brown University: "Generally, I use the case method in my teaching and it works well. I start with concrete facts in a real situation. The book we use includes stories and links well with students' service experiences. Much of the time, we are working from cases."

Other faculty have found it especially useful to begin with a film or other multimedia prompts. Dick Simpson's teaching assistant at the University of Illinois, Chicago, for example, said that one class on the politics of Chicago "began with the film *Lord of the Flies,* and the discussion was tremendous. In talking about the movie, students were really able to use the tools we had talked about regarding how democracy is shaped, what makes a prosperous democracy, and so on."

Face-to-face interaction among students can be an especially rich learning experience for a number of reasons. First, it requires students to become articulate orally and on the spot, skills that are given less emphasis in contemporary higher education than written work. Students seem particularly to appreciate the experience of engaging with each other directly on issues, rather than interacting solely through a professor.

The Urban Agenda component of the American government course provides an extended experience with this kind of interaction, working together in discussion sections to debate political issues facing their local communities and to develop strategies for addressing them.[3] Engaging with each other this way helps students learn to listen carefully, respond to critiques of their positions, manage their emotional reactions, and engage others with civility. Because face-to-face discussion is the most common way of engaging students in deliberation, many of the lessons of good practice that emerged from this project are connected with this mode of deliberation.

Most political discussions in the interventions involved students presenting their views in response to some kind of prompt, such as an issue, case presentation, speaker, or reading. The students would take positions, present evidence, and argue the issues through. In these discussions, students were most often presenting positions and views that they actually held, but sometimes were asked to make the case for a position they did not actually hold—as in a debate where the student must argue both sides or argue an assigned position, or when playing devil's advocate.

Discussion and Deliberation via Simulations

Some courses and programs involve discussion or deliberation in assigned or self-chosen roles in a simulation.[4] The Model United Nations program is an especially interesting example of simulated deliberation because each course is, in essence, a rich and extended experience with deliberation. As in the Model United Nations program more generally, students in Reitano's course at Vassar and Dutchess Community College introduce resolutions in a simulated United Nations General Assembly on behalf of the country they are representing and argue for their positions in mock committee sessions.

More frequently, the simulation is only one component of a course or program. Students in Rick Semiatin's Washington Semester Program, for example, role-play being political candidates or policymakers, trying out the process of decision making that they are learning about from speakers, readings, and other experiences in the program.

Technology-Enhanced Deliberations

Technology can be an important tool in classroom deliberations. Some faculty use a simple wand device, for example, that looks like a television remote control. When an issue has been discussed for a time, the faculty member can ask students to choose from among up to five options. They express their choices by pressing one of the buttons on their wand, and the results are immediately visible on a screen in the front of the room.

Many faculty also use Web-based interactions and discussions instead of face-to-face discussions and debates, or to supplement them, as a means for supporting deliberative skills and critical judgment. These kinds of exchanges provide students a bit more emotional distance and time to think before responding. They are sometimes seen as being at one remove from the classroom work and thus give students a feeling of more freedom to take risks in the positions they put forward or the arguments they make. Another advantage is that they make it easier for shy students to participate, and they offer essentially unlimited "airtime," unlike classroom discussions, in which it is not unusual for a few particularly vocal students to take more than their share of the available time. Morgan, for example, uses online discussions and feels they provide a good way for students to get feedback from each other on the views they put forward and on the quality of their arguments.

Writing Assignments

Writing can be an especially powerful way to learn careful deliberation and persuasion and is an important complement to oral argumentation. Most of the PEP courses and programs include experience with both written and oral deliberation. Written assignments that call for reasoned consideration of diverse viewpoints can take the form of a research report, a policy analysis, a position paper, or an essay. Like oral deliberation, these written assignments can be straightforward presentations of the students' own views, structured debates that attempt to make the case for two or more conflicting positions, or simulations in which students create documents as part of a role-play that represent some aspect of the political process.

In Duke's Service Opportunities in Leadership program, students create policy issue portfolios that include a policy recommendation paper or memo, in which they identify the key players and underlying structures and systems connected with the issue, consider existing policies and policy options, discuss which option is the most viable, make a case for the kind of leadership needed, and offer recommendations for action.[5] The Model United Nations offers an example of written deliberations in the context of a simulation. Among other things, the students in the Model United Nations course write position papers on topics assigned to each committee and council where their country is represented.

Lessons from the PEP Program

We quickly saw that the PEP faculty go well beyond simply creating assignments or activities. They take time to follow some practical steps to ensure the effectiveness of the experience:

1. Set ground rules for discussions at the outset of the course or program and maintain them throughout.
2. Directly teach students how to represent each other's views accurately.
3. Create a sense of community in the group.
4. Help students stand back from their deliberations to observe the process.
5. Teach students to moderate discussions.
6. Delay discussions until students have learned about the issues.
7. Use small groups as well as the class as a whole for deliberative discussions.
8. As much as possible, create discussion groups that are diverse.

Set Ground Rules

Both faculty and students talked about the importance of establishing guidelines for discussions and debates that stress making one's case with substantive arguments and avoiding prejudgment, labeling, and ad hominem arguments. As one Sorensen Institute student said: "Our disagreements were really over issues and not about people. That was important." Another student in the program elaborated on this point: "I think what really helped us—one of our first days there we sat down together and set guidelines for discussion and debating. And one of the things we said is be respectful—give your opinion but . . . always respect the other person. . . . We were able to each of us express our own point of view and know that it wasn't going to affect how they felt about us personally, but they could respect that we had this view, and we could respect theirs."

Teach How to Represent the Views of Others Accurately

Morgan shows students how to make sure that they understand each other before they respond. A student will make an argument, and Morgan will summarize the student's argument on a chalkboard for everyone in the class to see. He then asks the student whose view he is representing: "Is that what you meant?" This gives students time to reflect on what they've said and decide whether the summary matches their thoughts. Have they been misrepresented? Would they like a chance to restate their position, to revise the statements they have made?

Create a Sense of Community

If faculty can create a sense of community in the group, students are more comfortable expressing their opinions. A strong feeling of community increases mutual respect and attention even when students disagree with each other's views. Programs in which students spend a great deal of time together usually provide good opportunities to do this. Such programs include intensive summer institutes, living-learning communities, and semester in Washington programs. In these kinds of full-time programs, students get to know each other as friends, so they are less likely to dismiss out of hand positions with which they disagree. Programs like these, which build encompassing community for a period of time, offer especially fertile opportunities to learn deliberative skills because discussions can continue outside the formal sessions, allowing for greater depth of deliberation as well as a sense that exchanges will be respectful. A student in the Sorensen Institute's intensive summer program said that sometimes the heated discussions would continue "through dinner, or we would get together to have discussions during our free time so that we could continue discussing it if we didn't feel we'd had adequate time during the day. But it was never something that was carried over because someone was angry, or had something against another person—it was because we wanted to know where everyone was coming from, we wanted to understand their point of view."

Help Students Stand Back and Observe

The quality of the discussion benefits if faculty help students pay close attention to the ongoing process and character of their deliberations. When students are explicitly taught to pay attention to both the substance of the discussion and the quality and process of the deliberation, it helps consolidate their learning about the nature of productive deliberation and facilitates useful exchanges. This may mean helping students see that there are different kinds of rhetorical moves to make and roles to take in a complex interaction. For example, they may be taught to notice when someone is struggling to express his view and to step in and help make the case, even if the position they are arguing is one they do not agree with. Students as well as faculty can play the role of devil's advocate in a discussion, helping take responsibility for the overall quality of the discussion.

Teach Students to Moderate Discussions

It can be very useful to assign student moderators to keep discussions on track. Faculty are accustomed to watching the tenor and quality of discussions and taking steps to keep the conversation lively, bring it back to the point when it wanders, or restore a productive tone if some participants overstep the boundaries of civility. It is important for faculty to be attentive to these things, but they need not be the only ones to take responsibility for the quality of the discussion. Many of the PEP faculty teach students to take on explicitly the role of moderator or overseer of the discussion's productivity and tone. As we noted previously, for each class discussion in his Providence College course, Rick Battistoni assigns one student to be the discussion moderator and another to be what he calls a "vibeswatcher."[6] The very act of creating and using a role like this in discussions calls attention to the process and character of productive deliberation.

Students in the Sorensen Institute often mentioned the important role played by student moderators for ensuring civil and productive exchanges: "The student moderators would step in and say 'You know, maybe you need to look at this from a different perspective,' or 'Let's take a moment to calm down,' or we'd take a five-minute break, so everyone could take a moment to step back, relax, review what they've said or what others said, and then we would come back in and discuss again."

Some faculty assigned students to the role of moderator right away. Others felt it was better to shift the oversight to students more gradually, with faculty providing guidance and structure in the beginning, then stepping back as students got to know each other better and became more skilled in both deliberating and moderating.

This Sorensen Institute student felt that this gradual approach was important in helping students become comfortable with that role: "I think what helped with that was how the program leaders slowly, gradually worked us into that instead of just having students do it right from the beginning before we were really comfortable with one another."

Another student pointed out that faculty were careful about assessing students' readiness to take over the moderating role and adjusted the level of scaffolding to the expertise level of the group. "I think in the beginning [the program leaders] had more involvement with the political debate, but as they saw that we were maturing in our debating skills they stepped back more and more and allowed us to be the moderators and set the guidelines for each other."

Delay Discussions Until Students Have Learned About Issues

Discussions will be enriched if they take place after students have had time to develop more extensive knowledge of the issues. As we have said, deliberation can build on short common readings, a case presented in class, or a visiting speaker, and thus proceed usefully without extensive preparation. Students gain a different kind of deliberative experience, however, when they build a deeper knowledge base before engaging in discussions or other forms of deliberation. Because of the particular value of this more deeply grounded deliberation, many faculty try to include at least some experience of this sort in academic courses or institutes.

The Sorensen Institute program makes this explicit by structuring the whole summer institute around three "lenses": the informed citizen, the thoughtful citizen, and the active citizen. The program leaders make it clear to students that deliberation should be both informed and thoughtful, so they hold off on serious deliberation until students have had a chance to become more knowledgeable about issues, institutions, policies, and resources in the Commonwealth of Virginia. Students appreciate this approach, even if at first they sometimes resist it. As one student said: "At first, everyone wanted to get into debate, but they kept wanting to make us wait, because they started with lens one—informed citizen—informing us about what's going on. So they kind of put the debate off, which was good because that's when I was feeling, not necessarily intimidated, but not completely comfortable with my surroundings."

Use Both Small Groups and the Whole Class for Discussions

Full participation in deliberative discussions is often greater when the discussions take place in small groups rather than the whole class. Depending on the size of the group, it can be useful to break it into sections or small groups for deliberative discussions, especially in the beginning, when students are unfamiliar with the process and may be reluctant to speak in a larger group. Often students who are initially afraid to speak up in the larger group setting will begin to do so after they have had some positive experiences expressing their views in the smaller groups.

Create Diverse Discussion Groups

Discussions benefit from having a good mix of students with different backgrounds, styles, and points of view. Faculty seldom have much control over the backgrounds and characteristics of students who take their courses, but if they are establishing small groups for discussions or project-based deliberations, they can keep diversity of perspective and other variables in mind. As Craig Shinn said of his course at Portland State University, "Heterogeneity of values, backgrounds, and so on is a core concept of the class. A homogeneous class might be easier to teach in a classroom management sense, but in a class on deliberation, it helps to have something to deliberate."

Challenges in Teaching Political Deliberation

As we talked with PEP faculty and program staff, we learned that they face a number of challenges as they try to support their students in learning the various skills and qualities that characterize high-quality political deliberation. Indeed, most of these challenges are familiar to teachers with other goals or subject matter.

Lack of Deliberative Skills

Incoming students often have extremely limited deliberative skills, making it necessary to start at a very elementary level. This is not surprising, given the cognitive-developmental limitations of college students. In line with the research data on college students more generally, Morgan finds that many of his students lack some of the essential prerequisites for productive deliberation when they come into his course: "There are many students in the course who don't know what they believe, or if they do, they cannot say it in a cogent way. And if people can't do that, then they can't participate in political discourse. These students may have difficulty deliberating well all the way through the class, and it may turn out that many of them do not change much with respect to their deliberation skills by the time the ten-week course has ended."

Even at highly selective Brown University, Cheit finds that students have difficulty learning to deliberate about cases in a conceptually grounded way. As he said: "I think it is just inherently hard. I teach an intro class and say to the students, 'Can you conceptualize that?' and they don't know what I'm talking about. It's hard to get them to the point where they can do it. It's hard to work from cases to concepts, hard to put cases into a broader context."

Lack of Knowledge About Issues

Many students also lack the kind of rich knowledge base that supports effective deliberation. Although this is a widespread problem, Semiatin notes that even a small core group of knowledgeable students can raise the level of the discussion: "The knowledge base is key. When there are four to five students with a strong base, they bring the whole class up with them; it's like having teaching assistants." This has implications for both the structure of deliberative encounters and the choice of topics. If a core group of students can take responsibility for becoming better informed about a set of issues and then take a leadership role in the group's deliberations about those issues, it can help mitigate the more general lack of relevant knowledge. Allowing students to participate in choosing topics can also increase the chances that they will have some relevant knowledge or will be motivated to become more knowledgeable.

Uneven Levels of Readiness

Lack of knowledge and deliberative skills is further complicated because most classes are quite heterogeneous in terms of student preparation and sophistication. This variation is even more dramatic in programs that draw students from more than one college, as some extracurricular programs or collaborative academic courses do. This is a special challenge for Reitano's Model United Nations course, which draws students from a highly selective liberal arts college and an open-access community college. Faculty must pay significant attention to promoting useful interactions between students from these two very different institutions, especially because the course requires a lot of collaborative work.

Time Constraints

Lack of time for quality deliberation is another problem. If deliberations take place during a single class period, it can sometimes feel that the discussion ends prematurely, with no clear resolution or even full exploration of different points of view. As a Sorensen Institute student said, "Sometimes the discussions got cut short, and it was frustrating that people hadn't been able to make all the points they wanted to make." This experience can sometimes be a hidden blessing, though, encouraging students to continue the conversation beyond the artificial boundaries of the class period. This kind of spillover is more likely to happen in full-time programs where students spend time together outside class. After commenting on his frustration, the same Sorensen Institute student added: "Sometimes after class we'd continue the discussion in a more informal way, or after the speakers had left we'd talk over dinner and say, 'So what did you think about this or that part of the talk?'"

Because participation in Web-based deliberation happens outside class and is often optional, busy students can have trouble finding time to participate. As Morgan said, "Having enough time for this is a barrier. Students lack the time. This is an urban, blue-collar university with many first-generation college students, and it could be that 60 to 70 percent of students are working in addition to taking a full load of classes. Doing the reading and the writing on a course Web site takes time. It's also really important not to neglect the time that it takes to form an opinion and to rethink it—that's work! It takes time."

Web-based deliberations are also time-consuming for faculty, because most are active participants in the deliberation, following and responding to student comments. Many of these systems for online discussion or course-related chat rooms also require some technical maintenance, and this often falls on faculty as well.

Impatience

As important as deliberation is in its own right, some students become impatient if discussions do not lead directly to action. As one student in the Wayne State University Urban Agenda said: "The course made use of discussions to come upon a consensus and that was something that I had no previous experience doing and it expanded my way of doing things[7]. . . . They taught us to come up with a variety of views and try to combine those into some type of collaboration of ideals. But after that I felt—once I get this collaboration, what do I do with it?"

Addressing the Challenges

The well-known challenges we have outlined here are endemic to teaching, and there are no easy answers for resolving them. All can be mitigated in the immediate context of the course or program by setting realistic goals, planning activities carefully, and building up to the more demanding tasks as systematically and gradually as possibly. Stepping back a bit, though, it seems that to address these problems in a serious way one needs to take a more programmatic or institutional perspective.

When it comes to student frustration about lack of follow-up, for example, a longer-term perspective might suggest that, if handled well, this kind of impatience or frustration can properly be seen as a positive outcome. If students feel frustrated that a course does not take them far enough into the political process once their interest is awakened, they are expressing the kind of motivation that might energize their participation in additional courses or programs that build on those that came before.

This desire to go further underscores the importance of an overarching institutional strategy designed to expand and deepen students' necessarily limited experiences in any given course. A series of engagements that develop over a longer period of time can also help faculty struggling to foster sophisticated deliberative skills in students who come into their courses without the basics. The Duke Service Opportunities in Leadership program is one example, because it involves a spring preparatory course followed by a summer internship and then another course.[8] Each of the experiences strengthens and enhances the others. Of course, such an elaborate program is not always feasible. In such cases, if it is possible to collaborate with other faculty so that students are helped to build their deliberative skills over time, the curriculum will be a much better support to their mastery of these important capacities.

NOTES

1. In addition to its meaning in general usage, the term *political deliberation* has a more specialized meaning for political scientists and other scholars of politics. In this sense, the term refers to a particular kind of political dialogue in which people engage in reasoned consideration of multiple sides of an issue under conditions of mutual respect and equal inclusion in the conversation (Bohman, 1999; Dryzek, 2000; Elster, 1998; Gutmann and Thompson, 1996). Some political theorists have argued that the legitimacy of political decision making in a pluralist democracy rests largely on citizens' ability to engage in this kind of inclusive, reasoned debate about

complex issues. Research on public deliberation supports their claim that this process can help participants gain political knowledge, a more accurate understanding of the facts, and increased political tolerance, as well as lead to less extreme political views, more political involvement, wider consensus about the best course of action, and a greater sense of the legitimacy of political outcomes (Barabas, 2004; Ferejohn, 2006; Fishkin, 1995; Rosenberg, 2007).

2. For concrete examples of these different strategies, see the "Deliberation, Discussion, and Debate" section of the PEP document supplement at http://www.carnegiefoundation.org/educating_for_democracy/docs/.

3. For more on the Urban Agenda, see document 11 in the PEP document supplement online at the address shown in note 2.

4. For examples of a few such simulations, see documents 13 and 14 in the PEP document supplement online.

5. For a description of the various parts of the social issue research portfolio, and for an example, see documents 26 and 56 in the PEP document supplement online. Also, for a description of a policy-oriented writing assignment in the Citizen Scholars Program at the University of Massachusetts at Amherst, see document 10.

6. For Battistoni's own description of the moderator and vibeswatcher roles, see document 8 in the PEP document supplement online.

7. For Tony Perry's description of this process, see document 11 in the PEP document supplement online.

8. For a description of these three components of the Service Opportunities in Leadership program, see document 21 in the PEP document supplement online.

9

LEARNING THROUGH POLITICAL RESEARCH AND ACTION PROJECTS

IN OUR STUDY of courses and programs in the Political Engagement Project, we observed two teaching strategies that may seem quite distinct but in fact often overlap or shade into each other: political research and political action projects. Political action projects usually include a research phase, and political research projects are frequently designed to inform and lay foundations for future action.

Connecting the two activities is a powerful way to prepare students for political participation. Responsible and effective political action depends on up-to-date information, thoughtful exploration of alternatives, planning, and strategic considerations—all of which require some form of research or factual inquiry. For this reason, the political action projects in the PEP generally include some type of conventional research component, such as developing position papers and policy memos, strategy proposals, background briefings, and the like. Similarly, we saw that carrying out a political research project in courses focused on political engagement often involves practicing or preparing for political action—the projects are often designed to inform policy or other political decisions, shape organizational directions and procedures, or persuade others to support their recommendations.

In keeping with the broad definition of *politics* guiding the courses and programs in the PEP, the political research and action projects we studied included community engagement with a systemic dimension, participation in the work of nonprofits dealing with social and public policy issues, collective efforts to create outcomes of public value, and conventional politics at the local, state, and national levels. Of course, these political research and action projects were undertaken in the spirit of academic integrity and open inquiry.[1] Within these broad parameters, the PEP courses and extracurricular programs included a great variety of projects.

Types of Research and Action Projects

Although we saw political research and action projects as modest as a single day's participation in a city council meeting, we focus here on the more intensive types because they are especially useful in deepening students' understanding of issues that interest them—or that they have never considered. They also help students gain a better sense of the complexity of politics and public policy, as well as develop a host of skills and motivations. Although the array of political research and action projects we observed in the PEP does not lend itself to an exhaustive typology, five project types capture important aspects of the range of approaches we saw: real-world political action, simulated political action, research on political organizations, research for a political organization or community group, and research on political issues and policies.

Real-World Political Action

Many political action projects involve students in some form of actual (as opposed to simulated) political activity on or beyond the campus. A great strength of real-world focused projects is that working to accomplish tangible outcomes can increase students' desire to learn the knowledge and skills they need to succeed.

Marshall Ganz says the on-the-ground political action project for his Harvard University course on community organizing is the "core," providing motivation that drives students' learning: "Students become committed to learning because they are committed to accomplishing a purpose." A student in the extracurricular program Democracy Matters similarly described the empowering motivation that can arise from undertaking political action that involves "doing" something as opposed to just "learning" something: "While the lobbying trip to the state capital obviously is a really great educational experience, we also feel like we're there to get something done. . . . We are not just spending the time because we want to learn. We're *doing* something. Of course, we're learning by experience but, more importantly, we're actually working toward achieving something."

PEP faculty and program leaders created opportunities for real-world political activity by inviting students to formulate action or by organizing the projects themselves.

STUDENT-FORMULATED ACTION PROJECTS. In many of the PEP courses and programs, students worked individually or in groups to plan and carry out their own political projects that illuminate important course ideas. In Rick Battistoni's Democratic Theory and Practice course at Providence College, for example, one group of students chose to address a perceived lack of democracy on their campus. They organized a forum bringing together representatives from the faculty senate, student congress, student affairs office, and academic administration to discuss possible ways to increase students' input into decision making.

FACULTY-ORGANIZED ACTION PROJECTS. In other courses, the class participates together in some form of faculty-designed collaborative action that complements course material. Faculty develop the broad outlines of the political activity, but in this general framework, students can often bring their own particular interests to the task. This approach is exemplified by the Urban Agenda project in Otto Feinstein and Tony Perry's introductory American government course at Wayne State University. For their course project, students work together in discussion sections to debate political issues facing their local communities and develop strategies for addressing them. Small groups create and present five- to ten-point political action agendas identifying the issues they want to address and how they want to address them. After a series of deliberations, the class reaches a consensus on a single agenda for political action. This is presented at an annual Urban Agenda convention, to which the university and local community are invited. It is often also used to interview local politicians.[2]

EXTRACURRICULAR ACTION PROJECTS. Most colleges offer a number of politically oriented extracurricular experiences, such as Young Democrats and Young Republicans, and many campus groups and organizations address specific policy issues relating to the environment, education, religious concerns, or global human rights. These groups often provide an overarching framework in which students can create and pursue action projects aligned with the group's broader political goals.

One advantage of extracurricular political experiences is that they are ongoing rather than bounded by the quarter or semester, making possible more sustained involvement over longer periods of time. Although students benefit from the opportunities that "extracurriculars" offer for autonomy and leadership, strong guidance from faculty or staff can greatly enhance their learning opportunities. For example, Democracy Matters has a strong mentoring component: in its work on pro-democracy reforms, especially campaign finance reform, staff in the program's central headquarters at

Colgate University train students from many colleges to be campus coordinators. Those students create and spearhead Democracy Matters chapters
on their own campuses, where they develop projects for building awareness
of campaign finance reform and trying to influence public policies.[3]

Simulated Political Action

We also observed political action projects that involved simulating or role-
playing various political activities. These projects were usually structured
by faculty or program staff, but students were responsible for carrying
them out. In the Sorensen Institute's College Leaders Program, for example, students participate in a mock Virginia legislative assembly, during
which they negotiate for legislation they previously formulated through
group research on policy issues. Similarly, students in a Model United
Nations course role-play the responsibilities of United Nations delegates,
preparing committee reports, position papers, and resolutions and negotiating for their positions at the annual Model United Nations conference.

In political learning, as in other educational domains, simulations can
offer some advantages over participation in real-world situations. First,
they often make it possible for students to experience aspects of the political process and try out roles and activities that would not otherwise be
available to them at this stage in their lives, like those of state legislators.
A second benefit is that the learning experience in simulations is more predictable, enabling faculty to gauge how to use them effectively to teach
important concepts and skills and carefully prepare students for the experience. Finally, these projects are not dependent on action taking place in
"real time," such as the period when the legislature or city council meets.

Research on Political Organizations

One model of political research focuses on helping students gain a deeper
understanding of how government or community organizations work.
These projects often require students to choose a group or agency, and
then to observe, read documents, and interview staff in order to develop
a detailed write-up about the organization.

In Dick Simpson's course The Future of Chicago, for example, students
conduct research projects in which they simulate being a member of a new
mayor's transition team. They write a report informing the incoming
mayor of everything he or she should know about a single unit of government in Chicago or Cook County, including its work, its relation to
other groups and agencies, its strengths and weaknesses, and so on.[4]

Although the primary purpose of this kind of project is to help students gain a more complex understanding of how politically related organizations work, their research sometimes offers the satisfaction of real-world political consequences if it is used to shape the ideas and decisions of the organization or elected officials and their staff, as Simpson's students' reports often are.

Research for a Political Organization or Community Group

Some faculty develop projects that involve research designed to serve the needs of a community group or a government agency, which can include collecting and analyzing original empirical data or undertaking secondary research compiling existing information. In many cases, students design their research in collaboration with the organization, sometimes as part of a placement (often described as "research service learning" or "community-based research"). A student in Ross Cheit's Children and Public Policy course at Brown University, for example, was placed with the program evaluator for the Rhode Island Department of Children, Youth, and Families. The student was asked to write a report collecting and summarizing data on the relationship between academic achievement, school attendance, and recidivism of former juvenile offenders. This kind of project had real value to the organization and therefore was very satisfying to the student, who planned to continue his research after the course ended.

Research on Political Issues and Policies

Many courses seeking to educate for political understanding and engagement require students to conduct conventional library and Internet-based research on one or more public policy issues, individually or in groups. Students often produce written policy briefs or papers and may also present their findings orally. Research projects of this sort are sometimes used in conjunction with placements to deepen students' understanding of related policy issues and to connect the placement experience to academic learning. In the course that completes Duke's Service Opportunities in Leadership program, for example, students create a "social issue research portfolio" with several components: a research essay on a policy issue related to students' summer internships; an interview with a practitioner working in a relevant area of policy; and a policy recommendation memo that identifies key players and underlying structures, considers existing policies and policy options, and makes recommendations for action based on their analyses of viable options.[5]

Rewards of Research and Action Activities

Because these two teaching strategies are multifaceted and intersect with other key pedagogies of political teaching and learning, they can be deeply engaging for students and contribute to many goals of political development. Specifically, we saw that students' participation in research and action projects yielded a stronger base of political knowledge and understanding, and an array of political skills, particularly in research, writing, and critical thinking; communication; strategic thinking; collaborative work; and leadership. The students' participation in research and action projects also strengthened their political motivation, supported integrative learning, and enhanced their core academic learning. Perhaps most important, political action projects give students a taste of political engagement in action. As one Democracy Matters student commented about his political action project: "Now I have a more realistic sense of what politics is like . . . whereas before it was more impressionistic. . . . It's become striking to me how much harder a lot of things are than I may have originally expected. But there is a logical route from point A to B. Talking with people about how they passed the smoking ban or how they passed the bottle return bill. Those things took forever. They seem like these little meat-and-potatoes issues, but they take on a political life of their own and seeing that has been very instructive."

Deeper Political Knowledge and Understanding

Political research projects provide opportunities to develop a strong command of the knowledge base around particular policy issues or institutions, and action projects can help students learn political content and give them more nuanced understandings of political processes and institutions. In addition, the capacity of projects to connect theory and other academic knowledge with practice can solidify understanding of both. For example, students in Jim Farr's University of Minnesota course Practicing Democratic Education commented that applying the democratic theory they were learning in class to a practice setting through their Public Achievement projects made this one of the most effective courses they took in college.

A student in Democracy Matters echoed this point, emphasizing the intellectual synergies between coursework and his extracurricular involvement in political action projects. This kind of valuable integration of learning across the academic and student life divide is all too rare: "As a political science major, I've looked at a lot of these issues—not just campaign finance reform—from an academic perspective. . . . Democracy Matters is a very positive complement to that because it asks you to practice those beliefs and ideals."

Stronger Political Skills

Political skill-building is one of the greatest benefits students identify from their PEP experiences. As a student of the Sorensen Institute's College Leaders Program said, "I feel like I know how, if I want to get involved, I would know where to go, how to get involved. . . . I didn't know that before." Political research and action projects are one of the best ways to learn political skills, through practice, in context, with informative feedback. As Ganz says of the organizing projects in his course, "Without projects, there would be no skills learning. . . . Projects bring the whole thing alive."

RESEARCH, WRITING, AND CRITICAL THINKING. Political research projects enlist many broad-based intellectual skills: reviewing, evaluating, and synthesizing published scholarship or empirical studies, collecting and analyzing original data, interviewing experts on the issue under consideration, and communicating the findings both orally and in writing. At some institutions, these powerful academic dimensions can help political engagement work receive support from administrative leaders. At Duke University, for example, the president and deans identified research service learning as a priority for undergraduate education across the disciplines.

In democratic politics, the ability and inclination to investigate an issue before acting on it provides the basis for informed and responsible engagement. A student in Brian Murphy's Politics of San Francisco course underscored that political research projects can enhance informed engagement by helping participants feel "prepared to find out what I need to know about community issues." As he put it, the course "gave me a comprehensive sense of how to do research, how to find information about the community and community issues, how to see issues through others' eyes, not just my own. This was the first project of this kind I had done."

Useful political research need not involve writing a twenty-five-page report. Farr emphasizes that small-scale, informal fact-finding missions can stem from recognizing that "there is a broader world out there that deserves our attention and inquiry" and that "views of politics are informed by facts and points of view." Farr wants students to learn how to investigate the broader political world through basic research like "using the Internet, making phone calls, and so on."

COMMUNICATION. Communication skills are among the most frequently noted outcomes of political research and action projects. To carry out the projects, students must often use discussion and deliberative skills: articulate positions clearly, make cogent arguments for them, be persuasive in other ways, and listen carefully to others. These skills are broadly valuable across life experiences as well as for effective political engagement. Research and action projects can also help students learn strategic skills and an array of specific political skills, such as formulating issue agendas, lobbying, writing policy briefs or speeches, and obtaining press attention for their work.

Farr stresses the interconnections among the collaborative and communication skills undergraduates gain from coaching younger students on action projects, which is a key component of the Public Achievement Program at the University of Minnesota. A central goal is to help students practice a host of deliberative and action skills through "learning by doing." Farr underscores that skills gained through Public Achievement projects enhance students' abilities to engage in meaningful public action. Deliberating, listening, asking questions, negotiating and compromising, are essential for any form of democratic decision making because "all of our interests cannot be realized as we individuals wish them, but we must compromise. It's not about giving up one's authenticity, it's part of negotiation."

And because of the importance of negotiation and persuasion in working on political goals, skills of public speaking are also crucial—being able, as Farr says, to "wrangle an argument and turn a phrase." Public speaking is extremely difficult for most people—many identify it as one of their major fears—so Farr tries to create many opportunities for students to practice speaking before a group.

STRATEGIC THINKING. In addition to these kinds of foundational communication skills, research and action projects can foster students' abilities to think strategically and formulate realistic goals—"to sort out what is and isn't politically realistic," as students from Duke University put it. Farr describes strategic thinking as a critical complement to other skill sets; to recognize the power dimensions of politics and to prevent deliberation from being no more than "happy talk," students need to "see how steps lead to a certain end," even though strategic thinking can remove some of the "rosy glow" from idealistic goals.

COLLABORATIVE WORK. When students work together with peers on their projects or collaborate with members of the community, they also learn many teamwork and group process skills so important for many forms of political engagement. In addition to skills gained working together with fellow classmates or group members, some PEP programs help students learn tools of collective political action involved in building alliances with other organizations around shared agendas. Democracy Matters students describe using these alliance-building skills when working on campaign finance issues:

> I put a good amount of effort into the group and getting to know other organizations. For instance, being able to have a close tie with the woman who is president of the League of Women Voters in Mankato and getting them involved in our second event. And having a close tie with another organization called Minnesota Alliance for Progressive Action and knowing one of the members from there. . . . And just having these nonprofit organizations that are really well-known in Minnesota be a sponsor on our events. I think my effort of talking to these people face-to-face and on the phone, instead of just e-mailing or leaving a message, is bringing the student organizations to know the local community organizations. . . . Most of our group can now contact the League of Women Voters and also other organizations in the area. We can collaborate. That was one thing I was happy about.

Action projects can also lead students to collaborate with people different from themselves. Knowing how to do this is extremely valuable for democratic participation, given the increasing diversity of the United States, the press of globalization, and the polarization of electoral politics. When students participate in courses and programs that are diverse in political ideology, ethnicity, class, or other dimensions, they often remark on how much they learn about ways to cooperate and bridge those gaps in order to work together productively. Indeed, some students spoke of the opportunity to work with students whose views ranged across the political spectrum as particularly eye-opening and inspiring. Another student in Democracy Matters talked about forming an alliance around campaign finance reform with a more politically conservative organization:

> We got to work with people we don't usually work with, which was also nice. Especially, we worked with a group called USINPAC, which, nationally, is a right-wing organization designed to improve the military relationship between India and the United States. . . . You're working with a bunch of kids who care about something, and that's special. That's something to be cherished. In this case, we were working with

a particular ethnic group [Indian-Americans], which was really interesting for us. And it was something where we teamed up. We cospon-
sored this event and I thought, I don't want to have anything to do
with these people's [other political goals], but on a personal level,
they're very nice, they're very interesting, they're very committed.

Students' powerful teamwork experiences in their PEP courses and programs can influence *how* they can imagine getting involved in politics in
the future as well as *whether* they can imagine political involvement. A
student of Meta Mendel-Reyes at Berea College, who was already quite
politically aware before the course, said that she would now be much
more inclined to work with a group than to act individually, and she
would even be interested in becoming a "core leader, not just a member
of the group." Our survey results confirmed that many students had significantly shifted their willingness to work together with political groups
after completing their PEP experiences.

LEADERSHIP. Participating in political action projects can also help students learn how to discern common interests and motivate others to do
their part, skills central to leadership in multiple domains. Ganz's course
on organizing involves readings and discussions in which students think
about the role of political values, goals, and personal stories in motivating others for collective political action: "It's about becoming articulate
about your own moral sources, and not only what empowers you, but
also what allows you to engage others more clearly. This unleashes an
enormous amount of energy. . . . This last week there was a breakthrough
moment when people realized that the way you move others is not by
going to universal claims, but by getting to particulars about what moves
people. Then people have more access to you than if you just say, 'I'm for
justice.'"

Sometimes helping students develop concrete leadership skills involves
confronting discomfort with leadership: some young people are reluctant
to try to lead or exert authority over their peers. Adam Weinberg comments on the need to help students see that sometimes taking leadership
is a practical necessity for accomplishing political goals:

> Most students come into Democracy Matters with zero political
> skills. . . . What they're really poor at and struggle with the most is
> the task of organizing their peers. And we work a lot on really simple
> things like how do you hold a meeting. It sounds silly but it's one
> of the most important things they need to do, and they don't know
> how to do it. We use a model that may be a little more authoritarian,
> not because we think that's the only right way to do it but because our

students are really brought up with the idea that "no one should be in a position of power." But somebody's got to organize it, and they have a tendency to bring people together in a room and say "What do you want to talk about?" and no one talks about anything. So we need to get them to understand that structure is OK.

Stronger Political Motivation

Political research and action projects, especially those that include opportunities for real-world political action and influence, speak to many important dimensions of political motivation from political interest to hope and inspiration. Gerald Shenk and David Takacs use historically informed political projects as the centerpiece of their course on the environmental history of California at California State University, Monterey Bay.[6] They use these research and action projects to build students' sense of political efficacy and politically engaged identity: "Getting students to see themselves as political actors is the best way to develop their efficacy, their sense that they can do something politically. And once they have taken action, they see themselves differently—as someone who takes action and who can act. Seeing yourself in action is important, and so is seeing yourself as part of a group in action."

Likewise, Adam Weinberg talks about the impact that Democracy Matters can have on motivating students. Often young people remain politically inactive either because "they don't know what it means to get active, no one's modeled it for them, they don't have parents who are active, and so on" or because they're cynical "they don't believe it's going to make a difference." Democracy Matters works hard to "get them excited that they can really make our country democratic. . . . All you have to do is get someone active once, and once they take that first political action then they get 'bit by the bug.'"

Interviews with Democracy Matters students affirm Weinberg's perceptions about the impact that engaging in political action projects can have. For example, one student said, "The more effort we put in, the more we want to go out and do it some more. It's a system of positive feedback. . . . The more effort we put in, the more fun and gratifying it is, and so we keep going."

More Integrative Learning

Integrating learning across content areas, contexts, and time is essential for deep understanding, creativity, and persistence of learning and is widely understood to lie at the heart of a high-quality college education, but it is often elusive without guidance (Huber and Hutchings, 2004). Research and action projects are well-suited to creating linkages between multiple components and political learning goals, and many faculty rely on them for that purpose. Alma Blount, director of Duke's Service Opportunities in Leadership program, uses the Social Issue Research Portfolio in the final course to weave together the program's summer internship placements with its coursework: "Students have to identify a social issue that came up in their summer experience, frame it into a coherent problem, investigate it, and create a leadership policy memo. . . . Through this, all the students are involved with direct experience, discussion, and research—the process makes the connections for them. Otherwise, [the summer internship] would just be community service."

Enhanced Core Academic Learning

One of the great strengths of high-quality education for political engagement is that it does not require sacrificing other academic goals and can often contribute significantly to students' academic motivation and accomplishment. A student in Brian Murphy's course talked about how her research and action project heightened her interest in statistics:

> Numerical analysis was hard for me. Working on the project with this group helped me on that. . . . I love political theory, but political statistics is tough. I had to learn to focus. It's just like in sports—I love to hit, but if I want to play I have to learn the whole game. And others were there to help me. In other classes, statistics were not engaging, but here they were. They were real—not just a math problem in a book. It is really satisfying to work on your weakness, and the people I was working with made all the difference.

Likewise, a student in Takacs and Shenk's course talked about how the course's political research–action project changed her perspective not only on political engagement but also on the importance of historical research. She "never liked history" in the past, "I hated it in high school and never thought it was valuable. This project made me realize how crucial it is to understand the history of an issue before you become politically active; to make you more effective, to know what you're really fighting for."

Strategies for Effective Political Research and Action Projects

Although the research and action projects we saw used in the Political Engagement Project were thoughtful, innovative, and substantive, we realized that the gains in student learning and political engagement—knowledge, skills, motivation, and participation—were also the result of the faculty's approach to teaching or their pedagogical skills.

From our interviews and observations, we extracted seven "ground rules" for making the most of research and action projects:

1. *Be clear.* Tell students from the outset about your learning goals, process, standards, and the challenges of the project.
2. *Be realistic.* Help students choose a project that is both right for them and "doable."
3. *Monitor progress.* Provide feedback, coaching, and trouble-shooting; help students change direction when their projects are going offtrack.
4. *Encourage reflection.* Help students be reflective about both the process and substance of their projects.
5. *Go public.* Find ways to make projects public—to classmates, the campus, or the community.
6. *Make it enjoyable.* Help students have fun with their projects.
7. *Connect.* Where possible, connect the research or action projects with a national program.

Be Clear

When faculty or program leaders clearly identify the learning goals and how they believe projects will help students achieve those outcomes, students learn more from the projects. Greg Werkheiser is just one of many PEP leaders who stressed the value of this kind of transparency, or not "hiding the ball." He notes: "We tell the students what we're doing while we're doing it with them. So instead of just saying, 'Here's this culminating project, go to it,' we talk about where we think the project fits in terms of the scheme of civic education. We talk about what we intend for them to get out of it so that they understand that and can measure their own progress, not just in terms of how many pages they've written but in terms of our big picture goals. During the first two days . . . we lay it all out for them."

Clearly formulating goals and relating them to teaching methods and assignments not only helps students see where things are heading but also makes the teaching more reflective and intentional. Ganz described the process of creating a training manual for teaching assistants as a major advance in making learning goals more visible to everyone involved with his course. This involved being explicit about the pedagogies being used and why they are important.

In research or action projects that involve collaboration with a community partner, the community organization needs to be clear about what the project will entail from their end, what the student's role will be, and how these elements intersect with features the faculty and student consider essential from an educational standpoint. This requires clear communication, which can be facilitated by an ongoing relationship between the faculty member and the organization, and in some cases, by written contracts laying out the expectations for all parties.[7]

Be Realistic

Although political action and research projects can be successful when faculty assign topics they think are likely to yield good results, many courses and programs encourage students to find projects that intrigue them or excite their passion. Using a structured process to help students explore their interests and design viable projects can be very helpful. In Takacs and Shenk's course, students build up slowly to their historically informed political projects, gradually honing their conceptions of political action and the connection with their personal concerns. In the end, as Shenk noted, "Students love that they are able to pursue what they are passionate about."

Ganz's course also uses a deliberate process to help students shape their projects, including discussions that help students "anchor" their projects in their values and convictions, including their own histories with the issues: "As students go through the process of selecting their organizing project, we force them to do it with intentionality. A genealogy or archaeology emerges, where you are eventually getting people to talk about their experiences. . . . The success of the course depends on the extent to which we can help people align a project with their values."

Shaping the focus of group projects can be somewhat more complicated because it involves working together to find common ground—a project that, as much as possible, all can care about and believe in. Some PEP faculty ask students to be self-consciously democratic in creating the project design and then to reflect on the process as well as implement the project itself.[8]

Another important part of helping students design projects that are educationally valuable is working with them to define a realistic scope based on the time and resources available. Ganz, for example, helps students identify clear and well-defined methods and outcomes for their community organizing efforts: "There is a whole process of discerning what you can hope for by the end of the semester—somewhere between holding one meeting and achieving world peace. An important part of the learning is understanding the relationship between the significant and the doable."

Weinberg stresses the same point. Although subject to less severe time constraints than course projects, extracurricular projects must also be doable: It's "not getting 'clean money' [campaign-finance reform] in Albany next year, but changing the view of one or two Assembly members.'"

Monitor Progress

Students usually learn most from political action and research projects when faculty, program leaders, or skilled teaching assistants monitor their progress, offer personalized feedback frequently along the way, and help them make adjustments when the project seems to be going seriously off-track. As Weinberg suggests, a pedagogy of "coaching" that combines political action with ongoing feedback can work in much the same way as an athletic coach shapes the performance of his or her athletes.

It is also commonplace in the PEP courses and programs to include structured ways for students to provide guidance and feedback to each other, generally under faculty supervision.[9] Peer feedback can be especially valuable, because students learn a great deal from the careful evaluation of each other's work as well as from their fellow students when they present and receive comments on their projects.

For the social issues research project at Duke University's Service Opportunities in Leadership program, students' consultation with and presentations to peers is a key part of the learning. Students work together on thematically related portfolios as each develops his or her individual project. Then the group teaches a two-hour class around the theme, which may involve creative presentations such as a panel discussion, for example, or a series of presentations followed by a general discussion of crosscutting themes. Alma Blount encourages the group to really critique the students' presentations: "I tell them, 'Don't be too polite. Let people know if they are not being clear or if you don't buy their assumptions or analyses.'"

Ganz's course also uses a structured process to help students evaluate their projects. One method is reflection papers that help students examine their action projects through conceptual lenses drawn from the course. A second method is "midstream interventions" designed to help students adapt or shift direction when the project is struggling: "We use the midterm paper [and presentations] as a place to make an argument about whether the project is working or not. This is very useful because it forces students to reflect on their own and then readjust. . . . Students are supported in making the evaluation feel less like a judgment and more like useful information. We have to deal with people's defensiveness, and the presentation really helps."

These and other kinds of group debriefing or reflection sessions can help integrate learning and also provide a valuable opportunity for troubleshooting, maintaining morale, and sharing insights and tips for running a successful project. As one student pointed out, there is a risk that, without careful attention, debriefing sessions can turn into "gripe sessions," which are much less helpful for students. Skillful leadership from faculty, teaching assistants, or self-monitoring from students is usually needed to help shift the conversation in a constructive direction when it begins to degenerate into a litany of complaints. This is a way in which awareness of group process itself becomes important.

Encourage Reflection

Encouraging students to reflect on the *process* of political action can also be an important learning experience. In the Public Achievement projects in Farr's course, students use a democratic process to establish rules of behavior in the group. Students first consider the theoretical notions of liberty or freedom—that "you are free insofar as you make the laws that you live by"—then they "establish their own rules and commit them to paper," and finally they hold each other accountable for following them. Farr sees attending to the democratic process of establishing and maintaining group norms as an important source of learning for both political understanding and political skills.

Go Public

Making projects public can increase students' motivation to remain engaged in public life. This can take many forms, ranging from acknowledging the value of the projects and the hard work that went into them, to sharing the substance of the projects with classmates, to actual implementation of recommendations by an agency or organization. For faculty like Murphy, this public dimension is an essential feature of research and action projects: "All of the projects have to be conceived of as public interventions—competent to be shared in a public setting, not just a class. So if they're doing a demographic analysis of a neighborhood, they have to figure out how they're going to share it with the politicians running for office in that district or creating a document viable in the community-based planning process. They're creating something that is a public document, not simply a university document."

A student in Cheit's course conducted interviews with young people in the juvenile detention facility as part of a larger report to the facility. This student, like many others with whom we spoke, found it extremely gratifying that her research had real significance: "[Working on the report] allowed me to leave the class with a much more optimistic outlook, because it not only looked at what was wrong with the current system but it made real-life, concrete recommendations for how to improve the system for the people affected by it."

In other cases, making students' work public is more modest: thoughtful acts of explicit recognition from faculty can bolster students' enthusiasm. A young man in the Sorensen Institute's intensive summer program described how memorable it was to have the groups' projects publicly celebrated by program leaders: "At the end of the program, when cumulative projects were due, I wasn't the happiest person. . . . I was just kind of frustrated. . . . Then we went to 'graduation' the next day, and Greg Werkheiser [the director] spoke, and he's such a great speaker, and my family was there and I felt really, really proud. And the way Greg described everything we'd done. Now I feel I wouldn't change anything."

Make It Enjoyable

If done right, research and action projects can be really fun for students, and this has value far beyond students' short-term enjoyment. Research from Wendy Rahn (2000) and others suggests that promoting students' motivation for political engagement requires imparting a sense of playfulness as well as passion about politics: what students really need to learn about politics is "a love of the game and a sense of sportsmanship." If they do that, the question of whether they are making a difference with each specific act is less central and their sense of political efficacy can better weather the inevitable defeats all politically engaged people face. Students can especially enjoy engaging deeply with topics they really care about and sharing their passion with peers. Alma Blount notes that many of her students describe their research projects as "the most fun they've ever had at Duke." She thinks this is because students are choosing an issue "they are passionate about" and "know from the beginning [of the project] that they will be teaching the others about those issues."

Weinberg suggested that having fun with the work of Democracy Matters is a key mechanism for overcoming students' initial cynicism:

> [We try to overcome students' cynicism with] two things. One is with the truth—get them to understand that they are absolutely right that they are not going to change every law and make the United States

fully democratic in the next six months. It ain't gonna happen. . . . It's never happened—even in the civil rights movement. A lot of what we do is just relay history to them so they understand that it's a slow, fun process. . . . [And we] get them to understand that this is fun and just something that you do.

Connect

Embedding particular curricular or extracurricular projects into a larger or national effort can provide structure, resources, and a reference group for participating students, along with a sense of continuity and stability in the effort to accomplish the project's goals. This is very important for programs like the Model United Nations, where each course or campus group is one piece of a larger mosaic. Being part of the national structure gives students a sense of being part of something larger than their local effort, increasing their excitement, stamina, and sense of competence.

Students in Democracy Matters mentioned the value of the national character of their program and the enjoyment gained from "the feeling of being part of a broader coalition and the concrete benefits that provides," including being able to do things like "attend the annual conference . . . and hear from other students who are involved." Another Democracy Matters student appreciated being part of a well-established national group: "I've always wanted to get involved in politics but I never knew how to start or where to start from. This was an already established platform. I was easily drawn to it, and they made it clear there would be a lot of support if I had any questions, and a lot of help and a lot of knowledge. So I was drawn to it and knew it would be good."

Challenges of Using Research and Action Projects

Like any ambitious and demanding activity, political research and action projects come with inherent challenges. Some of these challenges are typical of active-learning pedagogies; others are particular to taking political action in the real world. As PEP faculty insights and our observation suggest, students' lack of preparation, their uneven levels of commitment, time pressures, and unrealistic expectations can undermine the most well-intentioned, well-designed projects. In addition, helping students maintain interest and motivation in the wake of unsuccessful outcomes is critical if they are going to hold on to what they have learned despite feelings of disappointment, frustration, or even failure. We also learned from the PEP faculty and students that, fortunately, many of these challenges can themselves become productive learning experiences if they are handled well.

Lack of Preparation

Political research and action projects focused on political engagement are not a familiar part of the academic or extracurricular landscape, so the PEP courses and programs are likely to be students' first experience with them. This confirms the importance of these opportunities, but it also indicates that students need a lot of scaffolding and coaching in order to gain the skills they need and learn to be effective. Even political research projects require skills many students do not have, especially if they involve collecting information in one or more communities. Blount comments on the lack of adequate preparation for research projects even among students at highly selective institutions like Duke University: "The Social Issue Research Portfolio project requires them to develop Web research skills. When they come in, the students don't really know how to do Web research but they think they do, so we team up with the librarian to help them with that. They get a lot of critical feedback on their projects as well as training on how to do policy memos in connection with these research projects."

Uneven Commitment, or "Collective Action Problems"

Group projects often involve uneven participation. Several students noted that even the logistics of finding mutually convenient times to sit down and talk about a project was difficult, often because some participants in the group did not make the project a high priority. As one faculty member lamented, "Some students just don't work very hard. . . . I had a couple of students last semester that really were not pulling their weight and that was really hard to deal with."

PEP faculty often use this kind of problem as an avenue into ethical issues of responsibility and fairness. As Mendel-Reyes said about her Berea College students, "They realize that people are depending on their work." Likewise, Farr noted: "There are duties and responsibilities that students owe each other in terms of attendance. They owe it to each other and to the group [of middle-schoolers] they're coaching. This raises ideas of accountability, attentiveness, openness to ideas—these are political and ethical qualities we try to teach. In the learning-by-doing of coaching, we try to pass this on. If students miss sessions, we have to show them what they are doing and what the implications are. Younger kids remember the things you do and do not do."

For some students, their peers' lack of commitment, although frustrating, can spur them to take on a greater leadership role, revealing that action projects can sometimes foster leadership capacities in unplanned ways. A student in Murphy's course on the politics of San Francisco commented: "People would say they would show up and then wouldn't. I wasn't appointed as leader, but the person who was chosen was not up to the challenge so I just became the leader. . . . People contacted me when they couldn't make it. I just did what I could to get through."

A Democracy Matters student also described assuming a leadership role and trying to set an example for less responsible students through his own strong commitment: "Sometimes I feel like I'm one of the few that is really fired up for it. It's very hard to get something to work when it's just you that's working on it. It's also good when they see that I'm really trying. . . . It's going to show them that I'm really dedicated to it, and next time, they will see how serious I am. And at the meeting, I'll tell them, 'Don't sign up for anything if you're not really going to do it. I'm not trying to work with little kids.'"

Time Pressures

Time constraints make it hard for students to complete meaningful research and action projects within the time frame of short courses and programs. The process of developing, implementing, and reporting on projects often must be telescoped into a short period of time. This is one reason why multicourse programs and extracurriculars can offer special benefits for promoting political engagement.

In our survey, we found that, for some students, the short duration of their research and action projects limited their value—some projects felt too short to lead to deep learning or any sense of mastery. This was the case for some students in the Youth Urban Agenda Forum in Feinstein's American government course. As one student said, he felt he needed to have more experience: "I'd need to have more discussions and more questions that required me to analyze and provide feedback about these things," and that he thought there "should have been things like [the Forum for debating political issues] the whole time."

To deal with this challenge, faculty try to plan and monitor project design and implementation carefully, helping students shape projects well-suited to the time available. The pressure to act quickly is not entirely a bad thing, however. In the political realm, it is sometimes possible to plan action slowly and deliberately, but there are also times when a need or opportunity arises unexpectedly and one needs to take fast-paced, imperfect action. With this in mind, Murphy tries to make a virtue of necessity in the way he frames the time limitations for his students:

> Time limitation plays a salutary destructiveness at some level. People
> have to learn the limits of what they think they know. And I mean that

affectionately. We've had people who really know survey research data management stuff, for instance, and they can't get that kind of project done in a semester. You just don't have the time. So the question is, what's another version of it that's not as analytically pure that would be useful. And so, I think those are very useful in thinking through— "What can I get done practically that's intellectually viable and still get it done?" It forces people to wrestle with the applicability or utility of what they think they've learned. And not to become skeptics, but just to become realists—"I know how to do all these fancy statistics. . . . OK, how do I use it?"

Some faculty address time constraints by arranging for interested students to continue their projects after completion of the course. Indeed, many students with whom we spoke were doing just that, a testament to the value students find in this kind of work.

Unrealistic Expectations

As we noted in our discussion of political efficacy, students can become overwhelmed, discouraged, or disappointed when they undertake the kinds of activities involved in political action projects. The issues they are trying to influence may simply be too large for them to see that they are contributing to meaningful change. The passion and enthusiasm they have for the cause or candidate may not be widely shared in the community. The realities of the political process are often unpleasant.

Sometimes the scope of the social problems students are trying to confront through their small-scale projects is overwhelming. Takacs found this to be an issue for some of the students in his Social and Environmental History of California course at California State University, Monterey Bay: "We want to link students' commitment to issues—such as children's issues—to action and reality, in systems of power, to understand what are the systemic forces that make children poor in Salinas or make soil erode in Salinas. And sometimes they see how unfair the world is and the more they dig into that the more they realize how big the problem is, and that can feel very dispiriting."

Faculty use two key strategies to address this demoralization and prevent students from giving up. The first is to give students realistic expectations about what they can hope to accomplish within the limits of their projects. The second is to help students learn to take pleasure and pride in the process of action, in the incremental progress they are able to make. Peer support, debriefings, and opportunities to share their experiences help students work through their feelings of discouragement and maintain their stamina.

One of Farr's students said she and many other students had "grandiose visions" when they began their action projects. Working through her initial disappointment involved a gradual attitude adjustment rather than an "aha" moment of saying "OK, today I'm going to stop being disappointed about this." She described this process as a kind of "acclimation" and as "growing like a team should" that was assisted by weekly debriefing sessions in which students "could talk about issues we wanted to bring up, problems, disappointments. . . . It helped to know that others were also going through similar frustrations." Students can find their lack of expertise and disappointment more tolerable if they are given ongoing support and coaching during their projects.

Unsuccessful Outcomes

Sometimes the problem is not that the students have only a limited amount of time to make a difference or that they expect more far-reaching changes. Sometimes the project simply does not lead to any change. The legislature votes the other way. The city council has a more pressing agenda, and the effort is tabled. The candidate for whom the students are campaigning loses. When the inevitable happens, faculty need to be ready to help students hold onto not only the motivation they developed but also the skills and knowledge they worked so hard to gain.

To protect against the demoralizing effect of disappointing outcomes, Feinstein recommends that "you have to bring it back and then work with the students to evaluate what happened. You don't want to lose them. . . . You have to show them that they have the ability to address issues and then lose and come back and refine their approach and move forward."

Faculty can guide students in framing the definition of success differently, so that they have a sense of accomplishment even if they do not achieve their most significant goals. Shenk talks about this strategy as a way to counter discouragement in his students at California State University, Monterey Bay: "Another student concerned with the Salinas River and pollution runoff got a group of stakeholders together to talk about it. That student didn't solve the problem of runoff but he felt a great deal of pride and sense of accomplishment for the effort and progress he did make. This illustrates an important point. This student didn't achieve his ultimate goals but was satisfied with the first, successful step he did take. All big projects must be taken incrementally. That's what politics is like. This is a very valuable lesson."

Another way to maintain stamina in the face of seeming defeat is to help students make an honest assessment of what they might have done differently. Shenk and Takacs try to focus their discussions on tangible strategies for what the students might do next time, and they also ask students what is likely to happen if they just give up.

A Democracy Matters student said this kind of concrete reevaluation can breathe new life into flagging spirits: "The staff helped us to see how to have efficient tactics. Like they taught us how to make flyers that really stand out and attract people's attention, even little events like showing political movies. Because sometimes, you'll just be like, 'This is tiring; it feels like we're not really getting anywhere,' but you actually are. The only way to really notice what's going on is by thinking about what you've done and coming out more efficient with it, more fresh, with something that will keep it fun."

NOTES

1. For examples, see the "Research/Action Projects and Simulations" section of the PEP document supplement at http://www.carnegiefoundation.org/educating_for_democracy/docs/.

2. For Perry's description of the Urban Agenda, see document 11 in the PEP document supplement online at the address shown in note 1.

3. For more information on Democracy Matters and the role of the campus coordinator, see documents 27, 28, and 29 in the PEP document supplement online.

4. For Simpson's instructions for this report, and for a model, see documents 19 and 20 in the PEP document supplement online.

5. For a more detailed description of the Social Issue Research Portfolio, and for excerpts from a completed portfolio, see documents 26 and 56 in the PEP document supplement online.

6. For more on the Historically Informed Political Project, see documents 17 and 18 in the PEP document supplement online.

7. For examples of two such written contracts, see documents 30 and 37 in the PEP document supplement online. For a note about expectations that the Service Opportunities in Leadership program provides to host organizations, see document 34.

8. For a description of an intentionally democratic group project, see document 15 in the PEP document supplement online. For an example of a student group's report based on the project, see document 54.

9. For an example of one such structured venue for peer feedback, see document 18 in the PEP document supplement online.

LEARNING THROUGH
SPEAKERS AND MENTORS

IF AN IMPORTANT GOAL of a course or program is to promote political engagement, when and under what circumstances can interactions with outside speakers or mentors help? How should political practitioners or others of political relevance be chosen, and what purposes does their participation serve? In what ways can they enhance the understanding, motivation, and skills of political engagement? What do faculty have to do to prepare the political practitioners, and to prepare their students so that they are confident those aims will be realized? These are issues that faculty and staff need to address when they call on individuals external to the course or program to participate in some way.

Both faculty teaching academic courses and staff who oversee extracurricular programs have found that connecting students with individuals who are especially knowledgeable about, experienced in, or passionate about some aspect of politics can be helpful to student learning—especially their political understanding and motivation—in ways not accomplished by readings and class discussions. Most often, faculty invite these political actors to visit for one class session to speak about their experiences or issues of particular concern to them and to interact with students. Sometimes invited speakers or mentors visit the course or program several times or have more sustained interaction with students.

In other cases, students visit the practitioners in their offices to get a feel for the speaker's institutional context or learn about the work of an agency, branch of government, or other organization from several firsthand perspectives. The Engalitcheff Institute, which brings students to Washington, D.C., for the summer, calls these visits "site briefings." Students find these visits exciting and learn a great deal from them. One student said that site briefings were "one of the best parts of the program, I think, because most interns don't get to do that. We went to the White House, the Federal Reserve—and with the Federal Reserve we sat in the Board of Governors' room and had one of the governors speak to us. We went to Capitol Hill and had representatives from five different states talk to us. Things like that, where you really get a feel for what D.C. life is and you get to see each of the different parts of government—it was tailored for our interests."

Among the twenty-one courses and programs we studied, all but four involved at least one brief interaction with a political speaker. About a third incorporated political speakers in a relatively modest way, perhaps inviting a single political speaker to class or requiring students to attend one political talk on campus. A third of the faculty provided opportunities for students to listen to or engage with political figures somewhat more extensively than listening to one political talk, and three of the courses and programs specialized in using political speakers as a major component of students' learning. A few engaged politically knowledgeable and active figures to serve as something like short-term mentors to students in the context of the course or program.

The range of political experience speakers and mentors bring to the courses and programs with which they engage is extremely varied, reflecting the broad definition of *political engagement* that informs these programs. Speakers and mentors include elected and appointed officials; community activists; staff of nonprofit organizations; civil servants at local, state, and federal levels; and interested parties in policy debates.

Rewards of Involving Political Speakers and Mentors

Involving outside speakers in a course or program can provide specific kinds of learning about political institutions, processes, and issues—learning that is qualitatively different from the knowledge and understanding students gain through reading. Having the opportunity to speak or interact directly with an individual who currently is working in the political or policy arena makes very concrete and real what otherwise seems to students like a distant abstraction. Speakers almost always tell stories as well as share their knowledge, and this narrative approach, if the stories are compelling and engaging, makes the material particularly memorable.

Class sessions with invited speakers are usually designed to be very interactive so that students' questions and comments help shape the conversation, which is directed to their special interests and concerns. And speakers often connect with students in ways that feel quite personal.

They can be role models—helping to motivate and inspire students and showing them what they could become or do.

In some ways, what students gain from mentors is quite similar to what they gain from good speakers: inspiration, models of political participation and commitment, understanding of both content and process. But mentors can also offer a different kind of guidance and support, because they connect with students one-on-one over a longer period of time. Faculty and staff in the PEP stressed three key purposes that outside speakers and mentors can serve: enhancing political understanding, increasing political motivation, and building skills of deliberation.

Enhanced Political Understanding

Deepening students' knowledge and understanding of various aspects of politics is always a key aim for faculty, and it is often the goal they think of first when they invite practitioners into their courses or connect students with mentors. Instructors want students to gain understanding about many dimensions of politics and they choose guests who bring to the class a rich background of knowledge and experience. Outside speakers and mentors can be especially helpful in the following four areas of political understanding.

A MORE REALISTIC VIEW. A common goal of faculty teaching for political understanding is for their students to understand better the various processes involved in electoral politics, policymaking and implementation, and grassroots political action. Entering students often bring a schematized and overly simple understanding of political institutions and the political process, and faculty are eager for them to learn more about how politics "really works."

Rick Semiatin, for example, in his class on American politics, part of the Washington Semester program at American University, stresses that a major goal of his course is for students to understand that politics in Washington is messy. They do not come to see this simply by reading, though some carefully selected readings can contribute to this understanding and offer a valuable complement to the visiting speakers. His students hear and talk with a large number of people engaged in the messy business of politics, and the kaleidoscope of their perspectives reinforces lessons that might not otherwise take hold. The practitioners tell stories about politics as it is in Washington, and their stories enable the students to understand how key aspects of our political system, such as the separation of powers, actually work in practice and what can happen when they are threatened.

The Engalitcheff Institute's site briefings also give students a more concrete feeling for various departments of the federal government and their place in the political process. As one student said, "We got to go to the State Department, which was really interesting for people like me who are definitely focused on international issues, and to see how our government is supposed to diplomatically relate to others. I thought that was a great aspect of the program."

Because of the nature of their courses, the location of their institutions, and their particular learning goals, some faculty are more likely to invite grassroots political activists than elected or appointed officials. At Berea College, in Appalachia, Meta Mendel-Reyes finds that local community activists have particularly compelling stories of effective political action to share with her students. Among other things, these speakers illustrate that political power can be exerted from the bottom up as well as from the top down, and they convey a tangible sense of how this kind of political action works. There is a world of difference between electoral politics at the federal level and local community organizing and collaborative public work. If students can vividly experience how democratic decision making includes a myriad of processes at many different levels operating simultaneously, they begin to appreciate the complex and dynamic nature of political systems.

AN APPRECIATION OF DIVERSE ROLES. Part of helping students move beyond an oversimplified, schematized, or civics textbook conception of the structure and workings of political institutions is showing them in a compelling way the many and varied roles political actors play. At best, students are only dimly aware of the critical contributions of people who are not highly visible. When students meet and talk with people who fill those roles, hearing from them about what their work actually entails, what kind of impact it has, and how they interact with people in other roles, they gain a concrete sense of the many different kinds of work that help shape political outcomes.

So, for example, students may read that White House staff are key in presidential decision making, but that knowledge comes alive when a White House staff member tells how he or she shaped a decision memorandum for the president, as speakers in Semiatin's program do. Semiatin is careful to include both elected officials and staff members as invited speakers so that students can begin to appreciate their different yet interlocking roles.

This approach to exposing students to a range of political figures who play different roles not only contributes to a better understanding of the political realm but also broadens the options for students who would like to consider a career in politics. In Doug Morgan's Portland State University course Civic Initiative: The Ethics of Leadership, at least half the speakers are career bureaucrats. This is enlightening to students, because, as he says, "Most students don't understand that career administrators do much of the real work of public policymaking." He notes that few of his students will run for public office but many could end up in appointed or other staff positions.

Greg Werkheiser wants to leave his Sorensen Institute students with very much the same message: "Some of you will ultimately be elected to political office, and that's great, and some of you will never be elected or appointed to political office, but you'll be a private-sector citizen who has an extremely influential role in deciding the future of the state." To help students gain this understanding, to really learn the message, he brings in many different types of people—some public policymakers, both elected and appointed, some advisers to politicians, and many who work in non-profit organizations or academic centers that seek to analyze or influence public policies. All are involved in some aspect of Virginia politics. Together these practitioners give students a rich, textured understanding that there are many different kinds of roles in politics, that each involves a distinct set of responsibilities and expertise, and that each offers its own opportunities, satisfactions, and demands.

DEEPER KNOWLEDGE. In addition to teaching students about political process, roles, and institutions, invited speakers can also provide a deeper and more memorable understanding of important substantive issues, including both policy issues and aspects of the economic, demographic, scientific, international, or other contexts that bear on those issues. Invited speakers can talk about policy issues that are important at many different levels in the political system. Some focus on local concerns, whereas others talk about problems and proposed solutions that face both local communities and the nation as a whole. Mendel-Reyes's students, for example, told us how much they learned from invited speakers about environmental hazards in their local area, and about ways members of the local community had worked to resist the expansion of those hazards.

Civil servants bring to the classroom a wealth of knowledge about the implementation of policy. The speakers Ross Cheit invites to his Brown University course on children and public policy exemplify the kind of deep expertise that comes with years of experience in an area and the good judgment that is needed when grappling with the difficult decisions they face daily in their work. One student commented that the class had had a visit from the woman who "has run child protective services in Rhode

Island for fifteen years. And she just knows everything about child protective services and what's best for children."

Some faculty invite several speakers with experience in the same area, in part to provide multiple perspectives but also to achieve greater depth and breadth of coverage. The Engalitcheff Institute, for example, organizes some of its guest speakers into a series stretching over several weeks. A regular series on foreign policy is particularly engaging to many students in this Washington, D.C.–based program.

A diverse array of speakers can help students understand political perspectives and social-cultural contexts different from their own, the different impacts particular policies have on people in different occupations, social classes, or regional locations, and the issues that are salient in contexts with which the students have little or no familiarity. A politically liberal California State University, Monterey Bay, student appreciated the opportunity to look at political issues from the very different perspective of a politically conservative speaker who visited the class: "We had . . . the mayor of Marina. She had a military background and was from the South. Her political views were very different from [another invited speaker] and it was interesting to hear her speak and to understand where she came from and to look through her eyes and say, 'OK, I can understand why you think that even though I still don't agree with you.'"

Other faculty invite speakers who can help students understand the tensions involved in public policy. In his four-course, one-semester program in Minneapolis serving students from a number of campuses (a program sponsored by the Higher Education Consortium for Urban Affairs, or HECUA), Phil Sandro seeks to help students learn about the various tensions underlying some pressing policy issues, especially with regard to government regulation of industry. So he also invites speakers from the corporate world. HECUA students enjoyed learning from a Honeywell executive about the reasons corporations do the things they do and the inescapable need for businesses to make a profit. Similarly, students in the Engalitcheff Institute hear from representatives of the pharmaceutical industry about the costs of research and development and their perspective on government regulation of the industry.

UNDERSTANDING OF ETHICAL ISSUES. Students gain a greater appreciation of the ethical issues in political life and the kinds of dilemmas faced by elected officials, civil servants, and others in public life. A more sophisticated understanding of these issues is important in its own right and can also help reduce naïve cynicism about politics. Many students explain their disengagement from politics in part by referring to their usually fairly vague sense that politics is corrupt, that politicians are often hypocritical and untrustworthy. Mendel-Reyes is one of many faculty who mentioned this barrier to engagement: "I think there are a lot of students who don't see politics as being capable of making any changes, and they see politicians as corrupt."

Of course, this skeptical view is not entirely erroneous. Furthermore, as we have discussed, research in political science has shown that people who combine low levels of social trust with a strong sense of political efficacy are the most likely to be politically engaged. But for many undergraduate students, cynicism and distrust of the political system serve as excuses for disengagement. Furthermore, their skeptical attitudes are seldom based in knowledge of what kinds of ethical issues are likely to arise in public life, exactly what (in a given circumstance) would count as an ethical or unethical response, and what pressures and constraints individuals in public life need to manage when they confront such dilemmas.

When speakers address in a frank way some of the ethical issues they have faced, it can build understanding, enabling students to be more discriminating in their judgments about politics and politicians, more knowledgeable about the kinds of ethical problems most likely to arise (such as conflict of interest and other issues around money in politics), and more thoughtful about how systemic conditions might contribute to or reduce the incidence of corruption. A speaker who visited David Takacs and Gerald Shenk's course at California State University, Monterey Bay, for example, has a reputation for holding especially high ethical standards, and he spoke about how one can compromise on an issue without compromising one's integrity. This was a distinction that few of the students had thought about before, and they found the conversation very enlightening.

Although students enjoy engaging with ethical questions when real issues are presented honestly, and can often respond well to idealism, they do not welcome preachy messages. Semiatin underscores how important it is to avoid speakers with heavy-handed, didactic rhetoric. He works hard to prevent his guests from "coming in and giving the 'civic duty speech.' Students are tired of being lectured to [about their democratic failings] and see it as patronizing. When speakers tell them how great things would be if 'we could all get together,' this just turns students off. They don't want to hear it."

Occasionally, speakers will turn out to have some ethically questionable incidents in their backgrounds that come to light only after visiting the class. Instead of treating the visit as a mistake or an embarrassment to the professor who made the invitation, these (fortunately rare) incidents can be used as powerful teachable moments. Werkheiser talks about a time when Virginia's Speaker of the House talked to the students at the Sorensen Institute's summer program. The individual had been in office for almost thirty years, and when he talked about his experiences, he emphasized the importance of public service and honesty as an integral part of that service. Soon after his visit, the front page of the *Washington Post* revealed that he had settled, outside of court, several sexual harassment claims with women who were much younger than he was and inferior to him in bargaining power. When this became public, a career that had taken thirty years to build crashed down in twenty-four hours. As Werkheiser put it, "This was an interesting lesson for the students. It was a 'wow' moment."

Increased Political Motivation

Political speakers and mentors are especially suited to fostering a number of dimensions of political motivation. Well-chosen speakers can spark interest, reduce cynicism, and evoke emotional responses of concern and inspiration. Speakers and mentors can help develop students' desire to become politically engaged and committed to stay engaged in the face of setbacks, in ways that are difficult if not impossible for traditional classroom teaching to accomplish. They do this by representing models of engagement that students can identify with, leading the students to feel that they, too, might make a difference on issues they care about.

A SENSE OF POLITICAL EFFICACY AND IDENTITY. Faculty and program leaders use political speakers and mentors as a powerful way to help students come to believe that what they think and do politically matters and could potentially make a difference—that is, to give them a stronger sense of internal political efficacy. Speakers and mentors can also change the ways that students think about who they are and who they want to be—their political identities. If speakers or mentors are very engaging, students can come to see being politically interested and active as personally appealing, making it more likely that these qualities will become more central to what psychologists Markus and Nurius (1986) call their *desired selves*—their sense of who they would like to be. The two outcomes (politically engaged identity and sense of internal political efficacy) are closely related: If students can identify with the politically active people who speak in their classes or serve as mentors, they find it easier to imagine themselves becoming active (politically engaged identity) and believe they can make a difference (sense of political efficacy).

Politicians and other political practitioners often seem remote and mysterious to students, so having real people come in and talk about their day-to-day experiences in political life makes that world more concrete, and political engagement seem more "doable." Especially when they talk personally and informally with students, speakers and mentors show that they are real people struggling with real issues. They *embody* the previously abstract role of *politician* or *political activist,* and that makes the role seem less distant and forbidding, and more accessible.

When speakers are similar to the students in important ways—age, gender, and ethnic or social class background, for example—this increases the chances that students will identify with them and feel that they might play such roles themselves. At Mills College, Joe Kahne hopes students will come to see themselves as having the potential to become the successors to those he invites to class, which means identifying with political leaders and coming to think, "I could be like that" or "This is the kind of person I want to be." Kahne chooses political practitioners to speak to his class who are not particularly famous but have nonetheless made a difference in their communities and helped shape public policies in demonstrable ways. He finds that it is easier for students to identify with people from a background similar to their own and who are only a decade (or less) older, so he takes this into account as well.

Another way that speakers bolster students' feeling that political roles are accessible to them, and thus their sense of political efficacy, is by telling stories about the various steps they took as they became more involved politically over time. These stories convey that there are numerous entry points, paths, and trajectories, and that many begin with modest steps that students have already taken or can imagine taking. A student from Dick Simpson's Future of Chicago course at the University of Illinois, Chicago, commented on one of the speakers from local politics: "He helped me see that a career in politics is made up of small steps and not necessarily some grand plan. . . . I guess it's putting a face on political leaders. I felt more engaged."

INSPIRATION. Speakers can generate emotional engagement, interest, and inspiration because they "make it real"; students see that political outcomes actually affect them. As we have discussed, students, like others, need to experience political engagement as a private or personal good as well as a public good for democratic processes to really flourish in America. There are several ways that political practitioners engaging with students as speakers or mentors can help students experience political engagement as a private good. One key is enabling them to see that public policies and other political decisions affect them personally. Some speakers are extremely effective in conveying the message that out of sheer self-interest it ought to matter to students what happens in the political realm both locally and nationally. Meta Mendel-Reyes invites speakers to her course at Berea College as a means, in part, for showing students how political issues and practices affect them, with the aim of motivating them to become engaged themselves. One local activist, for example, described some serious environmental hazards near where the students lived and went to school and talked about the work she and others were doing to mitigate those hazards. The speaker thus made it clear not only that these environmental problems warranted immediate attention but also that political action could make a very concrete difference in local conditions that directly affected the students' welfare.

Speakers can also spark students' positive emotional connection with the issues even when their immediate self-interest is not obviously at stake. Inspiration is known to be a powerful motivator of action (Haidt, 2000) and is clearly one of the most salient reasons for engaging speakers. Students in virtually all the courses that invited speakers said they felt inspired by the visitors, more interested in the issues raised, and more likely to want to do something to address them.

To underline the importance of public policy for people's lives and thereby make political issues more emotionally compelling, Sandro invites speakers to the HECUA program who talk about their direct experience on one side or another of current policy debates. For example, students hear from a welfare recipient how difficult it is to deal with the various agencies with which she has to interact to receive her benefits and the importance of programs that aim to make the system more flexible and accommodating.

Besides helping students see how politics affects them or inspiring them about an issue, another way to help make political engagement a private good is to show students how exciting and fun it can be to get involved in political action. Political scientist Wendy Rahn (2000) talks about the importance of imparting to young people "a love of the game" of politics. If they really enjoy being involved, the question of whether they are making a difference with each specific act is less central.

Speakers are often able to bring to the classroom their joy in politics, their sense of exhilaration in a campaign for a candidate or policy agenda. As Brian Murphy commented: "We have a lot of [speakers] whose lives have been lived in the service of their communities. These are valuable lives; these are things worth doing. . . . Here are people that have chosen out of their own personal reasons to commit their lives to serious public work, and it's cool rather than boring or depressing." This kind of narrative presentation contrasts with analytical discussions, which can offer disinterested examinations of the issues but sometimes miss the feeling of exhilaration that politics can provide.

Along with showing students that politics can be fun, speakers can challenge students' assumption that being politically involved requires enormous personal sacrifice. Simpson says that speakers who come to his course on Chicago politics often use their own experiences to illustrate that one can be politically engaged and still "have a life." Politics need not be a "24/7" occupation.

Stronger Skills of Deliberation

Speakers and mentors can be especially useful in helping students develop skills of political deliberation. Skillful deliberation involves learning to ask probing questions, listening to diverse perspectives, and developing one's own judgments. Speakers often function as a launching point for spirited deliberation, both during the visit and as a later follow-up.

For Simpson, bringing in political speakers is an important way to teach students how to engage others in sustained, well-informed deliberation on political issues. This means that the students need to prepare in advance of a speaker coming to class, learning about the issues that will be discussed and forming tentative views on those issues. With this background, they are ready to question the speakers to gain further insights. Simpson's guest speakers also serve as catalysts for later discussions among the students, further contributing to the development of their deliberative skills.

Practitioners can also motivate students to gain other political skills and sometimes even help enhance those skills, though they can usually accomplish this to a meaningful extent only as mentors, not as presenters. Classroom speakers can make it clear to students that a range of skills is needed for the kind of political engagement they represent, but visiting speakers are not well positioned to help students master those skills. Mentors are better able than speakers to provide feedback on practice, because they engage with students over time, often around political action projects. Democracy Matters, for example, uses mentors effectively to help students learn political skills. Former director Adam Weinberg stresses the importance of students' carrying out various political actions and then using the program's advisers as coaches to talk through problems and offer suggestions and other feedback.

Special Benefits of Mentors

When political figures or practitioners not only come to a class, or even several classes, but also are available to work with students over longer periods of time, they can provide a powerful learning experience. Several PEP courses and programs engaged collaborators to connect with students in a sustained way in mentorship or in quasi-mentorship roles. Sometimes this is a clearly demarcated component of the program—a formal mentorship program. In other cases, the arrangements are less obviously structured mentoring programs but serve some of the same functions.

The context changes as well. Sometimes students "shadow" their mentors; in other cases, they meet with a mentor several times to talk about that individual's work and the student's career interests and goals. In some programs, mentors advise students on political research or action projects, working closely with students as they plan and carry out their projects.

At the Institute for Civic Leadership, mentorship is a key component of a program that brings fifteen women from colleges across the country to Mills College for a semester. While at Mills, the students are immersed full-time in a multipronged program designed to support their development as leaders—fostering skills, knowledge, and other leadership qualities. The mentorship program connects each participating student with an experienced leader in civic affairs. Mentors include elected officials, nonprofit leaders, and other political practitioners.

Although not all institute students take full advantage of their mentors, those who do often find the relationship to be a powerful growth experience. As one of them put it, "My mentor was awesome. . . . I met with her every two to three weeks because she was very interested in what we were doing, and in providing support and talking about things going on in the community. That was really helpful to me. And she also shared her own experience, so I was able to see different ways of going about making change, leaving yourself open to what happens and [new ideas about] how you can be most useful."

Quasi-mentorship relationships include those with program staff who work closely with students over time. Democracy Matters engages individuals with different kinds of political experience to act as advisers to the various campus chapters, working especially to guide and support the student coordinators of the many campus chapters.[1] Some of these advisers are based at the Democracy Matters headquarters at Colgate University and connect with students through telephone and e-mail. Others are regional directors of the program, who visit the campuses and hold regional meetings as well as interact through telephone and e-mail. Students in Democracy Matters are encouraged to connect with advisers and collaborators both on and off campus, and they mention these relationships as extremely helpful as well. One student, for example, spoke of how useful it was for him to form an ongoing relationship with the chief of staff to the mayor of New Haven, Connecticut, as part of his work with Democracy Matters.

While teaching his course, The Politics of San Francisco, at San Francisco State University, Brian Murphy used a very different approach to connect the matriculated students in the course with community activists. He enrolled in the course a number of midlevel staff of community-based organizations and city agencies. (These students are taking courses in the College of Extended Learning and are not pursuing a degree.) The intention of the course is for these staff members to work closely with the regular students on various policy and political issues in the local communities. Reciprocally, the matriculated students are a resource on academic issues to the staff members, most of whom have no college experience. This kind of mutual teaching and learning between peers with very different areas of expertise can be considered another kind of quasi-mentorship, and it has a number of positive outcomes for both groups of students.

Murphy also connects students in the course on San Francisco politics with leaders in the community who are not themselves taking the course but who are willing to mentor his students not only in course-related activities but also, and sometimes more importantly, to help as those students work through issues concerning their careers and their future political engagement. During the many years he taught this course, Murphy was able to accumulate a steadily expanding group of community leaders willing to work with his students.

Strategies for Using Political Speakers and Mentors

As we suggest in the opening paragraph of this chapter, an invitation to speak or mentor is not something to be done casually. We observed that the faculty and staff leading the PEP courses and programs put a great deal of effort into this strategy. In particular, they followed these practical steps:

- ○ Choose carefully.
- ○ Prepare the speakers.
- ○ Prepare the students.
- ○ Ensure interaction.

○ Follow up.

○ Evaluate.

○ Work carefully to incorporate mentoring.

○ Be prepared for the challenges.

Choose Carefully

The sine qua non for using outside speakers and mentors effectively is to choose them carefully. Morgan, like other PEP faculty, stresses that "speakers need to be chosen with exactly the same care that readings are chosen. The instructor needs to know exactly what he or she hopes to accomplish with the speaker. If one doesn't have that degree of intentionality, it will have the same effect as randomly choosing your readings."

Of course, finding the right speakers and mentors is not as simple as choosing products from a catalog. Choices are constrained by faculty members' familiarity with the various kinds of people who might be available, the breadth of their contacts with relevant people, and whether they can induce busy people to participate. Despite these challenges, it is extremely important to begin not by locating the most readily available visitor but instead by thinking through as clearly as possible why political practitioners and others are being asked to join the class. There are a number of things to think about in choosing speakers for maximum impact.

BE SPECIFIC. Although it is not possible to predict exactly what students will gain from interacting with a particular speaker or mentor, the experience is more likely to be productive if faculty think carefully about their specific goals for student learning and use those goals to guide their choices. When the goal is to help students understand better the wide range of different roles that are important in the political process, invited speakers must represent this diversity. If they are chosen carefully, a series of speakers can expose students to the major branches of government and the relationships among them or the interplay among elected officials, political appointees, legislative and executive staff, civil servants, lobbyists, and nongovernmental policy analysts. Within the federal government, for example, there are more roles than one would have time to include in a semester or summer program. Similarly, programs that focus on state and local issues have a wide array of roles to choose from, and what students learn will depend on what roles are represented in the series.

Clearly, the mission or purpose of the course or program and its location have significant effects on the kinds of speakers faculty invite. A focus on speakers from the federal government is almost always central for semester (or summer) in Washington programs, for obvious reasons. In contrast, it makes more sense for Mendel-Reyes to invite local community activists from the Appalachian region of Kentucky where Berea is located to speak in her course on service, citizenship, and community.

When faculty want to maximize students' identification with the speaker—which is often, though not always, a key goal—they generally look for guests who come from similar backgrounds to the students and who are still quite young. In contrast, speakers' personal backgrounds are less important when the primary aim is to show a range of ways to contribute to public life. Broadening students' thinking about the array of options can be key to helping them see a place for themselves in public life. With this in mind, Werkheiser invites to the Sorensen Institute a mix of speakers; some are engaged in politics full-time, as he hopes some of his students will be, and some are involved as private citizens—as he wants all of his students to be.

TAKE STUDENTS TO THE SPEAKERS. In most cases, it is easier to invite speakers to visit the classroom than to take the students to the speakers because of the logistics involved in transporting a group of students. Sometimes, though, speakers prefer to have students visit them or offer it as an option. Visiting practitioners in their home settings can be an especially memorable experience if the setting itself is a source of learning, as it is when the students in the Washington, D.C.–based Engalitcheff Institute visit the State Department and other government offices.

PRESENT A RANGE OF PERSPECTIVES. The Sorensen Institute stresses the importance of citizenship that is deeply thoughtful and invites speakers who represent different ways of being thoughtful about politics and its practice. They include people who are known in the state for offering middle-ground solutions as well as "firebrands" on each side of some issues. This helps students see that extreme positions are not necessary in political life but also that being thoughtful is "not about being a political moderate or blasé."

When courses and programs offer speakers with a wide range of positions, students often comment on the value of being exposed to diverse opinions. A student in Dick Simpson's Chicago politics course is a case in point: "It was interesting because there were so many different leaders, and they all had different points of view. Some were Democrat, some were Republican. I enjoyed learning what different issues were important to them and seeing how they would help us even when their points of view were different [from ours]."

Achieving this kind of diversity is not easy, however. Naturally, faculty tend to know and admire like-minded people, so it is often easiest to invite speakers from this pool of fellow travelers. Representing a limited range of the political spectrum does not go unnoticed, however, and students complain when they feel the invitation list is skewed to the left or the right. As one student said, "One thing I didn't like was that the instructor did not show the other side. He [the professor] and the speakers were mainly liberal. . . . We didn't get speakers from the conservative side. Landlord-tenant issues is an example. We didn't hear from landlords. Just from people who are for rent control."

The Engalitcheff Institute is explicitly focused on an ideology of free market capitalism, and students know this before they choose to participate. For this reason, it seems quite legitimate for the program to present a less neutral or balanced point of view than programs that portray themselves as nonpartisan. Even so, some of the students expressed a wish for more political diversity among the invited speakers. As one student said, "The speakers were basically all conservatives. There may have been moderate conservatives, but they were basically all conservatives. . . . I came with somewhat conservative ideas, but not entirely—it depends on the issue. For me, it's been interesting to look at things and say, like, 'Well, I disagree with this conservative perspective even though I'm conservative on some issues.' But I didn't hear liberal perspectives on things, so maybe I agree with things now after this program because I only heard one side."

INVOLVE STUDENTS. Sue Briggs, at the living-learning program CIVICUS at the University of Maryland, follows a different approach from most other PEP course and program leaders in that she lets students choose speakers from a list that she and her colleagues prepare. She believes this gives the students a greater sense of investment and commitment in preparing for the speakers, and helps ensure that they make the most of the visits.

Programs that use mentors and advisers often provide a number of distinctly different options for students to choose from and let them select mentors with whom they would like to work. This selection role for students is especially important when matching students with practitioners they will spend more time with than a onetime classroom visitor. In a longer-term relationship, it is important to optimize the fit between individual students and their mentors or quasi-mentors, and allowing students to choose is more typical in these circumstances.

Some faculty use a combination approach: invitations by the professor and follow-up by the students. In this approach, the faculty member invites to class a series of practitioners from a range of backgrounds and political perspectives, with the idea that some of those speakers will then mentor students who choose to work with them. At California State University, Monterey Bay, Takacs and Shenk have used this model successfully. Over the period of a semester, five politically engaged activists with a spectrum of views hold discussions with the class as a whole. The speakers are available to mentor students in connection with their political research and action projects during the rest of the semester at the students' request.

Prepare the Speakers

It is important to let speakers know exactly what is expected from them well in advance of their visits. This involves talking about why they are being invited, what it is hoped students will learn, what background reading, if any, students will be doing, and how the presentation fits into the course or program as a whole. It is extremely useful to confirm the main points of that conversation, as well as dates and logistical arrangements, in writing, after the conversation.

Instructors should be as precise as possible about what the speakers should plan to cover during their talk, how the session will be structured (including how long their presentation should be), and what kind of interaction is hoped for. So, for example, the instructor might say that he hopes the speaker will talk about certain aspects of the political process, particular areas of substantive expertise, stories about how he or she became involved in this kind of work, what the challenges have been and how he or she has handled them, how the speaker has maintained his or her stamina in the face of defeats, or other issues of interest for the class.

At Portland State University, Doug Morgan emphasizes that he works hard to ensure that speakers are well-informed about the objectives of the class, what it has been doing, and how he expects the session with the speaker to fit in with the course's larger goals. To make sure all this is clear, Morgan gives speakers a page of briefing notes outlining the topics he wants discussed. This is intended not to control the content of the speaker's comments but to help shape the themes and questions discussed by the class. He finds that rather than being put off, speakers are grateful for this kind of guidance.

In addition to communicating with visitors about the content and format of the session, it is also important to make the experience as easy and gratifying as possible for the speakers. Obviously, they need clear directions to the venue, information about parking, and other logistics. After the visit, personal thank-you notes not only from the professor but also from one or more students who especially enjoyed the session can increase the chance that the speaker will feel the visit was worthwhile and agree to come back.

Prepare the Students

Courses and programs vary a great deal in the kind and extent of preparation required of students before a speaker visit, but some preparation is essential if students are to engage in serious and sustained dialogue. Students should be knowledgeable participants in the event, interacting actively with the speaker, asking good questions, and connecting issues the visitor raises with things they have already discussed in the course or program.

This means that, at the very least, students should be well-informed about who the visitor is and notable aspects of his or her background, role, and institution. In some cases this means that students read material on the speaker's topic in advance, either background readings suggested by the speaker or material chosen by the faculty member. This kind of preparation helps ensure that the students are a knowledgeable audience, prepared to engage the practitioners in substantive discussion.

Ensure Interaction

Outside practitioners are generally most effective when they educate students through interactive modes, rather than by giving long speeches. Class sessions with visiting speakers or site briefings in which students visit the speaker often include a relatively brief talk followed by discussion. When the event is structured this way, it is critical to build in enough time for questions and discussion and to enforce time limits tactfully if the speaker goes on for too long.

This approach is not universal, however, and some meetings with visiting speakers are interactive from the outset. The Sorensen Institute uses the latter approach, as Werkheiser notes: "It is important for everyone to understand that it's not a lecture environment. Guest speakers are in interactive mode, not giving speeches." A key to making either approach work effectively is to make sure that expectations are clear on all sides.

While remaining in the bounds of courtesy and respect, it is important for students to feel free to ask questions on any issues they want to pursue and even challenge the speaker if they disagree with something or a statement doesn't ring true. Students in the PEP courses and programs frequently mentioned how much they appreciated having the chance to ask speakers questions of particular interest to them and sometimes said they wished they had had more time for this kind of exchange.

Follow Up

Students need to spend time not only preparing for the class visits of political practitioners but also reflecting on those visits afterward. Structured opportunities for reflection—discussions after the practitioners leave and written reflections in journals or papers—are key to ensuring that students think about what they have learned and connect it with other aspects of the course. Postspeaker discussions often surface differing reactions to the speaker and conflicting points of view on the issues raised. When students have the opportunity to engage the professor and other students about their reactions to the speaker session, they come to notice important ideas, implications, and connections with the course that they missed, to think more critically about arguments they too readily accepted at face value, or to take more seriously some of the proposals or arguments they dismissed without thinking them through.

In Morgan's course, students write analytic papers about some of the speakers' presentations, gathering more information in their evaluation of the speakers' arguments and approach. This can be especially worthwhile when the visitors are candidates for elective office, as some of them are, because it gives students experience evaluating candidates in preparation for deciding whether to support the campaign or vote for the candidate.

Evaluate

Each political practitioner should be assessed in terms of the course goals after the appearance in class. This should include students' judgments as well as the faculty member's. Some instructors wait until the end of the course to ask students to evaluate the speakers. That way, they can comment on all the visitors at once, thus streamlining the process and making it comparative. Others review each speaker immediately after the class visit. Combining a quick initial evaluation that captures immediate reactions with a comparative overview at the end is ideal.

The evaluation should address not only content, style, and relevance of the presentation but also questions about whether the session would have benefited from a different structure, clearer guidelines for the speaker, or more or different preparation for the students. Thorough evaluations of speakers, along with clear records of those evaluations, can help faculty develop a roster of visitors with a strong track record who can be invited back every year or every other year, thus making the process progressively easier.

Work Carefully to Incorporate Mentoring

As we noted earlier, the PEP programs follow two basic models for using mentors, and each has several variants. In the first model, each student develops an ongoing personal relationship with a civic leader or other political practitioner. In the second, practitioners work with one or more students, usually individually, on projects, offering guidance as the students develop and carry out their political research or action projects. It is critical when engaging mentors to make expectations as clear as possible, just as it is with invited speakers.

In fact, when working with mentors, it is a very good idea to create written agreements that capture the mutual expectations.[2] If prospective mentors are not able to commit as much time and energy as needed, it is important to know that ahead of time and remove those individuals from the pool. Some PEP courses were able to provide the mentors with small stipends, as Takacs and Shenk have done in their course, and this arrangement may help to ensure a sense of commitment on the part of mentors. Likewise, the staff who act as mentors and guides for Democracy Matters students are paid for this work.

Because establishing personal relationships is central to the first model of mentoring, faculty sometimes take active steps to increase the chances that a relationship will develop. Key principles for accomplishing this intersect with guidelines for using outside speakers effectively, but go beyond them in several areas. Whereas only a few PEP faculty engage students in helping choose speakers, most programs that foster ongoing mentoring relationships stress the importance of students taking an active role in finding the mentor with whom they would like to connect. Of course, students need help in doing this, including suggestions of people or categories of people to consider; contacts and ongoing good relationships between the prospective mentors and the program, institution, or faculty member; and administrative and logistical support such as help with letters of introduction and memoranda of understanding. Students need to find someone whose work they personally find interesting and exciting and with whom they feel comfortable.

Commenting on the Mills College Institute for Civic Leadership's mentorship program, in which each student is paired with a civic leader in an ongoing relationship, Kahne reports that "the mentoring relationships are tough because the mentors tend to be very busy and personal relationships are hard to engineer. It's not something we assume will work with every-body, but we'd like it to work with a good percentage of the students. . . . There's a lot of need for communication, setting expectations, making time for those first connections to work and structuring some events [to support the developing relationship] so that it's easier to make those con-nections until a relationship can build a little bit so that students can then make more of a connection."

In preparing both students and mentors for the experience, it is useful to encourage them to explore a wide array of fairly personal issues, such as work-family balance, passions and other motivations for one's work, and how one deals effectively with difficulties, as well as strictly work- or content-related issues. From his experience with Democracy Matters, Weinberg stresses that program faculty and staff can serve in mentoring roles in this way: "We talk to them openly about the lives we've led and choices we've made—that the choices are not just the extremes of living to make money or being hippie activists living in dire poverty. It's a lot more complicated than that."

In this kind of relationship, Democracy Matters mentors serve as role models and support students' personal explorations and aspirations, but they also offer very practical nuts and bolts guidance to help students think through their projects on campaign finance reform and master the range of skills they need to carry out the work. Both the director and the students of Democracy Matters stressed the importance of both general and very concrete advice in the mentoring relationships within that program.

Be Prepared for the Challenges

It is no surprise that the biggest challenge in using speakers to support political development is finding political practitioners and others who are strong speakers in the many ways we have laid out in this chapter. Dick Simpson reflected the thinking of many PEP faculty who use speakers when he said: "The greatest weakness is the hit-or-miss of speakers—some are better than others; some are more topical than others." A visiting speaker may be disappointing or problematic in three main ways.

"CANNED" OR PAT PRESENTATIONS. In spite of advance communica-tion, some practitioners may come to class and give pat campaign speeches or other well-rehearsed, generic routines. Some tell stories of their battles that seem to have no point other than self-congratulation. Simpson suggests that speakers be given a particular topic that connects with the course material to minimize the risk that they will recycle tired litanies that have long since lost their spark. Encouraging students to be a tough, sharp, well-informed audience can help too, as long as they are respectful and reasonably humble. As we suggested earlier, a careful evaluation of each speaker will place those who cling to their canned presentations on the "don't invite back" list.

Sometimes, even though speakers have been asked to interact with students, they avoid responding directly to student questions or give answers that feel like public relations efforts. In one of Simpson's classes, for example, the Illinois lieutenant governor was speaking, and a student asked him what he thought about the outsourcing abroad of white-collar jobs. The lieutenant governor said it was a great question but proceeded to skirt around the issue. Another student raised her hand and went back to the question, pressing successfully for a more precise answer. This would not have happened if the students had not been prepared with background material about the speaker and the issue, and if the speaker had not been advised that real interaction was expected.

It is important that students be prepared to challenge speakers who seem evasive, because if they sense that the speaker is not being candid, they often become increasingly cynical. The goal is to separate justified from unwarranted skepticism and to prevent justified mistrust from becoming generalized cynicism or an excuse for disengagement. Active analysis, critique, and polite confrontation helps keep students engaged with the issues and the process even when they are uneasy about a particular speaker.

OFFENSIVE PRESENTATIONS. Occasionally, visiting speakers are particularly opinionated or outspoken and their aggressive argumentation can be offensive or hurtful to some students. This risk is especially high when the speaker makes strong or challenging statements about sensitive issues such as race or religion. A case in point was a visit by a professor of African American studies to Mendel-Reyes's class. The speaker said that African Americans are forced "to step out of their comfort zones all the time" on matters of race, and reach out to whites, but that whites do not have to reach out and usually do not, which he saw as a problem. A white student in the class responded by saying that she and other white students were reluctant to reach out to African American students because if they did, then:

> African Americans would want to know what our motives are, like if we went over to sit with a group of black students in the dining hall, they would wonder why we were doing that. There was a lot of controversy in the class when I said that. The speaker told me that it

wasn't true. I really got hit down. The black students were very accepting of what he was saying, but I didn't agree. I said nothing can make
up for what they've been through but I felt that what I had said had
some truth but they don't want to admit it. I was really upset and
started crying.

Whether or not this young woman had reason to be this upset, the incident underscores the importance of holding debriefing meetings after
speakers' visits. In some cases, the debriefing needs to include not only
intellectual analysis of the controversies raised in the speaker session but
also emotional support for students who may have been offended or hurt.
In this case, both Mendel-Reyes and other students, including some
African American students, were very supportive to the student whose
feelings had been hurt, and she recovered quickly. The incident does illustrate, however, a particular challenge presented by some visitors, especially if they are not open to opposing views raised by the students.

INSUFFICIENT INTERACTION. Most speakers have a great deal of both
substantive material and personal anecdotes to offer the class and it is easy
for them to fill a class session, leaving little time for questions and discussion. A common complaint from students is that they wished they had
more time for back-and-forth with the speaker. If it is possible to schedule a longer session than a typical class period, it is well worth doing.
Sometimes a visit to the practitioner in his or her own work setting facilitates a longer visit, outside the narrow constraints of the classroom. If
this is not possible, the best alternative is to hone the focus in conversation with the speaker ahead of time, so that time will not be wasted on
topics that are less relevant for the class.

LOGISTICS, TIME, AND SCHEDULING. The logistics of identifying political practitioners and others who are relevant to the course material, effective at engaging with students, and willing to take part are among the
most significant drawbacks to using outside speakers. The challenges are
even greater when the practitioners are asked to mentor students. The
time, energy, and effort of the faculty member is greatest if she is working with speakers for the first time to ensure that they understand the
goals of the course and how best to contribute to those goals. An assistant can help significantly, though PEP leaders found that they needed to
make the initial contacts themselves.

Programs with mentors must find practitioners who are not only willing to contribute their time but can be available to students at times that

work for the students. Although the details of finding mutually convenient meeting times is best left to students and their mentors, it is essential to have a general sense that the timing will work before the mentor is engaged. The principle difficulty in using mentors is that they are almost always extremely busy, and it is hard for them to live up to their good intentions of spending time with students. Furthermore, it is impossible to ensure that the chemistry of this one-on-one relationship will be right, so there are no guarantees that the mentoring will develop into a meaningful partnership. As Kahne noted, both students and mentors have trouble making the meetings a top priority, and this kind of relationship is also socially awkward at first.

A POSITIVE, CONSTRUCTIVE TONE. Despite the best efforts to prepare both speakers and students, sometimes the tone becomes unpleasant. It is not easy for students to strike just the right balance of tough-minded questioning, courtesy, and appreciation. And the faculty host cannot prevent the speaker from becoming defensive or belligerent if the tension rises. A student in Morgan's class described an occasion that took a negative turn: "[The speaker] wasn't as charismatic as we may have hoped he would be and I think that turned everyone off and put him in a more defensive mode and it got real hostile in class." Clearly, faculty intervention is called for if the tone becomes distinctly negative.

Debriefing after class can also be useful, especially if it involves analyzing the style of interaction and how the class might have handled the discussion differently. Of course, instructors must avoid using the debriefing conversation to complain about the speaker or blame particular students for the degeneration in tone.

NOTES

1. For more information about the close mentoring relationship that exists between Democracy Matters staff and campus coordinators, see document 27 in the PEP document supplement at http://www.carnegiefoundation.org/educating_for_democracy/docs/.

2. For examples of two such written agreements, see documents 30 and 37 in the PEP document supplement online at the address shown in note 1. For a description of the expectations that the Service Opportunities in Leadership program provides to community organizations, see document 34 in the PEP document supplement online.

LEARNING THROUGH PLACEMENTS, INTERNSHIPS, AND SERVICE LEARNING

IN *DEMOCRACY AND EDUCATION,* John Dewey warned that education should not be merely the "subject matter of the schools, isolated from the subject matter of life experience" ([1916] 1961, pp. 10–11). Dewey, one of the most outspoken champions of the democracy-enhancing value of experiential learning, recognized the value of enriching academic learning with applied work experiences that are related to the academic subject matter students are learning. In line with this perspective, many PEP faculty bring politics and policy issues to life by arranging for students to spend time interacting with organizations whose purposes connect with the objectives of the course or program through community placements, internships, and service learning activities. These experiences incorporate a wide variety of time configurations, sites, and student responsibilities and activities.

Whatever the setting or configuration, placements or internships are paired with complementary classroom experiences, and the faculty or staff explicitly and meaningfully connect the academic focus, the practical experiences, and the community or organizational setting. Thus, students' reading and other classroom-based activities help them make sense of what they are seeing in their internships or placements, and their placement experiences help them understand more deeply the academic substance of the course or program. If placements are used effectively, the overall result is powerful learning across the arenas of academic and political understanding, skill, and motivation.

Types of Internships and Placements

The sites for internships and placements vary considerably, depending on the particular nature and focus of the course or program.[1] In many cases, placement sites are community organizations or other nongovernmental nonprofit groups that focus on issues of community development, organizing, refugee and immigration matters, health, the environment, and other aspects of social welfare. They may be either direct service organizations or organizations addressing a particular cluster of public policy issues, conducting research on those issues, and advocating for policy change.

Most placement sites in the courses and programs we studied addressed a relatively focused set of needs or issues. Among those represented in the PEP courses were the American Civil Liberties Union, the Federalist Society, a welfare-to-work program, a church-based community arts program, labor unions, Catholic Charities of New Mexico, and a law office representing foster children. There were also offices of elected officials and government agencies that implement policy.

In Ross Cheit's Brown University course on children and public policy, for instance, students spend several hours a week in one of the state agencies that administers policies affecting children, such as the Family Court or the Department of Children, Youth, and Families. The Mills College Civic Leadership program and Siegrun Freyss's American government course at California State University, Los Angeles, are fairly typical in that their placement sites include both community organizations and offices of public officials who are committed to the education and development of civic leaders. Engalitcheff Institute students are placed in various Washington, D.C.–based policy organizations and governmental offices.

These hands-on political experiences range in intensity and length, level of student contribution, and time commitment. Some are full-time for a month or more, usually during the summer. Others include a significant time commitment for a semester or summer but are not full-time. These more significant time commitments allow students to accomplish more ambitious goals. Time-intensive internships or placements are possible only in special summer programs, multisemester programs that include a summer component, or full-time programs that last for a semester or more.

Obviously, standard academic courses are not compatible with a half-time or full-time placement, so students in these courses spend less time in their placements, usually only a few hours a week. Even so, there is evidence that placements can support significant learning as long as they include at least three hours a week of direct experience (Eyler and Giles, 1999). Another limitation is that placement commitments in academic courses almost always end, at least in a formal sense, at the end of the quarter or the semester. Many faculty make arrangements for interested students to continue in their placement sites afterward, and students often become so engaged and committed that they are eager to pursue this option. When the course ends, though, the placement activities are usually no longer linked with classroom experiences.

Student Activities in Internships and Placements

The wide variety we observed in student placement experiences derives from the extensive range of their activities and responsibilities as well as in the amount of time they invest and the kinds of organizations in which they work. Many faculty believe that the work students do in their placements must contribute to the organization in a real way, so the trick is to define responsibilities that will be challenging learning experiences and also meet the organization's needs. In some internships, however, students are not actually working for the organization to any significant degree but instead are there primarily to learn by shadowing an assigned mentor or other key staff, joining meetings and other activities as an observer, or talking with their mentors about the mentor's career path and current work and about their own career aspirations.

The exact nature of the work students do can be different from one site to another, so even students in the same course or program will have quite divergent experiences if the program uses multiple sites, as most do. Placement sites also vary a great deal in their responsiveness to the faculty member's request to give students challenging, meaningful work, so some students spend their time doing clerical work, despite efforts to prevent that.

Placements and Other Active Pedagogies

In many cases, placements are integrated with other active pedagogies. In fact, placements are almost always accompanied by structured reflection on the experiences, often using several different kinds of reflection.[2] Political research and action projects are also frequently linked with placements. Placement supervisors sometimes assign students a role in an ongoing research project or ask a student to design and lead a small study. In other cases, students bring their own research ideas to their placements. In either case, the research is usually undertaken to serve a need of the placement organization. In Duke's Service Opportunities in Leadership program many students conduct what director Alma Blount calls "research service learning,"[3] and all students in the program carry out research projects in the course that follows the placement. These subsequent projects are intended to deepen students' learning about the issues raised by the activities pursued during the placement.[4] In community organizing placements, the projects are more likely to involve political action than research, although some involve both.

The Difference Between Political Placements and Service Learning

Probably the best-known pedagogy for connecting academic courses or programs with civic or political experience is community service learning. In fact, some people are surprised to hear that service learning is not the only way to educate college students for civic or political engagement. Typically, in community service learning, students work for several hours a week in an organization or through some other arrangement to meet the needs of the organization or serve the community directly. To be considered service learning, this volunteer work must be directly connected with the content and goals of an academic course, serve both student learning and community needs, and include structured reflection as the link between the service and the rest of the course.

In some of the PEP courses and programs, the placements clearly represent service learning, and the faculty refer to them as such. In others, it seems fairly clear that the placements are not significantly service-oriented, and the faculty do not think of them as service learning experiences. For example, when students primarily observe the work of the organization, talk with mentors about their own career futures, and so on, but do not serve the needs of the organization in a serious way, the placement does not represent service learning.

Just as some placements used to educate politically are not service learning, service learning is not always designed to enhance students' political development. Of course, we are interested in placements that support political learning, whether they are properly understood as service leaning or not. In truth, the boundaries between service learning and other kinds of placements are blurry, and for our purposes the distinction is not critical. In any case, the service learning literature is rich with insights and examples that illuminate the effective use of placements, and we draw on that literature in our suggestions for using placements effectively.

Rewards of Political Placement Experiences

There is much research on the important role participating in community and political groups, volunteering, and other kinds of hands-on experiences have in supporting community and political involvement in the general population (Putnam, 2000; Verba, Schlozman, and Brady, 1995). Studies have also demonstrated the positive effects that hands-on learning experiences such as community service can have on high school and college students (Barber, 1991; Eyler and Giles, 1999; Glanville, 1999; Niemi, Hepburn, and Chapman, 2000). However, these experiences do not usually include opportunities for explicit political learning, so it is important to strengthen their political dimensions if they are to support that learning. In the Political Engagement Project, we saw that hands-on political experiences yield specific learning contributing to political understanding, motivation, and skills. Moreover, these experiences spur personal growth.

Political Understanding

We saw that students gain a more specific and concrete understanding of the political process and issues from their placements and internships. Several aspects of this increased understanding stand out as especially important.

SUBSTANTIVE KNOWLEDGE OF POLICY ISSUES. Students gain considerable knowledge of the issues addressed by the organizations with which they work. Simply being immersed in the work for an extended period of time is almost certain to deepen their understanding of these issues, such as civil liberties, social welfare, the justice system, and immigration. Furthermore, given the complexity and richness of issues like this, students' growing sophistication in a particular area often carries with it increased awareness of related issues, contextual factors, and implications for other areas of social and public policy.

A GREATER UNDERSTANDING OF THE POLITICAL PROCESS. Students who work in offices of elected officials or their staff and those who work with organizations pursuing other forms of political action can learn a great deal about how political processes of various sorts actually work. This more grounded and concrete understanding contrasts with the abstract or schematized understanding of these processes that students are likely to gain from readings, lectures, and academic discussions.

Sometimes these experiences illuminate components of the political process that are not visible to most young people. An Engalitcheff Institute student was enthusiastic about her summer internship at Senator Edward Kennedy's press office, for example: "The cool thing about working in a press office is that everything, every policy issue, has to get filtered through there so they can come up with a spin. I've never been in such a fast-paced, pressured environment or seen the sense of teamwork they were able to maintain."

THE NATURE OF POLICY IMPLEMENTATION. Placement sites that involve direct service or implementation of policy offer experience seeing what policy issues look like "on the ground" in a concrete way. Students learn how policies really work in practice, and become aware of complexities of application and unintended consequences that would be less likely to emerge in academic study. Students working in programs that help implement social policies, such as Family Court, learn why judgment is needed when applying an established policy to the messy reality of a case and the problems that can arise when "street-level bureaucrats" (people who work on ground-level implementation) are not as thoughtful as they might be. This kind of experience often provides a concrete explication of a general principle that has been discussed in class, making the principle much more real.

For example, a general principle that Ross Cheit and others teach is that policy formulation and implementation require difficult trade-offs between one set of desirable goals and another. In their placements, students see how hard these trade-offs can be in individual cases and how indeterminate or sometimes even misguided the operating principles seem to be. A class discussion might ask students to engage hypothetically with how one should weigh parents' interests against children's welfare, for example. In their placements, such as in a juvenile detention facility, students see many variants of how difficult dilemmas are resolved. As one student in that course commented, "So many of the things we studied seemed so far removed until you actually see kids go through it."

UNDERSTANDING ORGANIZATIONAL DYNAMICS AND COMPLEXITY. Students also learn about the functioning of organizations in ways that are hard to capture vividly without some hands-on experience. As Kristi Schutjer-Mance commented about the internships for students in the Mills program, "These internships provide students with an opportunity to see organizations successfully working toward change. Students begin to see how that organization's structure is set up and how to implement change processes, to see what systems in society will make a difference."

In some placements, students gain a much deeper understanding of organizational and contextual complexity and the impact of institutional dynamics on outcomes for the organization's constituents. While working in a youth detention facility, one of Cheit's students became acutely aware of the role that the guards' labor unions play in this kind of facility, commenting on the alliances, behind-the-scenes coalitions, and power struggles that take place, the conditions that seem to spawn these dynamics, and the implications for students entering such a complex system. But the student also saw the issues from the guards' point of view: "At times, the juvenile prison workers seem like they're kind of building this odd network, and it seems more of a game, like a mental game they're playing. In a sense, they're forced to because they don't really have the resources they need to do their jobs as effectively as they could be doing them."

INTEGRATION ACROSS LEARNING CONTEXTS. Integrating learning from qualitatively different contexts into a deeper and more usable understanding that is greater than the sum of its parts is often cited as an important goal of a liberal education—indeed, of any high-quality undergraduate education. Yet we know that it is not often accomplished and that when students do succeed in integrating learning across contexts, they usually do so with little help from their teachers. Placements that really connect with academic courses seem to be an exception.

When asked what they most valued in their PEP courses, students often mentioned that they had learned to integrate across contexts and make connections between theory and practice. Placement experiences not only can help students understand better the theoretical conceptions presented in class, but bringing those conceptual frameworks to their placement experiences can help them see things in that context that otherwise would have been virtually invisible. Cheit suggests one mechanism by which this integration seems to take place for his students: "The social worker might say, 'I would love to be able to do this or that but I can't.' Students come back and ask why they can't. I know the service placement is working when it generates questions they want answered. It raises macro questions about micro things they encounter. When working in foster care, they come back really interested in foster care policies. Otherwise they wouldn't be."

Political Motivation

We also saw students develop stronger political motivation through their hands-on experiences. It is well-known that most college students today feel more engaged by direct service volunteer work than by politics. Alma Blount believes that placements are ideally suited to take advantage of that enthusiasm and use it to engage students more fully in politics. She notes that her program's summer internships create energy in part because they involve direct service to individuals in need, and this energy makes students eager to learn about the political dimensions of issues they confront in their service placements.

Many students entered the PEP courses and programs with very little interest in politics, yet gained dramatically in political motivation as a result of participating. Because Siegrun Freyss's American government course fulfilled a university requirement, many of her students chose to take it despite relatively little initial interest in politics. One young woman in the course worked with the League of Women Voters and found that the dedication and commitment of the women she worked with intrigued her and piqued her interest enough that she decided to continue helping them with a survey of likely voters well beyond the conclusion of the course.

SENSE OF POLITICAL EFFICACY. A central goal for faculty in virtually all of the PEP courses and programs was to increase students' sense of political efficacy, focusing especially on internal efficacy, their sense that what they think and do politically matters, that they are capable of grasping complex political issues, and that they have a role to play in the political process. This is particularly important for Freyss, because her students, many of whom are low-income and immigrants, feel very disconnected from the political process. Freyss talked about how the placements help to change this: "It's about strengthening their belief that they can influence the political system by participating in it—a sense that the system is not closed, that it is open, that they belong in it, and they can influence it. . . . Service learning is the critical step for bringing them along."

When we talked with students from the course, it appeared that Freyss's message was getting through. As one student noted: "I wasn't aware of how I could make a difference, now I am. . . . I learned that if the issue is big enough, you can join an interest group or form voting blocs or do things that will get the attention of your representative so that he or she will do something about it."

POLITICALLY ENGAGED IDENTITY. Several faculty talked about how the new experiences students have in their placements can be especially effective in helping them broaden their understanding of what kind of person they are and want to be and building a politically engaged sense of self. As one of them said: "It's very hard to imagine yourself as something you've never seen yourself being but if you see yourself engaged in a political sense, it becomes more possible to think of yourself as a political person or as politically capable. If you see yourself organizing a meeting, it's therefore possible to imagine yourself as someone who can run things."

Placements can also help students think about the best fit between various ways of contributing politically and their own talents and interests. This kind of self-knowledge is another aspect of political identity, contributing to a more enduring motivation to be politically engaged. This sorting out can result from dissatisfaction with the placement as well as positive experiences but, as Joe Kahne explains about the Mills College program, even a negative experience can lead students to political engagements that are better suited to their own interests and talents: "We had one student who was very clear that the experience she had in her internship taught her what kind of work she *didn't* want to do. I think she was right. She had an authentic experience and realized through it that she wants to contribute in other ways, through policy work rather than grassroots work."

COMPASSION, HUMILITY, AND SOLIDARITY. In a discussion about sense of political efficacy as a key goal of many PEP courses and programs, Cheit said that in his ultra-high-achieving Brown students, he more often notices a lack of humility and compassion than a deficit in sense of efficacy or agency. This comment is telling because it highlights the important differences between the many kinds of institutions and students represented in the Political Engagement Project. Many of Freyss's students exhibited exactly the opposite pattern from Cheit's—too much deference, along with a weak sense of efficacy.

Consistent with this kind of contrast, Blount works hard to give her Duke University students, many of whom are very privileged,

> [A] real sense of solidarity and reciprocity with the less privileged communities they work in. This is hard because Duke students have a noblesse oblige approach. It is hard for them to see this and they don't think they have it, but they have many layers of noblesse oblige and paternalism that we need to peel away. Many are from privileged backgrounds and if they are not, they become entitled by being at Duke. They need to learn the value of listening to the members of the community before they jump in. They need to understand that we need everybody; we're in it together.

It is not terribly surprising that Freyss did not mention this goal in describing her course: her students mostly come from just those less privileged communities to which Blount is referring.

Blount's comment about solidarity and interdependence illustrates that, especially for students from more privileged backgrounds, a central benefit of placements can be greater compassion and empathy for people unlike themselves. This often involves changing their preconceptions about institutions and people or breaking down their stereotypes. This was evident in the students in Cheit's course who interned at the youth detention facility, for example. More than one made comments like this: "I didn't know what to expect there. And then when you go in there, and they just really are still kids. It's amazing that they've done these [serious crimes]. And like when I go and I interview them, they're shy and they don't know what to say. And they're like looking down and looking around, and they don't know what they want to do with their lives. And they really are kids. And it's sad, too, because you go into the interviews, and you can tell which kids will probably be back in here."

One might think there would be an inverse relationship between humility and sense of political efficacy, so that increasing students' humility would run the risk of undermining their political self-confidence. But, properly understood, a mature humility about one's place in the world relative to others is, in fact, a very valuable, if far from universal, trait for leadership. The capacity to communicate and collaborate with people from a wide range of backgrounds is important for political effectiveness. Genuine leadership requires a focus on the task at hand and collective efforts to accomplish it rather than on rewards to one's own sense of self-importance. It is this sort of humility to which faculty refer when they highlight this quality as a goal. In fact, some students pointed to increased humility as one of the most valuable things they learned through the courses and programs. One Duke student spoke about her internship in South Africa and how impressed she was by the resilience and hopefulness of those who had suffered most under apartheid: "To see how they still believe in the goodness of people is indescribable and so humbling. . . . The humility is important in whatever leadership position I have in the future. . . . Realizing that it's not about me."

MOTIVATION STEMMING FROM INCREASED OR DECREASED FAITH IN THE SYSTEM. It should not be too surprising that students' experiences in their placements can sometimes increase their faith in the political system or institutions that are part of that system and can sometimes undermine that faith. Of course, which of these reactions prevails depends in large part on the nature of the placement setting. In truth, there are real things about political institutions and aspects of the political process that reasonable people will despair about as well as celebrate. If students learn to see political realities more clearly and understand them better through their placements, then they will see both the negatives and the positives. Somewhat more surprising, perhaps, are student comments that reveal that either of these reactions, if handled well, can increase their motivation to become and remain politically involved.

The Engalitcheff Institute student in Senator Kennedy's press office came away with a more optimistic attitude toward politics: "Kennedy does so many things that I support so full-heartedly that it was exciting to feel part of the office's machine. . . . I guess I was feeling very frustrated and very alienated from the political system, and it was really exciting for me to see that there are people working on issues that I support and care about. In that respect, I have a little bit more faith in the political system and have found a place where my voice could be productive."

Students who make less positive evaluations often consider the time they spent to be valuable learning experiences nevertheless because the placement helped dispel the simpleminded idealism or naïveté they brought to it. As they understand better the dynamics of the organization or system, this means in some cases they come to see the system's serious structural problems. In a sense, they are achieving a more textured understanding of political realities. When the experience is intense enough, this can lead students to feel frustrated and disillusioned. But this is not necessarily a bad thing for their long-term political stamina or engagement. Political motivation that derives from idealism based in a misperception of reality is likely to be fragile, because engaging politically often involves confronting less rosy realities. Motivation that is not based on overblown idealism is likely to be tougher, more robust.

Adam Reich was originally a student in Cheit's course and went on to become his teaching assistant. Reich points to the paradoxical increase in inspiration that some students feel at the very time that they are becoming more pessimistic or cynical: "People's idealism about social change and work related to social justice might get tempered [in the placements]. It's hard, it's depressing to work with some of those organizations. . . . On the other hand, these same people are also more inspired to go out and work on these issues. It's an interesting tension."

Students in the course confirmed this impression. One student described his feelings of frustration and powerlessness but then went on to say that he and his friends planned to remain in their placements well beyond the end of the course. In essence, this student was pointing to his low sense of *external* efficacy (sometimes called expectations of government responsiveness), but for him the low external efficacy seemed to be accompanied by high levels of concern and political self-confidence. Studies of political action show that this combination can be a powerful motivator of political action (Levi and Stoker, 2002).

Political Skills

Acquiring skills requires practice guided by informative feedback. This means that placements can help students develop politically relevant skills if they gain experience with those skills in the placement and are given some guidance in using them effectively. One advantage of having students carry out tasks that are important to the placement organization is that staff will be invested in seeing that they accomplish the tasks correctly, and so are more likely to provide guidance. Of course, *which* skills students learn depends on exactly what they are doing in the placements.

POLITICAL ACTION SKILLS. Students who mention skills as a central part of what they gained from their placements had often conducted some kind of political action in the context of the placement. As one young woman from the Mills Institute for Civic Leadership said: "I had an internship with ACLU while I was there and that was a really great experience. I spent a lot of time phone banking, handing out fliers and bumper stickers, standing on street corners talking to people. That was good in terms of building those grassroots campaign skills, like getting comfortable approaching people and asking if they want a flyer. It was nice to see that grassroots campaigning can work—we were outspent on both campaigns and still won. Then we thought about, 'Here's what worked, and how do we replicate this in the future?'"

POLITICAL RESEARCH SKILLS. It is also common for students who conduct research of some kind during their placements to comment on the valuable skills they acquired. In addition, the more routine work assigned in some placements often constitutes a kind of participant observation research even when the student is not actually engaging in a formal research project.

CROSS-CULTURAL SKILLS. One issue that has received significant attention in both liberal arts and professional education is the need for students to learn to operate in increasingly culturally diverse American and international settings, as demographic shifts and globalization continue. Because placement sites often expose students to both coworkers and clients from backgrounds very different from their own, these experiences often help students become more skilled in functioning in unfamiliar cultural contexts.

In many cases, this involves middle-class, often white, students engaging with low-income or more racially diverse populations. If handled well, this kind of experience can be one of the great benefits of service learning. In contrast, at colleges that draw primarily first-generation college students, many of whom are immigrants or racial and ethnic minorities, the students may experience working in primarily white, middle-class, or professional class settings for the first time. Freyss highlighted this feature of service learning for her California State University, Los Angeles, students.

ADMINISTRATIVE SKILLS. Many placements involve a range of administrative tasks that help the organization pursue its mission. These are new experiences for students who have not worked in an organization before, and they appreciate the chance to acquire these skills, which are valuable in both political and other contexts. Joe Kahne mentions, for example, that students learn things like how to run a meeting. Often the administrative experience students gain in their placements also contributes to their ability to formulate action plans that will support the accomplishment of political goals.

Despite the positive value of some kinds of administrative experience, faculty need to be careful to ensure that students are not assigned exclusively to routine, clerical responsibilities that have little potential to enhance their learning. Such clerical tasks are important, of course, for any organization, but they should not be allowed to dominate student placements.

Personal Growth

Students who participated in the PEP courses and programs not only reported important academic and political learning as a result, but often also felt they had become more personally mature and responsible and had acquired understanding and skills that would contribute directly or indirectly to their future career success while also strengthening their capacity to contribute as citizens. High-quality placements are particularly well-suited to serve this configuration of goals.

MATURITY, SENSE OF RESPONSIBILITY, SELF-CONFIDENCE. It was quite common for students to report that their placement experiences had led to a greater sense of responsibility, self-confidence, and assertiveness. As one of Cheit's students said: "When I first went to Brown, I was kind of shy, had problems putting myself into new situations. So I try to get classes that have community involvement, because it kind of pushes my limits. Definitely the internship in the jail did that. I think every time I do that [push myself], I get a little bit better, a little more comfortable, and that's an intense situation to go into. . . . I think I'm now more comfortable in more situations because of that."

CAREER PREPARATION. Internships are well-known to today's college students as part of their career preparation, although they are more likely to be in businesses or other organizations where the students hope to work after graduation than in the kinds of public service organizations where PEP students are placed. Even so, it was not unusual for PEP students and faculty to mention the value of placements for students' future careers. Freyss is quite intentional in helping students use their placement experiences to become better prepared for the world of work:

> On the first day I tell them to treat it as a job placement. So they had to write a resume and I had a counselor from our Center for Career Planning and Placement do a half hour session on resume writing, providing handouts. Then students drafted their resumes and I looked at them and the Career Center looked at them before faxing them out to the organizations where they wanted to do the service learning project. Some of the organizations, like Senator Boxer's office, want to look at the resumes and do interviews before choosing students. And talking about that can be a good learning experience for the students, helping them understand that if the organizations have poorly motivated or poorly trained employees in their offices, their constituents or voters would notice and get a bad impression. So I'm combining a little career training with the civic education.

Another aspect of career preparation and personal development internships provide is the opportunity to talk with mentors about how these busy people negotiate the demands of their personal and family lives along with their professional obligations. Although most young women today expect to have both careers and families, and most young men expect to have wives who work, few college students, at least those entering college shortly after high school, have thought very hard about how to manage these potentially conflicting responsibilities. Kahne highlighted this as an important learning experience for the young women in the Mills Institute for Civic Leadership—a kind of collateral benefit because it was not one of the institute's explicit goals.

Strategies for Using Political Placements and Internships

Summing up her view of an effective placement, Alma Blount said: "This is what it means for an internship to work: The student has an intense learning experience. She is in over her head but able to do something productive, make a contribution. It must include direct service experience with face-to-face connections with clients. There has to be a good relationship with the supervisor with honest feedback. The supervisor may rein in the student when it is needed. And the student comes back in chaos mode." Although not all faculty would agree with this characterization, there is a near consensus on some key aspects of implementation:

1. Establish clear learning objectives.
2. Select placement sites carefully.
3. Set clear expectations and develop explicit agreements.
4. Attend to the logistics of site selection.
5. Consider the students' safety.
6. Prepare the students for the experience.
7. Establish strong mechanisms for students to reflect on the experience.
8. Evaluate the sites and the students' experiences regularly.
9. Prepare for the particular challenges of placements and internships.

Establish Clear Learning Objectives

All teaching benefits from clear forethought about what the teacher hopes students will learn from the course and from each of its component parts. It is also valuable in most cases for students to be aware of these learning objectives. It is therefore important that faculty articulate to themselves and to students their reasons for including external placements or other hands-on learning experiences in the course: what they specifically hope students will gain from participating in the placements, and how the goals for the placements fit into the larger set of goals for the course or program as a whole.[5] Unless the objectives are clearly articulated, it will be hard to know what constitutes a high-quality, relevant placement site and how to connect students' placement activities productively with other assignments.

Select Placement Sites Carefully

Once the course and placement objectives are clear, it is critical to choose sites that are most likely to provide productive learning experiences and are aligned with the objectives of the course. Some important considerations hold true in choosing a site for any course; others relate to the alignment between the site and the particular goals of that course.

LEARNING AND SERVING. In order to choose high-quality sites, it is important to find out as precisely as possible what students will be doing and to choose only those where students will engage in challenging activities that represent serious learning experiences. As we noted earlier, some placements, especially those called internships rather than service learning, involve activities that support student learning without contributing to the work of the organization in a serious way, but most faculty believe that students should be doing tasks that serve real organizational needs.

Phil Sandro stresses that it is "important to have a relationship with the community partner that has integrity and reciprocity." As one clue to the quality of the learning experience, he suggests using organizations "in which knowledge is shared among staff—as through regular staffwide meetings—and therefore more likely to be shared with students." He also asks himself whether the internship is likely to help students learn about community organizations more broadly, not just this organization's special niche. This dual assessment—of students' organizational contribution and the placement's learning value—is important because some responsibilities that help the organization, such as clerical work or very simple direct service activities, are not highly conducive to student learning.

RESPONSIBLE SUPERVISION. Another important consideration in choosing a site is whether someone will be available to supervise the student for the duration of the placement. Ideally, the supervisor should understand the goals of the course or program and try to ensure that the placement is a rich learning experience that furthers those goals.

POLITICAL, SYSTEMIC, AND POLICY DIMENSIONS. Besides providing challenging learning experiences and sustained supervision, placements must also involve experiences that support the course or program's particular goals. In the case of the PEP courses and programs, this means there must be some kind of political or policy dimension to the placement experience or at least some way to connect the experience productively with political or policy considerations. This requires the faculty member or program leader to be intentional about choosing sites and creating reflection mechanisms that support the development of *political* understanding, skills, and motivation.

The most straightforward way to accomplish this is to choose sites where students are involved in the practice of politics or activities designed to influence or implement public policy. This was the case for many of the

PEP placement sites: offices of elected officials, government agencies, policy institutes, and the like. But across the diverse placement sites that were used, we saw a continuum in the degree to which the political or policy focus was explicit.

In addition to those that are clearly political or policy-focused, the sites included many organizations that are less obviously political in nature, yet find ways to build a systemic or policy focus into the placement experience itself or into the way it connects with the rest of the course. In these settings, supervisors direct students' attention to organizational priorities and challenges and also to policy issues connected with the organization's mission. Thus, the policy focus is built into the placement experience even though the site itself could be considered a direct service organization. As David Schimmel says about the Citizen Scholars Program at the University of Massachusetts:

> If they're working at a soup kitchen, we hope they'll [not only be serving food but also will] be working with the director of the soup kitchen to understand what's involved in working with volunteers and with clients and in paying people and in getting the grants, things that they would not otherwise understand. And also it's important to get students involved with policy, both doing research, finding out how other communities have faced these problems and what the legislation has done, what is the research on this and policy proposals, and to take a stand and become an advocate.

In other cases, the policy dimensions are developed mostly through strategies implemented by the faculty member rather than the placement supervisor. The bridges that connect the students' placement experiences with the rest of the course or program provide the political or policy coloration. Both Alma Blount and Brian Murphy describe their students' placements as direct service, which is then tied to systemic issues through scaffolding from their teaching, assigned readings, and other course assignments.

As Blount said: "The *process* [of coaching and mentoring, discussion, research, and so on] makes the connection to the systemic level. Otherwise the summer internships would just be community service." This range of explicitness in political focus points to the fact that a wide range of placement sites can support political learning if faculty are thoughtful and intentional about weaving in a political/policy focus. But without this attention, many placement experiences will provide only community service rather than *political* learning.

THE FIT WITH SPECIFIC COURSE GOALS. Of course, incorporating a systemic dimension is not the only priority of the PEP courses and programs. Each also has its own unique substantive goals. Many faculty talked about choosing placement sites carefully so they support these goals. Cheit is extremely selective when evaluating prospective sites. They not only have to be welcoming, of interest to students, and generally relevant to the topic of the course—which is children and public policy—but also need to reliably raise issues that parallel the key policy considerations that Cheit hopes students will learn. He drops placement sites from the roster if they do not engage students in serious contemplation of those issues.

MATCH WITH STUDENT INTERESTS. Many faculty and program leaders also place a high priority on matching placement sites with the interests and goals of each student. Blount has developed a wide array of internship opportunities over a period of years.[6] "The key thing," she said, "is that the placements are customized. . . . We don't use cookie-cutter internships. If we want to quicken their leadership development, we need to put a lot of effort into finding goodness of fit."

Different kinds of courses and programs have different degrees of latitude in the extent to which they can tailor placement sites to students' particular interests. For some, the internships or other placements are drawn from a very wide range of topics, whereas other courses, such as Cheit's, are focused on particular substantive issues. Clearly, in topic-focused courses, it makes sense to match sites to student interests only in the constraints of the subject matter being addressed.

Kristi Schutjer-Mance talks about the process that the Mills Institute for Civic Leadership uses to match students with internships, emphasizing that a great deal of planning is needed to make sure the internships work well. Mills students commented on how much they valued being placed in settings of particular interest to them. As one student said, "I was excited about the internship we designed because it fit right in with all my interests—art and social change, community art processes. I got placed in a community arts program at a church, which was good because I'm also interested in faith-based nonprofits. It was exciting for me . . . really invigorating."

Clarify Expectations and Agreements

Clear expectations on the part of both site supervisors and students provide the basis for a mutually satisfying experience.[7] In the Higher Education Consortium on Urban Affairs (HECUA), once a placement site is chosen, each student develops a learning agreement, which is approved by both the external placement supervisor and the HECUA internship coordinator. The agreement may be amended as goals become clearer or circumstances change, and students are evaluated in part based on the degree to which they have met the goals outlined in the agreement.

A comment from a HECUA student underscores the importance of using learning agreements not only to plan the activities of the internship but also to guide and evaluate learning throughout the semester. The agreement is not set aside after it is developed but instead remains a key element in a dynamic process, designed to keep student learning on track:

> Before we started our internships, we had to make a learning agreement in which we listed goals we had for the semester in terms of personal development, skills, knowledge, and stuff, and we constantly checked back with that to see if we were in line with our goals, so that helped keep track. For example, I hated public speaking, so that was one of my learning objectives. Throughout the term my supervisor would make sure that I'd speak in high schools and just keep working on my skills. . . . The learning agreement was important. I signed it and my supervisor looked at it and then the internship coordinator at HECUA also looked at it. Then we'd have a midterm evaluation of our progress and also a final evaluation.

Choose Appropriate Sites

Given the many factors to consider, the process of enlisting appropriate placement sites is a significant undertaking. Fortunately, most campuses that are serious about encouraging students to be engaged in their communities, particularly in community service learning courses and programs, have a center or institute designed to promote that end. A first step is usually an audit of the organizations that might provide placement opportunities that connect with the learning objectives of the course or program. Centers are often very helpful in providing information on a wide range of possibilities. Then the center staff or the faculty member talks with contacts in the organizations to find out whether (a) the organization is interested, (b) the placement can provide challenging work for participating students, (c) a supervisor would be available to work with each student, and (d) arrangements can be made for regular evaluation of students in the placement.

At some colleges and universities, the center and its staff take the lead in contacting organizations being considered as placement sites and opening conversations about what that will entail. Otherwise it is the responsibility of the faculty to make the contacts and work out the necessary arrangements, including learning agreements between students, faculty, and site supervisors. In some cases, faculty prefer to make the initial connections even if a service learning center is available to do it. For example, Freyss says that she does this because she feels that the placements go more smoothly when she has talked directly with people at high levels of authority in the organization to gain their cooperation.

Service learning centers can also provide help with practical issues such as transportation to sites, liability issues, forms for defining the contractual relationship with the site, and so on. Whether or not this assistance is available, faculty need to consider logistics such as how students will get to their sites, whether public transportation or parking is available, the cost of parking, and so on. For some students, even modest expenditures can be prohibitive, so this needs to be taken into account.

Many faculty and program directors stress the value of developing long-term relationships with placement sites and using the same ones over and over again. There are many advantages to maintaining long-term relationships with placement sites. First, faculty can be confident that the sites understand the goals and requirements of the course or program, engage students in challenging work, and provide high-quality supervision. In addition, maintaining a core set of placement sites over time means that the laborious process of identifying and assessing sites does not have to be repeated in a full-scale way after the first year or two.

Consider Safety

Naturally, faculty and program leaders are careful not to put students at risk, and sites being considered need to be evaluated with this in mind.[8] These evaluations are not entirely straightforward, though. It is easy to assume that low-income neighborhoods are more dangerous than they really are, and this kind of bias carries an important message in itself.

Freyss told a story showing how her assumptions about a seemingly dangerous neighborhood came close to offending one of her students: "When a student described his assignment of leafleting an area in Los Angeles that is known as a high-crime area, I got concerned and was about to say that he should not go into areas that are not safe, when he mentioned that it was *his* neighborhood, that he was living three blocks away from the resource center where he had his placement."

It is important to distinguish between neighborhoods that pose real risks and those that might make students uncomfortable if they have lived only in affluent areas. In fact, one thing many students gain from their placements is learning to feel comfortable in settings that used to seem threatening.

Prepare for the Experience

It has become quite common for colleges and universities to offer, or even require, "gateway courses" that prepare students for community engagement before they participate in service learning. Stanford University, for example, offers a course called The Ethics and Politics of Public Service. The purpose, which we describe in *Educating Citizens* (Colby, Ehrlich, Beaumont, and Stephens, 2003), is to prepare students for responsible and thoughtful service and help them learn how to integrate their service experiences with their academic life. With similar goals in mind, Duke's Service Opportunities in Leadership program requires students to take a half-credit course—Civic Participation and Community Leadership—during the spring before their summer internships.[9]

When this kind of extensive preparation is not an option, faculty can prepare students for their placements in the service learning course. From his vantage point as former director of the Urban Institute at San Francisco State University, which handles some three thousand community placements each year, Brian Murphy stressed the importance of this preparation: "We just know from talking to professor after professor that where we have not done orientation to the environment they're going into, students can get lost; they can be overwhelmed."

Often the preparation addresses ethical issues, especially proper conduct in the placement sites. Cheit, for example, describes his approach this way: "I have them write an essay on the second or third day, asking them to think about the ethical implications of community service. There are major ethical implications with these placements. The ethics around leaving, for example: Is the child prepared for that? These are children who have had lots of people in and out of their lives. We discuss it in class before they go. . . . I want them to confront the question: 'Are you using these people?'"

Freyss also prepares her students for the ethical challenges of their placements. She sees this as an opportunity for students to learn something about professionalism:

> Behaving in an ethical manner is a requirement for their service learning experiences. I tell them they must always maintain a professional

demeanor. This isn't just about dressing appropriately or watching their language, but also about not gossiping. They are mostly eighteen-year-olds, fresh out of high school, and that's an age where they just want to share everything they observed. I have to help them understand what it means to be a professional—that one has to distance one's personal observations from one's professional role. So I have to remind them to be cautious in their presentations, to present things as general observations, not naming names, for example. And that's actually quite challenging for this age group, to move into the role of a professional and think about professional ethics.

Establish Mechanisms for Reflection

The experiences students have in their placements can be extremely valuable, but of necessity they represent experience with a very particular set of issues. This is both their strength and their limitation. This particularity means that faculty need to find ways to make sure the specific experiences students have in the placements raise larger questions and suggest larger lessons.

This raises the question of how faculty can help students see this one very particular experience as "a case of" something larger. The experiences students have in placements often point to other things, and much of their value is in their power to do this in a compelling and vivid way rather than in those particular experiences per se. Faculty work to ensure this by helping students make sense of what they're experiencing in a broader framework of understanding, connecting specific micro events in the placements with macro principles, and understanding the wider significance of particular events they witness and in which they participate. There are lots of ways to do that, including various forms of verbal sharing and writing assignments.

By sharing their experiences through discussions or presentations, students can learn not only from their own placements but also from those of their classmates. As one HECUA student remarked: "I think a lot of what I learned about the political process came from looking at the experiences of other people in my class with their community placement sites that sometimes were more directly involved with organizing. . . . We talked about building power or taking it, so that was one skill of political engagement I learned. It came about through my own experiences as well as from the experiences of others in the class."

Evaluate

Community and other placements as sites for student learning should be evaluated regularly by students who work there, by the placement supervisors, and by the faculty in charge of a course or program. To be most effective, evaluation should be ongoing or at least periodic throughout the term of the placement. Freyss, for example, stays in regular touch with students' designated mentors. Through this process, she evaluates her students' placement experiences as the quarter goes along rather than waiting until the end. By staying in touch with what is happening in the placements, she is able to help students make changes in placements that are not going well or modify their goals to establish a better match with available experiences. Unless the placements are evaluated early, it will be too late to move students with irresolvable problems to different sites.

To illustrate the importance of regular communication and evaluation, Cheit recounts a time when one of his students began having emotional problems in the placement and did not let Cheit or the teaching assistant know about it. The student simply stopped going, without telling anyone. This not only had negative consequences for that student's learning and well-being but "burned a bridge" for the course's ongoing relationship with a valuable placement site. Cheit tells the story in class to stress the importance of communication about issues that come up and responsibility toward the site and the course.

This case was an exception, though. Cheit generally stays in close touch with students' placement experiences. First, students keep journals that chronicle their activities and reactions to those activities. The journals not only serve as a pedagogical tool to deepen students' learning but also make it possible for Cheit to monitor how students are doing in their placements, what they seem to be learning, and the kinds of issues each placement site tends to raise.[10] Regular discussions of the placements similarly serve multiple functions. In addition, students complete both a regular course evaluation form and a special evaluation form for their placement at the end of the course.[11]

Journals and other reflection activities, along with the evaluations of the site supervisors, also provide the basis for student assessment in the context of a course. As Cheit writes in an introductory note to his students, "The journals provide you with an opportunity to connect theory and practice and relate what you are seeing and experiencing. . . . Since there is no final exam, the journal will become a very real and tangible exhibition of the work that you are doing at your placement. Reading your thoughts, understanding your experience, and following your reactions to the work that you're doing will provide us with an opportunity to see how you are engaging yourself in your placement and that you are thinking and learning about how your experiences relate to the course."

Be Prepared for the Challenges

These opportunities for powerful learning also have a particular set of challenges, from the most practical—time and transportation—to complex issues of the emotional intensity of the experience.

TIME COMMITMENT. External political placements entail very significant time commitments for both students and faculty. Such time commitments can be overwhelming for some students. Juggling placement commitments on top of schoolwork can be especially difficult for those who work to support themselves or those with family responsibilities.

Using placement experiences can also represent a major time commitment for faculty, at least during the process of enrolling sites and placing students. Service learning centers can be very helpful in this process. In addition, some programs employ their own internship coordinators, who take responsibility not only for placing students but for monitoring placements and troubleshooting during the internships. Fortunately, once placements have been arranged and are successfully serving the needs of the course or program and the organization, the partnerships should grow steadily stronger with each year. Experience using placements, especially experience with the same sites over time, helps the faculty member, the on-site supervisor, and succeeding groups of students benefit from prior experiences.

LOGISTICAL PROBLEMS. Especially in areas that lack convenient public transportation and in institutions where most students do not have cars, transportation to and from sites and other seemingly simple logistical problems can be real stumbling blocks. Although there is no way to fully address this kind of challenge, planning ahead and being creative about scheduling can help. Service learning centers are also invaluable in helping faculty with logistical issues.

UNEVEN QUALITY OF SITES, UNSUCCESSFUL MATCHES. Unfortunately, care in selecting sites does not guarantee a high-quality placement experience. Some organizations do not live up to their promises. Some students are irresponsible or otherwise unable to take full advantage of the site's potential. Sometimes the chemistry is just wrong. Many organizations are struggling to address very difficult issues with limited funds and inadequate staffing, and their institutional challenges make placement experiences impossible to fully predict or control. Kahne told us that one of the Mills College internship sites went bankrupt a couple of months into the semester, for example. At some sites, there is not enough for students to do. Some site supervisors find it difficult to trust students enough to give them real responsibility. Students sometimes complain that the supervision is poor and the work is not challenging. As Cheit said: "If you teach this way, you have to start with the knowledge that some of them will not work out well. By the time you realize it, it may be too late to put the student somewhere else. It's always a challenge."

These kinds of problems underscore once again why it is so important to evaluate the placements along the way, especially early on if there is an option to move students to another site. As Kahne said: "There's always a balance between letting the student work it out and intervening. That's something the internship seminar is key for. There have to be really good lines of communication. Ideally you want the students to solve the problems themselves but sometimes you do have to intervene and the hope is that you do it soon enough that all the time isn't spent."

Sometimes nothing can be done to bring the placement experience up to expectations, and moving the student is not feasible. Then, the question becomes how to salvage student learning in spite of a disappointing placement. Fortunately, this can usually be accomplished fairly reliably if faculty notice and deal with the problem. When students share their experiences with each other in some depth throughout the course or program, they can learn from others' placements even if they learn less than they hoped from their own.

In addition, when students are resourceful in finding ways to learn from a thin placement, they not only learn substantively but also develop strategies for coping with difficult situations. One of Freyss's students reported an experience like this: "Although I was doing work that I considered at the beginning not important—like cutting out newspaper articles or things like that—I kind of turned it around and made it important by asking questions about why I'm doing things and how it affected the community and what would be done with the work I did and things like that."

EMOTIONAL INTENSITY. Part of the power of external political placements as learning experiences derives from the fact that they engage students emotionally as well as intellectually. Of course, placement sites vary in the extent to which they raise potentially unsettling issues. Those that provide direct service are especially likely to expose students to highly charged issues that are far outside their prior experience. In this kind of placement, students need help managing their emotional reactions to the things they encounter. One of Cheit's students, for example, said that he had not felt emotionally ready for the intensity of entering a detention facility and really needed the support he got from his instructor and fellow students.

Sometimes students are upset not only by what the agencies' clients are going through but also by their perceptions of the staff. As Cheit acknowledged, "At the case discussions these hardened professionals [the doctors, social workers, police] tell jokes. The students are bothered by that. . . . They talk about the hardened professionals who tell child abuse jokes. To the students they seem really callous. When the students talk it through together, they understand it better. Some say this is what these professionals have to do. It is a mechanism they need to have to be able to tolerate this kind of thing week in and week out, even though it is jarring to us."

Good and continuous communication about placement experiences puts faculty in a position to help students interpret what they see and hear in the placement. Cheit told us, for example, that when his students work with public defenders in child abuse cases, "They talk to people who have been arrested. These people all talk about how unfairly they have been treated and the students get taken in by that. They come back and say 'You wouldn't believe how this guy has been treated!' I say, 'That's right, I wouldn't. You need to take it with a grain of salt.'" Of course, giving this kind of advice about how to interpret events from a placement site assumes that the faculty member knows that context well. Faculty do not second-guess students' direct experience lightly; a comment like this can come only from deep, long-term experience with the particular placement site and the issues it raises.

INCREASED PESSIMISM, CYNICISM, AND FRUSTRATION. Both faculty and students point out that some placement experiences give students a negative view of the institutions in which they work, the staff of those institutions, or other aspects of the political system. In almost every program, at least a few students end up feeling that the kind of work they saw in their placements is not for them. As Kristy Khachigian says about internships connected with the Engalitcheff Institute, "The internships can sometimes make some students more cynical. If they have placements in a federal agency, they can experience it as a humongous bureaucracy full of lazy bureaucrats. Sometimes they wind up learning that they don't want to do this kind of work."

If this realization leads students to pursue another, more personally compatible, approach to political engagement, the experience can mean a better fit between available options and their own interests and inclinations.

In fact, this process of sorting out where one might best make a contribution is an important outcome of placement experiences, and particularly whether to work in or outside the mainstream political system. In most cases, moreover, there are a wide array of strategies to help turn a negative reaction into renewed interest and inspiration.

In our discussion of the learning goals supported by placement experiences, we pointed out the somewhat paradoxical motivating impact that increased cynicism and frustration seem to have on some students. Negative experiences can be productive if they get the students thinking. As one of Cheit's students said, "I was really inspired by working at the training school, and the negative things I saw inspired me to figure out how to change them or how to take what I saw and use that constructively." The question, then, is how to keep motivation high in the face of frustration and disillusion. There are many different strategies for doing this, including invited speakers who offer another perspective, discussions with classmates, and faculty sharing their own wisdom of experience.

NOTES

1. For examples, see the "Placements (Service Learning and Internships)" section of the PEP document supplement at http://www.carnegie foundation.org/educating_for_democracy/docs/. For more extensive lists of sites where PEP students worked, see documents 32 and 36 in the PEP document supplement.

2. For examples, see the "Reflection and Journals" section of the PEP document supplement at the site shown in note 1.

3. For a better sense of what research service learning entails, and how it fits into the SOL program as a whole, see documents 21, 22, 23, and 24 in the PEP document supplement online.

4. For more information about this project, see document 26 in the PEP document supplement online.

5. For examples of how Alma Blount of the Service Opportunities in Leadership (SOL) program at Duke spells out these objectives for summer placements, see documents 21 and 33 in the PEP document supplement online. For an example of how Phil Sandro of the Higher Education Consortium for Urban Affairs (HECUA) spells out these objectives for internships, see document 31.

6. For examples of some of these internship opportunities, see document 36 in the PEP document supplement online.

7. For examples of how PEP faculty use written agreements to clarify such goals and expectations, see documents 30 and 37 in the PEP document supplement online.

8. For an example of one program's security policy for summer internships, see document 35 in the PEP document supplement online.

9. For a description of the gateway course and its relationship to the other components of SOL, see document 21 in the PEP document supplement online.

10. For Cheit's rundown of the journal's purposes, as well as his expectations for the journal, see document 39 in the PEP document supplement online.

11. For the form that students in Ross Cheit's course use to evaluate their placement experience, see document 51 in the PEP document supplement online.

12

LEARNING THROUGH STRUCTURED REFLECTION

REFLECTION IS WIDELY CONSIDERED to be the core of higher education, especially liberal education, which was once playfully described as teaching students to analyze Freud from a Marxian perspective and Marx from a Freudian perspective. Our central question in this chapter is how to use structured reflection to help students consider their experiences through lenses that bring the political dimensions into focus. This kind of reflection plays a pivotal role in helping them understand and navigate the real world of political possibility, conflict, and uncertainty.

Structured reflection requires students to step back from their immediate experience to make sense of it in new ways. The object of their reflection could be a newspaper story or scholarly article, their observations while working in a government office or private nonprofit, some kind of political action, or some combination of these and other experiences. Making experiences into objects of reflection means simultaneously heightening their impact while attempting to understand them in connection with any number of other things: concepts, issues, or experiences arising from other course components; one's past academic learning or personal history, one's values, assumptions, and convictions; theoretical or other conceptual or analytic lenses, and the like. In the process, students observe, analyze, examine, and consider their political experiences from multiple points of view.

Of course, one can imagine an almost endless number of frames, lenses, or filters through which to reflect on a given experience, and the choice of frames helps determine the character of the meaning derived from reflection. Different aspects of the experience become salient and take shape. Considering the perceptual and cognitive power of alternative interpretive schemes underscores how important it is for faculty to help students consider their political experiences in terms that contribute to the overall purposes and goals of the course or program.

Reflection has the power to reframe experiences and events in new terms. As a result, even when some course or program experiences, such as working in a direct service environment, are not explicitly political in nature, guided reflection can help students recast them in political terms by connecting their direct service with relevant policy environments or systemic analyses of the needs the organization addresses. A Duke University student, for example, talked about how structured reflection on her internship at the refugee resettlement branch of the Catholic Charities of New Mexico led her to study immigration policy and the process of seeking refugee status.

A widespread misconception about structured reflection is that it entails simply sharing feelings or voicing opinions. Many people mistakenly see reflection as a "feel-good" experience that may be useful for building community but does not contribute to intellectual development. In fact, poor quality reflective activities do sometimes fit this description. In contrast, in well-conceived reflective activities, emotional responses and initial opinions may serve as starting points but not as ends. High-quality reflection calls for well-developed intellectual skill and perceptiveness richly grounded in knowledge and expertise. Although undergraduate students are not experts in the process of reflection any more than they are experts in the subject matter they are studying, well-conceived and well-structured assignments can help them develop greater expertise in the intellectual processes of reflection, analysis, and interpretation as they work toward greater subject matter expertise.

The importance of structured reflection is not simply an article of faith. Extensive research on community service learning shows that the quantity and quality of reflection is consistently associated with both academic and civic learning. Engaging regularly in structured reflection leads students to deeper understanding and better application of subject matter knowledge and increased knowledge of social agencies, increased complexity of problem and solution analysis, and greater use of subject matter knowledge in analyzing problems (Eyler and Giles, 1999). Reflective practices in the classroom have also been shown to help learners connect earlier experiences to new content in order to achieve better understanding of the new material (Lee and Sabatino, 1998).

Pedagogies of Structured Reflection

Faculty have developed many different ways to support and structure students' reflections on key aspects of their educational experiences.[1] These include both oral and written activities as well as online journals and conversations, which are a kind of hybrid of written and oral formats. Many faculty link these types of reflection, for example, by asking students to respond to written prompts or assignments and then share the products in a discussion with their classmates.

Few undergraduate students know how to reflect on their experience in a sophisticated and productive way, and it takes guided practice, faculty support, modeling, and feedback to learn this skill. For this reason, faculty who use structured reflection do so regularly throughout the course or program. Another reason why faculty include regular reflection in their courses or programs is to create a "culture of reflection" intended to engender lasting habits of reflecting systematically and self-consciously on one's experiences. This seems to work, and many students identified habitual reflectiveness and integrative thinking as qualities they expect to carry with them into the future as a result of participating in the course or program.

Reflective Discussion

All of the faculty teaching the courses we studied make time for reflective discussions of key texts and other learning experiences, such as community service placements and political action projects. They drew on several methods to structure discussion-based reflection. In some courses, faculty lead the whole class in reflection during the class session. In others, groups of students meet with teaching assistants for these discussions. In yet another approach, students in project teams meet to reflect on the work they have done together in their political action or research projects or other group activities. Many faculty use more than one of these approaches.

Reflective discussions are frequently used as a way for students to debrief after spending time in community service or other placements. This allows them to share insights, raise questions, express and make sense of emotional reactions, and very importantly, to connect what they are seeing and learning in their placements with key issues and themes highlighted in the course readings and lectures. Regular debriefing allows students to explore multiple perspectives and generates new insights that help group members address the complexity and uncertainty they encounter in their placements, internships, political action projects, and other experiences.

Sometimes in-class discussions involve talking about written reflections the participants have recently completed. For example, at Berea College, Meta Mendel-Reyes dedicates part of each class to reviewing students' written reflections about readings and activities, touching on key points she wants to make sure they understand. In addition, each week she *idea* assigns a different student to read through classmates' written reflections and make observations about them. "These are the things I noticed—there were quite a few who felt this way, but some . . . and so on." According to one of the students, the class felt that "this was a good way to start the discussion, because then another student would say, 'Actually, I do feel that way, but also. . . . ' and so on. It means that each student has to read everyone else's written reflections and lead the discussion at least once."

Written Reflection

Written reflection usually involves frequent short writing assignments such as journals, logs, or brief essays. Although faculty often use more than one form of written reflection, they almost always ask students to use each form a number of times so that they gain facility with it and the learning will be cumulative.

JOURNALS AND LEARNING LOGS. Faculty use collections of periodic or ongoing writing exercises in which students record thoughts, questions, and comments about their learning; make plans for future work; and give feedback to the instructor. The integration of learning from multiple sources is a central priority for the HECUA's Metro Urban Studies Term, so director Phil Sandro asks the students to write journal entries every three weeks about their internships, readings, and interactions with invited speakers.[2]

The format of journals or learning logs differs depending on the goals of the course or program. Many faculty use one or more of the following approaches:

- *Application of theoretical or conceptual frameworks to experiential learning.* What theories or other academic knowledge help me understand this experience or event? How do I understand the broader context of what I observed? How does this experience connect with other things I've studied or experienced?

○ *Direct reflection on experience.* What are the key things I learned from this experience or activity? What issues or questions did it raise? What reactions did it evoke—what was challenging, surprising, enjoyable, frustrating? Why did it evoke those reactions?

○ *Reflection on their own learning and development.* What do I still need to learn or work on? What is my strategy for making progress? How can my knowledge or skills be improved? What can I change or approach differently in the future?

Another way to structure students' responses to these kinds of questions is to ask them to write regular brief reports in the form of letters (for example, to a parent, friend, or their classmates) describing what they are experiencing and what they make of it. During their summer internships, students in Duke's Service Opportunities in Leadership program write weekly reflective "essay-letters," called "letters home," from their community placements to the program director, Alma Blount, who then replies to the letters.[3]

REFLECTIVE ESSAYS. Used frequently as a mechanism to support systematic reflection, essays are written in response to many different kinds of prompts and questions, often asking students to connect what they are learning across two or more components of the course. In the full-semester course that follows the summer internships in Duke University's program, students write a weekly reflective essay, each focusing on a different key concept. The concepts are grounded in reading assignments. Together they cover the central issues that Blount sees as critical in the development of political understanding and engagement. Some of the topics we noted during the year we studied this program were as follows: "navigating our way through a polarized political landscape—the liberal view, the conservative view"; "building power at the base—organizing across race, class, and political party differences"; and "the inner work of leadership." Each week, Blount chooses one or two of the students' essays, "not necessarily the best ones," to read to the class. The essays frequently stimulate lively discussions. In fact, as Blount puts it, the degree to which an essay opens up a full, rich discussion of the topic constitutes valuable feedback to the student author on the essay's depth and insightfulness.

Online Reflection

Some faculty use Web-based or online journals and discussions, which have both benefits and drawbacks. In one class, students wrote online journals with threaded discussions where classmates could see each other's contributions and respond to them electronically as well as have an in-class discussion about them. The professor reported that the online approach "didn't work well at first because students needed more technical training, so we had to provide that," but has evolved into a useful method. One student found online conversations more appealing than in class discussions because "it is hard to think on the spot [in reflective discussions], especially when you are listening to the other person." Being able to read and react online allows time for students to think about their responses. Another advantage of electronic conversations is that they can be conducted during out-of-class hours rather than taking up limited class time.

Goals and Benefits of Structured Reflection

Reflection is itself a goal for political development, as well as a set of learning activities or pedagogical strategies. As a goal for democratic citizenship, reflection includes certain intellectual skills—reflective and critical thinking of various sorts; it is also a habit of mind or inclination—a tendency to think about and take time to carefully consider, interpret, and integrate one's own experiences. Structured reflection activities contribute importantly to reflective thinking, as well as to many other key aspects of political learning. Reflection is an opportunity to promote deeper knowledge of political concepts, issues, and processes. It can strengthen students' sense of political identity and efficacy, as well as help them acquire and apply political skills. Reflection can help students think critically and purposefully about their political learning, judge the progress they are making toward goals, and plan or imagine realistic future political engagements. Perhaps most important, reflection can support the integration of learning across multiple contexts.

Political Understanding

Faculty members' primary reason for using structured reflection is to help students develop a better understanding of the substantive content of the course or program. Like most faculty, those who teach for political learning often observe that students have difficulty focusing on the main points of readings or projects, do not analyze the issues clearly and thoughtfully in papers or discussions, and need continuous prompting to think systematically and creatively about the course material. We learned from students that when reflection is structured to help them engage closely with course materials—and when they are encouraged to put real intellectual energy into it—they become more inquisitive and engage more actively with the texts and topics they are studying. As one student said: "It made me think a lot more than other classes [did]."

Teaching students to become more sophisticated political thinkers and writers involves helping them grapple with the complexity of political arenas, issues, and processes. For many students we talked to, reflective processes were a significant contributor to making them less simplistic in their approaches to social and political issues: "[Structured reflection] has made me think about social problems, definitely, on a deeper level than I was before. Before, I would try to break down issues to very simple cause and effect, like one cause, one effect to an issue. And now I tend to look more at underlying issues, aggravating factors, and political barriers to enactment of change, like ideological barriers." Structured reflection can lead students to more specific forms of understanding and knowledge, such as recognizing their own and others' underlying assumptions, deepening their learning from experiential learning activities, and integrating learning across the different components of the course or program.

RECOGNIZING UNDERLYING ASSUMPTIONS. Critical reflection can also help students recognize the unexamined assumptions that shape their thinking, locate the origins of those assumptions, and subject them to critical analysis (Cranton, 1996). A number of faculty use reflection to help students recognize and reconsider the stereotypes and pat judgments they bring to political engagement so they can begin to consider a wider array of interpretations. Sandro works to help his Metro Urban Studies students "become aware of the lenses they are using—how those lenses are socially constructed, [how they are] partial, who [the lenses] privilege, and so on. They need to come to grips with the lenses they are using. . . . No view is unmediated. Students see through lenses, and to the extent that they are aware of that, they can *test* their lens in the world."

MAKING SENSE OF EXPERIENTIAL LEARNING ACTIVITIES. Reflection is widely understood as a critical component for all forms of experiential learning, including those used to support political understanding and engagement: community service learning and internships, students' interactions with political leaders or mentors, and their involvement in political action projects and simulations. Many students said that even though reflection exercises were time-consuming and difficult, the effort was well rewarded because these exercises were so clearly essential for making sense of their internships, service placements, and political action projects.

Without reflecting on these experiences in a systematic way, students often do not know what to make of the action experiences and find that these experiences do not add up to anything they can take with them and build on. John Dewey considered reflection a key component of experiential learning and a critical part of the intellectual work of developing hypotheses and testing them through action (Dewey, [1910] 1933). Modern experiential learning theories also stress the role of reflection in translating experiences into concepts that can be used as guides for engaging in new experiences (Kolb, 1984).

Ethical questions are among the most compelling issues students grapple with as they attempt to make sense of their experiential learning. Kristi Schutjer-Mance, of the Mills College Civic Leadership program, noted that ethical issues emerge in relation to specific events that have taken place, often having to do with things like power conflicts or confidentiality. In the seminar that accompanies Mills students' internships, "Students bring in cases that arise in their placements and they will do role-plays focusing on ethical ways to respond, what are the options here, what is the best option, why is that the best option, and so on."[4]

Structured reflection can also add a political, systemic, or policy dimension to nonpolitical or direct service experiences. Faculty who use political internships or placements do not always use sites that are explicitly political in nature, such as legislative offices. Some place students in direct service organizations and are faced with the question of how to draw out the political or policy dimensions of the service experiences. Structured reflection that is designed specifically to make those links is critical for ensuring that this kind of placement contributes to *political* learning. A student at Berea College talked about how much she appreciated the broader, more policy-related context that the course's reflection exercises provided for her community service work: "It gave me the chance to reflect—what causes this problem, why do we need to do this service? In the class, we did a project on emergency food, which really opened my eyes—an analysis of the emergency food system. I always try to think through the things I do, but it is a relief for it to be part of an assignment."

INTEGRATING LEARNING. Students often have trouble connecting new knowledge with prior and concurrent learning on other social issues or disciplinary topics and with practical applications of that knowledge. This is a problem because fragmented knowledge and isolated bits of information are much less useful than knowledge and information that are connected and brought together in a more complex and powerful integration.

Structured reflection is an important method for helping students integrate their learning across time and different contexts, across different components of the course, and especially, to connect experiential learning with readings and lectures. One PEP student said that the feature of the program that stood out most vividly for him was the combination of critical questioning, applying common lenses to otherwise segmented experiences, and finally weaving it all together through structured reflection.

Faculty frequently use structured reflection to help students connect their experiential learning with other major components of the course or program, notably reading assignments and course lectures. The goal is for the various sources of learning to be mutually illuminating in an authentic way—not forced, artificial, or facile. When this is achieved, reflection forms a kind of connective tissue for supporting the integration of these different forms of knowledge and experience.

Reflection is particularly useful for helping students move between political theory and political practice or action. Faculty often describe the integrative process as one of moving between micro and macro levels of politics or between concrete and abstract representations. They point out that this is a two-way street, moving from practice to theory as well as from theory to practice. A simple "application of theory to practice" is not a true integration, because it does not take seriously the dynamics and complexities of real practice situations.

Theory necessarily abstracts a formal model from the uncertainty, specificity, and complexity of practice. Making judgments about which particularities can be abstracted out without undermining the usefulness of the theory is a key factor in developing and refining theory. For this reason, the process of reflecting on the kinds of lived experiences involved in political action projects or community placements often means that theoretical learning is challenged by the complexities of the political arena, where resource constraints, organizational dynamics, and inevitable conflicts between two or more valued outcomes pose thorny dilemmas and require judgment in the face of irresolvable uncertainty. Reflection does not always provide answers to those questions and dilemmas, but it does increase the likelihood that students will become aware of them and take them seriously.

Political Skills

When carefully designed and guided, structured reflection helps students develop some important political skills. They exercise the skills of good judgment, build skills of strategy and tactics, and begin to take responsibility for learning from experience.

GOOD JUDGMENT. Faculty often use reflection to help students think critically about their choices and actions, with the intention of fostering better judgment and decision making. For Sandro, every reflection exercise is intentionally "pointed toward . . . wiser action and habits of mind." He wants the HECUA students to pursue thoughtful, wise political action and believes that "reflection may help prevent students from going in a bad direction."

When students are taught to think consciously about their own political action in progress, about the decisions they are making as they grapple with difficult challenges, and about the dynamics and processes of the groups in which they are working, including their own role in the group—and when they are encouraged to employ this kind of reflection habitually—they begin to acquire the skill of critical reflection during action. Blount considers this to be a crucial leadership skill, and supporting its acquisition is one of the central goals of the Service Opportunities in Leadership program. She offers a compelling metaphor for this ability:

> Critical reflection is the ability to develop a reflective stance in the midst of action. It is the skill of doing "balcony dance floorwork" with groups—being in the middle of intense, demanding, and perhaps confusing experiences (on the dance floor) and at the same time stepping back to see the large patterns and contours of the group experience (going to the balcony). Balcony-dance floorwork helps you see more clearly, make sense of the mess, and strategize skillfully about where to go from here . . . to see the larger context of the work and one's options for effective action.

Like Blount, Marshall Ganz teaches his students to distance themselves from their immediate political action in order to observe their own practice and gain a perspective on the work. As Ganz said, they are "moving from self-consciousness to self-awareness." This reflective stance provides the basis for wiser, more considered judgment, which is important in a public arena characterized by uncertainty, conflict, and creative opportunity.

POLITICAL STRATEGIES AND TACTICS. An important subset of critical reflection in the midst of action is evaluative reflection on the political strategies and tactics students are using in their concurrent political activities. This kind of reflection involves sharing information about successful approaches, troubleshooting ineffective action, and refining political skills, especially when students debrief regularly during their political action projects, as Jim Farr's University of Minnesota students do each week of their Public Achievement practicum. The reflection groups hash through what is working and what is not, offering each other suggestions based on their own experiences and suggesting ways to refine important skills. By sharing their experiences with the same skills being applied in very different situations, group reflection increases the students' ability to transfer their skills to new problems or settings.

LEARNING FROM EXPERIENCE. Studies suggest that reflection involving what learning psychologists call *metacognitive processes,* in which students reflect on their own learning, can generate greater mastery and understanding of a subject. For example, math students who are asked to pause frequently during problem solving and ask themselves questions such as "What am I doing now?" are more strategic in their problem-solving and perform better than unreflective learners (Garner and Alexander, 1989; Schoenfeld, 1985, 1987).

Reflection can also encourage students to establish their own learning goals, to monitor their progress, and to ask for help when they are not accomplishing the goals. In this sense, students are taking responsibility for their own learning. As we pointed out in Chapter Eleven, some PEP programs, especially those that use placements, ask students to create learning contracts in which they clearly articulate what they want and expect to learn.[5] Through targeted reflection exercises, students evaluate their progress toward those goals and make changes where needed.

The desire to teach students how to learn from their own experience in political practices of various sorts is a driving force for some of the PEP faculty. For example, Ganz is well aware that his students will not become experts in community organizing during the semester that they take his course. Because their skills will still be rudimentary when the course ends, Ganz pays a lot of attention to teaching students how to learn from their own practice or experience. The conscious use of targeted reflection is the basis for this effort.

Political Motivation

With deeper understanding of political issues and concepts and stronger political skills, students are more likely to be motivated to participate politically after the course or program. Structured reflection can help them recognize and articulate their reasons for wanting to participate. In the course of reflection, they may voice the personal meaning they find in ideas or experiences, understand themselves as politically engaged, and reinforce their sense of efficacy, especially in the face of challenges.

PERSONAL MEANING. Just as in other college courses, students in the PEP courses learn about the subject matter as well as develop skills such as writing and analytic thinking. In most of the PEP courses and programs, it is also important for students to think through in a serious way what the material means for them, and to formulate their own (at least preliminary) conceptions, perspectives, and opinions both on political or policy issues and also on broader questions such as the nature of a democratic system.

Rick Battistoni of Providence College has this goal squarely in mind when he asks the students in his political science course, Ancients and Moderns: Democratic Theory and Practice, to keep an ongoing "democracy theory journal." In their journals, students draw from readings, lectures, and other course activities to build their own theories of democracy incrementally over the course of the entire semester.[6] Battistoni believes the journals give his students a sense of ownership of the course material, making it more personally meaningful to them and thus more useful in their lives as citizens. His students appreciate this personal dimension of the course, "being able to write about what *I* believed and *my* theory, versus writing a research paper about someone else's ideas."

POLITICALLY ENGAGED IDENTITY. Many of the PEP faculty use reflection to help students become more aware of their political values and identities, and in many cases, to reevaluate them in light of their current experience. These efforts to develop a deeper self-understanding focus on questions like, "Who am I? What kinds of forces shaped who I am now? Where am I heading, and what is important to me?" Prominent threads in these reflections are the students' beliefs about their roles as citizens, their responsibilities in a democratic system, and their political histories, values, and aspirations. Battistoni's "democracy theory journals," for example, push students to think about their own political commitments and responsibilities as well as political theory more generally.

In many of the PEP courses and programs, this self-examination is directed toward creating an alignment between one's history, important aspects of oneself, such as talents and interests, deeply held political and social values, and one's political aspirations and actions. To the extent that this kind of alignment can be achieved, it means that students' political actions will be grounded in their personal, cultural, and religious backgrounds, their awareness of their own individual strengths and inclinations, and stable, deeply held values, as well as new and ongoing learning and open-minded consideration of alternatives. Commenting on his course on the environmental history of California at California State University,

Monterey Bay, David Takacs explains that he uses reflection as an integral part of a cycle of self-awareness and action through which students "understand and plumb their own values," become more alert to the political and historical contexts of their lives, and "use what they learn to act politically in the world."

When reflection leads students to pay attention to the way new goals and beliefs fit with their prior understandings, they are prompted to resolve the tensions and inconsistencies between the two (Boud, Keogh, and Walker, 1985). The exploration of these tensions and inconsistencies among values and beliefs or between values and actions is an important part of working toward a more "examined life" and a more fully integrated sense of oneself as a civic and political person. A number of PEP students mentioned that reflective journal exercises, especially when they read and respond to each other's work, help them bring understanding, values, and actions into alignment. As one Berea College student said, the reflection process pushed her to "analyze my thoughts, actions, beliefs, values to make sure they're all in line."

Similarly, students learn to build their political values and commitments into their sense of who they are, thereby developing a strong sense of themselves as politically engaged people. One of the main goals of students' reflection on the practicum experience in Farr's course at the University of Minnesota is to "get students to reflect on their own roles as citizens—to establish a sense of 'civic self.'"

We saw this happening for the students in that course and others. A Duke University student, for example, told us that participating in Service Opportunities in Leadership created a "commitment to being engaged no matter what I'm doing careerwise later on." This happened in large part through a reflection process that involved "a lot of questioning in terms of how I should live my life and how I should choose my career. . . . I didn't really reach any definitive answers, but I think the answer I did reach was that no matter what, it needs to be making a positive contribution to the world around me."

All of this is supported by the introspection entailed in individual reflection and also by the social, collective process of group reflection. When students articulate their civic or political goals privately, it contributes to a stronger sense of commitment. And when they share their personal articulations of political aspirations, they often gain social support for their developing goals and commitments. A young woman from the Mills Institute for Civic Leadership (ICL) told us that a reflection exercise was critical in "steeling her commitment" to her goal of starting a nonprofit organization promoting self-help and mutual support among African Americans of all ages.

REINFORCED SENSE OF EFFICACY. As we observed in our discussion of placements and internships, the emotional or other personal challenges of experiential learning can be both exhilarating and demoralizing. The process of structured reflection can strengthen a feeling of efficacy despite the challenges.

Experiential learning—especially placements or internships and political action projects—often involves frustration, setbacks, disappointment, and disillusion. One of the key roles structured reflection plays is to support students during these challenges, in part by helping them make sense of what they have seen and experienced. Regular reflective discussions in which students describe the challenges they are facing and share strategies for dealing with them can enable students to maintain a positive, hopeful attitude toward engagement, rather than becoming cynical to the point of withdrawal or overcome with frustration. Ross Cheit's students at Brown University who spent the semester working in the youth detention facility, for example, were dismayed to find the system quite dysfunctional, while students in Family Court were distraught over the horrific accounts of child abuse they heard. In Cheit's view, the thing that kept them motivated in the face of all this was the chance to work through their perceptions and feelings with the other students in the course through regular section meetings devoted to reflection.

In the view of Schutjer-Mance, the biggest obstacles to students' achieving the goals of Mills' ICL program are their "despair and doubt about whether the political system is the way to go or frustrations with conflicts within the group or with people in the internship organization, or frustration with the politics of their nonprofit or government office internship site. But because the program's internship seminar provides opportunities to reflect on these disenchanting experiences and strategize and get feedback from the institute's faculty leaders, these obstacles are not insurmountable and students get through it pretty well."

One reason it is so important to help students work through their frustrations and disappointments as they occur is that, if they are not dealt with, these feelings undermine students' confidence and their capacity to maintain a sense of political efficacy in the face of setbacks. As students learn from upsetting experiences, talk through challenges and difficulties, and share their achievements and successes, they learn how to deal with unanticipated problems and gain confidence about surmounting difficulties in the future, thereby achieving a stronger sense of political efficacy.

Strategies for Fostering Structured Reflection

As we noted in the beginning of the chapter, if poorly planned, reflection exercises and activities can result in little more than a "feel-good" experience and do not contribute significantly to intellectual development. The faculty and staff in the Political Engagement Project worked especially hard to design and use structured reflection in ways that would be effective and meaningful to the students.

- o *Be clear.* Make sure the students understand the purpose and specific goals of the reflection assignments.
- o *Teach the process.* Teach students how to do structured reflection.
- o *Mix it up.* Use varied reflection strategies.
- o *Assess the work.* Assess student reflection, either formally or informally.
- o *Learn from the reflections.* Use students' reflections to assess and strengthen assignments and the course or program.
- o *Be prepared.* Anticipate the challenges of using structured reflection.

Be Clear

Creating opportunities for guided, intentional reflection is only the first step. It is also important to make clear to students the reasons behind the reflection assignments. Structured reflection can be used for many different purposes, and the purpose ought to shape the character of the reflection process. This means that both faculty and students need to be clear about their answers to questions like, "Reflection for what? Toward what ends? From what points of view?" Students often misunderstand the purpose of reflection, treating it as a rote exercise or a chance to share their feelings. For example, one student said she thought the purpose of the reflection was simply "to let [the professor] know that we read the chapter or participated in the event." Not surprisingly, she did not feel that she got much out of it: "My feeling is that if I am going to do it [read the text, go to the event], I will do it. Having to do the reflection didn't help much."

Teach the Process

It is equally important to explain to students precisely how the reflection exercises will work, tying the exact nature of this particular kind of reflection closely to the goals it is meant to serve. For in-class reflective discussions, it is important to begin by showing students what is expected. This involves setting out guidelines, helping students engage with each other, probing where appropriate, and modeling the kind of reflection sought. It can also help to explain and show how to use a heuristic or analytic framework that aids students to understand what kind of learning their reflections should involve and what kind of things would serve as evidence of that learning.

To help students understand what they are looking for in written reflection responses, many faculty create and distribute explicit guidelines for these reflection exercises.[7] The guidelines might point out, for example, that the instructor will look for evidence that students are connecting their action experiences with ideas from readings and other class materials, not just spouting stream-of-consciousness ruminations or offering personal opinions that are not conceptually grounded. Faculty also emphasize that it is not acceptable to focus entirely on personal feelings ("I felt very upset about. . . .") or to simply describe events without commenting on their significance or connecting them meaningfully to key issues in the course.

As already noted, few students come to college already knowing how to reflect on and integrate their various course experiences in thoughtful and productive ways. Teaching them how to do so is an integral part of using reflection pedagogies effectively. PEP faculty pointed out several facets of this process.

CREATE HIGH EXPECTATIONS. A critical first step in teaching students systematic reflection is to create high expectations for what reflection involves—that is, to convey and elicit intellectual rigor from the outset. Faculty often start by choosing terms for reflection assignments that convey the intellectual rigor they are seeking, calling the assignments field observation reports, personal observation reports, reflective essays, critical reflection papers, and the like. Farr, for example, calls the journals that his students write "thought books," a term taken from Hannah Arendt.

High standards can also be signaled by grading some or all reflection assignments, highlighting or sharing examples of good work, and building key points or issues raised in students' reflections into future lectures, discussions, or assignments. These practices show that the ideas students generate through reflective discussions and writing are taken seriously.

PROVIDE EXAMPLES. Modeling can be another powerful way to set high expectations and help students understand the kind of reflection you want them to engage in, including what it means to link reflection to course materials and other academic learning. John Reiff, of the University of Massachusetts Citizen Scholars Program, begins by telling students a story about his own racial awakening in college in the South and then asks students to apply a framework they have been learning in class to his story. After they have finished the analysis, he tells them, "This is the same process that I want you to use in making sense of your own stories and experiences." Others provide examples of well-crafted written reflections from previous years to help students understand what is expected. Before Duke University students set out on their summer internships, they read examples of especially thoughtful and well-written "letters home" from previous cohorts, which are posted on the Web.[8]

PROVIDE TIMELY, INFORMATIVE FEEDBACK. One of the best ways to ensure that students learn how to reflect with clarity and insight is to give them guidance not only at the outset but continuously as they move forward in practicing the skills of reflection. PEP faculty provide timely, substantive feedback on their students' reflections, pointing out connections students are missing and suggesting areas for useful future reflection. They also provide feedback on the argumentation and presentation: Do the students' conclusions truly follow from the analysis? Do the observations form a connected whole?

Some faculty even take the time to follow up on how students understand the feedback they have given. They write questions and comments about journal assignments or reflection papers—suggesting that students make some changes in the ways they carry out their reflections—and then ask them to respond to the feedback. Because this process is so time-consuming, some faculty offer feedback on only a subset of students' journal entries.

In reviewing students' written reflections, faculty are careful to respond to students' comments and queries, often discussing frequently occurring issues with the class. If students use their reflections to raise problems or challenges from their placements or projects, faculty find ways to address these individually or in the particular work group that is having the problem. Students told us repeatedly how important it was for them to know that faculty were reading their reflections and responding with instructive feedback. One student told us how helpful it was when her professor responded to a conflict in her internship about which she had written in her journal, even though the comment did not offer a concrete solution to the problem. "The professor wrote back and said, 'I hear you, I know where you're coming from. And It's OK to feel the way you do.' I really appreciated having that affirmation from her."

Mix It Up

In order to accomplish the full range of outcomes that structured reflection can lead to, it is helpful to include several different reflection strategies in a single course or program, varying the form and medium. Asking students to write regularly in a learning log or journal looking critically at their experiential learning as it proceeds is one of the most common methods, but it is far from the only way to structure reflection. Many faculty incorporate written and verbal reflection, individual and group activities, and assignments that draw on and develop a variety of skills, including analytic, expressive, integrative, evaluative, communicative, and strategic capacities.

TIMING. When structured reflection is paired with experiential learning, the timing of the reflection assignments depends on their goals. Reflection *before* learning activities helps students prepare for the project or placement, bringing existing knowledge to bear, planning strategically, and identifying skills they need to work on. Students find it useful to discuss the assumptions and expectations they bring to the task ahead, as well as articulate their hopes and the resources they can mobilize for the work.

Reflection *during* activities is used to make sense of the experience from multiple points of view, to think about the relationship of issues arising in the practice activities to prior and concurrent academic learning, and the like. Ongoing reflection can also help students monitor their progress and learning, address problems and challenges, and celebrate incremental achievements.

Reflection *after* activities, whether carried out individually or in groups, helps students process what they have learned, examine the relationship of new learning to prior understandings, assess their own performance, and set new goals. One way to do this is through a reflective report of some kind—a report to the class at the conclusion of a political research or action project or a report to a placement site that shares students' insights with the organization.[9]

DEGREE OF STRUCTURE. Another important dimension along which reflection assignments vary is the degree to which they are highly structured or more open-ended. There are advantages and disadvantages to each, and many faculty use assignments of both types, often moving from more structured formats early in the course or program to less structured formats later, when students have become more adept.

Almost all PEP faculty using reflection ask students to respond (in discussions or in writing) to specific questions or issues,[10] rather than offer free-form responses to their reading or applied experiences. Sometimes students choose from among several alternative prompts.[11] Especially in the beginning, asking students to respond to specific, concrete questions can help clarify what structured reflection entails. This can be particularly important for students who have not participated in reflection before or when they are being asked to do reflection involving a high level of abstraction or theorizing. Even when students are very experienced, some highly structured reflection tasks remain useful for particular purposes.

Another structured reflection assignment that many faculty find useful is a sentence completion exercise, which can be done in either written form or as the trigger for a discussion. Sentence stems are designed to get at issues that are important at a particular stage of the course, program, or project. For example: "The most important task ahead is. . . ." "We will know our action project is successful if. . . ." "The biggest challenge in my project is. . . ." "The most interesting thing about studying the election process so far has been. . . ." Another approach is to ask students to list the top five or ten questions they have about a topic: "Write the five most important questions you have now about education policy/campaign finance reform/role of interest groups in politics," and so on. It can be useful to have students write down their questions individually and then join a group discussion of the questions class members have listed.

Critical incident analysis is another useful, semistructured task. Students choose key events or experiences from their internships or action projects and write in colorful detail about what happened and also the "how, why, what, and when" of the event. They include their thoughts and feelings about the event, along with important connections to other course or program material.[12]

In addition to using prestructured tasks, most faculty also include more open-ended reflection assignments.[13] Students often appreciate having the freedom to choose their own topics for reflection, based on what they find most compelling, intriguing, or troubling. A student who had earlier complained that the directions for an assigned reflection journal were vague also commented that she actually liked the openness of the assignment:

"On the flip side, I kind of enjoyed the looseness of it because I got a chance to think freely." Students vary in the amount of structure they prefer, some wanting the instructor to define the task very precisely, others finding less structure liberating, a welcome contrast with most assignments in their other courses.

CUMULATIVE VERSUS DISCRETE TASKS. Another choice faculty need to make when they use structured reflection is whether to use assignments that are cumulative—in essence, repeated reflections on the same topic—or a collection of more discrete tasks or a series that uses a common format but addresses a new topic each time. The "democracy theory journal" that Battistoni uses is a prime example of the cumulative approach.[14] Over the course of the semester, students expand, rethink, and refine their thinking about democracy by responding to questions; drawing on course readings, lectures, and discussion; and connecting all that to their own values and beliefs. By the end of the course, they have created their own seventy- to one-hundred-page working models of democracy that Battistoni hopes will inform and shape their experiences as citizens during and after the course.

In addition to this kind of cumulative approach, almost all courses that use reflection include a variety of reflection tasks that cover a wide range of territory in both form and content rather than pursue a single set of issues in the same form over time, as the cumulative tasks do. This variety helps students develop many skills as well as flexibility in using a reflective mind-set in different ways. As always, the key to effective reflection is to match the form with the goals.

Assess the Work

Faculty who use written reflection in their courses often struggle with whether and how to grade the assignments. They want to send a message that the reflections constitute serious intellectual work and are an important part of the course. Assigning letter grades to students' reflections is a powerful way to accomplish this.

Not surprisingly, whether or not assignments are graded and how heavily those grades figure into the overall course grade makes a difference in students' effort and therefore what they learn from these assignments. As one student said when we asked her how much effort she put into this work: "Not as much as I should have. . . . I did the things that were given more weight in that class and other classes."

At the same time, faculty are aware that many reflection assignments include a strong personal dimension, which makes a grade seem like a judgment about the student's character. Faculty are understandably reluctant to have that kind of judgment play a role in the student's course grade. They also fear that formal assessment of the more personal types of reflection would discourage candor in the students' responses. Another factor mitigating against assigning letter grades is faculty workload. Some faculty ask students to write journal entries or other reflections frequently throughout the course, and it is not feasible to grade all of these assignments.

Faculty resolve this tension in a number of ways, usually depending on the nature of the reflection task. Generally, the stronger the personal dimension, the less likely the responses will be assigned letter grades. Reflection essay papers, such as those that centrally address substantive issues in the readings and lectures and integrate these with issues arising in experiential learning, are graded usually. More than half the PEP faculty whose students complete written reflections grade some or all of the work. Most use a pass-fail system for journals, with passing grades assigned to those who complete all of the journal or learning log assignments. These faculty often supplement the pass-fail system with written comments on a subset of the journal entries, asking probing questions and suggesting ways for students to strengthen their reflective analysis and writing.

Cheit requires students to keep an ongoing reflective journal about their placement experiences as they connect with issues from course readings and lectures. The journal includes three reflective essays.[15] Although Cheit does not grade each journal entry, he does grade each essay separately, and the overall grade for the three along with other journal entries accounts for 40 percent of the course grade. The "letters home" that Duke University students write during their summer internship are not graded, but the weekly reflective essays in the fall semester follow-up course are, and together the seven essays account for 25 percent of the course grade.

Learn from the Reflections

For most faculty, structured reflection is not only a teaching strategy that supports many aspects of student learning but also a way to find out how well students understand the course materials, how they are reacting to particular parts of the course or program, and what they are learning from the various components. For example, Cheit taps into student discussions of their placement experiences regularly to monitor how rich those experiences are and how well they raise the key issues addressed by the course. This kind of evaluative reflection can be an extremely effective way to find out whether students are getting out of assignments what the teacher intends, and to make adjustments or deal with problems along the way if things seem to be going offtrack.

Faculty also use student responses to reflection exercises to evaluate and strengthen their teaching. Some make the course-evaluation function of reflection very explicit. At the end of each class, the students in Ganz's course on community organizing spend about ten minutes doing what he calls a "plusses and deltas" exercise. This involves talking about what worked well in that class session (plusses) and what changes they would suggest as the course moves forward (deltas). This exercise can be used to identify what is working well or needs adjustment in the course as a whole or in particular components, such as students' projects.

Be Prepared

As with the other teaching strategies, being prepared for the particular challenges can ensure reflection's efficacy. The greatest challenges are poor quality of student efforts, the time these processes demand of both students and faculty, and students' discomfort sharing their thoughts and experiences.

POOR-QUALITY REFLECTION. The key challenge in using these pedagogies is to achieve reflections that are of high enough quality to support real learning. Faculty members often express dismay about the poor quality of their students' reflection. One told us, "I often don't get from students what I am seeking. . . . We often get 'Dear Diary, Today I did X, Y, Z.'" Students have the same concerns. One Providence College student was able to see that her theory journal entries were not up to par: "At some points I found that I kind of rambled on about whatever I was reading and thinking about."

Sometimes this poor-quality work results from lack of clarity in the assignment. Students often complain that the directions for reflective exercises are vague. Faculty may not realize how little they can take for granted in incoming students' reflection skills, so an explanation of the assigned task may seem crystal clear to them while being opaque and confusing for the students.

Another reason for poor quality is lack of motivation. It is a challenge to get students to put their best efforts into this activity. Some just do not buy into the task, primarily because they do not understand its value, or they believe that if it is not graded it is not important, or because they do not have time for everything they need to do and when they have to make hard choices, it is careful reflection that goes.

Developing expertise in reflection takes time, but students do make progress as they gain experience. Battistoni is not alone in seeing increasing sophistication in students' reflections as the course proceeds: "A lot of students begin with a narrow definition of democracy— 'It's what is done in the United States,' or 'We're the only true democracy'—but come to have much more nuanced views of different forms of democracy (direct participation versus representation, and so on) by the end of the course."

An excellent long-term strategy to provide more sustained experience with reflection is for faculty teaching different courses to work together to help students develop their reflective capacities cumulatively over the entire course of their college years. By coordinating efforts, faculty can build on each other's work, so that students in later years are not starting from scratch each time they are called upon to do structured reflection.

TIME LIMITATIONS. Another concern for faculty is the extensive time commitment structured reflection requires—time that could be used for additional readings, assignments, or activities. Similarly, students sometimes complain about the amount of time and work that goes into written reflections, even if they acknowledge benefiting from and enjoying it. The keys to keeping the task manageable—and palatable—for students have already been described in our guidelines for using reflection effectively: use some highly structured, quick, but productive tasks along with more time-consuming assignments; intersperse written reflection, which tends to be more demanding, with discussion-based reflection that takes place during class and thus does not increase students' workload; make it clear that it is more important for regular journal entries to be cogent and insightful than long; and make sure students understand the value of the work and develop some skill in doing it so that reflection will feel like time well spent.

Faculty are also concerned about how time-consuming reflection assignments are for *them*. Although there is no ideal solution to this problem, faculty do find ways to keep the workload within reasonable limits. Among the various strategies are extensive use of well-trained teaching assistants; establishing the expectation that students will receive feedback on a subset of their journal entries and other frequent written reflections, not on every entry; asking students to respond to each other's written reflections when the decision has been made to share them; and substituting reflective essays for other class papers rather than making them add-ons.

STUDENT DISCOMFORT. Students are accustomed to classroom discussions, so reflections that use this format do not usually raise any special problems. In fact, most students enjoy sharing their reactions to class readings and other experiences and learning from the reactions and thoughts of their classmates. Reflective discussions can sometimes feel more personal than the types of class discussions students have experienced before, however, and for those who are shy or who feel their perspectives may deviate from the norm, these discussions can provoke anxiety. For the sake of these students and others, it is essential to create an atmosphere of trust and mutual respect.

In some courses, faculty suggest that students share with each other at least some of their written reflections; in others, written reflections are read only by the instructor. When the course does involve sharing written reflections, reactions are divided. Not surprisingly, some students feel less comfortable sharing their written reflections—whether those are made public in electronic form or in the context of a class session—than they do expressing their thoughts during a group discussion.

Other students are entirely comfortable sharing what they have written, welcome feedback from peers, and are eager to read what their classmates have to say. One student commented that the best thing about the reflection process was the opportunity to read and respond honestly to what others in the class had to say. This student felt that the process revealed a multiplicity of fresh and enlightening perspectives and that her peers' responses to each other's work were "very tactful and professional, not mean. I would read and reflect one way and then would see another perspective, so it broadened all our perspectives." In fact, some students who were not asked to share their journal entries and other reflections regretted the lost opportunity.

This sentiment is not universally shared. As with almost any writing, reflections are written, at least implicitly, with a particular audience in mind. Some students write for themselves and their instructors even if they know their responses will eventually be shared more broadly. When the time comes to make their journal entries or other responses public, these students are sometimes acutely uncomfortable.

When students know their written reflections will be made public eventually, some write from the outset with the audience of the whole class in mind. This approach makes their writing easier to share, but it also has a widely acknowledged downside. Students commented that they did not feel they could be completely honest when they wrote from this point of view, when they were acutely aware that the others would be reading their reflections.

Students often need guidance as they learn to comment on each other's work diplomatically yet honestly, whether orally or in writing. It is also important to encourage students to challenge each other's interpretations and arguments. One student noted that making comments online after reflections are posted can be a "nonconfrontational way of sharing ideas," but also saw the lack of confrontation as a drawback, noting that learning to confront others' positions tactfully is a valuable skill.

These challenges are very much like those faced in fostering high-quality deliberation. In both cases, it is important to encourage frank exchange while maintaining an open-minded and respectful tone. Students need guidance and practice doing this, as well as a classroom atmosphere that values and supports these goals.

NOTES

1. For examples, see the "Reflection and Journals" section of the PEP document supplement at http://www.carnegiefoundation.org/educating_for_democracy/docs/.

2. For the guidelines for these praxis reflections, see document 44 in the PEP document supplement at the site shown in note 1. For examples of other assignments in the HECUA program that involve reflection about the internship, see documents 45, 46, 47, and 48.

3. For the guidelines for these letters home, and for an example, see documents 49 and 58 in the PEP document supplement online.

4. For the guidelines for these weekly journals, see document 43 in the PEP document supplement online.

5. For an example of a learning contract, see document 30 in the PEP document supplement online.

6. For Battistoni's description of this journal, see document 38 in the PEP document supplement online.

7. For examples, see documents 38, 39, 43, 44, 49, and 50 in the PEP document supplement online.

8. For one example, see document 58 in the PEP document supplement online.

9. For a description of one such reflective report, and for a student example, see documents 15 and 54 in the PEP document supplement online.

10. For examples of this more structured approach, see documents 38, 40, 42, and 46 in the PEP document supplement online.

11. For examples of this middle-ground approach, see documents 43 and 50 in the PEP document supplement online.

12. For an example of this critical incident approach, see document 44 in the PEP document supplement online.

13. For examples of this more open-ended approach, see documents 39, 41, and 49 in the PEP document supplement online.

14. Again, for a description of the democracy theory journal, see document 38 in the PEP document supplement online.

15. For a description of the journal and the three reflective essays, see documents 39, 40, 41, and 42 in the PEP document supplement online.

13

PUTTING THE
PIECES TOGETHER

HIGHER EDUCATION CAN—and should—do more to prepare college students for responsible democratic participation. Helping young people become more politically engaged not only benefits communities and American democracy writ large but is also extremely valuable for young people themselves, contributing to many developmental goals and helping them become more skilled and enlightened guardians of their own political interests and values.

As we noted at the outset of this volume, we do not expect or even hope to turn everyone into a superactivist, armchair pundit, or professional politician. Our conception of politics is very broad, allowing for great variety in modes of participation, some of which may not look much like conventional political activities. A generally informed and habitual voter fits this broad conception of responsible political engagement, but so does a faithful member of a neighborhood association or a person who participates in a social movement that is critical of political policies, leaders, or institutions.

Preparing Students for Political Participation

Contributing to the social good in some way is important to most adults (Rossi, 2001; Seligman, 2002), but there are many legitimate ways to do this. We recognize that people differ in their interest in politics and their desire to be actively engaged. Even for socially responsible people, the centrality of political participation in their lives varies enormously. These variations notwithstanding, we believe that a person's education is deficient if she has not developed at least a basic working knowledge of the political world in which she lives.

Preparation for informed citizenship should include some understanding of political institutions, processes, and issues, and it should include long-term interests, habits, and commitments that support at least a basic level of knowledge and engagement. It should also include the abilities to acquire and evaluate political information, to formulate and express opinions about important political issues, and to engage in conversation and cooperate with others around these issues, including those who have quite different views. Although these capacities can all be developed through informal as well as formal means, it would be hard to argue that people who lack them are well educated.

In our view, the quality of political engagement is at least as important as the frequency of engagement. Of course, what counts as quality in political participation is to some degree a subjective matter, and quality is arrayed along a broad continuum that ranges from multiple variants of the misinformed and misguided to equally varied embodiments of political expertise and wisdom. It does not seem sensible to set the bar for participation too high—it is better to be inclusive even in the absence of sophisticated understanding. But surely higher-quality participation is preferable, and undergraduate education should aspire to move students forward on the quality continuum, whatever their starting point.

What do we mean by quality? Ideally, participation should reflect wise judgment grounded in political knowledge and understanding, familiarity and comfort with a wide array of political skills and a strong strategic sense for when and how to deploy these skills, along with steadfast motivation, including the capacity to withstand setbacks and disappointments and a commitment to basic democratic principles such as equality, rights, and majority rule. It is at least as important to work toward a sense of political participation that is emotionally compelling, intellectually interesting, exciting, attractive, and personally consequential. Politics is, at best, an avocation rather than a career for most people. In order to stay involved over time, people have to feel that it is something they want to do, for their own sake and for the sake of others. An undergraduate education can make only a start toward these goals—none will be fully achieved. But a clear vision of the multidimensional nature of the goals will go a long way to ensuring that the endeavor is at least heading in the right direction. It will provide learning that lasts—as described in the next section.[1]

Learning That Lasts

Even if undergraduate education moves students forward on these various dimensions of political development, it cannot guarantee their continued political participation and growth in the years after college. For most people, the desire to contribute to the common good competes with many other desires and needs, which vary both individually and according to life-cycle stage and life situation. This hard reality raises the question of what college educators can do not only to develop these qualities but also to make them robust and stable enough to survive the vicissitudes of time and competing claims.

Based on developmental theory and research as well as common sense, we believe that the learning goals of the Political Engagement Project, if they are achieved, can form the basis of ongoing participation and learning well beyond college. This does not mean that taking part in any single course or program will be sufficient to foster lifelong political learning and engagement. But it does mean that if we frame political development in multidimensional terms—to include many aspects of deep understanding, personal transformation, and expertise—the chances are much greater that changes during college will constitute an early step of a trajectory that will be cumulative over time, diverging more and more from those of students who have not undergone these changes in early adulthood.

Some aspects of learning, including political learning, appear to be quite stable once they are achieved. Intellectual sophistication, including the capacity for critical thinking, the ability to engage in reasoned discourse, and the ability to marshal and evaluate evidence, does not appear to degrade significantly once it is achieved, at least in the absence of distinct pathology (Mentkowski and Associates, 2000). This is one of many reasons to address, in the political domain, reflective judgment and related cognitive processes that are universally acknowledged as central goals of higher education (see King and Kitchener, 1994, 2002).

Key concepts about political institutions and processes will also persist if students grasp them in a deeply experiential way. For example, if students enter a course thinking that democratic participation refers only to electoral politics in the narrowest sense but then meet people who are politically active and effective pursuing avenues that go well beyond voting or campaigning—or if they take part in such activities themselves—their understanding of the scope of political participation shifts. This understanding should not be lost once it is achieved. Likewise, if students experience directly the complexity of competing values that characterizes policy formulation and implementation, they will rarely go back to a simplistic, rule-bound conception of those processes.

Substantive content knowledge, so essential to wise judgment about real issues, tends to fade in memory or become outdated. Maintaining awareness of current issues, and of the evolving scientific, social, and economic contexts of political events, so essential for high-quality political participation, requires ongoing attention and engagement. Only those who develop long-term habits, interests, and inclinations, often referred to as *dispositions*, are likely to remain well informed about contemporary issues.

One important factor that explains why some changes in civic and political habits that take place in college persist and others do not is the degree to which they are incorporated into one's political identity. A number of studies have shown that the long-term impact of organizational and other political experiences on later political involvement is mediated by the development of an enduring sense of self as a socially concerned and politically responsible person. This politically engaged identity in turn motivates continuing action that is consistent with that sense of self (Colby and Damon, 1992; McAdam, 1988; Piliavin and Callero, 1991; Youniss and Yates, 1997).

Habits, interests, and inclinations that are deeply rooted in one's personal identity are more likely to persist for a number of reasons. First, there is a press to behave in a way that is consistent with deeply held values and beliefs in order to avoid a sense of internal contradiction (A. Blasi, 1995; Colby, Ehrlich, Beaumont, and Stephens, 2003). For example, if a person feels that it is essential for a responsible citizen to vote and that belief is a core feature of that person's own identity as a responsible citizen, then he is more likely to feel that he *has to* vote at election time, whether it is convenient to do so or not.

Second, core characteristics of an individual (those central to her sense of self) are likely to play a role in the activities and environments with which she chooses to engage, which then reinforces or even amplifies the characteristics that led her to choose that environment. Thus, people's deeply held interests and values often channel them into activities that further deepen those very qualities. So, for example, if staying politically well informed is a key part of a person's identity, she might develop a habit of following a favorite political blog, listening to public radio while driving in the car, or watching the news on television while making dinner. These experiences then make her better informed, she is more likely to feel confident joining conversations about current issues, and these activities further reinforce her sense of herself as an engaged and well-informed person.

Politically engaged identity is just one of several developmental goals that, if achieved, provide a strong foundation for continuing political learning and engagement. Similarly, a strong sense of political efficacy has been shown to increase active participation, which then further increases the individual's actual expertise and sense of efficacy.

Many political skills, once gained, are also likely to persist. Once people have learned how to negotiate and compromise in group decision making or how to run a meeting, it is not likely they will forget completely how to do so. They might choose not to compromise or negotiate in a given situation, they might feel a bit rusty if it has been a long time since they used these skills, or they might encounter more challenging circumstances for which their current level of expertise is not sufficient. But their abilities rarely revert to their pretraining level.

Teaching for Enduring Learning

We are convinced that the active and reflective pedagogies used in the Political Engagement Project are especially well-suited to accomplishing deep and enduring learning. They engage students simultaneously on several different levels: intellectually, emotionally, socially, and personally. They ask students to perform their understanding: students take key ideas learned in an academic setting and apply them to the complex and uncertain realities of political action, with important reciprocal impact from the realm of action back to their grasp of the intellectual subtleties of the classroom material. Furthermore, these pedagogies are effective because they offer ongoing assessment, coaching, and feedback, often self-consciously instilling in students the capacity for self-assessment and an active search for sources of guidance.

Finally, a special strength of these key pedagogies is that they connect students not only with ideas but also with *people*. Students interact with faculty and program staff and peers and also with mentors, speakers, staff at placement sites, clients or constituents of placement organizations—people who draw in students new to political engagement, deepening their engagement by making demands on them, inspiring them, personalizing and dramatizing the issues, offering solidarity in a common quest, and leading them to new identifications that change their sense of who they are and who they want to be (Colby and Damon, 1992; Youniss and Yates, 1997).

Openness to Political Engagement

A number of recent surveys show increases in social and political concern and higher levels of political participation among undergraduates. For example, in its recent report on its 2005 survey of college freshmen, the Higher Education Research Institute (HERI), of the University of California, Los Angeles, was generally upbeat about young people's increasing interest in the political realm. That survey found feelings of social and civic responsibility among entering freshmen at their highest levels in twenty-five years. A record 49.7 percent had participated in an organized demonstration as high school seniors, and more than one-third (36.4 percent) believed it is important or essential to "keep up to date with political affairs," which is the highest rate since 1994 (Pryor and others, 2005; see also Harvard University Institute of Politics, 2005; Lopez and others, 2006.)

In this and other recent surveys, investigators often interpret the increases in political interest and engagement as reactions by students to major world events such as the September 11, 2001, terrorist attacks, the war in Iraq, and natural disasters such as Hurricane Katrina. At this point, there is no way to know whether this rebound in social concern is a temporary reaction to dramatic events or an indication of a more enduring shift in attitudes. However, it is quite likely that students' heightened awareness of the need for social solidarity and human concern will not persist unless it is reinforced by other experiences.

It is also worth noting that the level of political interest in this so-called Millennial Generation still leaves almost two-thirds of the students in the HERI study believing that it is *not* important to keep up with political affairs. Other political indicators in this study are also fairly low in absolute terms, even though they are higher in this cohort than they have been for many years (Pryor and others, 2005). In another study, voter turnout in the 2004 presidential election among those under age twenty-five was shown to have climbed eleven points since 2000, but that age group still trailed the next generation of voters (ages twenty-five to thirty-four) by nine points and the next (ages thirty-five to forty-four) by seventeen points (Lopez, Kirby, Sagoff, and Herbst, 2005).

Overall, we believe these data and the results of other recent surveys indicate a real openness among young people to political and civic learning and engagement, but they also suggest that large numbers of young people probably will not make a long-term democratic commitment without efforts by educators to capitalize on that openness.

High-profile events and issues that command young people's attention may not accomplish widespread change, but they do present valuable opportunities for learning. Even a modest and temporary increase in social and political interest offers a chance to engage students through activities and experiences that have the potential to build a more enduring sense of social and political concern. But without educational follow-up, young people's immediate concerns triggered by these issues and events will likely fade.

The Political Engagement Project offers a similarly optimistic picture of college students' openness to and potential for political development.

The PEP survey data show that it is possible to move students along the continuum of quality political engagement—or rather on the multiple continua that represent more specific goals in each of the three main clusters—understanding, skill, and motivation. (See Appendix B, "Survey Scales and Results.") These data make it clear that students can gain significantly in all these areas, and also in their expectations for future participation, even during a single summer or academic semester.

Participating students showed statistically significant gains in both foundational political knowledge and knowledge of current issues and events. Their skills of political influence and action and of political analysis increased, as did other skills relating to communication and teamwork. In addition, their interest in politics, their sense of political efficacy and politically engaged identity, and their intentions for future electoral participation and expression of "political voice" were significantly strengthened.

But does the PEP present an overly optimistic view? After all, the students who took part in these courses and programs did so because they chose these experiences over others. In that sense, they may not seem representative of the larger college population. Still, many chose to participate for reasons other than an interest in politics; indeed, as we have explained in this volume, many had little interest in politics at the outset. These students took courses and programs because they fit with a schedule or because they fulfilled a graduation requirement, for example. Yet these low initial interest students were those for whom the courses and programs had the greatest impact.

The lesson, then, for colleges and universities is this: even if it is not possible to provide all undergraduates on a campus with compelling educational experiences to promote political engagement, they can reach a much larger share of students than they are reaching now. Students are not given well-crafted opportunities to learn about and engage with the political realm nearly as often as they are encouraged and helped to engage in nonpolitical civic voluntarism. We believe they will respond to attractive opportunities for political engagement, because we have seen this happen in colleges and universities across the country.

Beyond Political Engagement

The HERI report on 2005 freshmen noted that the increases in civic responsibility and engagement indicated by the survey are correlated with improved practical and intellectual skills.

Increased Intellectual Development

Students in that study who showed a greater desire to contribute to society also had higher scores on a standard test of the disposition to think critically, the ability to see the world from someone else's perspective, and a willingness to think in complex ways about other people's behavior (Pryor and others, 2005). This association is not surprising: political learning both requires and contributes to the development of greater epistemological maturity, reflective judgment, critical thinking, research skills, oral communication skills, and writing ability.

A highly regarded instrument for assessing what students learn in college, the Collegiate Learning Assessment (CLA), illustrates the intersection of political learning with the kind of general intellectual development that is the hallmark of successful learning in higher education (Klein and others, 2005; Shavelson and Huang, 2003). The CLA, which the 2005 U.S. Secretary of Education's Commission on the Future of Higher Education features as one of the most promising new approaches to collegiate assessment, assesses students' critical thinking, analytic reasoning, problem-solving, and writing abilities, using performance tasks of several kinds.

To measure problem solving, the CLA uses tasks in which students are given multiple sources of information about a problem and are asked to evaluate and analyze the information and use it to draw and defend conclusions about the problem at hand. These problems are often questions of institutional or public policy, and their similarity to questions addressed in the PEP courses and programs is evident. For example, students must integrate information from newspaper articles, federal investigation reports, scientific studies, internal memos, and other documents to formulate a policy recommendation for an organization.

The CLA measures analytic writing through tasks requiring students to articulate a position on a complex issue, provide evidence in support of the position, and make a persuasive case for their view through effective writing. Again, several of the writing prompts focus on issues that arise in public life or controversial proposals for public policy. For example, one writing prompt asks students to explain why they agree or disagree with this statement: "There is no such thing as 'truth' in the media. The one true thing about the information media is that it exists only to entertain."

Although some educators have raised questions about the feasibility, cost, and proper uses of the CLA, to our knowledge no one has questioned the importance and relevance for undergraduate education of the outcomes it is designed to assess. Because it is clear that these outcomes are also central to education for political development, the compatibility between political and general intellectual learning is undeniable.

Learning for Work

Intellectual development is universally acknowledged as among the most important goals of higher education, but it is not the only goal. As we pointed out at the very beginning of this book, preparation for paid work is at least as salient in many students' thinking about the purpose and value of a college education. The majority of respondents (73 percent of women and 65 percent of men) in the 2005 HERI freshman survey said that they were attending college in order to pursue training for a specific career. Seventy-two percent of both women and men said they had decided to attend college in order to get a better job (Pryor and others, 2005). These findings, which are consistent with those of many other studies, raise the question of how compatible political learning goals are with preparation for work.

In this area, as in the case of intellectual development, we believe the answer is clear. Every occupation affects and is affected by the political, economic, and policy contexts in which it is located. Issues of professional licensing and accreditation, the institutional settings of work and regulations that affect them, workforce and compensation issues, and the complex of forces that shape the clienteles or other publics the occupation serves are just a small sampling of topics in the political domain, broadly understood, that students preparing for a particular occupation can benefit from studying.

In addition, virtually every occupation has the potential to serve the public good. An important longitudinal study that followed students during and after college found that six years after college, graduates' civic voluntarism that is unconnected with their work had fallen off significantly, but these alumni increasingly believe their work contributes to the greater good: "Two thirds (66.2 percent) of the study participants are satisfied or very satisfied with the opportunities to contribute to society through their job, and more than half (57.7 percent) report participating in volunteer service opportunities through their employer" (see Higher Education Research Institute, 2005). A survey by Cone, Inc. also found that "young people are extending their social consciousness to the workplace. Of the 28 percent of young people (ages 13 to 25) who are employed full-time, 79 percent said they want to work for a company that cares about how it affects or contributes to society" (Jayson, 2006).

A strong background in thinking about the public purposes of one's chosen work and the broader issues connected with the social impact of a range of institutions and occupations can help ensure that this desire for or perception of social contribution is more than wishful thinking or rationalization. That outcome would benefit the individuals themselves as well as contributing to the greater good. A study of paid work in a representative sample of American adults found that people who experience their work as contributing to the social good find their jobs more rewarding than those whose job satisfaction is limited to personal gratification, such as sociability or intellectual challenge. Those who spoke of the social contribution their work makes (usually along with personal gratification) also reported significantly higher psychological well-being and rated their lives as better overall (Colby, Sippola, and Phelps, 2001).

A Move Toward Open Inquiry and Political Tolerance

Colorful news reports of bitter political discord among college students and between students and faculty make it clear that the academy is no haven from the polarization and intolerance that characterize politics outside the academy. Those who are deeply engaged in political action care passionately about the issues, so it is not surprising that tempers often run high. In addition, for many politically active individuals, not only those in college now but also (maybe even especially) those who went to college during the Vietnam War, intolerance toward and vilification of the opposition are taken as signs of political commitment, integrity, and purity, indicating a strong resolve to resist the ongoing press to compromise one's principles for the sake of expedience. Open-mindedness and human understanding across political difference are not even aspirations or ideals among those who think this way. This "litmus test" phenomenon has been around for a long time, and it is not likely to yield easily to countersuggestions. Entrenched cultural values are hard to change.

Political passion, on the whole, is a good thing, and we have no desire to turn it into cool and distanced calculation. But in the PEP programs we have seen that it is possible to instill in college students passionate concern and commitment combined with openness to views different from their own. Many of these students achieve a gut-level understanding that those with opposing views are real people, not demonic caricatures. They come to recognize that some common ground often unites people whose interests are otherwise at odds and that both groups can benefit by cooperating around those shared goals. We were continually impressed by the ways these courses and programs were able to work toward political clarity and conviction combined with human understanding, tolerance, open-mindedness, and a sense of community that transcends ideological difference.

We are under no illusion that courses and extracurricular programs on college campuses, even if they become widespread, can quickly or easily shift the tone of public affairs more broadly. The dynamics of politics at all levels, from local to international, are extremely complicated and subject to implacable structural forces. But it may be possible to chip away at the polarization and narrow-mindedness that too often characterize politics both on and off college campuses if we can show large numbers of young people the moral and practical appeal of a more cooperative approach.

We also come away from the Political Engagement Project much encouraged about the troubling question of political bias on campuses and in the classroom. We wholeheartedly agree with critics of the academy that political indoctrination of students is not acceptable. And we believe that "some professors are intolerant of certain political or social viewpoints," to quote the survey conducted on behalf of the conservative American Council of Trustees and Alumni (Center for Survey Research & Analysis, 2006, n.p.). It stands to reason that a few faculty are politically intolerant and bring that intolerance into the classroom, whether wittingly or unwittingly. But intolerance comes from both conservative and liberal directions, and neither variety seems to have much impact on students' political views (Astin and Denson, n.d.; Beaumont, Colby, Ehrlich, and Torney-Purta, 2006).

We are also convinced that the great majority of faculty who take their students' political learning seriously recognize their responsibility to provide multiple legitimate perspectives on issues under consideration, to draw out differences of opinion among the students, and to help students think critically about evidence and claims, even when those claims are being put forward by the instructor. Students in these courses enjoy differences of opinion and value diversity of perspectives. A close look at the PEP courses and programs makes it clear that there are many viable ways to educate students for responsible democratic participation without imposing on them any particular ideology.

Importance of Quality Teaching

Throughout this book, we have presented a very hopeful picture of higher education's potential to foster political engagement that is inclusive as well as reflective, thoughtful, and open-minded—engagement that is both critical and self-critical but also committed, forceful, and active. But our optimism is contingent. These outcomes depend on colleges and universities' efforts to make opportunities for political learning more widely available and on the quality of teaching in the courses and programs they offer.

In many respects, good teaching for political development is simply a variant of good teaching more generally. Much of what we learned from the PEP faculty echoes the findings of research on teaching and learning and other writing that captures the wisdom of practice.

Teach Students What You Want Them to Learn

Again and again, we heard what seems to be the most important maxim: *Teach students what you want them to learn.* Surprisingly often, faculty do not think through fully what it is they do want students to learn, and their teaching is guided by other considerations—the structure and landscape of the field, their own interests and expertise, readily available texts, and so on. The assumption is that students will somehow pick up and retain whatever is most important to them from the breadth of material that is offered.

The importance of teaching what you want students to learn applies equally to deep understanding of concepts and to the learning of complex skills of practice. Fully grasping a concept implies that the student can explain it in his own words, provide examples that illustrate its meaning, extend its application to new contexts or situations, and represent it in multiple ways. The more directly students are taught to manipulate the concept in ways that constitute and reflect deep understanding, the more likely they are to attain that understanding. Likewise, if students are to develop skilled know-how, they need to be taught those skills directly through carefully chosen tasks that require the skills in question and guided practice in performing the skills.

This simple idea has a number of implications for education that aspires to support political development. For example, educators often assume that providing experience with nonpolitical *civic* engagement will prepare students for sophisticated and effective *political* engagement. This transfer does sometimes happen, but we cannot count on it. If you want students to learn about political and policy concepts and issues related to community experiences or academic subject matter, it is important to make those connections explicit.

It is also important to give students practice using the political concepts they are learning in ways that develop and reveal deep understanding, along with feedback on their efforts to do this. We saw a number of strategies for accomplishing this in the PEP courses and programs—for example, an ongoing theory journal, which draws on readings of classic political theory to develop a working theory that can guide students' own democratic participation. When students try to integrate the abstract theoretical ideas they are learning and apply them to contemporary experience, they understand those ideas more fully, remember them better, and are better able to use them in the future.

Other general guidelines are variants of the first. Most important: *Be clear with students about what you are after, what your expectations are for the course as a whole and for each assignment.* If faculty are clear in their own minds about their course goals and are intentionally teaching students what they want them to learn, it is natural for them to assume that this course framework will be transparently clear to the students as well. Often it is not. Students bring to class a long history of experience with schooling and are likely to assimilate new approaches to that history. Especially when using unfamiliar pedagogies such as simulations, real political action, political deliberations and debates, policy research and analysis, or placements in government or nonprofit agencies, it is helpful to spell out as fully as possible what is required of students, how their work will be evaluated, and why the assignments are structured as they are.

Yet another variant takes the general maxim one step further: *Explicitly teach students the intellectual skills they need, even if these skills seem too basic to require direct attention.* This includes things like how to listen carefully when others speak so as to represent what they are saying accurately; what the ground rules are for engaging in reasoned public discourse and why discourse is subject to these standards; how to deliberate with others about complex issues on which there are legitimate differences of opinion, even among experts; how to determine what kind of information will best illuminate the issue at hand; how to find that information and assess its quality; and how to reflect in a disciplined and structured way on course readings, classroom activities, and other experiences, whether in writing or through discussion. These intellectual skills often have become second nature to faculty, and it is easy to take them for granted. But college students often lack this expertise, or their skills are too rudimentary to support sophisticated political discourse or effective political action. If they are to gain this expertise, they need explicit guidance, repeated practice, and informative feedback.

For many assignments, whether classroom deliberations, group projects, or democratic decision making, it is fruitful to teach students not only how to carry out the task but also to stand back and reflect on the process by which they are pursuing it. Students can learn a great deal about the logic, rhetoric, and social process of political deliberation, for example, by observing the process even as they are engaged in it. When students reflect on the process of deliberation, it throws into relief key elements of deliberative expertise, which supports consolidation of their learning and its transfer to new situations. Similarly, teaching groups of students to step back and reflect on the learning process as they work together to plan and execute political research or action projects ensures that they are thinking about the work on several levels, adding significantly to its value for teaching political skills as well as substantive knowledge.

Finally, teaching directly what we hope students will learn requires explicit attention to the integration of learning across different components of the course or program. This can include connecting action projects or placements with course readings and lectures, a deeper investigation of policy issues that arise from experience in a summer internship, or connecting political theory with observations of politics in action. Making the various components of a course or program cohere toward deeper and more memorable and usable learning is a goal for all courses and programs that include assignments across multiple modalities. But this coherence does not happen automatically. When students are left to make the connections on their own, some accomplish that (usually implicit) goal, but many do not. They are left wondering what their placement activities had to do with the books and papers they read, often commenting that the connection seems tenuous at best.

Most of the PEP courses and programs address the issue of integration directly. Regular structured reflection, either in writing or through class discussions, can serve this purpose if it is used effectively. In order for this to work, the reflection must indeed be structured. That is, it needs to help students self-consciously apply conceptual and analytic lenses to their experiences, using common lenses to look across qualitatively different kinds of experiences in order to discern and articulate important patterns of consistency and contradiction. In this way, disciplined, structured reflection based in discussions and journals can go a long way toward helping students achieve integration across separate components of a course or program.

One commonly used strategy that is, in effect, a version of written reflection, is to ask students to write essays in which they pull together themes that crosscut two or more different components of the course. Especially when they write short essays at several points along the way, this strategy can be very effective in ensuring that students recognize and think through the ideas and issues that surface in various forms from different contexts. Thoughtful investigations into a common issue as it is reshaped and given new meaning in a different modality or setting can be an ideal way to deepen both conceptual sophistication and the subtleties of practical judgment.

Prepare for the Challenges

Just as teaching for political development draws on general principles that apply to many content areas, pedagogies, and educational contexts, this teaching also confronts some common challenges no matter what the subject matter or pedagogical approach. These challenges are not unique to political teaching and learning, but they do surface with regularity there, so they are worth some attention and thought.

STUDENTS' LACK OF BACKGROUND. In talking about the difficulties they face in teaching for political development, PEP faculty and program leaders mention most often students' lack of background and preparation for the work. The basic knowledge, skills, and cognitive capacities required to participate effectively in pedagogies like political deliberation, research and action projects, and structured reflection are often lacking in undergraduate students or are not consistently developed by their prior undergraduate experiences. Likewise, the intellectual, personal, and interpersonal capacities required to take full advantage of placements and invited speakers are unevenly distributed and generally far from optimal in most classrooms. These are, of course, perennial problems not only in higher education but for teachers at all levels.

This lack of necessary background knowledge and skills means that faculty need to teach these skills directly, as we have already suggested. It also has implications for the kind of ongoing support students need as they engage in unfamiliar pedagogies. Though labor-intensive for faculty, providing detailed feedback on student work pays significant dividends later in the course, especially if begun early in the course or program.

Ultimately, though, starting from scratch in each course is not the best way to optimize students' learning. Whether in the political domain or any other area of academic inquiry, it is preferable for students to encounter a need for the same fundamental skills and capacities regularly during their undergraduate years so that their expertise grows as they progress through college.

TIME CONSTRAINTS. Another common challenge for virtually all courses and many programs that use pedagogies of engagement such as projects and placements is lack of sufficient time to complete ambitious projects or attain the fullest benefits from placements. This is a serious problem for academic courses, because a quarter or a semester is a short time in which to plan and implement a project or placement experience. Time limits are also an issue for summer and semester-long programs because of their fixed schedules.

We have seen a number of different ways to address this problem. Some faculty teaching service learning courses or other courses with placements try to achieve greater continuity by arranging for interested students to remain in their placements after the course ends. Students take advantage of these opportunities fairly often. Alternatively, some programs are designed to continue over longer periods of time in order to support extended engagements with projects and placements. Most extracurricular programs have no predetermined time limits, so students can participate over a period of several years if they want to—sometimes pursuing a single line of work, which develops over the period of engagement. Other programs include both curricular and cocurricular components, providing a full-time experience for a semester or a longer engagement that is pursued along with a normal courseload of other commitments.

For many students, however, pressures to meet other commitments preclude involvement in a one- or two-year program. Even when continuing involvement beyond a quarter or semester is possible, and especially when it is not, faculty struggle to find exactly the right balance between time devoted to placement and project work and to course readings, lectures, and discussions. With experience, they learn how long a reasonable project takes and how much time students need to spend in a placement in order to achieve significant learning. This experience helps faculty as they work with students to set achievable learning goals for their placements or to define a project with the right scope for the amount of time available— somewhere between holding a meeting and saving the world, as one faculty member put it. Of course, choosing productive placement sites, defining students' roles carefully, and actively structuring reflections on placement experiences so as to maximize learning are also major factors in achieving significant student learning during a limited period of time.

GROUP PROJECTS. Group projects represent a special case of these first two challenges—lack of basic skills and time limitations—as well as presenting special challenges of their own. Students often find it hard to work together. They have trouble coordinating overcrowded schedules, they are unsure how to handle irresponsible group members or what feels like unfair division of labor, and they have little experience negotiating differences of opinion and achieving consensus. The more each of these difficulties can be used as a learning opportunity, the more productive the project will be. Teaching students to focus simultaneously on the work itself and on important dimensions of group process helps facilitate this productivity.

PEDAGOGIES OF UNCERTAINTY. Lee Shulman calls teaching strategies such as project-based learning and service learning "pedagogies of uncertainty" (2005). By this he means that faculty give up a certain amount of control when they use these pedagogies and outcomes are less predictable. Unlike lectures and reading assignments, these pedagogies of uncertainty often rely on the cooperation of partners outside the academic institution. Faculty have to count on invited speakers, institutional partners in community-based learning and placements, and outside mentors to do their part, and the quality of the experience for students depends on these collaborators' commitment, skill, and relevance to course objectives.

Faculty do not lack control entirely when working with community and other partners, however. Important points of leverage come before, during, and after the engagements. By clarifying expectations and roles as fully as possible when setting up these partnerships, the risks of using speakers, mentors, and community partners can be reduced considerably. Troubleshooting and quick intervention can sometimes put a problematic situation back on track. Finally, it is just as important to document each partnership after it is completed, using both student and faculty assessments, and to move on to other partners in the future if some do not seem to be working.

POTENTIAL FOR DISILLUSIONMENT. Pedagogical uncertainty often arises when students engage with the real world of politics, either inside or outside the academy. As we have mentioned, it is clear from the outset that the political world does not always cooperate with educational objectives. Some political action projects have unsuccessful outcomes, just as some placements expose students to troubling institutional dynamics. Political engagement often increases students' cynicism, at least temporarily.

In cases like this, projects and placements are often disillusioning primarily because of the inherent uncertainty and moral complexity of political institutions and processes. Coming to understand this and knowing how to deal with it is an important aspect of political learning—part of developing a tougher and more realistic grasp of what it means to be politically engaged. The best way to deal with this kind of challenge in a course or program is through searching, deeply thoughtful, and honest reflection. Connecting political projects, placements, mentors, and speakers with this kind of incisive reflection at every step along the way can turn a troubling or discouraging experience into a strong learning opportunity. When insightful reflection provides a new perspective on difficult experiences, strong negative emotions can become fuel for increased passion rather than sending students off the track into disengagement.

In other cases, the placement or project is discouraging not because it confronts the complicated and uncontrollable nature of political reality but just because it is not going well. A project may be ill-conceived or poorly executed, mentors or placement supervisors may be unavailable or unsupportive, and so on. The best way to minimize the negative impact of these problems is to pay close attention to how students' projects, placements, and other course-related activities are going so that it will be possible to see sooner rather than later if they are going astray. Frequent checks on students' progress, especially in the beginning, make possible midcourse corrections before it is too late.

Sometimes these corrections require a radical change—a new project focus or placement site, for example. In other cases a major shift may not be feasible. When that happens, creative strategies for turning a foundering project or placement into a rich learning experience can rescue even the least promising situations. One such strategy might be to shift the focus in a placement, so that a student assigned only menial tasks can do a kind of participant observation and analysis of the organization. Another approach would be for a student to act in a sense as a consultant to his own project, conducting a detailed investigation of what went right and what went wrong with a failed action project, outlining the factors that prevented its success, and writing a set of recommendations for future work.

The Institution's Responsibility

Almost all of the challenges and problems that confront teaching for political development point to the value of a more cumulative, institutionally integrated approach. Students' lack of preparation for the demands of political discourse and research, team-based projects, active political engagement, and structured reflection all point to the great value of cumulative learning through multiple experiences that build on each other over time. In the absence of cumulative learning, faculty are, in effect, starting over in each course.

If these kinds of basic capacities for engaged citizenship were adopted as overarching goals of an integrated undergraduate education, it would benefit not only students' political learning, but also their mastery of reflective

judgment and analytic thinking, persuasive writing and speaking, teamwork, and the use of multiple lenses through which to structure reflection
on a range of experiences. These are all essential to academic excellence and
to effective workforce participation as well as to political competence.

Curriculum

The curriculum is only part of the total undergraduate experience, but it
is the keystone in academic terms and so deserves particular emphasis in
terms of integration. The problem of severe time constraints on political
projects and placements would not be solved entirely by an integrated curriculum but it would be greatly mitigated. Students with training and experience in basic political capacities would have less groundwork to do and
so would be ready to move into political engagement activities more efficiently. In addition, some campuses have adopted curriculum-wide themes
for service learning strands so that students can remain on a single, developing path over two or more years rather than starting over in unfamiliar
domains each time they begin another service learning project. The same
approach could be adopted for politically focused service learning and for
other pedagogies of engagement connected with political learning.

An institutional approach also helps address the challenge of finding
reliable and productive sites for projects and placements with community
partners. Using the same community organization for multiple curriculum experiences can provide students with multiple lenses through which
to examine and understand political engagement. Many campuses have
community-based learning or service learning offices, which are extremely
valuable in providing time-tested information about local nonprofits and
other partners as well as a great deal of logistical help for faculty using
these pedagogies. Even in the absence of a formal community-based learning center, informal sharing of information among faculty doing this work
can be extremely useful.

We realize that creating a curriculum that pursues crosscutting long-
term goals in a cumulative way brings its own challenges—whether the
curricular focus is general education, the majors, or elective themes. On
most campuses, however, efforts to address some basic shared goals across
the curriculum are already in place, at least in theory, and the goals these
efforts usually pursue intersect to a significant degree with those that are
central to students' political development. It may take only a moderate
shift in focus to ensure that the major curricular goals are framed so as to
support high-quality preparation for democratic participation.

Ideally, curricular efforts to build a more cumulative, coordinated learning experience for undergraduates take place at several levels simultaneously. General education programs are an obvious location for some of this work. To make sure that the program makes a systematic, developmental contribution to political learning, it is very useful to review in some detail the goals and assignments of courses that are meant to contribute to this set of learning outcomes.

In addition, some academic departments might consider sequences in the major that build a knowledge and skills base connecting the discipline with political and policy issues. Properly conceived, these connections should enrich students' understanding of that discipline and its implications. In some cases, courses that teach the foundational capacities, such as deliberation and structured reflection, might serve as prerequisites for courses that come later in the sequence.

Efforts to thread the intellectual and practical skills as well as the substance of political learning more broadly throughout the curriculum will go only part of the way to an integrated approach, however, even in the curricular domain. It is well-known that students have trouble integrating what they are learning in their many courses into a coherent whole, or even a set of internally integrated segments (DeZure, Babb, and Waldmann, 2005; Huber, Hutchings, and Gale, 2005). Many institutions are now experimenting with strategies designed to support that integration directly. Student learning portfolios that include specifically integrative assignments all along the way are among the most promising approaches. Another strategy that is being adopted on many campuses is a senior capstone project that is designed explicitly to support the integration of learning in the major.

Cumulative, integrated learning in the curriculum can go a long way toward increasing the power of educational experiences for students' political development during their undergraduate years. But the curriculum is not the only source of teaching and learning. We wrote at some length in *Educating Citizens* (Colby, Ehrlich, Beaumont, and Stephens, 2003) about the importance of using three major sites of learning in higher education institutions to foster students' moral and civic development. The curriculum, the cocurriculum, and the campus culture all hold great potential for political learning. One clear advantage of campus-based rather than distance education is that students are learning from the totality of a much richer experience than the classroom alone. This learning is strongest when the educational potential of all three sites is used fully and when the three are aligned and dynamically interconnected.

Cocurriculum

The richest political learning is achieved when students participate in both curricular and extracurricular political learning activities. This can take place either in a fully coordinated curricular-cocurricular program or less formally through choices of individual students who participate in extracurricular activities that amplify their curricular learning (and vice versa).

Fortunately, many extracurricular activities support political learning on virtually every college and university campus, so students can choose those that most closely align with their interests. Some of these activities are obviously political in nature. Others, like film societies, environmental organizations, some community service programs, and many other clubs and organizations, make explicit connections between their concerns and political issues, broadly understood. Especially if students are given some guidance and encouragement, the realm of student life can be a very powerful site for political learning, especially for learning political skills and fostering political identity, efficacy, and other aspects of motivation.

Many colleges and universities encourage faculty members to serve as advisers for cocurricular programs. These arrangements can often foster natural links between a student's curricular and cocurricular experiences. When the experiences involve enhancing political engagement, the opportunities for learning can be deeper and richer than are possible in just one domain.

Campus Climate

The third important site for student learning is the campus climate or culture—the events; routines; explicit and implicit cultural messages; shared ideas, images, and stories; and symbolically important spaces and physical features of the campus. (See *Educating Citizens* for a more extended discussion of campus culture.) On some campuses, the climate is notably apolitical. This absence of political concern itself sends a powerful message of disengagement.

On other campuses, the political climate may be experienced by many students and faculty as a key element of the institution's identity but also as homogeneous and constraining. The political culture may even be seen as oppressive by those who do not share what they believe to be the dominant perspective. Yet other institutions are characterized by engagement that reveals significant diversity of opinion, which may or may not lead to high-profile political conflict that captures the attention of people both inside and outside that academic community. It is worthwhile for educators, together with students, to think about the political climate in their institution and to talk together about whether it might benefit from efforts to foster more political excitement, engender more openness of opinion, or work toward more civility—or sometimes even less civility if the current norms dictate an overly polite unwillingness to engage.

The goals of educating for political engagement should be stated directly to students by college and university administrators as well as by faculty members. If new students read in materials they receive before coming to campus, and then hear reaffirmed at freshman orientation programs, that they are expected to gain the understanding and skills to be engaged citizens of their communities, the likelihood is increased that these expectations will be realized. That likelihood is made more certain to the extent that students are exposed to role models of political engagement on a regular basis, in their classes and in campus events that are outside the curriculum. These are lessons that need to be stated and restated. Deep discussions of tough issues of public policy in an atmosphere of open inquiry are also extremely valuable. In short, there is no one intervention that is absolutely essential and none that, without reinforcement, can provide all the learning that is needed. Rather, multiple, reinforcing learning experiences over the course of undergraduate education are the best way to educate for political engagement.

* * *

Most campus mission statements include a mandate that graduates are to be prepared to be responsible and engaged citizens of their communities. Too few campuses succeed. We believe that meeting this challenge is both an opportunity and an obligation of higher education. Educating for democracy is difficult, demanding work. We have no question, however, that it is essential work if our political institutions and political processes are to function as they should and if our students are to be well prepared for democratic citizenship.

NOTE

1. The following heading echoes the title of Marcia Mentkowski's important book reporting on longitudinal research that tracks the longer-term impact of college learning, *Learning That Lasts* (Mentkowski and Associates, 2000).

APPENDIX A

COURSE AND
PROGRAM SUMMARIES

The following twenty-one courses and programs were included in the PEP. They are listed alphabetically, by instructor or program leader name.

RICK BATTISTONI: ANCIENTS AND MODERNS:
DEMOCRATIC THEORY AND PRACTICE

PROVIDENCE COLLEGE (PROVIDENCE, RHODE ISLAND)

Overview: This is a one-semester political theory course. Enrolls twenty to twenty-five students, mainly sophomore and junior political science majors.

Description: Battistoni's course links democratic theory to democratic practice, both inside and outside the classroom. He uses several "democratic pedagogies" that help students "learn democracy by doing democracy." Innovative pedagogical tools include a simulation in which students work in groups to create models of a perfectly democratic and a perfectly undemocratic classroom, a "democratic theory journal," and exercises that use several different democratic decision-making devices (such as selection by lot, direct democracy, and representative democracy). Students also complete a Theory into Practice component, which includes two options. The first is the Democratic Organizational Biography project, in which students work individually in a community organization and engage in participatory research, conducting interviews with key stakeholders. The second option is the Democracy in Action project, where students work in groups with the dual goals of organizing themselves democratically and creating and implementing a democratic action plan.

ALMA BLOUNT: SERVICE OPPORTUNITIES IN LEADERSHIP (SOL)

HART LEADERSHIP PROGRAM

DUKE UNIVERSITY (DURHAM, NORTH CAROLINA)

Overview: A two-semester interdisciplinary program, including a one-and-a-half-course sequence plus a summer internship. Enrolls a mix of twenty-two to thirty freshmen, sophomores, and juniors from a range of majors.

Description: The mission of this interdisciplinary program is to help students "become engaged citizens in a democratic society." SOL involves a sequence of one and a half courses and an internship that combines academic study, community service, mentoring, and leadership training. It begins with a preparatory half-credit "house course" in the spring, titled Service Leadership and Social Change, in which students explore concepts of service; learn basic tools of reflection, including documentary writing; and engage in a service project. After this course, students participate in summer internships working on social or political change projects for organizations across the country and abroad. When SOL interns return to Duke in the fall, they participate in a public policy research seminar that requires them to reflect on and integrate what they have learned in their internships by analyzing social and political issues related to their internships and identifying strategies to address those issues. Each student completes a Social Issue Investigation Portfolio, which includes an essay on an issue or problem related to their summer placements, an interview with a practitioner who has some connection to the issue, and a policy recommendation paper.

SUE BRIGGS: CIVICUS LIVING-LEARNING PROGRAM

UNIVERSITY OF MARYLAND, COLLEGE PARK

Overview: This is a two-year interdisciplinary living-learning program, including five courses and active residence hall involvement. Sixty first-year students enter each year; preference is given to social science majors.

Description: This two-year living-learning program involves collaboration between the College of Behavioral and Social Sciences, the Department of Residential Life, Undergraduate Studies, and

University Libraries. The program's theme is "creating a civil society," with an emphasis on citizenship, leadership, community service, and community building in a diverse society. Students, or "CIVICUS associates," live, study, and plan service activities together, and all of them play active roles in the CIVICUS administration. The five required courses include an introduction to the program that examines the roles of individuals, groups, and social institutions in a civil society; a sociology course on contemporary problems; an elective course that addresses diversity issues; Leadership in a Multicultural Society, where students examine issues of pluralism and diversity and prepare for the leadership challenges they present; and a capstone course in which students complete an internship or a "discovery"/research project.

ROSS CHEIT: CHILDREN AND PUBLIC POLICY
BROWN UNIVERSITY (PROVIDENCE, RHODE ISLAND)

Overview: This is a one-semester public policy course, including work with a state agency that addresses policy issues concerning children and families. Enrolls twenty-five to thirty students, mainly sophomores and juniors, from a mix of majors.

Description: A political science and public policy service learning course in which students are required to work a few hours each week in a state agency dealing with children's issues: the Family Court, the Department of Children, Youth and Families, or the Rhode Island Training School. Cheit helps students connect their work experience to readings and discussions about laws and policy issues related to children, including juvenile justice, students' rights, children's rights, voting, and the role of the state in shaping children's policy. Students keep a journal in which they reflect on their work experiences and respond to questions and prompts about specific policies. For instance: "After considering the position of parental rights groups (from the readings), sketch out and defend your own conception of parental rights." Students also complete a research project related to their work, make oral presentations to the class about their experiences, and write several essays connecting their placement experiences with material covered in the course.

JIM FARR AND ROBERT HILDRETH: PRACTICING DEMOCRATIC
EDUCATION AND THE PUBLIC ACHIEVEMENT PROGRAM

UNIVERSITY OF MINNESOTA, TWIN CITIES

Overview: A two-semester political theory course, including one
semester of coursework combined with a two-semester practicum
in democratic education. Enrolls about twenty students, mostly
junior and senior political science majors.

Description: This upper-level political theory course meets for
one semester and includes a practicum in democratic education
that extends across two semesters. After studying major texts in
the history of Western political thought that address concepts of
citizenship and political education, students put their learning
into practice by serving as Public Achievement "coaches" at a
local middle school. The goal is to help middle-schoolers research
and develop action plans based on their own concerns about
social issues in and around their school. The projects vary widely,
from working to change school rules on uniforms, to organizing a
peace march, to laying the groundwork for a neighborhood play-
ground. In the Public Achievement Program, young people learn
how to become informed and involved citizens who engage in
"public work."

OTTO FEINSTEIN AND ANTHONY PERRY:
INTRODUCTORY AMERICAN GOVERNMENT
AND THE URBAN AGENDA–CIVIC LITERACY PROJECT

WAYNE STATE UNIVERSITY (DETROIT, MICHIGAN)

Overview: This is a one-semester political science course required
for graduation. Draws three hundred students, mainly sophomores
and juniors, representing all majors.

Description: Feinstein designed the course to involve students in
the Urban Agenda–Civic Literacy project, which includes theory
building for civic literacy, creating an urban agenda, and civic
participation, including voter registration and political education.
For the civic literacy and civic skills component, students work
together in small groups to debate political issues facing their
local communities, develop five- to ten-point political action agendas, and present these agendas to others in the class. Then, after
a series of deliberations, the class as a whole reaches a consensus

on a single agenda for political action. This is presented at an
annual Urban Agenda convention, to which the university and
community are invited. This process of agenda-building is intended
to prepare students for their roles as participants in a democratic
society. The course also includes a civic action component that
involves a series of individual and small group voter registration
projects on the campus and in the Detroit community. The UACL
project has strong partnerships with community organizations,
educational leaders, city and county politicians and officeholders,
community and religious leaders, teachers, and students.

SIEGRUN FREYSS: GOVERNMENT AND AMERICAN SOCIETY
CALIFORNIA STATE UNIVERSITY, LOS ANGELES

Overview: This one-quarter, introductory political science course,
meeting general education requirements, includes service learning
in a political organization. Limited to twenty-five students, mainly
freshmen and sophomores, from a range of majors.

Description: Freyss teaches one of ten sections of this introductory
course at CSULA. Hers is the only section that includes a service
learning component, for which students work eighteen hours in a
political advocacy organization or in the office of an elected offi-
cial and keep a journal of their activities and learning. In class,
they study the basics of American and California government and
politics, and reflect together on the meaning of advocacy work and
constituency service in the context of the political system and civic
culture. Her course draws a range of students, most of them possessing little initial knowledge of or interest in politics. Many come
from the Los Angeles neighborhoods served and affected by the
political organizations in which they work, allowing them to see,
often for the first time, how political processes and issues affect
their own communities and families.

MARSHALL GANZ: ORGANIZING: PEOPLE, POWER, AND CHANGE
HARVARD UNIVERSITY (CAMBRIDGE, MASSACHUSETTS)

Overview: This one-semester graduate-level course includes a
major organizing project. Enrolls about sixty to seventy students,
including graduate students from the Kennedy School of Government, Divinity School, and School of Education, as well as
undergraduates.

Description: Ganz's course focuses on what de Tocqueville called "knowledge of how to combine": how people organize to turn their values into action. Ganz uses tools of reflective practice rooted in an understanding of power to teach students to develop leadership abilities, build relationships, motivate participation, devise strategies, and mobilize resources. Each student commits an average of six hours per week to a semester-long organizing project that requires mobilizing others to achieve a measurable outcome by the end of the semester. Some students work with an ongoing project of a community or campus group; others initiate their own projects. Using an analytic framework offered in lectures and enhanced by readings drawn from social science, history, and practice, students learn to analyze their experience in weekly reflection papers, presentations, and discussions. They begin to develop their own praxis of organizing, as well as an appreciation of the organizing tradition and its links to social movements and political institutions.

JOE KAHNE, AJUAN MANCE, AND KRISTI SCHUTJER MANCE: INSTITUTE FOR CIVIC LEADERSHIP

MILLS COLLEGE (OAKLAND, CALIFORNIA)

Overview: This one-semester interdisciplinary program includes four courses, an internship, and a mentor program. Enrolls fifteen women per semester, mostly juniors, representing a range of majors and several different colleges.

Description: The Institute for Civic Leadership is a semester-long program for women from Mills and other colleges that combines discipline-based analysis of civic leadership and social justice with ten hours per week of internships, in which students work on projects linked to public policy and social change. The program includes four courses: Civic Leadership and Social Text looks at novels, essays, and other literature that address the issue of leadership in a democratic society; Social Science, Civic Participation, and Democratic Change explores research and theory connecting civic participation to the strength and effectiveness of political institutions; Community Internship and Seminar: Theory and Practice has students participate in internships, reflect on their internship work, compare different approaches to leadership, and consider possibilities for social change; a fourth course is an advanced seminar in the student's major with a term paper connecting the content of her internship with relevant issues and learning from her discipline. All students in the program are also paired with mentors who are experienced leaders in civic affairs.

ARTHUR KEENE, JOHN REIFF, AND DAVID SCHIMMEL:
CITIZEN SCHOLARS PROGRAM

UNIVERSITY OF MASSACHUSETTS, AMHERST

Overview: This two-year interdisciplinary program includes five courses and a minimum of sixty hours of community service per semester. Up to twenty students per year enter the program as sophomores or juniors, representing a mix of majors.

Description: Preparing students for lives of engaged citizenship, with a social action edge, is the dominant theme of this intensive two-year interdisciplinary program run by the Honors College. Students take a sequence of five courses (one course for each term in the program plus one elective) with an emphasis on service learning. The course sequence includes: The Good Society, which examines visions of the good society and explores issues involved in working toward the common good; Tools for Change, which explores tools for bringing about structural change, including public policy, political mobilization, and participatory action research; Organizing for Change, in which students work in the community to conduct research, identify a problem, and develop a proposal for structural change; Public Policy and Citizen Action, in which students implement the proposals they designed in the organizing course; and an elective service learning course.

KRISTY KHACHIGIAN: ENGALITCHEFF INSTITUTE
ON COMPARATIVE POLITICAL AND ECONOMIC SYSTEMS

THE FUND FOR AMERICAN STUDIES

GEORGETOWN UNIVERSITY (WASHINGTON, D.C.)

Overview: This seven-week summer program includes two courses and a public policy internship. About one hundred students from many different colleges participate in the institute each summer, mostly rising juniors and seniors, and mostly political science or economics majors.

Description: The Engalitcheff Institute is an intensive seven-week summer program sponsored by the Fund for American Studies, an educational nonprofit organization that prepares "young people for honorable leadership by educating them in the theory, practice, and benefits of a free society." The Engalitcheff Institute draws undergraduate students from campuses all over the United States. Its goal is to provide future student leaders with hands-on experience in domestic and international policy work and to teach them the value of capitalism and the founding democratic ideals of the United States through internships and coursework at Georgetown University. Internships are thirty hours a week in a Washington, D.C., organization involved in politics, government, economics, or international affairs. Students also complete two three-credit courses: Comparative Economic Systems, which explores free market economics, and The Transformation of American Politics, which focuses on the history of American political thought. Weekly dialogues are arranged with leaders in foreign policy and economics, and students also attend briefings by officials at government institutions, including the White House, House of Representatives, State Department, and the Federal Reserve.

META MENDEL-REYES: INTRODUCTION TO SERVICE, CITIZENSHIP, AND COMMUNITY

BEREA COLLEGE (BEREA, KENTUCKY)

Overview: This one-semester general studies seminar includes service projects and placements. Enrolls eight to twelve students, mostly sophomores, representing a range of majors.

Description: Founded by abolitionists, Berea College has a long-standing commitment to interracial education and to serving low-income students from Appalachia. All students at the college come from low-income families and hold jobs in addition to their coursework. Mendel-Reyes teaches an introductory course in service and citizenship with a particular focus on Appalachian issues and communities. Topics covered include democratic citizenship; racial, gender, and economic inequalities; different approaches to service; and the relationship between service, citizenship, and community, with an emphasis on local, grassroots democracy. Each student completes an individual or group service project, and engages in sustained reflection about her work. After the terrorist incidents of September 11, 2001, for example, students led a workshop on conflict resolution for an assembly of seventy-five fifth graders and gave a presentation at the local library on issues facing Afghan women.

DOUGLAS MORGAN AND CRAIG SHINN:
CIVIC INITIATIVE: THE ETHICS OF LEADERSHIP;
CIVIC ENGAGEMENT: THE ROLE OF SOCIAL INSTITUTIONS
PORTLAND STATE UNIVERSITY (PORTLAND, OREGON)

Overview: Both of these one-quarter courses fall in the Leadership for Change cluster of courses at Portland State University. Both draw sophomores and juniors from a range of majors, and typically enroll twenty to twenty-five students per course.

Description: These two courses are among a group of more than twenty courses that fall under the umbrella of PSU's interdisciplinary Leadership for Change cluster. The Leadership for Change cluster is one of twenty-five clusters that fulfill the university's general education requirements. Students are required to take four courses in their chosen cluster, most of which are completed during the sophomore and junior years. In Morgan's Ethics of Leadership course, students learn how to use ethical frameworks and criteria of effective leadership to develop ethical standards for public leaders. The course includes an extensive speaker series, with political and administrative leaders from throughout the state and region. Shinn's Civic Engagement course uses the theme of civic dialogue to introduce students to two historical models of the common good: the representative republic model, which relies on elected officials and the formal processes of government, and the civic republic model, which relies on face-to-face communication, such as neighborhood groups, voluntary associations, and advocacy groups. Students assess the relative merits of these approaches through field-based projects.

BRIAN MURPHY: THE POLITICS OF SAN FRANCISCO
SAN FRANCISCO URBAN INSTITUTE, SAN FRANCISCO STATE
UNIVERSITY (SAN FRANCISCO, CALIFORNIA)

Overview: This one-semester course includes internships in community-based organizations and city agencies. Enrolls thirty-five to fifty students; half of whom are regularly matriculated university students, mostly junior political science majors. The remainder are staff members of community-based agencies and organizations, enrolled through the university's College of Extended Learning.

Description: This course is team-taught by a former deputy mayor of San Francisco, three longtime community activists, and a university instructor (Murphy). Students learn about the city's recent economic and political history and intern in nonprofit social and economic development agencies. Students work collaboratively on research-action projects designed to assist public dialogue in San Francisco neighborhoods. These projects integrate census data, public opinion surveys, and economic development analysis, linked to a current planning or political issue. Each student group produces an analytic paper and a public presentation. This is one of several courses offered through the Urban Curriculum Project, a joint project of two community organizations and SFSU.

RICHARD REITANO: THE NATIONAL MODEL UNITED NATIONS

DUTCHESS COMMUNITY COLLEGE AND VASSAR COLLEGE (POUGHKEEPSIE, NEW YORK)

Overview: This one-semester course includes preparation for and involvement in the weeklong annual National Model United Nations Conference in New York. Enrolls a mix of twenty to thirty students from Dutchess Community College and Vassar College. Dutchess students are mainly sophomores enrolled in the liberal arts humanities programs; Vassar students are typically sophomores, juniors, and seniors, and are mainly political science or international studies majors.

Description: For many years, Reitano has taught a course that prepares a combined group of students from Dutchess Community College and Vassar College, known as the "Hudson River Group," to attend the National Model United Nations Conference and other regional conferences. The first half of the course involves in-depth learning about the United Nations and the particular country the class has been assigned to represent. The second half prepares students for the NMUN national conference, a five-day conference during spring break that serves as a kind of "weeklong final exam." Students' preparation involves extensive research on the history and foreign policy of the country they will represent, writing position papers on the topics assigned to each committee and council with which their country is affiliated, developing resolutions that they will introduce during the simulation, and holding mock committee sessions. The NMUN conference is the largest student conference in the United States, drawing more than two thousand students each year from more than two hundred different college campuses, including thirteen foreign countries.

PHIL SANDRO: METRO URBAN STUDIES TERM

HIGHER EDUCATION CONSORTIUM FOR URBAN AFFAIRS (HECUA) (ST. PAUL, MINNESOTA)

Overview: A one-semester, four-course credit-bearing program sponsored by HECUA, a consortium of fifteen midwestern colleges and universities. The program includes three seminars and a twenty-hour-per-week internship. Draws about twenty to twenty-five students per semester from consortium schools, who are sophomores through seniors.

Description: The Metro Urban Studies Term focuses on urban poverty and inequality and the structures and behavior that influence these problems, especially the economy, education, and welfare. The program consists of four integrated components that connect theory and practice. A three-day-per-week internship focuses on social and political change. The reading seminar explores alternative theoretical perspectives on the roots and dynamics of urban inequality, poverty, and social change. The field seminar directly links theoretical work in the reading seminar to meetings with community organizers, union organizers, community activists, policymakers, urban planning advocates, educators, residents, and corporate executives. The integration seminar draws together students' internship experiences with the reading and field seminars through group discussions, structured writing, group study projects, papers, and a portfolio. The program provides a holistic experience by encouraging students to integrate their social analysis and action with their thoughts about how the world should be and their role in creating that world.

RICHARD SEMIATIN: WASHINGTON SEMESTER PROGRAM

AMERICAN UNIVERSITY (WASHINGTON, D.C.)

Overview: This one-semester program includes a double American Politics class (the credit equivalent of two courses) and an internship in a Washington, D.C., political or policy office. Draws twenty to thirty students per semester from many different colleges, mainly junior political science majors.

Description: Semiatin teaches an American politics course that is one of several offered at the Washington Semester Program at American University. Students from various colleges, and often some from overseas, enroll in the program. They spend three days a week in Semiatin's "double" class, and two days per week interning in a Washington, D.C., political office or policy organization. The first half of the course focuses on elections and the policymaking institutions of government. The second half focuses on the political, legal, and social impact of various policies. During the semester, students learn from approximately fifty guest speakers, who speak on issues directly related to what students are reading about and studying in class. About half of the students also complete a directed research seminar during which they write research papers based on in-depth personal interviews as well as secondary source material.

GERALD SHENK AND DAVID TAKACS:
SOCIAL AND ENVIRONMENTAL HISTORY OF CALIFORNIA
CALIFORNIA STATE UNIVERSITY, MONTEREY BAY

Overview: This is a one-semester interdisciplinary course. Draws forty students, representing a cross section of years and majors.

Description: This interdisciplinary course looks at how ethnic communities in California affect and have been affected by California's diverse landscapes. Shenk and Takacs teach students to use a cycle of action and reflection to help them become "informed, ethical, and effective participants in the civic lives of their communities." The course's central component is the Historically Informed Political Project (HIPP), a political research and action project that focuses on a California issue with social and environmental dimensions. To complete their HIPP, students conduct historical research, invest at least ten hours in political action linked to the project, reflect on the values and assumptions they carry into the project and how these may change, and make a set of policy recommendations informed by both their historical research and their community experience. Students present their HIPP to the class at the end of the semester.

DICK SIMPSON: THE FUTURE OF CHICAGO

UNIVERSITY OF ILLINOIS AT CHICAGO

Overview: This one-semester course includes a project examining local government agencies. Enrolls fifty to sixty students, mainly sophomores and juniors, from a range of majors.

Description: Simpson has been very involved in Chicago politics and held local elected office himself at one point. His Future of Chicago course uses about fifteen speakers—from scholars, to activists, to politicians at all levels of government—to provide different perspectives on the issues and challenges that Chicago faces. The experiential component of the course is a research project in which students are told to imagine that they are part of a new mayor's transition team and need to write a report informing the incoming mayor of everything she needs to know about a particular unit of government in Chicago or Cook County. Students choose an agency they are interested in, and after conducting library research and looking at public documents and annual reports to get a baseline understanding of how the organization works, they conduct interviews with leaders and other personnel. More than sixty of these student reports have been included in publications used by actual transition teams when there has been a change of mayoral or other political leadership.

ADAM WEINBERG: DEMOCRACY MATTERS

COLGATE UNIVERSITY (HAMILTON, NEW YORK)
AND OTHER CAMPUSES

Overview: This yearlong noncredit course is for students who create and lead Democracy Matters chapters on their campuses. The training program draws about seventy students per year, representing a range of years, majors, and campuses. A total of eight hundred to one thousand students participate through the campus chapters throughout the year.

Description: Democracy Matters is a nonprofit, nonpartisan organization focused on pro-democracy reforms, especially campaign finance reform. The program trains students to be campus coordinators, who then create and lead Democracy Matters chapters at their schools. It is run by several Colgate professors. The program

consists of four phases. The first is Learning the Issues and Acquiring Political Skills, in which students work through a Web-based
tutorial that includes readings, exercises, and reflection pieces.
Democracy Matters staff run the tutorial as an interactive correspondence course: responding to questions, sharing answers, and
offering reflections. In the next phase, Generating Campus Politics,
students return to their campuses and create local Democracy Matters chapters. Through these chapters, students develop their own
strategies for building awareness and organizing their campuses.
Reflection and Strategy is the third phase. At the end of the semester, the campus coordinators write a summary of the semester's
work. They present these at a two-day "student summit" at the
start of the winter semester, during which outside faculty are also
brought in to lecture and run seminars. The final phase, Engaging
in Community Politics, takes place during the spring semester.
Campus chapters continue their work with a focus on linking to
communities and other chapters. At the end of the year, each chapter issues a report that assesses its work and outlines plans for the
next year.

GREG WERKHEISER: COLLEGE LEADERS PROGRAM

SORENSEN INSTITUTE (FORMERLY VIRGINIA
CITIZENSHIP INSTITUTE)

UNIVERSITY OF VIRGINIA, CHARLOTTESVILLE

Overview: This thirty-day residential program is held each summer. It provides civic leadership training to thirty Virginia college
and university students.

Description: The College Leaders Program (CLP) brings together
thirty students from across Virginia for an intensive monthlong
experience focused on state-level politics and public policy. The
Sorensen Institute, a nonpartisan, nonprofit organization dedicated
to civic education, sponsors the CLP. The curriculum centers on
the "Three Lens Approach." The first component is the Informed
Citizen Lens, in which students gain a basic knowledge of politics
and public policy in Virginia by mapping the state's political to-
pography (institutions, agencies, interest groups, and so on) and
by learning the ways in which Virginians identify and debate
issues. Next is the Thoughtful Citizen Lens, in which students
consider questions about the purposes and goals of government

and the role of values in public policy. Last is the Active Citizen Lens, in which students acquire practical knowledge and skills of political engagement. Experiential programs—including guest lectures, debates, panel discussions, and workshops—are offered in addition to the approximately four hours spent in classroom learning. Toward the end of the program, students take part in a mock state assembly session, in which they work in teams to try to pass legislation. Students also work on final projects in groups of ten, researching an area of Virginia public policy and presenting thirty-minute policy briefings. They write comprehensive reports detailing key issues, possible remedies, cost-benefit analysis, and the political backdrop and mobilization issues related to passage of the policy proposals.

SURVEY SCALES AND RESULTS

Table 1. Student Background and Demographics

Sex	Percent	Number (N = 612)
Male	39	238
Female	61	367
Parents' Educational Attainment (Average of Both Parents' Educational Attainment)		
High school diploma, GED, or less	16	96
AA degree or vocational education past high school	22	129
BA degree	15	85
Beyond BA degree	13	74
Graduate or professional degree	34	204
Racial or Ethnic Group (Choose All That Apply)		
American Indian or Native American	1	8
Asian American or Pacific Islander	11	68
Black or African American	12	73
Hispanic, Latino, or Spanish origin	10	60
Middle Eastern	5	28
White/Caucasian	68	413
Respondents who selected only White/Caucasian category	63	383
Other/additional (please specify)	5	31
Immigration Status		
Born outside the U.S.	15	91
One or both parents are immigrants	32	192

Table 2. Survey Scales[1] and
Items, Questions, and Response Options

A. POLITICAL KNOWLEDGE AND UNDERSTANDING	
Foundational Political Knowledge Scale	
Q: *Please rate your knowledge of the following topics:*	*(6-point Likert scale ranging from no knowledge to in-depth knowledge)*
1. Organizations that work on social and political problems	
2. Theories about politics and democracy	
3. Political institutions and how they work	
Current Events Knowledge Scale	
1. Current national or international political issues, such as those on the front page of major newspapers	
2. Current local or state political issues, such as those dealt with by city councils or state agencies	
3. Political leaders and their roles	
4. Current economic issues	
B. POLITICAL INTEREST AND MEDIA ATTENTION	
Interest in Politics Item	
Q: *Some people seem to follow what's going on in government and public affairs most of the time. How often would you say you follow what's going on in government and public affairs?*	*(6-point Likert scale ranging from never to most of the time)*
Media Interest (Newspaper Attention) Item	
Q: *Listed below are some ways that people get news and information. In a typical week, how often do you. . .*	*(7-point Likert scale ranging from 0 to 7 days per week)*
1. Read about public affairs and politics in a newspaper (print version or on-line)	

Table 2. Survey Scales[1] and
Items, Questions, and Response Options, Cont'd

C. CIVIC AND POLITICAL SKILLS	
Skills of Political Influence and Action Scale	
Q: *Listed below are some skills that people use in various situations. Please rate how well you can do each.*	*(6-point Likert scale ranging from cannot do this to can do this very well)*
1. Know whom to contact to get something done about a social or political problem.	
2. Develop strategies for political action.	
3. Organize people for political action.	
Skills of Collaboration Scale	
1. Reach a compromise.	
2. Help diverse groups work together.	
3. Deal with conflict when it comes up.	
4. Talk about social barriers such as race.	
Skills of Political Analysis Scale	
1. Recognize conflicting political interests.	
2. Write well about political topics.	
3. Weigh the pros and cons of different political positions.	
Skills of Leadership and Communication Scale	
1. Articulate my ideas and beliefs to others.	
2. Assume the leadership of a group.	
3. Make a statement at a public meeting.	
D. POLITICAL IDENTITY AND VALUES	
Party Identification Item	
Q: *Generally speaking, do you think of yourself as a . . .*	
Republican, Independent, Democrat, or other (specified)	

Table 2. Survey Scales[1] and
Items, Questions, and Response Options, Cont'd

Political Ideology Continuum Item	
Q: We hear a lot of talk about conservatives and liberals these days. Here is a scale on which the political views that people hold are arranged from extremely liberal to extremely conservative. Where would you place yourself on this scale?	(6-point Likert scale ranging from extremely liberal to extremely conservative)
Politically Engaged Identity Scale	
Q: How important to your sense of who you are is each of the following characteristics?	(6-point Likert scale ranging from not central to my sense of self to very central to my sense of self)
1. Concerned about international issues	
2. Politically involved	
3. Concerned about government decisions and policies	
E. POLITICAL EFFICACY	
Internal Political Efficacy Scale	
Q: Please use the following scale to respond to the statements.	(6-point Likert scale ranging from very strongly disagree to very strongly agree)
1. I feel that I have a pretty good understanding of the political issues facing this country.	
2. I believe I have a role to play in the political process.	
3. When policy issues are being discussed, I usually have something to say.	
4. I think I am better informed about politics and government than most people.	
5. I consider myself well qualified to participate in the political process.	

Table 2. Survey Scales[1] and
Items, Questions, and Response Options, Cont'd

Efficacy in Political Institution Contexts Scale	
Q: Working with others, how hard would it be for you to accomplish these goals?	*(6-point Likert scale ranging from impossible to get this done to easy to get this done)*
1. Getting the town government to build an addition to the local senior center	
2. Influencing a state policy or budget decision	
3. Influencing the outcome of a local election	
Efficacy in Community Contexts Scale	
1. Organizing an event to benefit a charity	
2. Starting an after-school program for children whose parents work	
3. Organizing an annual cleanup program for a city park	
Efficacy in Campus Contexts Scale	
1. Solving problems on your campus	
2. Changing academic offerings or requirements on your campus	
3. Influencing decisions about who teaches on your campus	
F. CIVIC AND POLITICAL INVOLVEMENT	
Expected Conventional Electoral Activities Scale	
Q: Following is a list of items. In the future, what do you expect that you will do?	*(6-point Likert scale ranging from will certainly not do this to will certainly do this)*
1. Vote in future national and local elections.	
2. Work with a political group or for a campaign or political official.	

Table 2. Survey Scales[1] and
Items, Questions, and Response Options, Cont'd

3. Wear a campaign button, put a sticker on your car, or place a sign in front of your house.	
4. Give money to a political candidate or cause.	
Expected Political Voice Activities Scale	
1. Contact or visit a public official—at any level of government—to ask for assistance or express your opinion.	
2. Contact a newspaper or magazine to express your opinion on an issue.	
3. Call in to a radio or television talk show to express your opinion on a political issue, even if you didn't get on the air.	
4. Take part in a protest, march, or demonstration.	
5. Sign a written or e-mail petition about a political or social issue.	
6. Buy a certain product or service because you like the company's social or political values or not buy something or boycott it because of the conditions under which it is made, or because you dislike the conduct of the company.	
7. Work as a canvasser going door to door for a political candidate or cause.	
Expected Political Discussion Item	
1. Discuss political problems with friends.	
Expected Community Involvement Item	
1. Work together with others to solve a problem in the community where you live.	

[1] *We derived our survey scales through a two-stage process, first using exploratory factor analysis (principle factor analysis in SPSS) to create preliminary scales and then using confirmatory factor analysis (structural equation modeling in EQS) to examine and further refine those scales. Details on scales can be found in the document supplement. Cronbach's alphas for scales reported here were above .64. With the exception of the "expected political voice activity" scale developed by Keeter, Zukin, Andolina, and Jenkins (2002), the scales reported here met criteria for "good fit" in confirmatory factor analysis using Hu and Bentler's (1999) criteria.*

Table 3. Results from Analysis of Variance: Comparing Pre- and Post-Survey Means on Scales and Items for All Respondents and Groups with High and Low Initial Interest in Politics[1]

Survey Scales	N	Presurvey Mean	Presurvey SD	Postsurvey Mean	Postsurvey SD	Significance from ANOVA p	Effect Size d from Paired Sample T-Test d
Politically Engaged Identity Scale							
All respondents	464	4.2	1.2	4.4	1.0	< .001***	0.2
Low initial interest	229	3.5	1.1	4.0	1.0	< .001***	0.5
High initial interest	235	4.9	0.8	4.8	0.9	n.s.	

Significant pre-post main effect, Pillai's Trace = .060, $F_{(1, 462)}$ = 29.504, p < .001, with a significant interaction between time and initial political interest, Pillai's Trace = .081, $F_{(1, 452)}$ = 40.472, p < .001.

Survey Scales	N	Presurvey Mean	Presurvey SD	Postsurvey Mean	Postsurvey SD	Significance from ANOVA p	Effect Size d from Paired Sample T-Test d
Internal Political Efficacy Scale							
All respondents	464	4.3	1.2	4.6	1.0	< .001***	0.3
Low initial Interest	231	3.5	1.0	4.1	1.0	< .001***	0.6
High initial interest	233	5.1	0.7	5.1	0.8	n.s.	

Significant pre-post main effect, Pillai's Trace = .124, $F_{(1, 462)}$ = 65.306, p < .001, with a significant interaction between time and initial political interest, Pillai's Trace = .107, $F_{(1, 452)}$ = 55.186, p < .001.

Table 3. Results from Analysis of Variance: Comparing Pre- and Post-Survey Means on Scales and Items for All Respondents and Groups with High and Low Initial Interest in Politics[1], Cont'd

Survey Scales	N	Presurvey		Postsurvey		Significance from ANOVA	Effect Size *d* from Paired Sample T-Test
		Mean	SD	Mean	SD	*p*	*d*
Efficacy in Campus Contexts Scale							
All respondents	457	3.4	0.9	3.5	1.0	.002**	0.2
Low initial interest	228	3.2	0.9	3.5	1.0	< .001***	0.3
High initial interest	229	3.5	0.9	3.6	1.1	n.s.	

Significant pre-post main effect, Pillai's Trace = .021, F(1, 455) = 9.799, p = .002, and a significant interaction between time and initial political interest, Pillai's Trace = .011, F(1, 455) = 5.158, p=.024.

Survey Scales	N	Presurvey		Postsurvey		Significance from ANOVA	Effect Size *d* from Paired Sample T-Test
Efficacy in Political Institution Contexts Scale							
All respondents	457	2.8	0.9	3.2	0.9	< .001***	0.4
Low initial interest	230	2.6	0.9	3.1	0.9	< .001***	0.6
High initial interest	227	3.0	0.9	3.3	0.9	< .001***	0.3

Significant pre-post main effect, Pillai's Trace = .128, F(1, 455) = 67.047, p < .001, with a significant interaction between time and initial political interest, Pillai's Trace = .014, F(1, 455) = 6.375, p = .012.

Media Interest (Newspaper Attention) Item

All respondents	471	5.3	2.1	5.5	2.0	.005**	0.3
Low initial interest	236	4.1	1.8	4.5	1.9	.001	0.2
High initial interest	235	6.4	1.7	6.5	1.5	n.s.	

Significant pre-post main effect, Pillai's Trace = .017, F(1, 469) = 8.122, p= .005, with no significant interaction between time and initial political interest (Pillai's Trace = .007, F(1, 469) = 3.409, p = .065).

Foundational Political Knowledge Scale

All respondents	463	3.9	1.2	4.3	1.0	<.001***	0.4
Low initial interest	231	3.2	1.1	3.9	1.1	<.001***	0.7
High initial interest	232	4.6	0.8	4.7	0.8	.038*	0.1

Significant pre-post main effect, Pillai's Trace = .161, F(1, 461) = 88.258, p < .001, with a significant interaction between time and initial political interest, Pillai's Trace = .094, F(1, 461) = 48.047, p < .001.

Current Events Knowledge Scale

All respondents	463	3.7	0.9	4.0	0.9	<.001***	0.4
Low initial interest	232	3.1	0.8	3.6	0.9	<.001***	0.6
High initial interest	231	4.3	0.7	4.5	0.8	.015*	0.2

Significant pre-post main effect, Pillai's Trace = .141, F(1, 461) = 75.425, p < .001, with a significant interaction between time and initial political interest, Pillai's Trace = .067, F(1, 461) = 33.241, p < .001.

Table 3. Results from Analysis of Variance: Comparing Pre- and Post-Survey Means on Scales and Items for All Respondents and Groups with High and Low Initial Interest in Politics[1], Cont'd

Survey Scales	N	Presurvey Mean	Presurvey SD	Postsurvey Mean	Postsurvey SD	Significance from ANOVA p	Effect Size d from Paired Sample T-Test d
Skills of Political Influence and Action Scale							
All respondents	465	3.5	1.2	4.0	1.1	< .001***	0.4
Low initial interest	232	3.0	1.1	3.6	1.1	.005***	0.6
High initial interest	233	4.1	1.1	4.3	1.0	.002**	0.2

Significant pre-post main effect, Pillai's Trace = .134, F(1, 463) = 71.490, p < .001, with a significant interaction between time and initial political interest, Pillai's Trace = .042, F(1, 463) = 20.322, p < .001.

Survey Scales	N	Presurvey Mean	Presurvey SD	Postsurvey Mean	Postsurvey SD	Significance from ANOVA p	Effect Size d from Paired Sample T-Test d
Skills of Political Analysis Scale							
All respondents	464	4.3	1.1	4.7	0.9	< .001***	0.3
Low initial interest	232	3.8	1.0	4.3	0.9	< .001***	0.6
High initial interest	232	4.9	0.7	5.0	0.8	.028*	0.2

Significant pre-post main effect, Pillai's Trace = .126, F(1, 462) = 66.886, p < .001, with a significant interaction between time and initial political interest, Pillai's Trace = .052, F(1, 462) = 25.532, p < .001.

Skills of Collaboration Scale

All respondents	456	4.5	0.9	4.6	0.8	<.001***	0.2
Low initial interest	229	4.4	0.9	4.6	0.8	<.001***	0.2
High initial interest	227	4.6	0.8	4.7	0.7	n.s.	

Significant pre-post main effect, Pillai's Trace = .029, $F(1, 454) = 13.493$, $p < .001$, with no significant interaction between time and initial political interest, Pillai's Trace = .005, $F(1, 454) = 2.48$, $p =.116$).

Skills of Leadership and Communication Scale

All respondents	466	4.5	1.0	4.7	0.9	<.001***	0.2
Low initial interest	236	4.2	0.9	4.5	1.0	<.001***	0.3
High initial interest	230	4.8	1.1	5.0	0.9	.008**	0.1

Significant pre-post main effect, Pillai's Trace = .078, $F(1, 464) = 39.171$, $p < .001$, with a significant interaction between time and political interest, Pillai's Trace = .013, $F(1, 464) = 6.215$, $p =.013$).

Expected Conventional Electoral Activities Scale

All respondents	452	4.2	1.2	4.3	1.1	<.001***	0.1
Low initial interest	227	3.7	1.1	4.0	1.1	<.001***	0.3
High initial interest	225	4.7	1.1	4.7	1.1	n.s.	

Significant pre-post main effect, Pillai's Trace = .027, $F(1, 450) = 12.669$, $p < .001$, with a significant interaction between time and initial political interest, Pillai's Trace = .021, $F(1, 450) = 9.653$, $p = .002$.

Table 3. Results from Analysis of Variance: Comparing Pre- and Post-Survey Means on Scales and Items for All Respondents and Groups with High and Low Initial Interest in Politics[1], Cont'd

Survey Scales	Presurvey			Postsurvey			Significance from ANOVA	Effect Size d from Paired Sample T-Test
	N	Mean	SD	Mean	SD		p	d
Expected Political Voice Activities Scale								
All respondents	444	3.6	1.1	3.8	1.1		.001***	0.1
Low initial interest	222	3.3	1.0	3.6	1.1		<.001***	0.2
High initial interest	222	3.9	1.0	3.9	1.1		n.s.	

Significant pre-post main effect, Pillai's Trace = .023, F(1, 442) = 10.323, p < .001, with a significant interaction between time and initial political interest, Pillai's Trace = .017, F(1, 442) = 7.666, p = .006.

Survey Scales	Presurvey			Postsurvey			Significance from ANOVA	Effect Size d from Paired Sample T-Test
Expected Political Discussion Item								
All respondents	462	5.2	1.2	5.4	1.0		<.001***	0.2
Low initial interest	232	4.6	1.3	5.0	1.2		<.001***	0.3
High initial interest	230	5.7	0.7	5.7	0.6		n.s.	

Significant pre-post main effect, Pillai's Trace = .037F(1, 460= 17.570, p < .001, with a significant interaction between time and initial political interest, Pillai's Trace = .037, F(1, 460) = 17.570, p < .001.

Expected Community Involvement Item

All respondents	464	4.6	1.3	4.7	1.2	.019*	0.1
Low initial interest	233	4.4	1.4	4.6	1.3	.014*	0.2
High initial interest	231	4.9	1.1	4.9	1.1	n.s.	

Significant pre-post main effect, Pillai's Trace = .012 F(1, 462) = 5.508, p = .019, with no significant interaction between time and initial political interest, Pillai's Trace = .003, F(1, 462) = 1.316, p = .252.

[1]Results from multivariante tests for repeated-measures analysis of variance (ANOVA) with one within-subject effect tested (time or presurvey compared to postsurvey) and one between-subject effect tested (level of political interest or low initial political interest compared to high initial political interest). Significance level * = p < = .05; ** = p < = .01; *** = p < .001. Effect size (ES) refers to indices that measure the magnitude of a treatment effect, and unlike significance tests, are independent of sample size. We report ES as the standardized differences between the pre- and posttest means, using pooled standard deviation (Rosnow and Rosenthal, 1996). To interpret the magnitude of ES, we rely on Cohen's (1988) recommendation that d = .2 is small, d = .5 is medium, d = .8 is large. See document supplement for further information on effect sizes.

REFERENCES

Abramson, P. R. *The Political Socialization of Black Americans: A Critical Evaluation of Research on Efficacy and Trust.* New York: Free Press, 1977.

Aldrich, J. H. "Rational Choice and Turnout." *American Journal of Political Science,* 1993, 37(1), 246–278.

Almond, G. A., and Verba, S. *The Civic Culture: Political Attitudes and Democracy in Five Nations.* Princeton, N.J.: Princeton University Press, 1963.

Althaus, S. L. "Information Effects in Collective Preferences." *American Political Science Review,* 1998, 92(3), 545–558.

Amadeo, J., and others. *Civic Knowledge and Engagement: An IEA Study of Upper Secondary Students in Sixteen Countries.* Amsterdam: International Association for the Evaluation of Educational Attainment, 2002.

American Association of University Professors. "On Freedom of Expression and Campus Speech Codes," 1994. Retrieved Sept. 2006, from http://www.aaup.org/AAUP/pubsres/policydocs/speechcodes.htm?wbc_purpose=Basic&WBCMODE=PresentationUnpublished.

American Council of Trustees and Alumni. "Survey Reveals Pervasive Political Pressure in the Classroom," Nov. 30, 2004. Retrieved Jan. 2005, from http://www.goacta.org/press/Press%20Releases/11–30–04PR.htm.

American Council on Education. "Statement on Academic Rights and Responsibilities," June 23, 2005. Retrieved Dec. 2005, from http://www.acenet.edu/AM/Template.cfm?Section=Search&template=/CM/ContentDisplay.cfm&ContentID=10672.

American Council on Education and others. "Addressing the Challenges Facing American Undergraduate Education: A Letter to Our Members," Sept. 21, 2006. Retrieved Sept. 2006, from http://www.nasulgc.org/six.nextsteps.letter.0906.pdf.

Anaya, G. "College Impact on Student Learning: Comparing the Use of Self-Reported Gains, Standardized Test Scores, and College Grades." *Research in Higher Education,* 1999, 40(5), 499–526.

Anderson, L. F., Jenkins, L. B., Leming, J., MacDonald, W. B., Mullis, I.V.S., Turner, M. J., and Wooster, J. S. *The Civics Report Card: Trends in Achievement from 1976 to 1988 at Ages 13 and 17; Achievement in 1988 at Grades 4, 8, and 12.* Princeton, N.J.: Educational Testing Service, 1990.

Applebaum, B. "Social Justice, Democratic Education, and the Silencing of the Words That Wound." *Journal of Moral Education*, 2003, *32*(2), 151–162.

Associated Press. "Anti-War Protesters Go Digital," Mar. 27, 2003. Retrieved June 2006, from http://www.cnn.com/2003/TECH/ptech/03/27/digital. protesters.ap/index.html.

Association of American Colleges and Universities. "Academic Freedom and Educational Responsibility," Jan. 6, 2006. Retrieved Mar. 2006, from http://www.aacu.org/about/statements/academic_freedom.cfm.

Astin, A. W., and Denson, N. "Long-Term Effects of College on Students' Political Orientation." Los Angeles: Higher Education Research Institute, University of California, unpublished research paper under review 2007.

Astin, A. W., Vogelgesang, L. J., Ikeda, E. K., and Yee, J. A. *How Service Learning Affects Students*. Los Angeles: Higher Education Research Institute, University of California, 2000.

Bahr, A. M. "The Right to Tell the Truth," May 6, 2005. Retrieved May 2005, from http://chronicle.com/weekly/v51/i35/35b00501.htm.

Bandura, A. *Self-Efficacy: The Exercise of Control*. New York: Freeman, 1997.

Barabas, J. "How Deliberation Affects Policy Opinions." *American Political Science Review*, 2004, *98*(4), 687–701.

Barber, B. R. *Strong Democracy: Participatory Politics for a New Age*. Berkeley: University of California Press, 1984.

Barber, B. R. "A Mandate for Liberty: Requiring Education-Based Community Service." *The Responsive Community*, 1991, *1*(2), 46–55.

Barry, B. *Sociologists, Economists, and Democracy: Themes and Issues in Modern Sociology*. London: Collier-Macmillan, 1970.

Bartels, L. M. "Uninformed Votes: Information Effects in Presidential Elections." *American Journal of Political Science*, 1996, *40*, 194–230.

Bartels, L. M. "Partisanship and Voting Behavior, 1952–1996." *American Journal of Political Science*, 2000, *44*(1), 35–50.

Battistoni, R. M. "Service Learning and Democratic Citizenship." *Theory into Practice*, 1997, *36*(3), 150–156.

Baxter Magolda, M. *Knowing and Reasoning in College: Gender-Related Patterns in Students' Intellectual Development*. San Francisco: Jossey-Bass, 1992.

Beaumont, E., Colby, A., Ehrlich, T., and Torney-Purta, J. "Promoting Political Competence and Engagement in College Students: An Empirical Study." *Journal of Political Science Education*, 2006, *2*(3), 249–270.

Beaumont, E., Greene, J., and Torney-Purta, J. "The Nexus of Political Efficacy and Political Learning: An HLM Analysis of the Development of Political Engagement." Paper presented at the Midwest Political Science Association annual conference, Chicago, Apr. 2007.

Bennett, S. E. "The Persian Gulf War's Impact on Americans' Political Information." *Political Behavior,* 1994, 16(2), 179–201.

Bennett, S. E., and Bennett, L.L.M. "Reassessing Higher Education's Effects on Young Americans' Civic Virtue." Paper presented at the International Conference for Civic Education Research, New Orleans, Nov. 2003.

Berelson, B. R., Lazarsfeld, P. F., and McPhee, W. N. *Voting: A Study of Opinion Formation in a Presidential Campaign.* Chicago: University of Chicago Press, 1954.

Berry, J. M., Portney, K. P., and Thompson, K. *The Rebirth of Urban Democracy.* Washington, D.C.: Brookings Institution Press, 1993.

Blasi, A. "Moral Understanding and the Moral Personality: The Process of Moral Integration." In W. Kurtines and J. Gewirtz (eds.), *Moral Development: An Introduction* (pp. 229–253). Needham Heights, Mass.: Allyn and Bacon, 1995.

Blasi, G. L. "What Lawyers Know: Lawyering Expertise, Cognitive Science, and the Functions of Theory." *Journal of Legal Education,* 1995, 45(3), 313–397.

Bohman, J. *Public Deliberation: Pluralism, Complexity, and Democracy.* Cambridge, Mass.: MIT Press, 1999.

Bohman, J., and Rehg, W. (eds.). *Deliberative Democracy: Essays on Reason and Politics.* Cambridge, Mass.: MIT Press, 1997.

Bollinger, L. C. "Cardozo Lecture on Academic Freedom," Mar. 24, 2005. Retrieved Mar. 2005, from http://www.columbia.edu/cu/news/05/03/cardozo_lecture.html.

Boud, D., Keogh, R., and Walker, D. "Promoting Reflection in Learning: A Model." In D. Boud, R. Keogh, and D. Walker (eds.), *Reflection: Turning Experience into Learning* (pp. 18–40). London: Kogan Page, 1985.

Bowen, W. G. (1988). "The Politics of the Faculty." In *Ever the Teacher: William G. Bowen's Writings as President of Princeton* (pp. 323–336). Princeton, N.J.: Princeton University Press.

Boyte, H. C. *The Backyard Revolution: Understanding the New Citizen Movement.* Philadelphia: Temple University Press, 1980.

Boyte, H. C. "The Citizen Politics of Public Work," 2001a. Retrieved Mar. 2006, from http://www.publicwork.org/pdf/speeches/Wisconsin_2001.pdf.

Boyte, H. C. "A Tale of Two Playgrounds: Young People and Politics," 2001b. Retrieved Mar. 2006, from http://www.publicwork.org/pdf/speeches/TaleofTw.pdf.

Boyte, H. C. *Everyday Politics: Reconnecting Citizens and Public Life.* Philadelphia: University of Pennsylvania Press, 2004.

Brady, H. E. "Political Participation." In J. P. Robinson, P. R. Shaver, and L. W. Wrightsman (eds.), *Measures of Political Attitudes* (pp. 737–801). Orlando: Academic Press, 1999.

Bransford, J. D., Brown, A. L., and Cocking, R. R. *How People Learn: Brain, Mind, Experience, and School.* Washington, D.C.: National Academies Press, 2000.

Brehm, J., and Rahn, W. M. "Individual-Level Evidence for the Causes and Consequences of Social Capital." *American Journal of Political Science,* 1997, *41*(3), 999–1023.

Brickhouse, T. C., and Smith, N. D. *Plato's Socrates.* New York: Oxford University Press, 1994.

California Campaign for the Civic Mission of Schools. "The California Survey of Civic Education," 2005. Retrieved July 2006, from http://www.cms-ca.org/civic_survey_final.pdf.

Campbell, A., Converse, P. E., Miller, W. E., and Stokes, D. E. *The American Voter.* Hoboken, N.J.: Wiley, 1960.

Campbell, A. L. *How Policies Make Citizens: Senior Political Activism and the American Welfare State.* Princeton, N.J.: Princeton University Press, 2003.

Center for Civic Education. "National Standards for Civics and Government," 1994. Retrieved June 2006, from http://www.civiced.org/index.php?page=stds.

Center for Information and Research on Civic Learning and Engagement. "National Youth Survey 2002," Mar. 4, 2002. Retrieved Oct. 2002, from http://www.civicyouth.org/research/products/national_youth_survey.htm.

Center for Survey Research & Analysis. "Politics in the Classroom: A Survey of Students at the Top 50 Colleges & Universities," Feb. 2006. Retrieved May 2006, from http://www.atr.org/content/pdf/2006/feb/020206Politics%20in%20the%20Classroom.pdf.

Chickering, A. W., and Gamson, Z. F. "Seven Principles for Good Practice in Undergraduate Education." *American Association for Higher Education Bulletin,* 1987, *39*(7), 3–7.

Chong, D. *Collective Action and the Civil Rights Movement.* Chicago: University of Chicago Press, 1991.

Cohen, J. 1988. *Statistical Power Analysis for the Behavioral Sciences* (2nd ed.). Mahwah, N.J.: Erlbaum, 1988.

Colby, A., and Damon, W. *Some Do Care: Contemporary Lives of Moral Commitment.* New York: Free Press, 1992.

Colby, A., Ehrlich, T., Beaumont, E., and Stephens, J. *Educating Citizens: Preparing America's Undergraduates for Lives of Moral and Civic Responsibility.* San Francisco: Jossey-Bass, 2003.

Colby, A., Sippola, L., and Phelps, E. "Social Responsibility and Paid Work in Contemporary American Life." In A. S. Rossi (ed.), *Caring and Doing for Others: Social Responsibility in the Domains of Family, Work, and Community* (pp. 463–501). Chicago: University of Chicago Press, 2001.

Conover, P. J., and Searing, D. D. "A Political Socialization Perspective." In L. M. McDonnell, P. M. Timpane, and R. Benjamin (eds.), *Rediscovering the Democratic Purposes of Education* (pp. 91–124). Lawrence: University Press of Kansas, 2000.

Converse, P. E. "The Nature of Belief Systems in Mass Publics." In D. E. Apter (ed.), *Ideology and Discontent* (pp. 206–261). New York: Free Press, 1964.

Craig, S. C., Niemi, R. G., and Silver, G. E. "Political Efficacy and Trust: A Report on the NES Pilot Study Items." *Political Behavior,* 1990, *12*(3), 289–314.

Cranton, P. *Professional Development as Transformative Learning: New Perspectives for Teachers of Adults.* San Francisco: Jossey-Bass, 1996.

Creighton, J. A., and Harwood, R. C. *College Students Talk Politics.* Dayton, Ohio: Kettering Foundation, 1993.

Dahl, R. *Who Governs? Democracy and Power in an American City.* New Haven, Conn.: Yale University Press, 1961.

Dahl, R. *Democracy and Its Critics.* New Haven, Conn.: Yale University Press, 1989.

Delli Carpini, M. X., and Keeter, S. *What Americans Know About Politics and Why It Matters.* New Haven, Conn.: Yale University Press, 1996.

Dewey, J. *How We Think: A Restatement of the Relation of Reflective Thinking to the Educative Process.* Lexington, Mass.: Heath, 1933. (Originally published 1910)

Dewey, J. *Democracy and Education: An Introduction to the Philosophy of Education.* New York: Macmillan, 1961. (Originally published 1916)

Dewey, J. *The Public and Its Problems.* Athens, Ohio: Swallow Press, 1988. (Originally published 1927)

Dewey, J. "Creative Democracy: The Task Before Us." In J. A. Boydston (ed.), *The Later Works of John Dewey, 1925–1953* (Vol. 14; pp. 224–230). Carbondale: Southern Illinois University Press, 1988. (Originally published 1939)

DeZure, D., Babb, M., and Waldmann, S. "Integrative Learning Nationwide: Emerging Themes and Practices." *Peer Review,* 2005, *7*(4), 24–28.

Dryzek, J. *Deliberative Democracy and Beyond: Liberals, Critics, Contestations.* New York: Oxford University Press, 2000.

Dumont, R. G., and Troelstrup, R. L. "Exploring Relationships between Objective and Subjective Measures of Instructional Outcomes." *Research in Higher Education,* 1980, *12*, 37–51.

Dye, T. R., and Ziegler, L. H. *The Irony of Democracy: An Uncommon Introduction to American Politics.* Belmont, Calif.: Wadsworth, 1970.

Easton, D. "A Reassessment of the Concept of Political Support." *British Journal of Political Science,* 1975, *5*(4), 435–457.

Easton, D., and Dennis, J. "The Child's Acquisition of Regime Norms: Political Efficacy." *American Political Science Review,* 1967, *61*(1), 25–38.

Ehman, L. "The American School in the Political Socialization Process." *Review of Educational Research,* 1980, *50,* 99–119.

Elster, J. (ed.). *Deliberative Democracy.* Cambridge, U.K.: Cambridge University Press, 1998.

Ericsson, K. A. (ed.). *The Road to Excellence: The Acquisition of Expert Performance in the Arts and Sciences, Sports, and Games.* Mahwah, N.J.: Erlbaum, 1996.

Ericsson, K. A. "Exceptional Memorizers: Made, Not Born." *Trends in Cognitive Sciences,* 2003, *7*(6), 233–235.

Ericsson, K. A., and Charness, N. "Expert Performance: Its Structure and Acquisition." *American Psychologist,* 1994, *49*(8), 725–747.

Ericsson, K. A., Krampe, R. T., and Tesch-Romer, C. "The Role of Deliberate Practice in the Acquisition of Expert Performance." *Psychological Review,* 1993, *100*(3), 363–406.

Euben, J. P. *Corrupting Youth: Political Education, Democratic Culture, and Political Theory.* Princeton, N.J.: Princeton University Press, 1997.

Eyler, J., and Giles, D. E. *Where's the Learning in Service-Learning?* San Francisco: Jossey-Bass, 1999.

Ferejohn, J. "The Citizens' Assembly Model," Feb. 2006. Retrieved June 2006, from http://www.hhh.umn.edu/img/assets/19781/citizens%20assembly%20model.pdf.

Finkel, S. E. "Can Democracy Be Taught?" *Journal of Democracy,* 2003, *14*(4), 137–151.

Fiorina, M. P. "Extreme Voices: A Dark Side of Civic Engagement." In T. Skocpol and M. P. Fiorina (eds.), *Civic Engagement in American Democracy* (pp. 395–425). Washington, D.C.: Brookings Institution Press, 1999.

Fisher, R., Ury, W., and Patton, B. *Getting to Yes: Negotiating Agreement Without Giving In.* New York: Penguin Books, 1991.

Fishkin, J. S. *The Voice of the People: Public Opinion and Democracy.* New Haven, Conn.: Yale University Press, 1995.

Fiske, S. T., Kinder, D. R., and Larter, W. M. "The Novice and the Expert: Knowledge-Based Strategies in Political Cognition." *Journal of Experimental Social Psychology,* 1983, *19*(4), 381–400.

Flanagan, C. A., and Sherrod, L. R. "Youth Political Development: An Introduction." *Journal of Social Issues,* 1998, *54*(3), 447–456.

Free Exchange on Campus. "Facts Count: An Analysis of David Horowitz's 'The Professors,'" Sept. 5, 2006. Retrieved Sept. 2006, from http://www.freeexchangeoncampus.org/index.php?option=com_docman&task=cat_view&gid=12&Itemid=25.

Galston, W. "Political Knowledge, Political Engagement, and Civic Education." *Annual Review of Political Science,* 2001, *4,* 217–234.

Gamson, W. *Power and Discontent.* Homewood, Ill.: Dorsey Press, 1968.

Garner, R., and Alexander, P. A. "Metacognition: Answered and Unanswered Questions." *Educational Psychologist,* 1989, *24*(2), 143–158.

Gerber, A. S., Green, D. P., and Shachar, R. "Voting May Be Habit Forming: Evidence from a Randomized Field Experiment." *American Journal of Political Science,* 2003, *47*(3), 540–550.

Gilens, M. "Political Ignorance and Collective Policy Preferences." *American Political Science Review,* 2001, *95*(2), 379–396.

Glanville, J. L. "Political Socialization or Selection? Adolescent Extracurricular Participation and Political Activity in Early Adulthood." *Social Science Quarterly,* 1999, *80*(2), 279–290.

Gorney, C. *Articles of Faith: A Frontline History of the Abortion Wars.* New York: Simon & Schuster, 1998.

Gould, J. B. *Speak No Evil: The Triumph of Hate Speech Regulation.* Chicago: University of Chicago Press, 2005.

Gray, M. J., Campbell, N. F., Ondaatje, E. H., Rosenblatt, K., Geschwind, S., Fricker, R. D., Goldman, C. A., Kaganoff, T., Robyn, A., Sundt, M., Vogelgesang, L., and Klein, S. P. *Combining Service and Learning in Higher Education: Evaluation of the Learn and Serve America Higher Education Program.* Santa Monica, Calif.: Rand Education, 1999.

Green, D. P., Gerber, A. S., and Nickerson, D. W. "Getting Out the Youth Vote in Local Elections: Results from Six Door-to-Door Canvassing Experiments," June 25, 2004. Retrieved Oct. 2006, from http://www.youth vote.org/info/YouthVote2001YaleReport.pdf.

Grossman, P. L., and Compton, C. M. "The Anatomy of Professions: The Decomposition of Practice." Paper presented at the American Educational Research Association annual meeting, Montreal, Quebec, Canada, Apr. 2005.

Gutmann, A. "Democratic Citizenship." In J. Cohen (ed.), *For Love of Country: Debating the Limits of Patriotism* (pp. 66–71). Boston: Beacon Press, 1996.

Gutmann, A., and Thompson, D. *Democracy and Disagreement: Why Moral Conflict Cannot Be Avoided in Politics, and What Can Be Done About It.* Cambridge, Mass.: Belknap Press, 1996.

Gutmann, A., and Thompson, D. *Why Deliberative Democracy?* Princeton, N.J.: Princeton University Press, 2004.

Haidt, J. "The Positive Emotion of Elevation," Mar. 2000. Retrieved Jan. 2002, from http://content.apa.org/journals/pre/3/1/3.

Hanson, R. L., and Marcus, G. E. "Introduction: The Practice of Democratic Theory." In G. E. Marcus and R. L. Hanson (eds.), *Reconsidering the*

Democratic Public (pp. 1–32). University Park: The Pennsylvania State University Press, 1993.

Harvard University Institute of Politics. "October 2003 Survey," Oct. 2003. Retrieved Jan. 2004, from http://www.iop.harvard.edu/pdfs/survey/ fall_2003_topline.pdf.

Harvard University Institute of Politics. "Redefining Political Attitudes and Activism: A Poll by Harvard's Institute of Politics," Nov. 16, 2005. Retrieved Feb. 2006, from http://www.iop.harvard.edu/pdfs/survey/ fall_2005_execsumm.pdf.

Harwood Group. *Citizens and Politics: A View from Main Street America.* Dayton, Ohio: Kettering Foundation, 1991.

Hess, R. D., and Torney, J. V. *The Development of Political Attitudes in Childhood.* Hawthorne, N.Y.: Aldine de Gruyter, 1967.

Higher Education Research Institute (HERI). "Volunteering and Community Involvement Declines After Students Leave College," 2005. Retrieved Dec. 2006, from http://www.gseis.ucla.edu/heri/PDFs/Atlantic_PR.pdf.

Hitlin, S. "Values as the Core of Personal Identity: Drawing Links Between the Two Theories of Self." *Social Psychology Quarterly,* 2003, 6(2), 118–137.

Hoffman, M. "Is Altruism Part of Human Nature?" *Journal of Personality and Social Psychology,* 1981, *40,* 121–137.

Horowitz, D. "Academic Bill of Rights," July 1, 2006a. Retrieved July 2006, from http://www.studentsforacademicfreedom.org/abor.html.

Horowitz, D. "In Defense of Intellectual Diversity," Feb. 13, 2004a. Retrieved Apr. 2006, from http://chronicle.com/weekly/v50/i23/23b01201.htm.

Horowitz, D. "It's Time for Fairness and Inclusion in Our Universities," Dec. 14, 2004b. Retrieved Apr. 2006, from http://www.frontpagemag.com/ Articles/ReadArticle.asp?ID=16301.

Horowitz, D. *The Professors: The 101 Most Dangerous Academics in America.* Washington, D.C.: Regnery Publishing, 2006b.

Hu, L., and Bentler, P. M. "Cutoff Criteria for Fit Indices in Covariance Structure Analysis: Conventional Criteria Versus New Alternatives." *Structural Equation Modeling,* 1999, 6, 1–55.

Huber, M. T., and Hutchings, P. *Integrative Learning: Mapping the Terrain.* Washington, D.C.: Association of American Colleges and Universities, 2004.

Huber, M. T., Hutchings, P., and Gale, R. "Integrative Learning for Liberal Education." *Peer Review,* 2005, 7(4), 4–7.

Huckfeldt, R., and Sprague, J. *Citizens, Politics, and Social Communication: Information and Influence in an Election Campaign.* New York: Cambridge University Press, 1987.

Huckfeldt, R., and Sprague, J. "Political Parties and Electoral Mobilization: Political Structure, Social Structure, and the Party Canvass." *American Political Science Review,* 1992, 86(1), 70–86.

Huntington, S. P. "The United States." In M. Crozier, S. P. Huntington, and J. Watanuki (eds.), *The Crisis of Democracy: Report on the Governability of Democracies to the Trilateral Commission* (pp. 59–118). New York: New York University Press, 1975.

Huntington, S. P. *American Politics: The Promise of Disharmony.* Cambridge, Mass.: Belknap Press, 1981.

Hurtado, S., Engberg, M. E., Ponjuan, L., and Landreman, L. "Students' Precollege Preparation for Participation in a Diverse Democracy." *Research in Higher Education,* 2002, 43(2), 163–186.

Iyengar, S. "Subjective Political Efficacy as a Measure of Diffuse Support." *Public Opinion Quarterly,* 1980, 44(2), 249–256.

Jacobson, J. "Penn State Reverses Intolerance Policies," June 2, 2006. Retrieved Dec. 2006, from http://chronicle.com/weekly/v52/i39/39a02003.htm.

Jamieson, K. H. *Everything You Think You Know About Politics. . . And Why You're Wrong.* New York: Basic Books, 2000.

Jaschik, S. "Fact-Checking David Horowitz," May 9, 2006. Retrieved May 2006, from http://insidehighered.com/news/2006/05/09/report.

Jayson, S. "Generation Y Gets Involved," Oct. 23, 2006. Retrieved Nov. 2006, from http://www.usatoday.com/news/nation/2006-10-23-gen-next-cover_x.htm.

Jennings, M. K. "Education and Political Development Among Young Adults." *Politics and the Individual,* 1993, 3(2), 1–23.

Jennings, M. K. "Political Knowledge Over Time and Across Generations." *Public Opinion Quarterly,* 1996, 60(2), 228–252.

Jennings, M. K., and Niemi, R. G. *The Political Character of Adolescence: The Influence of Families and Schools.* Princeton, N.J.: Princeton University Press, 1974.

Jennings, M. K., and Niemi, R. G. *Generations and Politics: A Panel Study of Young Adults and Their Parents.* Princeton, N.J.: Princeton University Press, 1981.

Jennings, M. K., and Stoker, L. "Dynamics of Social Capital: A Longitudinal Multiple Generation Analysis." Paper presented at the annual meeting of the American Political Science Association, San Francisco, August-September 2001.

Jones, A. "The One-Sided University (Part One): UCLA Employee Donations," Jan. 5, 2006a. Retrieved May 2006, from http://www.uclaprofs.com/articles/contributions.html.

Jones, A. "The One-Sided University (Part Two): UCLA Professor Political Party Affiliation," Jan. 5, 2006b. Retrieved May 2006, from http://www.uclaprofs.com/articles/affiliation.html.

Keeter, S., Zukin, C., Andolina, M., and Jenkins, K. "The Civic and Political Health of the Nation: A Generational Portrait," Sept. 19, 2002. Retrieved

Feb. 2003, from http://www.civicyouth.org/research/products/Civic_Political_Health.pdf.

Kelly-Woessner, A., and Woessner, M. "My Professor Is a Partisan Hack: How Perceptions of a Professor's Political Views Affect Student Course Evaluations." *PS: Political Science & Politics,* 2006, *39*(3), 495–501.

Keohane, N. O. "President Keohane Responds to Ad Placed by Duke Conservative Union," Feb. 11, 2004. Retrieved Feb. 2004, from http://www.duke news.duke.edu/2004/02/ad_0204.html.

King, D. C. "The Polarization of American Parties and Mistrust of Government." In J. S. Nye Jr., P. D. Zelikow, and D. C. King (eds.), *Why People Don't Trust Government* (pp. 155–178). Cambridge, Mass.: Harvard University Press, 1997.

King, P., and Kitchener, K. *Developing Reflective Judgment: Understanding and Promoting Intellectual Growth and Critical Thinking in Adolescents and Adults.* San Francisco: Jossey-Bass, 1994.

King, P., and Kitchener, K. "The Reflective Judgment Model: Twenty Years of Research on Epistemic Cognition." In B. Hofer and P. Pintrich (eds.), *Personal Epistemology: The Psychology of Beliefs About Knowledge and Knowing* (pp. 37–61). Mahwah, N.J.: Erlbaum, 2002.

Klein, D. B., and Stern, C. "How Politically Diverse Are the Social Sciences and Humanities? Survey Evidence from Six Fields," Nov. 18, 2004. Retrieved Jan. 2006, from http://swopec.hhs.se/ratioi/abs/ratioi0053.htm.

Klein, D. B., and Western, A. "How Many Democrats per Republican at UC-Berkeley and Stanford? Voter Registration Data Across 23 Academic Departments," Nov. 18, 2004. Retrieved Jan. 2006, from http://swopec.hhs.se/ratioi/abs/ratioi0054.htm.

Klein, S. P., and others. "An Approach to Measuring Cognitive Outcomes Across Higher Education Institutions." *Research in Higher Education,* 2005, *46*(3), 251–276.

Knefelkamp, L. *Developmental Instruction: Fostering Intellectual and Personal Growth in College Students.* Unpublished doctoral dissertation, University of Minnesota, 1974.

Kolb, D. A. *Experiential Learning: Experience as the Source of Learning and Development.* Upper Saddle River, N.J.: Prentice Hall, 1984.

Kuh, G. D. "In Their Own Words: What Students Learn Outside the Classroom." *American Educational Research Journal,* 1993, *30*(2), 277–304.

Kuh, G. D. "The National Survey of Student Engagement: Conceptual Framework and Overview of Psychometric Properties," Nov. 8, 2003. Retrieved Oct. 2005, from http://nsse.iub.edu/pdf/conceptual_framework_2003.pdf.

Kuh, G. D. "Imagine Asking the Client: Using Student and Alumni Surveys for Accountability in Higher Education." In J. C. Burke and Associates (eds.),

Achieving Accountability in Higher Education: Balancing Public, Academic, and Market Demands (pp. 148–172). San Francisco: Jossey-Bass, 2005.

Kuh, G. D., and others. *Involving Colleges: Successful Approaches to Fostering Student Learning and Development Outside the Classroom.* San Francisco: Jossey-Bass, 1991.

Langton, K. P., and Jennings, M. K. "Political Socialization and the High School Civics Curriculum in the United States." *American Political Science Review,* 1968, 62(3), 852–867.

Langton, K. P., and Karns, D. A. "The Relative Influence of the Family, Peer Group, and School in the Development of Political Efficacy." *Western Political Quarterly,* 1969, 22(4), 813–826.

Lee, D., and Sabatino, K. "Evaluating Guided Reflection: A U.S. Case Study." *International Journal of Training and Development,* 1998, 2(3), 162–170.

Leighley, J. "Group Membership and the Mobilization of Political Participation." *Journal of Politics,* 1996, 58(2), 447–463.

Levi, M., and Stoker, L. "Political Trust and Trustworthiness." *Annual Review of Political Science,* 2002, 3, 475–507.

Lindholm, J. A., Szelenyi, K., Hurtado, S., and Korn, W. S. *The American College Teacher: National Norms for the 2004–2005 HERI Faculty Survey.* Los Angeles: Higher Education Research Institute, University of California, 2005.

Lipset, S. M. "Introduction." In R. Michels (ed.), *Political Parties: A Sociological Study of the Oligarchical Tendencies of Modern Democracy* (pp. 15–39). New York: Collier, 1962.

Long, S. E. "The New Student Politics: The Wingspread Statement on Student Civic Engagement" (2nd ed.), 2002. Retrieved May 2006, from http://www.compact.org/wingspread/wingspread-web.pdf.

Longo, N. V., and Meyer, R. P. "College Students and Politics: A Literature Review," May 2006. Retrieved June 2006, from http://www.civicyouth.org/PopUps/WorkingPapers/WP46LongoMeyer.pdf.

Lopez, M. H., Kirby, E., Sagoff, J., and Herbst, C. "The Youth Vote 2004 (with a Historical Look at Youth Voting Patterns, 1972–2004)," July 2005. Retrieved Dec. 2005, from http://www.civicyouth.org/PopUps/WorkingPapers/WP35CIRCLE.pdf.

Lopez, M. H., and others. "The 2006 Civic and Political Health of the Nation: A Detailed Look at How Youth Participate in Politics and Communities," Oct. 2006. Retrieved Oct. 2006, from http://www.civicyouth.org/PopUps/2006_CPHS_Report_update.pdf.

Lord, C. G., Ross, L., and Leeper, M. R. "Biased Assimilation and Attitude Polarization: The Effects of Prior Theories on Subsequently Considered Evidence." *Journal of Personality and Social Psychology,* 1979, 37(11), 2098–2109.

Lummis, C. D. *Radical Democracy.* Ithaca, N.Y.: Cornell University Press, 1996.

Lupia, A., and McCubbins, M. D. *The Democratic Dilemma: Can Citizens Learn What They Need to Know?* Cambridge, U.K.: Cambridge University Press, 1998.

Luskin, R. C. "Explaining Political Sophistication." *Political Behavior,* 1990, *12*(4), 331–361.

Lutkus, A. D., Weiss, A. R., Campbell, J. R., Mazzeo, J., and Lazer, S. *NAEP 1998 Civics Report Card for the Nation.* Washington, D.C.: U.S. Department of Education, 1999.

Madsen, D. "Political Self-Efficacy Tested." *American Political Science Review,* 1987, *81*(2), 571–582.

Makdisi, S. "Witch Hunt at UCLA," Jan. 22, 2006. Retrieved Jan. 2006, from http://www.latimes.com/news/opinion/sunday/commentary/la-op-makdisi 22jan22,0,2020503.story?coll=la-home-sunday-opinion.

Mann, S., and Patrick, J. J. (eds.). *Education for Civic Engagement in Democracy: Service Learning and Other Promising Practices.* Bloomington, Ind.: ERIC Clearinghouse for Social Studies/Social Science Education, 2000.

Mansbridge, J. J. *Beyond Adversary Democracy.* Chicago: University of Chicago Press, 1983.

Mansbridge, J. J. "On the Idea That Participation Makes Better Citizens." In S. L. Elkin and K. E. Soltan (eds.), *Citizen Competence and Democratic Institutions* (pp. 291–325). University Park: The Pennsylvania State University Press, 1999.

Markus, H., and Nurius, P. "Possible Selves." *American Psychologist,* 1986, *41*(9), 954–969.

Mason, J. L., and Nelson, M. "Selling Students on the Elections of 2000." *Chronicle of Higher Education,* Sept. 22, 2000, p. B16.

McAdam, D. *Freedom Summer.* New York: Oxford University Press, 1988.

McAdam, D., and Paulsen, R. "Specifying the Relationship Between Social Ties and Activism." *American Journal of Sociology,* 1993, *58*(3), 640–667.

Mentkowski, M., and Associates. *Learning That Lasts: Integrating Learning, Development, and Performance in College and Beyond.* San Francisco: Jossey-Bass, 2000.

Mill, J. S. *Considerations on Representative Government.* New York: Harper and Brothers, 1862. Retrieved Sept. 2004, from http://www.gutenberg. org/etext/5669.

Mill, J. S. "On Liberty." In J. B. Schneewind (ed.), *The Basic Writings of John Stuart Mill* (pp. 1–119). New York: Modern Library, 2002. (Originally published 1859)

Miller, W. E., and Shanks, M. *The New American Voter.* Cambridge, Mass.: Harvard University Press, 1996.

Moats, D. *Civil Wars: A Battle for Gay Marriage*. Orlando: Harcourt Brace, 2004.

Murphy, J. B. "Against Civic Schooling." *Social Philosophy and Policy*, 2004, 21(1), 221–265.

Mutz, D. "Cross-Cutting Social Networks: Testing Democratic Theory in Practice." *American Political Science Review*, 2002, 96, 111–126.

Mutz, D., and Mondak, J. J. "The Workplace as a Context for Cross-Cutting Political Discourse." *Journal of Politics*, 2006, 68(1), 140–155.

National Association of Secretaries of State. *New Millennium Project-Phase I: A Nationwide Study of 15–24 Year Old Youth*. Alexandria, Va.: The Tarrance Group, 1999.

Neuman, W. R. *The Paradox of Mass Politics: Knowledge and Opinion in the American Electorate*. Cambridge, Mass.: Harvard University Press, 1986.

Newton Jr., R. D. "Academic Advocacy. Appeals and Abuses." *Teaching Ethics*, 2003, 3(2), 1–25.

Nie, N. H., and Hillygus, D. S. (2001). "Education and Democratic Citizenship." In D. Ravitch and J. P. Viteritti (eds.), *Making Good Citizens: Education and Civil Society* (pp. 30–57). New Haven, Conn.: Yale University Press.

Nie, N. H., Junn, J., and Stehlik-Barry, K. *Education and Democratic Citizenship in America*. Chicago: University of Chicago Press, 1996.

Niemi, R. G., Craig, S. C., and Mattei, F. "Measuring Internal Political Efficacy in the 1988 National Election Study." *American Political Science Review*, 1991, 85(4), 1407–1413.

Niemi, R. G., Hepburn, M. A., and Chapman, C. "Community Service by High School Students: A Cure for Civic Ills?" *Political Behavior*, 2000, 22(1), 45–69.

Niemi, R. G., and Junn, J. *Civic Education: What Makes Students Learn*. New Haven, Conn.: Yale University Press, 1998.

Ober, J. *Political Dissent in Democratic Athens: Intellectual Critics of Popular Rule*. Princeton, N.J.: Princeton University Press, 1998.

Pascarella, E. T., and Terenzini, P. T. *How College Affects Students: Findings and Insights from Twenty Years of Research*. San Francisco: Jossey-Bass, 1991.

Pascarella, E. T., and Terenzini, P. T. *How College Affects Students: A Third Decade of Research*. Vol. 2. San Francisco: Jossey-Bass, 2005.

Pateman, C. *Participation and Democratic Theory*. Cambridge, U.K.: Cambridge University Press, 1970.

Perry, J. L., and Jones, S. G. *Quick Hits for Educating Citizens: Successful Strategies by Award-Winning Teachers*. Indianapolis: Indiana University Press, 2006.

Perry, W. *Forms of Intellectual and Ethical Development in the College Years: A Scheme*. San Francisco: Jossey-Bass, 1970.

Peter D. Hart Research Associates. "Making a Difference, Not a Statement: College Students and Politics, Volunteering, and an Agenda for America," April 2001. Retrieved July 2006, from http://www.panettainstitute.org/hart_research.html.

Petrovic, J. E. "Can We Forget to Censor Silence? A Rejoinder to Applebaum." *Journal of Moral Education,* 2003, 32(2), 163–166.

Piliavin, J. A., and Callero, P. L. *Giving Blood: The Development of an Altruistic Identity.* Baltimore: Johns Hopkins University Press, 1991.

Plutzer, E. "Becoming a Habitual Voter: Inertia, Resources, and Growing in Young Adulthood." *American Political Science Review,* 2002, 96(1), 41–56.

Pollock III, P. H. "The Participatory Consequences of Internal and External Political Efficacy: A Research Note." *The Western Political Quarterly,* 1983, 36(3), 400–409.

Popkin, S. L., and Dimock, M. "Political Knowledge and Citizen Competence." In S. Elkin and K. Soltan (eds.), *Citizen Competence and Democratic Institutions* (pp. 117–146). University Park: The Pennsylvania State University Press, 1999.

Pryor, J. H., and others. *The American Freshman: National Norms for Fall 2005.* Los Angeles: Higher Education Research Institute, University of California, 2005.

Putnam, R. D. *Making Democracy Work: Civic Tradition in Modern Italy.* Princeton, N.J.: Princeton University Press, 1993.

Putnam, R. D. *Bowling Alone: The Collapse and Revival of American Community.* New York: Simon & Schuster, 2000.

Rahn, W. M. "The Decline of National Identity Among Young Americans: Diffuse Emotion, Commitment, and Social Trust." Unpublished manuscript, University of Minnesota, 1992.

Rahn, W. M. Panel discussion at the advisory board meeting of the Civic Identity Project, Grand Cayman, Bahamas, 2000.

Rahn, W. M., Aldrich, J. H., and Borgida, E. "Individual and Contextual Variations in Political Candidate Appraisal." *American Political Science Review,* 1994, 88, 193–199.

Ricks, V. "Introduction: How Not to Teach Moral Relativism." Paper presented at the Teach-In on Moral Relativism, Stanford University, Stanford, Calif., May 1999.

Riker, W., and Ordeshook, P. "A Theory of the Calculus of Voting." *American Political Science Review,* 1968, 62(1), 25–42.

Rimmerman, C. A. "Teaching American Politics Through Service: Reflections on a Pedagogical Strategy." In G. Reeher and J. Cammarano (eds.), *Education for Citizenship: Ideas and Innovations in Political Learning* (pp. 17–29). Lanham, Md.: Rowman & Littlefield, 1997.

Robinson, T. "Dare the School Build a New Social Order?" *Michigan Journal of Community Service-Learning,* 2000, *7,* 142–157.

Rosenberg, S. W. (ed.). *Can the People Decide? Theory and Empirical Research on Democratic Deliberation.* London: Palgrave Macmillan, 2007.

Rosnow, R. L., and Rosenthal, R. "Computing Contrasts, Effect Sizes, and Counternulls on Other People's Published Data: General Procedures for Research Consumers." *Pyschological Methods,* 1996, *1,* 331–340.

Rossi, A. S. (ed.). *Caring and Doing for Others: Social Responsibility in the Domains of Family, Work, and Community.* Chicago: University of Chicago Press, 2001.

Rothman, S., Lichter, S. R., and Nevitte, N. "Politics and Professional Advancement Among College Faculty," Jan. 2005. Retrieved Jan. 2006, from http://www.bepress.com/cgi/viewcontent.cgi?article=1067&context=forum.

Sax, L. J. "Citizenship Development and the American College Student." In T. Ehrlich (ed.), *Civic Responsibility and Higher Education* (pp. 3–18). Phoenix: Oryx Press, 1999.

Sax, L. J. "Citizenship Development and the American College Student." *New Directions for Institutional Research,* 2004, *122,* 65–80.

Sax, L. J., and others. *The American Freshman: National Norms for Fall 2003.* Los Angeles: Higher Education Research Institute, University of California, 2003.

Schachter, H. L. "Civic Education: Three Early American Political Science Association Committees and Their Relevance for Our Times." *PS: Political Science & Politics,* 1998, *31*(3), 631–635.

Schlozman, K. L. "Citizen Participation in America: What Do We Know? Why Do We Care?" In I. Katznelson and H. Milner (eds.), *Political Science: The State of the Discipline* (pp. 433–461). New York: Norton, 2002.

Schlozman, K. L., Verba, S., and Brady, H. E. "Civic Participation and the Equality Problem." In T. Skocpol and M. P. Fiorina (eds.), *Civic Engagement in American Democracy* (pp. 427–459). Washington, D.C.: Brookings Institution, 1999.

Schneider, B. "Netroots Activism Arrives," Aug. 5, 2005. Retrieved Aug. 2005, from http://www.cnn.com/2005/POLITICS/08/05/bloggers/.

Schoenfeld, A. H. *Mathematical Problem Solving.* Orlando: Academic Press, 1985.

Schoenfeld, A. H. "What's All the Fuss About Metacognition?" In A. H. Schoenfeld (ed.), *Cognitive Science and Mathematics Education* (pp. 189–216). Mahwah, N.J.: Erlbaum, 1987.

Seligman, M.E.P. *Authentic Happiness: Using the New Positive Psychology to Realize Your Potential for Lasting Fulfillment.* New York: Free Press, 2002.

Shapiro, R., and Bloch-Elkon, Y. "Political Polarization and the Rational Public." Paper presented at the Annual Conference of the American Association for Public Opinion Research, Montreal, Quebec, Canada, May 2006.

Shavelson, R. J., and Huang, L. "Collegiate Learning Assessment Conceptual Framework," 2003. Retrieved Nov. 2006, from http://www.cae.org/content/pdf/CLA.ConceptualFramework.pdf.

Shulman, L. S. "Pedagogies of Uncertainty." *Liberal Education*, 2005, *91*(2), 18–25.

Smith, E. "The Effects of Investments in Social Capital of Youth on Political and Civic Behavior in Young Adulthood: A Longitudinal Analysis." *Political Psychology*, 1999, *20*(3), 553–580.

Snyder, R. C. "Should Political Science Have a Civic Mission? An Overview of the Historical Evidence." *PS: Political Science & Politics*, 2001, *34*(2), 301–305.

Somin, I. "Knowledge About Ignorance: New Directions in the Study of Political Information." *Critical Review*, 2006, *18*(1–3) 255–278.

Stewart, J. H. "Letter to the Hamilton Community: President Discusses Kirkland Project/Ward Churchill Event," Feb. 9, 2005. Retrieved Nov. 2005, from http://www.hamilton.edu/news/more_news/display.cfm?ID=9073.

Student PIRGs' New Voters Project. "Student PIRGs' New Voters Project Posts Huge Vote Increases," Nov. 8, 2006. Retrieved Dec. 2006, from http://www.newvotersproject.org/new-voters-project-posts.

Talcott, W. "Modern Universities, Absent Citizenship? Historical Perspectives," Sept. 2005. Retrieved Oct. 2005, from http://www.civicyouth.org/PopUps/WorkingPapers/WP39Talcott.pdf.

Thompson, D. F. *The Democratic Citizen: Social Science and Democratic Theory in the Twentieth Century.* Cambridge: Cambridge University Press, 1970.

Torney-Purta, J. "Evaluating Programs Designed to Teach International Content and Negotiation Skills." *International Negotiation*, 1998, *3*, 77–97.

Torney-Purta, J., Barber, C., and Wilkenfeld, B. "Differences in the Civic Knowledge and Attitudes of U.S. Adolescents by Immigrant Status and Hispanic Background." *Prospects*, 2006, *36*(3), 343–354.

Torney-Purta, J., Lehmann, R., Oswald, H., and Schulz, W. *Citizenship and Education in Twenty-Eight Countries: Civic Knowledge and Engagement at Age Fourteen.* Amsterdam: International Association for the Evaluation of Educational Achievement, 2001.

Torney-Purta, J., Oppenheim, A. N., and Farnen, R. F. *Civic Education in Ten Countries: An Empirical Study.* Hoboken, N.J.: Wiley, 1975.

Trosset, C. "Obstacles to Open Discussion and Critical Thinking: The Grinnell College Study." *Change*, 1998, *30*(5), 44–49.

Truman, D. B. *The Congressional Party: A Case Study.* Hoboken, N.J.: Wiley, 1959.

Truman, D. B. *The Governmental Process: Political Interests and Public Opinion.* New York: Knopf, 1971.

U.S. Department of Education, National Center for Educational Statistics. "Fast Facts: Postsecondary Enrollment," 2006. Retrieved Aug. 2006, from http://165.224.221.98/fastfacts/display.asp?id=98.

Uslaner, E. M. *The Decline of Comity in Congress.* Ann Arbor: University of Michigan Press, 1993.

Verba, S., Schlozman, K. L., and Brady, H. E. *Voice and Equality: Civic Voluntarism in American Politics.* Cambridge, Mass.: Harvard University Press, 1995.

Walker, T. "The Service/Politics Split: Rethinking Service to Teach Political Engagement." *PS: Political Science & Politics,* 2000, 33(3), 646–649.

Wolfe, A. *Does American Democracy Still Work?* New Haven, Conn.: Yale University Press, 2006.

Yates, M., and Youniss, J. "Community Service and Political Identity Development in Adolescence." *Journal of Social Issues,* 1998, 54(3), 495–512.

Young, I. M. "Communication and the Other: Beyond Deliberative Democracy." In S. Benhabib (ed.), *Democracy and Difference: Contesting the Boundaries of the Political* (pp. 120–136). Princeton, N.J.: Princeton University Press, 1996.

Young, I. M. *Inclusion and Democracy.* Oxford, U.K.: Oxford University Press, 2000.

Youniss, J., McLellan, J. A., Su, J., and Yates, M. "The Role of Community Service in Identity Development." *Journal of Adolescent Research,* 1999, 14(2), 248–261.

Youniss, J., McLellan, J. A., and Yates, M. "What We Know About Engendering Civic Identity." *American Behavioral Scientist,* 1997, 40(5), 620–631.

Youniss, J., and Yates, M. *Community Service and Social Responsibility in Youth.* Chicago: University of Chicago Press, 1997.

Zaller, J. *The Nature and Origins of Mass Opinion.* Cambridge, U.K.: Cambridge University Press, 1992.

Zinsmeister, K. "Diversity on Campus? There Is None," 2005. Retrieved Nov. 2005, from http://www.taemag.com/issues/articleID.18346/article_detail.asp.

Zukin, C., and others. *A New Engagement?: Political Participation, Civic Life, and the Changing American Citizen.* Oxford: Oxford University Press, 2006.

NAME INDEX

A

Abramson, P. R., 142
Aldrich, J. H., 48, 57
Alexander, P. A., 260
Almond, G. A., 142
Althaus, S. L., 13, 108
Anaya, G., 124
Andolina, M., 3, 124
Applebaum, B., 70, 71
Aristotle, 58
Astin, A. W., 3, 53, 79, 81, 82, 286

B

Bahr, A., 66, 88
Bandura, A., 142
Barabas, J., 27, 162
Barber, B. R., 7, 29, 58, 226
Barber, C., 50
Barry, B., 139
Bartels, L. M., 13, 27
Battistoni, R. M., 36, 168, 261, 269
Baxter Magolda, M., 54
Beaumont, E., 2, 145, 242, 279, 286, 295
Bennett, L.L.M., 4, 52
Bennett, S. E., 4, 52, 108
Berry, J. M., 58
Blasi, A., 279
Blasi, G. L., 135
Bloch-Elkon, Y., 27, 48
Blount, A., 99, 114, 135–136, 146, 189, 191, 225, 230–231, 236, 238, 239, 254
Bohman, J., 30

Bollinger, L., 89, 91, 94

Borgida, E., 48
Boud, D., 262
Bowen, W., 91
Boyte, H. C., 7, 29, 30, 97, 106, 114
Brady, H. E., 7, 27, 29, 30, 36, 37, 47, 50, 58, 59, 123, 143, 226
Bransford, J. D., 132, 135
Brehm, J., 141
Brickhouse, T. C., 1
Briggs, S., 102, 160, 213
Brown, A. L., 132, 135
Bush, G. W., 47

C

Callero, P. L., 279
Campbell, A. L., 26, 29, 58
Chapman, C., 226
Charness, N., 124
Cheit, R., 39, 112, 117, 153, 171, 191, 202, 223, 227, 228, 230, 231, 232, 239, 242, 244, 246, 247, 248, 263, 270
Chong, D., 31
Churchill, W., 97
Clinton, B., 47
Cocking, R. R., 132, 135
Colby, A., 2, 89, 242, 279, 280, 285, 286
Compton, C. M., 136
Converse, P. E., 26, 29
Craig, S. C., 142, 143, 144
Cranton, P., 256
Creighton, J. A., 32, 34, 41

SUBJECT INDEX

A

Academic Bill of Rights, 91–92
Academic discourse: maintaining civility during, 67–73; standards of, 63–67
Academic Freedom: definition of, 62–63; setting limits for, 65; setting limits for students, 65–67; standards of academic discourse, 63–65
"Academic Freedom and Educational Responsibility" (AACU), 64
Academic values: academic freedom, 62–63; civility, 67–73; implicit in academic discipline, 83–85; intellectual pluralism and diversity of perspective, 61–62, 78; standards of academic discourse, 63–67, 97–98
Action project strategies: be clear, 187–188; be realistic, 188–189; connect, 192; encourage reflection, 190; go public, 190–191; make it enjoyable, 191–192; monitor progress, 189–190
Action projects: challenges of using, 192–197; political engagement through, 150–152; real-world type of, 176–178; research type of, 178–180; rewards of, 180–186; simulated, 178; strategies for effective, 186–192
Active listening, 158
Administrative skills, 234
Advocacy: forms of teaching-based, 74; PEP faculty experience with, 74–75

American Association of University Professors, 69
American Civil Liberties Union (ACLU), 223, 233
American Council of Trustees and Alumni (ACTA), 79, 286
American Council on Education (ACE), 3, 76, 91
American flag issue, 103–104
AmeriCorps, 124
Apology (Plato), 1
Associated Press, 32
Association of American Colleges and Universities, 64, 91

B

Berea College, 152, 184, 193, 201, 207, 212, 262
Bill of rights, 109
Brown University, 171, 202, 223

C

California Campaign for the Civic Mission of Schools (2005), 46
California State University, Los Angeles, 223, 234
California State University, Monterey Bay, 195, 196, 203, 204, 214, 261–262
Campus climate, 296–297
Career preparation issues, 235
Catholic Charities of New Mexico, 223